Communications in Computer and Information Science 1507

More information about this series at https://link.springer.com/bookseries/7899

Enrico Borgogno-Mondino ·
Paola Zamperlin (Eds.)

Geomatics and Geospatial Technologies

24th Italian Conference, ASITA 2021
Genoa, Italy, July 1–2, 9, 16, 23, 2021
Proceedings

Springer

Editors
Enrico Borgogno-Mondino (iD)
DISAFA - University of Torino
Grugliasco, Italy

Paola Zamperlin (iD)
University of Pisa
Pisa, Italy

ISSN 1865-0929   ISSN 1865-0937 (electronic)
Communications in Computer and Information Science
ISBN 978-3-030-94425-4   ISBN 978-3-030-94426-1 (eBook)
https://doi.org/10.1007/978-3-030-94426-1

This Springer imprint is published by the registered company Springer Nature Switzerland AG
The registered company address is: Gewerbestrasse 11, 6330 Cham, Switzerland

Preface

ASITA, the Italian Federation of Scientific Associations for Territorial and Environmental Information, for over two decades has brought together scholars, public administrators, and professionals with the Italian Conference on Geomatics and Geospatial Technologies. After the decision to cancel the 2020 event, in this time of COVID-19 global disruption and uncertainty, the Scientific and Executive Committees of ASITA committed to hold the conference online. The traditional organization was significantly modified, making the event a distributed one along a longer period. Five thematic days, one per week, were therefore programmed. They took place between July 1 and July 23, 2021, under the name of Asita Academy 2021. The decision proved to be successful. Communities committed to similar topics were attracted by the highly-focused program, which was designed to gather thematically connected contributions for presentation on the same day. Authors and audience were therefore able to meet and discuss advances in geomatics theory and practice in their specific field of interest.

A total of about four hundred people connected to the online sessions, with an average number of participants per session of about a hundred people.

In total, 140 contributions were submitted to the conference. During a first review round, the Program Committee selected 36 papers that were consistent with the CCIS proceedings requirements. These were then submitted to a second round of evaluation by national and international reviewers in a single-blind review process. Finally, 28 papers were recommended for the publication in this volume.

As editors, we thank all reviewers for their support during the review process and, more broadly, the researchers whose work and commitment can be found in these proceedings.

While organizing this volume, chapters were built considering the different disciplines, methodologies, and research approaches within the ASITA Federation — Cartography, Geodesy, Remote Sensing, Photogrammetry, Geodatabase, GIS, and so on. Five chapters were finally populated, namely Remote Sensing Applications (five papers); Geomatics and Natural Hazards (six papers); Geomatics for Cultural Heritage and Natural Resources (four papers); Sensors Performance and Data Processing (eight papers); and Geomatics and Land Management (five papers).

In light of the accepted contributions, the editors proudly recognize that the volume is successfully compliant with ASITA's goals. It gathers solid and up-to-date scientific papers that move, in most cases, towards a high-level technology transfer. The book provides insights into the current and ongoing experiences and applications in geomatic tools and skills in Italy. The resulting framework is an encouraging one that certifies that proper competences can be found to support the economic recovery that is warmly encouraged and expected at both national and global level in response to the COVID-19 pandemic.

Geomatics is proving, once more, that it can certainly provide a significant and needed contribution in supporting territorial analysis, land planning, and cultural heritage representation and management, increasingly consistent with the green transition and resilience requirements cited in this specific historical moment.

The editors wish to thank the dedicated Program Committee members and all the other reviewers for their valuable contributions.

September 2021

Enrico Borgogno-Mondino
Paola Zamperlin

Organization

Program Chairs

Enrico Borgogno-Mondino   DISAFA - University of Torino
Paola Zamperlin   University of Pisa, Italy

Program Committee

Maria Antonietta Dessena   ENAS, Italy
Fabio Naselli   Epoka University, Albania
Andrea Fiduccia   AMFM GIS Italia, Italy
Antonio Ganga   AMFM GIS Italia, Italy
Alberto Giordano   Texas State University, USA
Francesco Guerra   Università Iuav di Venezia, Italy
Francesco Nex   University of Twente, The Netherlands
Stefano Nicolodi   SIFET, Italy
Filiz Sunar   Istanbul Technical University, Turkey
Paolo Dabove   Politecnico di Torino, Italy
Sandro Bimonte   INRAE, France
Francesco Pirotti   University of Padua, Italy
Domenico Sguerso   University of Genova, Italy
Maria Teresa Melis   University of Cagliari, Italy
Stefania Bertazzon   University of Calgary, Canada
Tiago Gil   University of Brasilia, Brazil
Elena Dai Prà   University of Trento, Italy
Cinzia Podda   University of Sassari, Italy

Contents

Geomatics and Land Management

Remote Sensing Applications

Copernicus Users Uptake: An Overview of Downstream Applications

Lorenza Apicella[1]([⊠]) ⓘ, Alfonso Quarati[1] ⓘ, Silvia Gorni[2], Roderic Molina[2], and Monica De Martino[1]([⊠]) ⓘ

[1] Institute for Applied Mathematics and Information Technologies, National Research Council, Genoa, Italy
{lorenza.apicella,alfonso.quarati,monica.demartino}@ge.imati.cnr.it
[2] GISIG, Geographical Information System International Group, Genoa, Italy
{s.gorni,r.molina}@gisig.it

Abstract. The European Programme Copernicus is one of the main sources of free and open Earth Observation (EO) data and information services, aimed at sustaining important social and economic advancements to the European Union with Remote Sensing (RS) practices. To achieve these goals User Uptake initiatives have been undertaken: aimed at increasing Copernicus awareness, dissemination and competences, thus supporting the development of downstream applications. The paper introduces the ongoing activity of the EO-UPTAKE project, funded by Liguria Region, aiming to bridge the skills gap between intermediate and end-users involved in the downstream sectors and promoting the use and integration of Copernicus data and services. It presents an overview of the Copernicus Programme and the European User Uptake initiatives, and provides a survey about the downstream applications based on academic literature, by outlining thematic sectors involved, the developed applications, their users, and data integration practices. Benefits and obstacles are discussed.

Keywords: Copernicus programme · Users uptake · Downstream applications · Core services

1 Introduction

Launched in 2014 by the European Commission (EC) with the European Space Agency (ESA), Copernicus[1] is the European EO Programme, equipped with a constellation of satellites, called Sentinels, which acquire data in a wide variety of wavelengths for atmospheric, oceanic and terrestrial monitoring. High-resolution data covering Europe and a large portion of Earth are made available via free and open data policy, thus establishing a crucial paradigm shift in EO's policies towards global environmental management and security [14]. Almost 150 terabytes of data are delivered daily to users from the central Copernicus Open Access Hub[2], to tackle more and more societal, environmental and

---

[1] www.copernicus.eu.
[2] www.scihub.copernicus.eu.

© Springer Nature Switzerland AG 2022
E. Borgogno-Mondino and P. Zamperlin (Eds.): ASITA 2021, CCIS 1507, pp. 3–14, 2022.
https://doi.org/10.1007/978-3-030-94426-1_1

economic challenges, and allowing to open new market opportunities. About this, the 2019 EC Market Report [31] forecasts economic benefits in the 2018–2020 period between Eur 16.2 and 21.3 billion, for the intermediate and end-users. The Report also estimates a 162,000 users-base that could benefit from Copernicus, which could grow by at least 780,000 users in the future. To ensure that the expected societal benefits materialize [31], Copernicus data and services have effectively to be used. In fact, just publishing Open Data *per-se* does not necessarily grant their reuse [32, 34], and Open Data have value only if used [33, 46, 51]. To this purpose, a User Uptake strategy [18] has been launched in 2016 by EC and many initiatives have recently been undertaken to raise user awareness, with the aim of increasing the competitiveness and the dissemination's skills. However, the heterogeneity of users communities, as well as the geographical peculiarities of public authorities make user uptake initiatives complex to manage. The current experiences highlight the need for a systematic and integrated framework to ensure the continuity and sustainability of these initiatives [50].

The paper presents the ongoing activity of the EU funded Italian project EO-UPTAKE[3], whose main objective is to increase the widespread of Copernicus competences fostering the collaboration between scientific training and the productive sector. The expected results will materialize in a series of procedures and guidelines for the access, use, and integration of Copernicus data by heterogeneous user communities. The paper focuses on the initial project activity related to the state of the art on the use of Copernicus resources. A preliminary overview of downstream applications (i.e. products using Copernicus data with social and economic potential) and thematic sectors presented in the recent academic literature is provided and described for the users, the data integration practices, the related benefits and obstacles.

2   Copernicus Background

Copernicus is an EO programme addressing the provision of environmental information, for land and oceans, climate and global changes and their effects on civil security. The objective of Copernicus is to monitor and forecast the state of the environment on land, sea and in the atmosphere, to support the climate change mitigation and adaptation strategies, the efficient management of emergencies, and the improvement of citizen security. As a publicly-funded EU Programme, Copernicus data are for the most part free and open. By mandate of the EU, their production and distribution are ensured by selected institutions across Europe, called Entrusted Entities. Data from the Sentinels are distributed by the ESA and the European Organisation for the Exploitation of Meteorological Satellites (EUMETSAT). Copernicus data and information are available in different ways: the Copernicus Open Access Hub for Sentinel data, the Copernicus

---

[3] www.gisig.eu/projects/eouptake.

Core Services[4] for value-added information and the Data and Information Access Service[5] (DIAS) cloud platforms for resources processing.

The following six Core Services are provided to support a broad range of environmental and security applications, transforming raw data into value-added information such as informative maps and datasets:

– *The Copernicus Atmosphere Monitoring Service*(CAMS), allows a continuous monitoring of Earth's atmospheric composition at global and regional scales through the provision of near real-time data and forecasts products. It is used for health, renewable energy, or climatology issues.
– *The Copernicus Marine Environment Monitoring Service*(CMEMS) provides systematic information about the physical state and dynamics of the ocean and marine ecosystems. Its products cover the global oceans and the European regional seas, through the provision of observations and forecasts.
– *The Copernicus Land Monitoring Service*(CLMS) provides information on land cover and land use over the years, vegetation state and the water cycle.
– *The Copernicus Climate Change Service* (C3S) responds to changes in the environment and society associated with climate change, through the provision of information for monitoring and predicting climate change and the support to adaptation and mitigation strategies.
– *The Copernicus Emergency Management Service* (CEMS) encompasses an early warning component about the risk assessments of floods and forest fires, and a mapping component which provides map and geo-information products for all types of natural and man-made disasters.
– *The Copernicus Security Service* (CSS) is addressed to crisis prevention, preparedness and response in three domains: border surveillance, maritime surveillance, and support to EU External Action. It is used to support related EU policies by providing information in response to the security challenges; the data provided for this service is restricted to authorized users [31].

Copernicus services process information from Sentinels' constellation, as well as tens of third-part satellites known as "contributing space missions", complemented by in-situ measurement data. Maps and statistics are retrieved from Sentinels products and can be used for generating indicators for researchers and end-users providing information on past, present and future trends. At present, three complete couples of satellite are in orbit plus an additional single satellites, Sentinel-5P and Sentinel-6 monitoring the various environmental compartments. Table 1 provides a synthetic view of Sentinel features [3].

---

[4] www.copernicus.eu/en/copernicus-services.
[5] www.copernicus.eu/en/access-data/dias.

Table 1. Sentinel Constellation features.

Satellite	Sensor	Resol.	Revisit	Domain
Sentinel-1 (2014)	Synthetic aperture radar	4–40 m	6 days	Oceans, ice and land, emergency
Sentinel-2 (2015)	Multispectral Optical imagery	10–60 m	5 days	Land and vegetation cover
Sentinel-3 (2016)	Radar altimeter, Optical imagers, infrared radiometer, imaging spectrometer	300–1200 m	<2 days	Land cover and ocean
Sentinel-5P (2017)	Spectrometer, IR Atmospheric Sounder	7–68 km	1 day	Global atmospheric pollution
Sentinel-4	Spectrometer on Meteosat	8 km	60 min	European air quality
Sentinel-5 (2021)	Spectrometer carried aboard the MetOp Second Generation satellites	7.5–50 km	1 day	Global air quality
Sentinel-6 (2020)	Radar altimeter and a microwave radiometer	300 m	10 days	Global sea-surf, height, oceanography, climate

3   EO-UPTAKE Project Outline

EO-UPTAKE is funded under the European Social Fund, Liguria Region 2014–2020, Axis 3, specific objective 10.5, to support the User Uptake strategy for maximising the adoption of Copernicus data and information in Europe.

3.1   User Uptake Strategy Activities

The EC report Copernicus User Uptake [18] on 2016 provides the building blocks of an effective user engagement strategy into the operational phase for the Copernicus Programme. The key objectives support an ecosystem of service providers, public or private, that transform space data into accessible and usable information, and promote the use and uptake of Copernicus data, products, services, and good practices among a wide range of user communities. In particular, as expressed in the 2016 Space Strategy, the EC focused on three key objectives: (i) to increase the awareness about Copernicus; (ii) to facilitate access to Copernicus resources; (iii) to support downstream actors. To meet these objectives, numerous EC initiatives are promoted, such as the Copernicus Relays and the Copernicus Academy Network which foster Copernicus awareness by respectively local user communities and academic communities [50].

Figure 1 shows a synthetic view of the User Uptake strategy and the Copernicus data value chain from the upstream sector related to satellite data acquisition, to the downstream sector. It points out the distinctions between intermediate users (i.e. technical) and end-users (i.e. non-technical). Intermediate users, with specific expertise in RS processing and analysis and/or geographic information system (GIS) databases, are involved in exploiting the EO-space data and providing EO-related products and services to end-users (i.e. citizens, Public Administration, i.e. PA, and private companies).

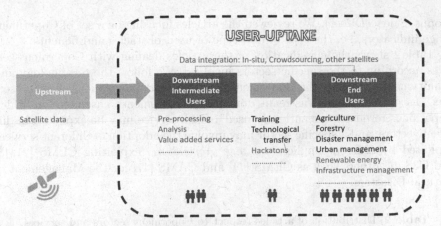

Fig. 1. Copernicus User Uptake and downstream sectors (re-elaboration of [31]). Font in black outlines activities and targets of the EO-UPTAKE project.

3.2 EO-UPTAKE Project

EO-UPTAKE is a two-year project, started in November 2019, promoting the development and the dissemination of competencies related to Copernicus data and services usage. It aims to bridge the gap between intermediate and end-user by strengthening the existing ecosystem of skills and promoting the use and integration of data and services supporting innovative applications for end-users. Focused on meeting the different end-user needs for Copernicus data access and use, one of the EO-UPTAKE main missions is to strengthen the competitiveness of the Italian Liguria Region through a new strategy which increases interactions between science and tertiary sector, research and innovation. EO-UPTAKE's core activity concerns the identification of practices and definition of a set of procedures and guidelines for access, use, and integration of Copernicus resources regardless of domain. The project will provide processing workflows for the realization of concrete examples of applications in different sectors: agriculture, forestry, urban monitoring and management of natural disasters. One of the missions of the project is the assignment of a research grant for training a young researcher, aiming at the transfer of technological skills in the EO sector, from research centres to companies potentially interested in the downstream sector.

4 Overview of Copernicus Downstream Applications

4.1 Literature Analysis

As starting project activity, we carried out an overview of the downstream applications based on a literature review to gather insights about the state of play of Copernicus resources research and use. We selected 41 recent (after 2014) peer-reviewed articles from well known scientific databases (i.e. Web of Science,

Scopus, ScienceDirect). We reviewed the articles focusing on a set of Copernicus usage indicators, i.e. the type of use, type of user, obstacles and benefits.

Table 2 shows the classification of the articles dealing with Copernicus services according to the specific sectors involved. We follow the terminology and definitions described in the Copernicus Market report [31], which refers to "sectors" as "promising downstream domains/user segments ensembles in which Copernicus resources are currently used". Each service may be exploited in different sectors, and a specific sector may involve the adoption of different services exploited by different applications, e.g. *Agriculture*, exploiting CLMS [21,48] and C3S [9], others such as CEMS [44] and CAMS [47] for the Management of Natural Disasters.

Table 2. Distribution of articles respect to Copernicus sectors and services.

Theme (service)	Sector	References
Climate (C3S)	Agriculture	[9]
	Climate	[8,30,39,41,45], [7,15,23,27,38]
	Coastal and marine exploitation and preservation	[43]
Atmospere (CAMS)	Air quality management	[22,23]
	Forestry	[20]
	Management of natural disasters	[47]
	Monitoring air quality	[1,2,5,17,28,40]
Emergency (CEMS)	Management of natural disasters	[10,13,16,23,35,44]
Land (CLMS)	Agriculture	[11,21,23,25,48]
	Forestry	[11,25,29]
	Urban monitoring	[11,24]
Ocean (CMEMS)	Coastal and marine exploitation and preservation	[4,6,12,19,23,26], [36,37,42,45,49]

4.2   Discussion

Type of Use. According to the type of use, we categorized articles as *Research* or *Product*. *Research* papers focus on research issues of the intermediate actions in the Copernicus data value chain: *e.g.* data processing and analysis [6,19], algorithms [13,20,42,43], services comparison or general documentation [15,23, 38]. *Product* are papers discussing the implementation of innovative applications based on Copernicus services. They deal with practices in specific sectors and address the final step of the data value chain. From Fig. 2, showing articles' distribution with respects to the Copernicus services and the type of use, we notice that most of the articles refer to products, thus confirming the relevance of Copernicus resources to face the environmental and social issues requiring the development of new resources. The ongoing release of spatial data supplies useful time series to support climatic studies. Not surprisingly, considering that Climate affects all the Earth system, we see from Fig. 2 that C3S is among the most exploited services. We found that it is used by downstream applications in different sectors: climate change monitoring [30,39], health [41], and climate forecasts for decision planning in agriculture [8].

Sentinel data integration with other satellite data, in-situ data, and data derived from numerical models, is a common and effective practice in the products' implementation to achieve some improvements such as:

- Enhancing temporal resolution of Sentinel data with the integration of other satellite data provided by non-European missions e.g. Landsat, MODIS, Sea-WiFS and Jason-3 missions [22] or other missions managed by NASA [9,10,24] or other EU missions e.g. Meteosat [2] for agricultural purposes [48], change detection in urban areas [11], and in emergency situations [10].
- Increasing the reliability of products thanks to the integration of *in-situ data*. Besides the usual calibration of Copernicus data, higher precision and accuracy, especially for specific parameters whose values are derived from existing indices and maps, may be achieved [4,49].
- Improving the ability to forecast and to simulate real-world conditions thanks to the aid of numerical hydrology or weather models [17].

From our study emerges that most of the data integration practices are in the meteorological field, especially for weather and atmospheric applications [2,26, 44,47]. Although weather models have been used since the second half of '900 for the study of atmospheric conditions, the assimilation of satellite-derived dataset integrated with in-situ data represents a revolutionary approach allowing achieve more precise weather forecast.

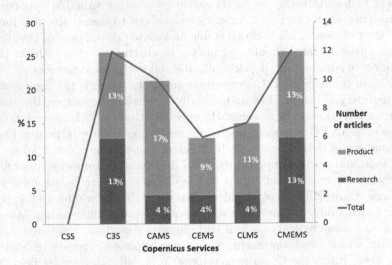

Fig. 2. Distribution of articles respect to the Copernicus services and their type of use (*Research* or *Product*).

Type of Users. Our study highlights the involvement of different type of users according to their roles in the data value chain and their levels of skills in EO or other scientific fields. For instance, EO-experts' skills are required in research topics about Land and Urban monitoring [24,45]. EO knowledge is used at an intermediate level by GIS users in application areas such as geology, or meteorology [11,26,44,47], where the goal is not to implement the resource but to reach a sector-specific final product. The required expertise may also be related to social and governance issues, involving end-users such as PA, target communities and citizens. This is the case of high-level decision organs processes as the ones dealing with climate change effects mitigation [9,30], as well as the local authorities in charge of disasters management [10,16,41] and air quality management [1,2,40]. Disregarding users competencies, Copernicus resources may be beneficial in social and health sectors supporting safer life programs addressing the continuous expansion of urbanized areas. It is therefore of primary importance to provide each user with information and uptake instructions according to its level of knowledge.

Benefits and Obstacles. The analysis of the literature highlights some social, economic, and technological benefits as well as obstacles related to technological, business, and policy issues in the Copernicus use.

Understanding user needs is the starting point for the planning, management and development of any Copernicus downstream application and the related benefits. The importance of a user-driven approach has been highlighted in many articles analysed [17,29,39]. Thus, a proper communication strategy with citizens, public and private institutions is needed to enhance the potential of Copernicus and to facilitate the use of its resources creating valuable opportunities and becoming a precious tool for decision-makers to assess the full implications of their choices. This boosts a stable and steady development. Besides, the upstream space industry should provide the downstream sector with the proper information to support and develop suitable and exploitable services.

The main challenge that Copernicus is currently facing is the fragmentation of the resources. This fact has undoubtedly a negative impact on the strategy of engaging new users. For newcomers, especially those with basic or intermediate knowledge of EO science, Copernicus may appear quite intricate. There is a huge number of data access portals, different Copernicus product stores, processing tools and managing platforms. This decreases the opportunity of finding the proper resources. As well, many of the Copernicus data borne applications allow users of any skill to exploit added-value data, thus providing useful applications for Earth monitoring systems, which are money and time-saving. Moreover, many *in situ* measurements, as well still required nowadays, combined with RS data, allow wider areas monitoring with fewer expenses. From a technological point of view, RS in the Copernicus ecosystem is still a developing field. Many implementing techniques, such as machine learning and deep learning processing image methods, have still much potential but are not yet fully exploited. On the other hand, the management and storage of the huge amount of data produced by the ongoing missions is still a challenge and have been partially solved in the Copernicus Programme.

5 Conclusions

In the context of EO-UPTAKE project, this paper analytically describes the use of Copernicus data and services for the implementation of downstream applications, their strengths and weaknesses. It represents the first step towards a new definition for the uptake strategy pointed at a wide range of users. A systematic literature review is performed providing an overview of the use of Copernicus resources. The analysis according to some usage indicators highlights the effective social and economic benefits of Copernicus use in many sectors. However, it also shows the heterogeneity of user communities involved in the downstream applications: from the EO expert to the end-user without technological skill. Thus, to benefit from the opportunity provided by the Copernicus ecosystem, it is necessary to bridge the knowledge gap between technical and domain expert users. This paves the way for future works addressed to enhance the uptake strategy. The next activity will study real use cases and user requirements to define the guidelines for Copernicus resources access and use.

Acknowledgment. This work is supported by the European Social Fund, Liguria Region 2014–2020, Axis 3, specific objective 10.5.

References

1. Adame, J., Notario, A., Cuevas, C., Lozano, A., Yela, M., Saiz-Lopez, A.: Recent increase in no2 levels in the southeast of the Iberian peninsula. Sci. Total Environ. **693**, 133587 (2019). https://doi.org/10.1016/j.scitotenv.2019.133587
2. Alfadda, A., Rahman, S., Pipattanasomporn, M.: Solar irradiance forecast using aerosols measurements: a data driven approach. Solar Energy **170**, 924–939 (2018). https://doi.org/10.1016/j.solener.2018.05.089
3. Ayazi, R., d'Auria, I., Tassa, A., Turpin, J. (Eds.): The ever growing use of copernicus across europe's regions (2018)
4. Bensoussan, N., et al.: Using CMEMS and the Mediterranean marine protected areas sentinel network to track ocean warming effects in coastal areas. J. Oper. Oceanogr. (2019). https://doi.org/10.1080/1755876X.2019.1633075
5. de Blas, M.: Summertime high resolution variability of atmospheric formaldehyde and non-methane volatile organic compounds in a rural background area. Sci. Total Environ. **647**, 862–877 (2019). https://doi.org/10.1016/j.scitotenv.2018.07.411
6. Bonaduce, A., Benkiran, M., Remy, E., Le Traon, P.Y., Garric, G.: Contribution of future wide-swath altimetry missions to ocean analysis and forecasting. Ocean Sci. **14**(6), 1405–1421 (2018). https://doi.org/10.5194/os-14-1405-2018
7. Buontempo, C., et al.: What have we learnt from Euporias climate service prototypes? Clim. Serv. **9**, 21–32 (2018). https://doi.org/10.1016/j.cliser.2017.06.003
8. Buontempo, C., Hewitt, C.: Euporias and the development of climate services. Clim. Serv. **9**, 1–4 (2018). https://doi.org/10.1016/j.cliser.2017.06.011

9. Buontempo, C., Hutjes, R., Beavis, P., Berckmans, J., Cagnazzo, C., et al.: Fostering the development of climate services through copernicus climate change service (c3s) for agriculture applications. Weather Clim. Extremes (2019). https://doi.org/10.1016/j.wace.2019.100226

10. Caballero, I., Ruiz, J., Navarro, G.: Sentinel-2 satellites provide near-real time evaluation of catastrophic floods in the west mediterranean. Water **11**(12) (2019). https://doi.org/10.3390/w11122499

11. Cole, B., Smith, G., Balzter, H.: Acceleration and fragmentation of corine land cover changes in the united kingdom from 2006–2012 detected by copernicus image2012 satellite data. Int. J. Appl. Earth Obs. Geoinf. **73**, 107–122 (2018). https://doi.org/10.1016/j.jag.2018.06.003

12. Delory, E., Pearlman, J.: Chapter 5 - innovative sensor carriers for cost-effective global ocean sampling. In: Challenges and Innovations in Ocean In Situ Sensors, pp. 173–288. Elsevier (2019). https://doi.org/10.1016/j.scitotenv.2016.01.020

13. DeVries, B., Huang, C., Armston, J., Huang, W., Jones, J.W., Lang, M.W.: Rapid and robust monitoring of flood events using sentinel-1 and landsat data on the google earth engine. Remote Sens. Environ. **240** (2020). https://doi.org/10.1016/j.rse.2020.111664

14. Doldrina, C.: Open data and earth observations: the case of opening up access to and use of earth observation data through the global earth observation system of systems. J. Intell. Prop. Info. Tech. Elec. Com. L. **6**, 73 (2015)

15. Donnelly, C., Ernst, K., Arheimer, B.: A comparison of hydrological climate services at different scales by users and scientists. Clim. Serv. **11**, 24–35 (2018). https://doi.org/10.1016/j.cliser.2018.06.002

16. Doxani, G., Siachalou, S., Mitraka, Z., Patias, P.: Decision making on disaster management in agriculture with sentinel applications. Int. Arch. Photogramm. Remote Sens. Spatial Inf. Sci. (2019). https://doi.org/10.5194/isprs-archives-XLII-3-W8-121-2019

17. Eskes, H., et al.: Validation of reactive gases and aerosols in the MACC global analysis and forecast system. Geosci. Model Dev. **8**(11), 3523–3543 (2015). https://doi.org/10.5194/gmd-8-3523-2015

18. European Commission: Copernicus User Uptake - Engaging with public authorities, the private sector and civil society. Final Version (2016)

19. Garcia, D.A., et al.: An identification and a prioritisation of geographic and temporal data gaps of mediterranean marine databases. Sci. Total Environ. **668**, 531–546 (2019). https://doi.org/10.1016/j.scitotenv.2019.02.417

20. García-Haro, F.J., et al.: Derivation of global vegetation biophysical parameters from eumetsat polar system. ISPRS J. Photogramm. Remote Sens. **139**, 57–74 (2018). https://doi.org/10.1016/j.isprsjprs.2018.03.005

21. Gomarasca, M.A., et al.: Sentinel for applications in agriculture. Int. Arch. Photogramm. Remote Sens. Spatial Inf. Sci. (2019). https://doi.org/10.1109/IGARSS.2018.8518494

22. Huijnen, V., et al.: Fire carbon emissions over maritime Southeast Asia in 2015 largest since 1997. Sci. Rep. **6** (2016). https://doi.org/10.1038/srep26886

23. Jutz, S., Milagro-Pérez, M.: 1.06 - copernicus program. In: Liang, S. (ed.) Comprehensive Remote Sensing, pp. 150–191. Elsevier, Oxford (2018). https://doi.org/10.1016/B978-0-12-409548-9.10317-3

24. Lefebvre, A., Sannier, C., Corpetti, T.: Monitoring urban areas with sentinel-2a data: application to the update of the copernicus high resolution layer imperviousness degree. Remote Sens. **8**(7), 606 (2016). https://doi.org/10.3390/rs8070606

25. Marco, E., et al.: Improvement of existing and development of future copernicus land monitoring products - the ecolass project. ISPRS Int. Arch. Photogramm. Remote Sens. Spatial Inf. Sci. **XLII-2/W16**, 201–208 (2019). https://doi.org/10.5194/isprs-archives-XLII-2-W16-201-2019

26. Minnett, P., et al.: Half a century of satellite remote sensing of sea-surface temperature. Remote Sens. Environ. **233**, 111366 (2019). https://doi.org/10.1016/j.rse.2019.111366

27. Monfray, P., Bley, D.: JPI climate: a key player in advancing climate services in Europe. Clim. Serv. **4**, 61–64 (2016). https://doi.org/10.1016/j.cliser.2016.11.003

28. Naitza, L., et al.: Increasing the maturity of measurements of essential climate variables (ecvs) at italian atmospheric wmo/gaw observatories by implementing automated data elaboration chains. Comput. Geosci. **137**, 104422 (2020). https://doi.org/10.1016/j.cageo.2020.104432

29. Piedelobo, L., et al.: Assessment of green infrastructure in riparian zones using copernicus programme. Remote Sens. **11**(24) (2019). https://doi.org/10.3390/rs11242967

30. Plummer, S., Lecomte, P., Doherty, M.: The ESA climate change initiative (CCI): a European contribution to the generation of the global climate observing system. Remote Sens. Environ. **203**, 2–8 (2017). https://doi.org/10.1016/j.rse.2017.07.014

31. France, P.C. (ed.): Copernicus Market Report. Luxembourg, European Union (2019)

32. Quarati, A., Raffaghelli, J.E.: Do researchers use open research data? exploring the relationships between usage trends and metadata quality across scientific disciplines from the figshare case. J. Inf. Sci. (2020). https://doi.org/10.1177/0165551520961048

33. Quarati, A., De Martino, M.: Open government data usage: a brief overview. In: Proceedings of the 23rd International Database Applications & Engineering Symposium, pp. 1–8 (2019). https://doi.org/10.1145/3331076.3331115

34. Quarati, A., De Martino, M.: Geospatial open data usage and metadata quality. ISPRS Int. J. Geo-Inf. **10** (2021). https://doi.org/10.1177/0165551520961048

35. Rossi, C., et al.: Early detection and information extraction for weather-induced floods using social media streams. Int. J. Disast. Risk Reduct. **30**, 145–157 (2018). https://doi.org/10.1016/j.ijdrr.2018.03.002

36. Rumson, A.G., Hallett, S.H.: Opening up the coast. Ocean Coast. Manag. **160**, 133–145 (2018). https://doi.org/10.1016/j.ocecoaman.2018.04.015

37. Staneva, J., Behrens, A., Gayer, G., Aouf, L.: Synergy between cmems products and newly available data from sentinel. J. Oper. Oceanogr (2019)

38. Stegmaier, P., Hamaker-Taylor, R., Jiménez Alonso, E.: Reflexive climate service infrastructure relations. Clim. Serv **17**, 100151 (2020). https://doi.org/10.1016/j.cliser.2020.100151, special issue on European Climate Services Markets - Conditions, Challenges, Prospects, and Examples

39. Swart, R., de Bruin, K., Dhenain, S., Dubois, G., Groot, A., von der Forst, E.: Developing climate information portals with users: Promises and pitfalls. Clim. Serv. **6**, 12–22 (2017). https://doi.org/10.1016/j.cliser.2017.06.008

40. Tchepel, O., et al.: Urban aerosol assessment and forecast: coimbra case study. Atmospheric Pollution Research (2020). https://doi.org/10.1016/j.apr.2020.04.006

41. Tompkins, A.M., et al.: Chapter 22 - predicting climate impacts on health at sub-seasonal to seasonal timescales. In: Sub-Seasonal to Seasonal Prediction, pp. 455–477. Elsevier (2019). https://doi.org/10.1016/B978-0-12-811714-9.00022-X

42. Tyler, A.N., Hunter, P.D., Spyrakos, E., Groom, S., Constantinescu, A.M., Kitchen, J.: Developments in earth observation for the assessment and monitoring of inland, transitional, coastal and shelf-sea waters. Sci. Total Environ. **572**, 1307–1321 (2016). https://doi.org/10.1016/j.scitotenv.2016.01.020

43. Tătui, F., Constantin, S.: Nearshore sandbars crest position dynamics analysed based on earth observation data. Remote Sens. Environ. **237**, 11155 (2020). https://doi.org/10.1016/j.rse.2019.111555

44. Van Hateren, T.C., Sutanto, S.J., Van Lanen, H.A.: Evaluating skill and robustness of seasonal meteorological and hydrological drought forecasts at the catchment scale-case catalonia (Spain). Environ. Int. **133** (2019). https://doi.org/10.5194/egusphere-egu2020-1491

45. Verron, J., et al.: The saral/altika mission: a step forward to the future of altimetry. Adv. Space Res. (2020). https://doi.org/10.1016/j.asr.2020.01.030

46. Viscusi, G., Castelli, M., Batini, C.: Assessing social value in open data initiatives: a framework. Fut. Internet **6**(3), 498–517 (2014). https://doi.org/10.3390/fi6030498

47. Vitolo, C., Napoli, C.D., Giuseppe, F.D., Cloke, H.L., Pappenberger, F.: Mapping combined wildfire and heat stress hazards to improve evidence-based decision making. Environ. Int. **127**, 21–34 (2019). https://doi.org/10.1016/j.envint.2019.03.008

48. Wolanin, A., Camps-Valls, G., Gómez-Chova, L., Mateo-García, G., et al.: Estimating crop primary productivity with sentinel-2 and landsat 8 using machine learning methods trained with radiative transfer simulations. Remote Sens. Environ. **225**, 441–457 (2019)

49. Van der Zande, D., et al.: Joint monitoring programme of the eutrophication of the northsea with satellite data user case. J. Oper. Oceanogr. **12**, 1–7 (2019)

50. Zeil, P., Ourevitch, S., Debien, A., Pico, U.: Copernicus user uptake-copernicus relays and the copernicus academy. In: GI Forum-Journal for Geographic Information Science, vol. 1, pp. 253–259 (2017)

51. Zuiderwijk, A., Janssen, M.: Open data policies, their implementation and impact: a framework for comparison. Gov. Inf. Q. **31**(1), 17–29 (2014). https://doi.org/10.1016/j.giq.2013.04.003

Land-Cover Mapping in the Biogradska Gora National Park with Very-High-Resolution Pléiades Images

Eleonora Cagliero[1,2]([✉]) [iD], Donato Morresi[3] [iD], Niccolò Marchi[1] [iD],
Laure Paradis[2] [iD], Walter Finsinger[2] [iD], Matteo Garbarino[3] [iD],
and Emanuele Lingua[1] [iD]

[1] Department of Land, Environment, Agriculture and Forestry (TESAF),
University of Padova, 35020 Legnaro, PD, Italy
eleonora.cagliero@phd.unipd.it
[2] University of Montpellier, ISEM, CNRS, IRD, EPHE, Montpellier, France
[3] Department of Agricultural, Forest and Food Sciences (DISAFA),
University of Torino, 10095 Grugliasco, TO, Italy

Abstract. Old-growth forests (OGFs) are extremely valuable relict ecosystems for studying natural disturbance dynamics. Small-scale disturbances caused by tree crown mortality of one or few individuals, i.e. gap dynamics, are the most frequent events occurring in OGFs. Understanding these processes requires information on the spatial arrangement of forest patches dominated by different tree species and forest canopy gaps at a fine spatial scale. Here, we aimed at mapping different land-cover classes including conifers, broad-leaved trees, and forest canopy gaps using two very-high-resolution satellite images, i.e. Pléiades images, in the mixed fir-spruce-beech OGF reserve of Biogradska Gora (Montenegro). Specifically, we coupled an Object-Based Image Analysis (OBIA) approach and a Random Forest classifier, trained with samples partly derived from field data. The adopted approach showed high accuracy for the main land-cover classes (conifers, broadleaved trees, grasslands, bare ground, and water), e.g. producer's and user's accuracy higher than 92% and 95%, respectively. Conversely, forest canopy gaps were classified with lower accuracy, e.g. minimum producer's and user's accuracies of 75% and 54%, respectively. Despite the exploitation of textural metrics during both image segmentation and classification, the lack of remote sensing data providing information on the vertical structure of the forest stand prevented us from accurately map forest canopy gaps.

Keyword: Very-high-resolution satellite imagery · Old-growth forest·
Land-cover map · Object-based image analysis · Forest canopy gaps

1 Introduction

Old-growth forests (OGFs) are ecosystems that have developed in the absence of anthropogenic influence and of stand-replacing natural disturbances for a period of time long

© Springer Nature Switzerland AG 2022
E. Borgogno-Mondino and P. Zamperlin (Eds.): ASITA 2021, CCIS 1507, pp. 15–27, 2022.
https://doi.org/10.1007/978-3-030-94426-1_2

enough (centuries-millennia) to develop peculiar structures and functions [1]. OGFs provide a wide range of ecosystem services, contributing to global biodiversity conservation and to mitigate climate change by carbon sequestration [1]. Moreover, OGFs act as reference systems for restoration and close-to-nature silviculture [2] because vegetation dynamics take place without direct human influence.

Depending on the predominant dynamics, OGFs have structural characteristics that vary among geographic areas. In temperate forests, large-scale natural disturbances are rare, and the stand dynamics are mainly characterized by small- to intermediate-scale forest canopy openings (gap dynamics) following the natural- or disturbances-caused mortality of single or small groups of dominant forest canopy trees [3]. The temporal and spatial interplay of type, size and frequency of disturbance events influences the species composition of the canopy layer and determines the creation of a heterogeneous mosaic of structural types [4] that is particularly developed in large OGFs (>1000 ha). However, presumably due to widespread millennial-long and increasing rates of land-use change [5, 6], large OGFs are rare today in Europe and mainly located in protected areas [6].

In the last decades, forest stand dynamics have been investigated mostly with terrestrial methods, such as representative sample plots (permanent or not), extensive field surveys, belt transects, and systematic grids [4, 7–10]. However, the structural heterogeneity of OGFs require a finer scale of analysis than terrestrial methods, which are expensive [11] and time-consuming, especially in OGFs, as these often are in remote places and difficult to access.

In this context, coupling remote sensing methods with field data as ground-control [3] is particularly valuable since it allows analyzing patterns (e.g. land-cover maps) and processes (e.g. gap dynamics) at the landscape scale in a shorter amount of time [3, 12, 13]. Moreover, remote sensing allows performing multi-temporal analyses to assess forest cover changes through time [14]. For instance, the extent and number of gaps continuously change due to (i) the formation of new ones and (ii) infilling by young trees and (iii) the expansion of older gaps. Even if the temporal dynamics can be deduced from field-based methods (by dendrochronology or repeated inventory in permanent plots), remote sensing analyses based on satellite imagery would be more cost-effective and could provide spatial information over broad areas.

However, the detection of fine-scale forest components, such as tree crowns and small forest canopy gaps, is constrained by the availability of very-high-resolution (c. <5 m) multispectral satellite imagery (e.g. Ikonos, Pléiades, QuickBird, Kompsat-2, WorldView-2) [3, 15]. To our knowledge, only few studies employed single very-high-spatial-resolution satellite images for mapping forest canopy gaps [3] while others took advantage of stereo aerial imagery [16] or integrated multispectral and LiDAR data [15]. Given the smaller pixel dimension with respect to the image objects of interest, a common approach adopted with high-spatial-resolution imagery is to perform Object-Based Image Analysis (OBIA) [17]. This technique aims at grouping neighboring image pixels with similar spectral and textural characteristics into objects, thus reducing their internal variability. OBIA avoids the "salt and pepper" noise commonly resulting in the classification compared to the traditional pixel-based methods and aims at delineating image objects that closely correspond to the size and the shape of real features [18].

Here we focused on the Biogradska Gora mixed beech-fir-spruce OGF (Montenegro), a forest landscape large enough to develop the whole natural temporal and spatial variability of forest dynamics [5]. Specifically, we aimed at mapping different land-cover classes including conifers, broad-leaved trees, and forest canopy gaps, using two very-high-resolution Pléiades images and coupling OBIA and a Random Forest classifier.

2 Methodology

2.1 Study Site

The Biogradska Gora National Park (Fig. 1) is located in the Dinaric Alps. The reserve area of the park (c. 6000 ha) includes a core area of strict protection of c. 2830 ha surrounded by a buffer zone (Fig. 1). In the core area, all land-use activities are prohibited except scientific research and controlled tourism. Instead, pastoral farming is allowed in the buffer zone, as meadows and shepherds' huts testimony. The reserve area is protected since 1885 CE as royal hunting reserve and since 1950 when the National Park was established. The climate is characterized by a mean annual temperature of c. 7 °C, and an annual average precipitation of 1962 mm with maximum values in November-December and minimum values in July-August. In the reserve area the overstorey is dominated by European beech, silver fir, and Norway spruce with lesser amounts of other tree species such as maples, common ash, and elms [5].

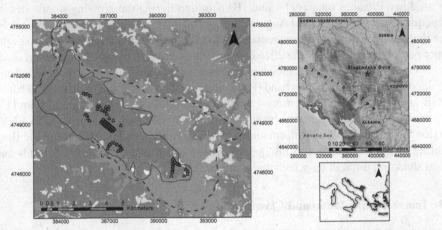

Fig. 1. Maps of the location of the study site at decreasing spatial scales and of the 81 forest plots (yellow triangles). Delimitation of the administrative boundary of Montenegro (red continuous line), of the reserve area (black dashed line) and of the core area of the Biogradska Gora National Park (blue continuous line). Reference system EPSG:32634 (WGS 84/UTM zone 34N). (Color figure online)

2.2 Field Surveys

To characterize the forest structure and the tree-species composition and to obtain ground control points for remote sensing analyses, we carried out field campaigns in May and

September 2019. We defined the location of the 51 survey plots (Fig. 1) using a forest map produced by Motta et al. [5] obtained by the classification of a SPOT5 image (acquired in May 2007) adopting an unsupervised classification algorithm (ISODATA) on three multispectral bands (G, R, and NIR). In each circular plot (area = 615.5 m^2; radius = 14 m) for all the living trees with a diameter at 1.30 m (DBH) $\geq$ 7.5 cm we recorded the species and DBH and for a sub-sample of individuals belonging to different species and diametrical classes we measured the height. We then measured the minimum and the maximum diameter and the length of the coarse woody debris (CWD) to assess the volume of dead biomass. We pooled the data of our 51 plots with the data of 30 plots surveyed by Motta et al. [5] in a 120-m grid network adopting the same field protocol. For each of the resulting 81 plots we derived typical forest stand parameters, such as mean and standard deviation of DBH, total tree density (De), and basal area (BA). We inferred the unmeasured tree heights using specie-specific hypsometric curves that we built based on the field data and computed the volume of living trees (V) using a local volume table.

2.3 Image Pre-processing

To map the distribution of six land-cover classes (conifer trees, broadleaved trees, grasslands-meadows, forest canopy gaps, bare ground, and water), we did an Object-Based Image Analysis (OBIA) on two very-high-resolution satellite images. Specifically, we used two Pléiades images (1A and 1B) acquired during the growing season of two subsequent years: on the 30th of August 2015 and on the 1st of August 2016, respectively. The images are spatially complementary, as the footprint of the 2015 image misses the upper part of the basin while the 2016 one was partly covered by clouds and cloud shadows over the forested area. The Pléiades images were provided already orthorectified and included a 0.5-m panchromatic band (PAN) and four 2-m resolution multispectral bands (RGB and NIR). We used the nearest neighbour diffusion (NNDiffuse) algorithm [19] to pan-sharpen the multispectral bands. The images were then co-registered in ENVI version 5.3.1 (Exelis Visual Information Solutions, Boulder, Colorado), using the Bing satellite image as reference. Subsequently, we masked invalid pixels, i.e. clouds and cloud shadows, through on-screen digitization.

2.4 Image Segmentation and Classification

We obtained image objects representing small groups of crowns using the Large-Scale Mean-Shift (LSMS) segmentation algorithm [20] implemented in Orfeo ToolBox version 7.0 [21] (Fig. 4). In particular, we set the following parameters in the LSMS algorithm: a spatial radius of 20 pixels, a range radius of 0.015 (as all rasters in the input stack assumed values ranging from 0 to 1) and a minimum region size of 200 pixels. We employed the Normalized Difference Vegetation Index (NDVI), the near-infrared band (NIR), and textural data derived from the mathematical morphology technique called opening as input rasters in the LSMS segmentation procedure. The opening procedure involves an erosion operation followed by dilation using a 2-dimensional structuring element (SE) [22], and it is applied to grey values of an image to eliminate objects smaller than the SE. Specifically, we used a 7-pixel diameter disc (corresponding to 3.5 m) as SE because this shape and size performed well to the smallest tree crowns recognizable in the Pléiades images. We performed the opening operation using grey values relative to the Value component of the Hue-Saturation-Value (HSV) transformation, which we applied to the red, green and blue bands of the Pleiades images. Since the Value component corresponds to the brightness of a surface, the opening procedure allowed us to maximize the contrast between sunlit crowns, generally located at the top of the forest stand, and darker portions in the background, corresponding to shorter trees and canopy gaps. We employed the Random Forest (RF) algorithm [23] implemented in the 'ranger' [24] R package (R Core Team 2019) to perform a supervised classification of the image objects. We created a set of 1457 training samples evenly distributed over the study area and stratified by land-cover class (Table 1) through on-screen photointerpretation of image objects intersecting the ground forest plots (groups of broadleaved trees, groups of conifer trees, forest canopy gaps) and of objects we did not survey (grasslands-meadows, bare ground and water). Predictor variables used in the RF classifier included several textural metrics together with reflectance values and selected spectral vegetation indices (Table 2).

We assessed the classification accuracy through a 5-fold cross-validation procedure and we analyzed each Pléiades image separately, merging classification results to obtain a unique land-cover map for the whole study area.

Since forest canopy gaps are areas temporary without a tree canopy cover (due to natural disturbances, gap dynamics), all the gaps permanently without tree vegetation due to limiting factors to tree growth (e.g. edaphic conditions, shallow water table) or human activities (e.g. pastures) that were erroneously classified as forest canopy gaps were filtered out in QGIS by a topological query before computing the number of gaps, size statistics and the gap fraction [25].

Table 1. Number of training samples in each land-cover class.

	Training samples		
	Image acquisition		TOT
Class	30th of August 2015	1st of August 2016	
Conifer trees	611	93	704
Broadleaved trees	435	137	572
Forest canopy gaps	18	11	29
Grasslands	66	19	85
Bare ground	32	27	59
Water	8	–	8

3 Results

The Biogradska Gora mixed fir-spruce-beech forest is characterized by the presence of large trees (DBH up to 150 cm, average DBH = 33.89 cm), and high volume of

Table 2. Details concerning the spectral and textural layers used to compute multiple summary statistics employed as predictor variables in the Random Forest (RF) model. NDVI = Normalized Difference Vegetation Index; EVI = Enhanced Vegetation Index; GNDVI = Green Normalized Difference Vegetation Index; MSAVI = Modified Soil Adjusted Vegetation Index; NDWI = Normalized Difference Water Index; SAVI = Soil Adjusted Vegetation Index; SR = Simple Ratio.

Spectral and textural layers	Summary statistics
Pléiades reflectance bands (PAN and MS)	Min; max; range; sum;
Spectral vegetation indices (NDVI; EVI; GNDVI; MSAVI; NDWI; SAVI; SR)	mean; variance; Gini
Morphological opening (kernels widths: 3; 5; 7; 9; 11; 13)	coefficient; standard
Simple Haralick textures (Energy; Entropy; Correlation; Inverse Difference Moment;	deviation; percentiles
Inertia; Cluster Shade; Cluster Prominence; Haralick Correlation)	(5th, 25th, 50th, 75th, 95th)

both living (907.3 m^3/ha) and dead biomass (251.57 m^3/ha). The forest stands show a complex horizontal and vertical structure, a high tree size diversification (DBH standard deviation of 22.74 cm), and a rotated sigmoidal DBH distribution.

The land-cover map derived from the Pléiades images (Fig. 2) confirmed on a small scale the spatial heterogeneity of the forest canopy. The overall good performance of the classifier is shown by high values of K and OA (Table 3). However, the classification accuracy differed greatly among classes. The Random Forest classifier performed better (in terms of both PA and UA) for conifers, broadleaved trees, grasslands, bare ground, and water classes while its accuracy was substantially lower for forest canopy gaps (Table 3).

Table 3. RF classification accuracy as assessed by means of overall (OA) and Cohen's Kappa (K) accuracies. Producer's (PA) and User's (UA) accuracies are grouped by land-cover classes.

| | Image acquisition | | | |
| | 30th of August 2015 | | 1st of August 2016 | |
Class	PA	UA	PA	UA
Conifer trees	95.8	96.1	92.9	97.8
Broadleaved trees	95.2	95.6	98.5	97.8
Forest canopy gaps	75.0	66.7	100.0	54.5
Grasslands	100.0	97.0	100.0	100.0
Bare ground	100.0	100.0	96.4	100.0

(continued)

According to the image classification (Fig. 2), the majority of the reserve area (61.09%) is covered by forest, followed by 33.56% of grasslands, 3.94% of bare ground,

Table 3. (*continued*)

Class	Image acquisition			
	30th of August 2015		1st of August 2016	
	PA	UA	PA	UA
Water	100.0	100.0	–	–
OA	95.6		96.5	
K	92.5		94.6	

1.15% of forest canopy gaps, and 0.25% of water. More in details, the core area consists mainly of forests (92.49%) while grasslands dominate (59.92%) in the buffer zone (Fig. 2). The inner part of the core area is dominated by coniferous trees while the surrounding area is dominated by mixed forest of beech-fir-spruce and by pure beech stands (Fig. 2). Forest canopy gaps were mainly found in conifer-dominated areas (99%).

Within the reserve area, 2638 forest canopy gaps were detected that cover a total of 67.95 ha, resulting in a gap fraction of 0.93% and a gap density of 0.45 #/ha (Table 4). The average size of gaps is 208.03 m^2 while the median value is 116.79 m^2 indicating that the majority of gaps are small, as confirmed by the negative exponential shape of the gaps size distribution (Fig. 3). In particular, 41% of gaps have a surface <100 m^2,

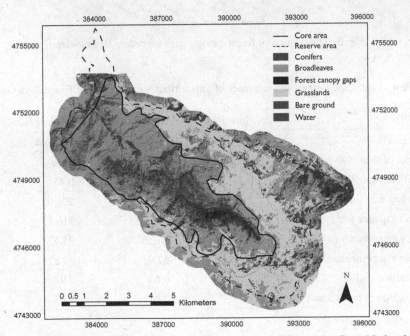

Fig. 2. Classification map of the land-cover classes of the Biogradska Gora National Park. Reference system EPSG:32634 (WGS 84/UTM zone 34N).

35% between 100 and 200 m^2, 18% between 200 and 500 m^2, and the remaining 6% are >500 m^2, whose 2% consists of gaps >1000 m^2 and only 0.15% are gaps >5000 m^2.

The core area and the buffer zones did not differ in terms of size (area), shape (perimeter), and frequency distribution of gaps (Table 4). On the other hand, the abundance of gaps was two times higher in the core area than in the buffer zone. However, since the buffer zone is characterized by a high proportion of grasslands (60%), the gap fraction relative to the forest area is higher in the buffer zone (Table 4).

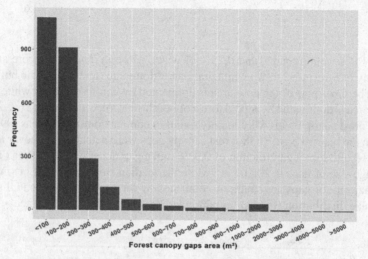

Fig. 3. Distribution of forest canopy gaps according to their size.

Table 4. Landscape metrics and summary of gap attributes in the OGF of Biogradska Gora.

Variables	Core area	Buffer zone	Reserve area
Total area (ha)	2834.27	3052.66	5886.94
Number of gaps (#)	1674	964	2638
Density of gaps (#/ha)	0.59	0.32	0.45
Mean gap area (m^2)	210.54	203.69	208.03
Median gap area (m^2)	119.78	111.85	116.79
Mean gap perimeter (m)	86.34	84.36	85.62
Median gap perimeter (m)	60.91	57.93	59.87
Gap fraction (%)	1.24	0.64	0.93
Gap fraction in forest area (%)	1.34	2.01	1.53

4   Discussion

The Biogradska Gora mixed fir-spruce-beech forest clearly shows old-growthness characteristics. The forest structure and the occurring gap dynamic place the forest among the largest old-growth forest remnants in South-Eastern Europe.

The combination of textural metrics with spectral data during the segmentation process is not a common practice as they are mostly employed in the classification phase [26], even if it has been shown to improve the classification accuracy of the land-cover classes in OBIA [17]. In our case, the use of textural metrics during the segmentation phase (Fig. 4) enhanced the identification of individual tree crowns and forest canopy gaps as they provided proxy information on the vertical forest structure. In fact, the opening procedure allowed us to distinguish between the circular-shaped and well-illuminated crowns of the dominant tree layer and the small trees and shrubs occurring in forest canopy gaps, characterized by lower brightness due to the shadow casted by the surrounding tree crowns.

Forest canopy gaps are more heterogeneous and with a rougher texture than the surrounding tree canopy cover [13, 18]. However, the classification shows lower accuracy in detecting forest canopy gaps compared to the other land-cover classes, as highlighted by a minimum producer's accuracy of 75% and a minimum user's accuracy of 54% (Table 3). The low producer's accuracy associated with forest canopy gaps can be affected by shadows, which we limited by employing the NDVI and the textural metrics in the segmentation and classification phases. Specifically, as a normalized index, NDVI is less affected by the proportion of canopy shadows than single reflectance bands and enhances the distinction between vegetation and bare ground [27].

The category of forest canopy gaps includes openings in the dominant tree canopy cover that can be already occupied by regeneration in various stages of growth. Conventionally, when the infilling trees reach heights equal to half of the height of the surrounding mature trees in the upper canopy [28], the area is assigned to the dominant tree-canopy cover. If the gap is small, the opening can be closed by the lateral growth of the edging tree crowns. This process is particularly evident when broadleaved species are involved, especially beech, since they have higher crown plasticity than conifers [29]. Of all observed gaps, only 1% were detected in broadleaved-dominated stands. This can be partially explained by the capacity of crowns to quickly close the gaps or reduce their size [7, 29]. The majority of gaps (99%) were found in coniferous stands, not only for the absence of lateral crown expansion of spruce and fir, but also since those stands showed the highest OGF characteristics. In OGFs, mortality is mainly occurring at the canopy layer, involving large and old, sometimes even individual, trees [1].

In the Biogradska Gora forest, canopy gaps are most often small (50–200 m^2), and large gaps (>1000 m^2) are rare (Fig. 3). The large gaps could have been generated by intense windstorm events or most probably by the expansion and fusion of neighboring gaps. This is supported by the shape analysis, which shows that large gaps are characterized by complex and heterogeneous shapes with a large perimeter.

Our analysis suggests that the gap fraction is small (<2%). Such small gap fraction values were also obtained in similar OGFs with remote sensing approaches using very-high-resolution images (Kompsat-2 and WorldView-2) [3, 12]. Such values are consistently lower compared to values derived from terrestrial methods (always >15%)

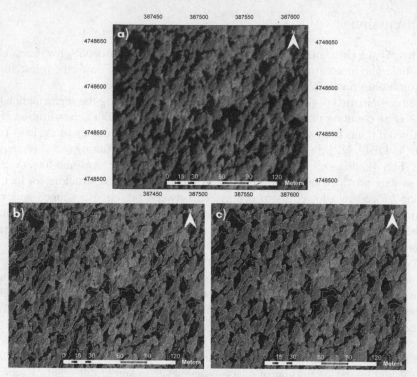

Fig. 4. Detail of the 2015 Pléiades-1B image displayed with false-color composite (R = NIR, G = Red, B = Green): original (a) and segmented either without (b) or with (c) the inclusion of textural information derived using the opening procedure. The parameters used in the Large-Scale Mean-Shift (LSMS) segmentation algorithm were held constant. Reference system EPSG:32634 (WGS 84/UTM zone 34N). (Color figure online)

[7–9]. It thus seems that the classification method substantially underestimates the fraction of the total forest canopy gaps. However, one should bear in mind that a broader range of gap ages and sizes are identified with field surveys [3]. With their finer detail of analysis, field surveys can better detect very small gaps, including those caused by a single tree-death. Moreover, field surveys can better detect old-formed gaps, including those that are almost closed or where regeneration is very high. Instead, the discrimination of gaps with remote sensing methods is hindered by the similar spectral response between the dominant tree canopy cover and the forest canopy gaps [26]. Conversely, remote sensing methods are suitable to detect recently formed gaps and large gaps in which the regeneration has not yet reached great heights or has not completely colonized the gap's surface. Moreover, remote sensing approaches are suitable to estimate the range of variability of disturbances over large areas. By contrast, terrestrial methods are often limited by the small size of the sampled area [8] and by expensive and time-consuming field inventories, especially in OGFs, which are usually located on steep slopes or in remote areas.

Our study reveals that the analysis of very-high-spatial-resolution satellite imagery alone is not sufficient to map forest canopy gaps and the complex forest structure of mixed

OGFs with high accuracy. Better results could be achieved using stereo-pair images or LiDAR data as they provide canopy heights, thereby allowing a better delineation of gaps [11, 12]. However, these approaches are more expensive due to image acquisition costs, especially in remote areas. Conversely, they achieve substantially higher accuracies (up to 96%) in gap detection [11]. Moreover, recent studies have shown the potential of combing optical and LiDAR data: LiDAR-derived Canopy Height Model allows to better isolate gaps during the segmentation phase. Simultaneously, the synergistic use of the two datasets can result in a more accurate classification map [15].

5 Conclusion

Coupling OBIA and a Random Forest classifier using two very-high-resolution Pléiades images provided high accuracy in mapping most land-cover classes with the exception of the forest canopy gap category. Even if the use of textural metrics during both the segmentation and classification phase enhanced gaps circumscription and the distinction between the dominant and the lower canopy layers, it was however not sufficient to obtain a good accuracy for this class. One reason for the low accuracy could be that the spectral indices (Table 2) derived from Pléiades MS bands (RGB and NIR) tend to saturate in dense vegetation conditions preventing an adequate distinction between young and mature crowns. Another possible reason could be the low number of training samples in the forest canopy gap category, since we used only the objects intersecting our field plot.

A reliable assessment of forest canopy gaps is extremely important to describe the complex forest structure and dynamics of mixed OGFs. Analyses based on single satellite imagery will lack the information on the vertical structure of the forests. Thus, to gain better results in terms of accuracy stereo-pair images, LiDAR data or a combination of optical and LiDAR data may be envisaged as better alternatives.

References

1. Wirth, C., Gleixner, G., Heimann, M. (eds.): Old-Growth Forests: Function, Fate and Value. Springer, Heidelberg (2009). https://doi.org/10.1007/978-3-540-92706-8_1. ISBN 978-3-540-92705-1
2. Bauhus, J., Puettmann, K., Messier, C.: Silviculture for old-growth attributes. For. Ecol. Manag. **258**, 525–537 (2009). https://doi.org/10.1016/j.foreco.2009.01.053
3. Garbarino, M., et al.: Gap disturbances and regeneration patterns in a Bosnian old-growth forest: a multispectral remote sensing and ground-based approach. Ann. For. Sci. **69**, 617–625 (2012). https://doi.org/10.1007/s13595-011-0177-9
4. Feldmann, E., Drößler, L., Hauck, M., Kucbel, S., Pichler, V., Leuschner, C.: Canopy gap dynamics and tree understory release in a virgin beech forest, Slovakian Carpathians. For. Ecol. Manag. **415–416**, 38–46 (2018). https://doi.org/10.1016/j.foreco.2018.02.022
5. Motta, R., et al.: Structure, spatio-temporal dynamics and disturbance regime of the mixed beech–silver fir–Norway spruce old-growth forest of Biogradska Gora (Montenegro). Plant Biosyst. **149**, 966–975 (2015). https://doi.org/10.1080/11263504.2014.945978
6. Sabatini, F.M., et al.: Where are Europe's last primary forests? Divers. Distrib. **24**, 1426–1439 (2018). https://doi.org/10.1111/ddi.12778

7. Bottero, A., et al.: Gap-phase dynamics in the old-growth forest of Lom, Bosnia and Herzegovina. Silva Fennica **45**(5), 875–887 (2011). https://doi.org/10.14214/sf.76
8. Drößler, L., von Lüpke, B.: Canopy gaps in two virgin beech forest reserves in Slovakia. J. For. Sci. **51**, 446–457 (2012). https://doi.org/10.17221/4578-JFS
9. Nagel, T.A., Svoboda, M.: Gap disturbance regime in an old-growth *Fagus-Abies* forest in the Dinaric Mountains, Bosnia and Herzegovina. Can. J. Forest Res. **38**, 2728–2737 (2008). https://doi.org/10.1139/X08-110
10. Petritan, A.M., Nuske, R.S., Petritan, I.C., Tudose, N.C.: Gap disturbance patterns in an old-growth sessile oak (Quercus petraea L.)-European beech (Fagus sylvatica L.) forest remnant in the Carpathian Mountains, Romania. For. Ecol. Manag. **308**, 67–75 (2013). https://doi.org/10.1016/j.foreco.2013.07.045
11. Vepakomma, U., St-Onge, B., Kneeshaw, D.: Spatially explicit characterization of boreal forest gap dynamics using multi-temporal lidar data. Remote Sens. Environ. **112**, 2326–2340 (2008). https://doi.org/10.1016/j.rse.2007.10.001.H
12. Hobi, M.L., Ginzler, C., Commarmot, B., Bugmann, H.: Gap pattern of the largest primeval beech forest of Europe revealed by remote sensing. Ecosphere **6**(5), art76 (2015). https://doi.org/10.1890/ES14-00390.1
13. Rich, R.L., Frelich, L., Reich, P.B., Bauer, M.E.: Detecting wind disturbance severity and canopy heterogeneity in boreal forest by coupling high-spatial resolution satellite imagery and field data. Remote Sens. Environ. **114**, 299–308 (2010). https://doi.org/10.1016/j.rse.2009.09.005
14. Torimaru, T., Itaya, A., Yamamoto, S.-I.: Quantification of repeated gap formation events and their spatial patterns in three types of old-growth forests: analysis of long-term canopy dynamics using aerial photographs and digital surface models. For. Ecol. Manage. **284**, 1–11 (2012). https://doi.org/10.1016/j.foreco.2012.07.044
15. Yang, J., Jones, T., Caspersen, J., He, Y.: Object-based canopy gap segmentation and classification: quantifying the pros and cons of integrating optical and LiDAR data. Remote Sens. **7**, 15917–15932 (2015). https://doi.org/10.3390/rs71215811
16. Zielewska-Büttner, K., Adler, P., Ehmann, M., Braunisch, V.: Automated detection of forest gaps in spruce dominated stands using canopy height models derived from stereo aerial imagery. Remote Sens. **8**, 175 (2016). https://doi.org/10.3390/rs8030175
17. Hossain, M.D., Chen, D.: Segmentation for Object-Based Image Analysis (OBIA): a review of algorithms and challenges from remote sensing perspective. ISPRS J. Photogramm. Remote. Sens. **150**, 115–134 (2019). https://doi.org/10.1016/j.isprsjprs.2019.02.009
18. Nyamgeroh, B.B., Groen, T.A., Weir, M.J.C., Dimov, P., Zlatanov, T.: Detection of forest canopy gaps from very high resolution aerial images. Ecol. Ind. **95**, 629–636 (2018). https://doi.org/10.1016/j.ecolind.2018.08.011
19. Sun, W., Chen, B., Messinger, D.W.: Nearest-neighbor diffusion-based pan-sharpening algorithm for spectral images. Optical Eng. **53**(1), 013107-1-013107-2 (2014). https://doi.org/10.1117/1.OE.53.1.013107
20. Michel, J., Youssefi, D., Grizonnet, M.: Stable mean-shift algorithm and its application to the segmentation of arbitrarily large remote sensing images. IEEE Trans. Geosci. Remote Sens. **53**(2), 952–964 (2015). https://doi.org/10.1109/TGRS.2014.2330857
21. Grizonnet, M., Michel, J., Poughon, V., Inglada, J., Savinaud, M., Cresson, R.: Orfeo ToolBox: open source processing of remote sensing images. Open Geospat. Data Softw. Stand. **2**(1), 1–8 (2017). https://doi.org/10.1186/s40965-017-0031-6
22. Soille, P.: Morphological Image Analysis: Principles and Applications, 2nd edn. Springer-Verlag, Heidelberg (2004). ISBN 978-3-642-07696-1
23. Breiman, L.: Random forests. Mach. Learn. **45**, 5–32 (2001)

24. Wright, M.N., Ziegler, A.: ranger: a fast implementation of random forests for high dimensional data in C++ and R. J. Stat. Softw. **77**(1), 1–17 (2017). https://doi.org/10.18637/jss.v077.i01

25. Schliemann, S.A., Bockheim, J.G.: Methods for studying treefall gaps: a review. For. Ecol. Manag. **261**, 1143–1151 (2011). https://doi.org/10.1016/j.foreco.2011.01.011

26. Kupidura, P.: The comparison of different methods of texture analysis for their efficacy for land use classification in satellite imagery. Remote Sens. **11**, 1233 (2019). https://doi.org/10.3390/rs11101233

27. Xu, N., Tian, J., Tian, Q., Xu, K., Tang, S.: Analysis of vegetation red edge with different illuminated/shaded canopy proportions and to construct Normalized Difference Canopy Shadow Index. Remote Sens. **11**, 1192 (2019). https://doi.org/10.3390/rs11101192

28. Tyrrell, L.E., Crow, T.R.: Structural characteristics of old-growth hemlock-hardwood forests in relation to age. Ecology **75**, 370–386 (1994). https://doi.org/10.2307/1939541

29. Muth, C.C., Bazzaz, F.A.: Tree canopy displacement at forest gap edges. Can. J. For. Res. **32**, 247–254 (2002). https://doi.org/10.1139/x01-196

UAV for Precision Agriculture in Vineyards: A Case Study in Calabria

Giuliana Bilotta[ID] and Ernesto Bernardo[✉] [ID]

Department of Civil, Energy, Environment and Materials Engineering (DICEAM), University Mediterranea of Reggio Calabria, Via Graziella, Feo di Vito, 89128 Reggio Calabria, Italy
`ernesto.bernardo@unirc.it`

Abstract. It is well known that nowadays remote sensing has a very crucial role in agricultural applications using in particular spectral indices as analysis tools useful to describe the temporal and spatial variability of crops, derived from processing of satellite images, each with different resolutions on the ground, according to the satellite of origin. It is also known that today such information can also be obtained through the use of sensors mounted on UAV (Unmanned Aerial Vehicle). In the present note we want to carry out a detailed analysis to define the condition of vigor of a vineyard situated in the province of Reggio Calabria (Southern Italy), comparing multispectral satellite images (Sentinel-2) with those provided by UAV platforms at low altitude, using as a parameter of effectiveness the relationship between the NDVI (Normalized Difference Vegetation Index) and the vigor of the crops. It is also proposed a GIS (Geographic Information System) for the management of agricultural land in order to build a system that can provide alerts in case interventions are needed depending on crop water stress.

Keywords: Precision agriculture · Satellite imagery · Unmanned aerial vehicle

1 Introduction

1.1 Precision Agriculture

In recent years, Precision Agriculture (PA) has received significant attention in the agricultural world. It enables automated management of portions of land on a "sub-apple" scale by integrating information technology and agronomic practices [1].

With the intention of integrating the concepts of business management and process automation, precision agriculture is a management strategy [2] that uses information technology to collect data from multiple sources in order to use them in decisions regarding field production activities [3].

Particularly interesting for this purpose is the crop monitoring that is based on observations carried out directly on crops in place in order to obtain data on phenological stages, nutritional status [5], phytosanitary status [6], production expectations [4, 7], production maps [8], etc. It is essential that this is automated given the large amount of data to be collected and processed [9].

© Springer Nature Switzerland AG 2022
E. Borgogno-Mondino and P. Zamperlin (Eds.): ASITA 2021, CCIS 1507, pp. 28–42, 2022.
https://doi.org/10.1007/978-3-030-94426-1_3

The crop monitoring, in particular, uses remote sensing data and is based on the link that exists between a series of parameters related to the leaf curtain [10] that can express the vegetative-productive responses of plants and evaluate the variability as a function of the different behavior of surfaces and bodies [11] to the phenomena of absorption or reflection of light in the visible and infrared [12].

Since the '70s, thanks to satellite remote sensing, large agricultural areas have been monitored for stock forecasting purposes [13], thus providing useful data for agriculture itself. Remote sensing techniques are very useful in fact to assess the state of vegetative health [14] thanks to the particular optical behavior of plants in the infrared radiation band [15]. The expensive flights of airplanes equipped with special cameras were soon supplanted by satellites that, continuously orbiting around the Earth, acquire data on the electromagnetic emission of objects on the Earth's surface, and therefore also of crops, with their multispectral sensors if passive, radar if active. Passive sensors in particular, however, have limitations in the necessarily diurnal acquisition and in the eventual cloud cover that constitutes an important obstacle. Also, the level of detail achievable does not allow certain types of analysis on small plots of land.

On the other hand, UAVs can be very useful by collecting more detailed georeferenced information with different types of sensors [16–19, 32].

In viticulture in particular, facing difficulties during production cycles by defining an adequate crop management, the PA approach has the final goal of improving vineyard yield and grape quality, while reducing all wastes, costs and decreasing environmental impact [20].

A correct knowledge of the spatial variability between and within crops is a fundamental factor for winemakers to estimate yield and quality results. Data provided by optical sensors in multispectral and hyperspectral imagery systems are exploited to calculate a broad set of crop-related indices (such as, for example, the LAI - Leaf Area Index [21]), of which the normalized difference vegetation index (NDVI) is one of the most widely used because it is related to crop vigor and, therefore, to estimated quantity and quality of field production.

MultiSpectral Instrument (MSI) of Sentinel 2 covers large areas and many satellite programs (i.e., Landsat, Sentinel-1 and Sentinel-2) now freely supply datasets, so promoting the exploitation of satellite imagery for many applications, agricultural too, including multisensor and multiresolution data fusion [22, 23]. Sentinel-2 from the European Space Agency (ESA) offers decameter resolution with six days revisiting time and efficient resolution in analyzing crop variability and conditions. But if we consider crops as orchards and vineyards (with discontinuities in layouts) remote sensing is more difficult. In fact, the existence of paths between yields and weedy vegetation within the cultivated land can greatly influence the overall calculation of spectral indices, resulting in a less accurate assessment of crop status. In order to overcome this criticality, new approaches and algorithms have been developed that also use multispectral data from UAVs [23, 24].

Low-altitude platforms, as UAVs with airborne sensors, by acquiring images with high resolution, having also flexible flight planning, allow to differentiate pure canopy pixels from other objects, even classifying details within canopies [25].

Specifically, it is possible to successfully combine an unmanned rotary-wing platform with a multispectral sensor in order to detect and monitor water-stressed areas of orchards, vineyards and olive groves [26].

NDVI index calculated by processing images taken in the infrared, is a parameter used in PA because it is directly related to the health of the vegetation, allowing to discover problems such as nutrient deficiency, the presence of parasitic infections or conditions of water stress. Early detection of such situations allows for targeted and effective intervention with cost savings and increased crop yield. Often infrared detection allows problems to be detected before they are visible to the naked eye [27, 28].

Multispectral sensors used on UAVs can record at least three channels like a normal camera but one of the channels is replaced by infrared. Although multispectral sensors can acquire in more than four bands, and multispectral cameras can record more than the 3 channels here defined, in this application each image will consist of two visible colors plus infrared [29, 30]. The NDVI index is thus calculated in a single image through a variant of the standard formula. The processing is done automatically in the GIS we used (QGis). The maps obtained after processing are false-color maps in which red represents areas of maximum vitality and are called "Vigor Maps" [31, 33].

In this paper, we are presenting an in-depth analysis of vineyards by comparing MultiSpectral Instrument (MSI) provided by a decameter resolution satellite and a low altitude UAV platform. The effectiveness of MSI from Sentinel-2 and UAV airborne sensors, with very high resolution, was evaluated considering the relationship between crop vigor and NDVI. UAV data were compared with satellite images, by calculating three NDVI indices to analyzing the contribution of the vineyard elements considering: (i) whole agricultural area; (ii) only vine canopies; and (iii) only inter-row soil [5, 34, 35].

Obviously, the proposed methodology can be extended to other types of crops grown in rows, where the crop canopies do not extend over the entire area or where the presence of grass or bare soil is significant [6, 36, 37].

2   Materials and Methods

Our study analyzed a vineyard situated in Bova Superiore, a small municipality in the province of Reggio Calabria (South Italy), locality Briga, covering an area of about 0.42 hectares. The cultivated territory is located in an area between latitudes [37.9855 and 37.9862'] and longitudes of [15.9142 and 15.917719'] and includes a series of parcels cultivated as vineyards, the most representative of which have respectively an extension of about 0.24 ha and 0.18 ha (Fig. 1).

The vineyard is located on a sloping land with a varied morphology, with an altitude ranging from 600 to 800 m above sea level and an orientation mainly facing south.

The interaxis between rows is 2 m, between one row and another there is a space of one meter while the width of the canopy of the row is about one meter. The planting dates back to 2016.

For the irregular land morphology as elevation, and soil characteristics, the considered vineyard is presumably characterized by variations in vine vigor within and between plots.

Fig. 1. Study area: Bova Superiore in Calabria, Southern Italy.

For extending the study to different phenological vine phases, we conducted survey campaigns (both satellite and drone) from May to September 2020. The vigor in fact varies throughout the phenological cycle, and consequently we acquired the images in four stages between flowering and ripening for considering various vegetative states [38]. However, some meteorological trends (including below-average rainfall) caused stress on crops by affecting the growth of plants [44].

Table 1. Characteristics of satellite Sentinel 2 imagery

Sentinel 2	
No. channels	13
Spectral bands used	B4 – Red 650–680 nm B8 – NIR 770–810 nm
Ground sampling distance (GSD) per band	10 m
Ground dimension of the image	100 km × 100 km

As satellite data were used Sentinel-2 Level 2A acquired on May 24, July 28, August 27 and September 21 2020 at 09:40 UTC (in Fig. 2 you can see an example) and in the Table 1 we report the image characteristics [39].

Fig. 2. Sentinel 2 false color image (RGB = bands 8, 4, 3) of a subset of the province of Reggio Calabria including the study area.

Regarding instead the multispectral images acquired by drone, it is noted that it was used the Parrot Bluegrass drone that integrates the multispectral sensor Parrot Sequoia, suitable for use in agriculture can capture images of crops in both the visible spectrum, both in the infrared. This system includes:

- A multispectral sensor recording crop images of crops in four spectral bands: Green (500 nm Bandwidth 40 nm), Red (660 nm Bandwidth 40 nm), Red-edge (735 nm Bandwidth 10 nm) and Near Infrared (790 nm Bandwidth 40 nm).
- An RGB camera (16 MP).
- An integrated 64 GB memory.
- A built-in brightness sensor ('sunshine' sensor) that records light situation and calibrates automatically the four multispectral sensors. The 'sunshine' sensor integrates an SD card slot to expand storage capacity.
- Sequoia also integrates GPS and IMU (Inertial Measurement Unit).

Table 2 shows UAV, sensor's image and characteristics.

Table 2. Platforms and sensors used: parrot sequoia multispectral camera

	No. channels	4
	Spectral bands	B2 – Red 640-680 mm B4 – NIR 770-810 nm
	GSD per band	5 cm
	Flight speed	30km/h
	Flight altitude	30m
	FOV – Field-of-view	70.6'' HFOV
	Ground Dimension of the Image	160m x 30m 100m x 35m

Figure 3 shows the parcels on the ground, with the superimposition of the hyperspectral camera images.

In Fig. 3 (a) are shown in false colors (NIR channels, red and green) the limits of the considered particles (marked by yellow polygons identified with "Area-A" and "Area-B"), returned by UAV. In particular the UAV-based multispectral images were processed with the Agisoft PhotoScan® software, processing imagery sequences of more than 1000 images acquired by a Parrot Sequoia® multispectral camera [40–42]. UAV flights were conducted on May 6, June 27, August 10, and September 15 at different hours.

The UAV route was designed to maintain flight height about 30 m above the ground by correctly defining waypoint sets. With this specification, the aerial GSD images measure 5 cm (Table 2).

Figure 3 shows the parcels on the ground, with the superimposition of the multispectral camera images, reference system is WGS84.

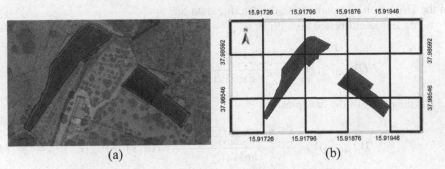

(a) (b)

Fig. 3. (a) Superimposition of the hyperspectral camera images on the surveyed parcels; multispectral imagery UAV-based, shown in false colours (Green, Red, NIR), of (b): "Area-A" and "Area-B". Reference system is WGS84. (Color figure online)

2.1 Data Processing

At this point we proceeded to comparing and analyzing the images obtained from the UAV and satellite with respective spatial resolutions after selecting from the Sentinel images the pixels fully enclosed in the limits of the 2 study areas considered "Area A" and "Area B" (Fig. 3).

In this regard, a procedure has been implemented to automatically determine the value of NDVI from satellite ($NDVI_{sat}$), to achieve homogenization of Sentinel and UAV data (through a downsampling of correlation between pixels s(i, j) from satellite and P(i,j) from UAV), to calculate the NDVI from UAV ($NDVI_{uav}$) and to calculate both the NDVI for the leaf canopies of the vines ($NDVI_{vin}$) and NDVI of inter-row area ($NDVI_{int}$).

In fact, important for evaluating the variability in the vineyard and therefore the vines vigor is NDVI index, thus calculated for the pixels of the Sentinel image s(i,j) thanks to the spectral data) in RED and NIR bands:

$$NDVI_{sat}(i,j) = \frac{n_N(i,j) - n_R(i,j)}{n_N(i,j) + n_R(i,j)} \tag{1}$$

A preliminary downsampling method of the high-resolution UAV images was done to allow the comparison of the UAV-based MSI and the Satellite imaging. So we proceeded to sampling the UAVs, data (at higher resolution) for comparing them with the corresponding satellite data, i.e. the set of UAV data D corresponding to P(i,j):

$$\mathcal{G}(i,j) = \{d(u,v) \in \mathcal{D} | \alpha_s(i, j+1) \leq \alpha_d(u,v) < \alpha_s(i,j),$$
$$\beta_s(i,j) \leq \beta_d(u,v) < \beta_s(i+1,j), \forall u,v\} \tag{2}$$

Thus the satellite data s(i,j) and UAV data P(i,j) show the same subset of the vineyard. Three NDVIs were analyzed from the VHR 2data from the multispectral sensor mounted on the UAV, then compared with the satellite data on:

(i) the entire cultivated area P(i,j):

$$NDVI_{uav}(i,j) = \frac{\sum_u \sum_v \frac{m_N(u,v) - m_R(u,v)}{m_N(u,v) + m_R(u,v)}}{\text{card } P(i,j)} \forall d(u,v) \in P(i,j) \tag{3}$$

(ii) the pixels of the canopies:

$$NDVI_{vin}(i,j) = \frac{\sum_u \sum_v \frac{m_N(u,v) - m_R(u,v)}{m_N(u,v) + m_R(u,v)}}{\text{card } P(i,j)} \forall d(u,v) \in P_{vin}(i,j) \tag{4}$$

(iii) the pixels of the inter-rows:

$$NDVI_{int}(i,j) = \frac{\sum_u \sum_v \frac{m_N(u,v) - m_R(u,v)}{m_N(u,v) + m_R(u,v)}}{\text{card } P(i,j)} \forall d(u,v) \in P_{int}(i,j) \tag{5}$$

In Fig. 4, (a) shows the $NDVI_{sat}$ map obtained the full set of pixels selected from Satellite imagery; (b) shows an $NDVI_{uav}$ map congruent (correctly aligned, at the same spatial resolution) to those derived from satellite imagery ($NDVI_{sat}$); (c) shows the complete $NDVI_{vin}$ map; (d) shows the $NDVI_{int}$ map of the inter-row ground, derived by processing the UAV images (Table 3).

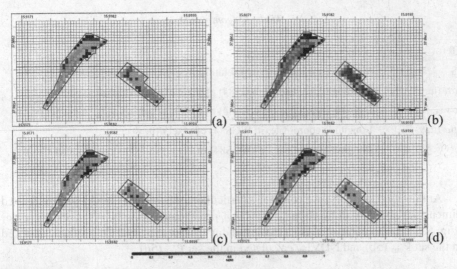

Fig. 4. Complete (a) $NDVI_{sat}$ map, with pixels fully included in "Area A" and "Area B", derived from satellite images S_2, and (b) $NDVI_{uav}$ obtained from UAV images D_2. (c) Vineyard $NDVI_{vin}$ map from UAV images D_2 obtained only on canopy pixels P_{vin}, (d) $NDVI_{int}$ map that consideres inter-row ground P_{int}.

Table 3. Nomenclature.

Term	Nomenclature
$d(u, v)$	Pixel in row u and column v of D, raster matrix
D	HIGH-resolution UAV multispectral image
$P(i, j)$	UAV pixels $d(u, v)$ depicting the area of satellite pixels $s(i, j)$
$P_{vin}(i, j)$	UAV pixels $d(u, v)$ showing only vines canopy
$P_{int}(i, j)$	UAV pixels $d(u, v)$ depicting only inter-row ground
$NDVI_{sat}(i, j)$	NDVI estimated using satellite images S
$NDVI_{uav}(i, j)$	Entire NDVI calculated on UAV pixels in $P(i, j)$
$NDVI_{vin}(i, j)$	NDVI calculated only on UAV pixels $P_{vin}(i, j)$ that represent vines canopy
$NDVI_{int}(i, j)$	NDVI calculated only on UAV pixels $P_{int}(i, j)$ showing inter-row ground
$mN(i, j)$	Reflectance values in the NIR band of pixels $d(u, v)$
$mR(i, j)$	DNs in the red band of pixels $d(u, v)$
$nN(i, j)$	DNs in the NIR band of pixels $s(i, j)$
$nR(i, j)$	DNs in the red band of pixels $s(i, j)$
$s(i, j)$	Pixels of row i and column j inthe raster matrix S

(continued)

Table 3. (*continued*)

Term	Nomenclature
S	Multispectral image 10 m resolution from Sentinel satellite
αd (u, v)	Latitude coordinate (in WGS84) of pixel d(u, v) centre
αs (i, j)	Latitude coordinate (in WGS84) of the upper left corner of pixel s(i, j)
βd (u, v)	Longitude coordinate (in WGS84) of pixel d(u, v) centre
βs (i, j)	Longitude coordinate (in WGS84) of the upper left corner of pixel s(i, j)

At this point, as in [5], we consider a particular study area of the vineyard of limited dimensions about 10 m by 10 m (size about 1 pixel) calculating $NDVI_{uav}$ in false color (Fig. 5a), $NDVI_{uav}$ in two classes canopy and inter-row (5b), $NDVI_{vin}$ value calculated in the set P_{vin} (5c) and $NDVI_{int}$ calculated in the set P_{int} (5d).

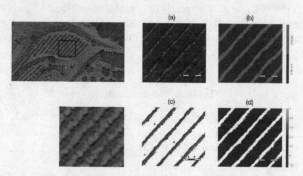

Fig. 5. Study area with 10 m ×10 m vineyard selection: (a) Enhancement of subset P(8, 20) of UAV map D2 in false colours (Green, Red and NIR); (**b**) pixels d(u, v) $\subset$ P(8, 20) classified into two classes: P_{vin} (green), vine canopies, and P_{int} (brown), inter-row ground; (**c**) NDVI values of P_{vin}, vine canopies; (**d**) inter-row ground P_{int}. (Color figure online)

3   Results

At this point, having available the NDVI values, both from UAV and satellite, we proceed to interpolate (correlation) the various data obtained, related to the categories $NDVI_{uav}$, $NDVI_{vin}$, $NDVI_{int}$, in order to assess whether the response from the two methodologies can be comparable [43]. For evaluating the comparison of satellite and UAV images effectiveness in depicting and evaluating the vigor value variability estimated relative to the vineyard, we calculated four NDVI maps over time:

- an $NDVI_{sat}$ map from satellite images;
- (i) an $NDVI_{uav}$ full map (spectral values from all the pixels showing both inter-row ground and vine canopies);

- (ii) an $NDVI_{vin}$ map of vine canopies;
- and (iii) an $NDVI_{int}$ map for paths between rows.

For comparing UAV-based images with satellite images (having 10 m GSD), UAV images - high-resolution - were decampioned as previously indicated.

The matching between each pair of spatiotemporal maps was examined using pair was examined with statistical comparison techniques, in particular Pearson's correlation coefficient, as measure of map similarity, after operating a normalization procedure focusing differences of the map pair.

With a preliminary investigation we examined the robustness of the set of data comparing $NDVI_{sat}$ map and $NDVI_{uav}$ full map, for the two Areas and four acquisition campaigns as can be seen by way of example from the correlation for the pair of images D1/S1, detailed for "Area A", "Area B" (note Fig. 6a–c where the $NDVI_{sat}$ map values (x axis) are correlated with:

- (a) the $NDVI_{uav}$ full map (y axis);
- (b) the NDVI values enhanced of $NDVI_{vin}$ map (y axis);
- (c) the leftover NDVI values of the $NDVI_{int}$ map (y-axis).

The values of the Pearson correlation coefficients obtained, referred to as $R_{Sat}/_{UAV}$, confirmed the consistency between the information obtained by the two platforms.

Table 4. Pearson correlation coefficient results of the NDVI map comparison procedure.

Map pair	$R_{sat/UAV}$				$R_{sat/vin}$				$R_{sat/int}$			
	D_1/S_1	D_2/S_2	D_3/S_3	D_4/S_4	D_1/S_1	D_2/S_2	D_3/S_3	D_4/S_4	D_1/S_1	D_2/S_2	D_3/S_3	D_4/S_4
Parcel A	0.58	0.68	0.61	0.58	0.33	0.31	0.40	0.45	0.58	0.66	0.59	0.52
Parcel B	0.59	0.66	0.64	0.62	0.42	0.40	0.42	0.42	0.63	0.66	0.54	0.61

Once the coherence of the chosen dataset was verified, the information quality offered by the two types of NDVI maps on vineyard vegetative condition was tested by comparing the $NDVI_{sat}$ and $NDVI_{uav}$ maps with the three-class field assessment of vigor performed by experienced vigor operators (Fig. 6). Statistical techniques based on analysis of variance did not show a significant difference between vigor groups.

The use of an image with a resolution of about 30 cm such as a WorldView-3, although not comparable to the drone data as resolution, would still allow a better definition of the vigor of the vines and, more generally, of the row crops.

WorldView-3 offers 31 cm ground sampling distance (GSD) for the panchromatic band and 124 cm for the 8 multispectral bands. With imagery from the WorldView-3 satellite, a much more accurate vigor analysis could be accomplished by proceeding as was done here with the UAV. In this case, since the inter-row areas are discriminable (those, acquired by decametric satellite sensor, lead to a bad understanding of the actual vigor of the vines), we could also provide a verification with Object Based Image Analysis (OBIA), operating firstly a segmentation of the canopies and inter-row areas, then

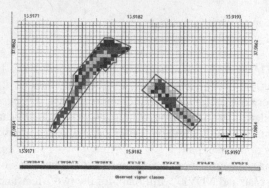

Fig. 6. Vineyard site classification into three vigor classes on the basis of the observed evaluation in field vigor. Classes "L", "M", and "H" related to low, medium, and high vigor.

proceeding separately to the classification of the vigor through the different NDVI found in the extraction of the objects formed with OBIA (extracting objects directly from satellite imagery is one of the strengths of OBIA, which is used in a wide range of applications [27]).

As a result of these analyses we realized a GIS (Fig. 7) for monitoring and managing agricultural land with Remote Sensing using, as input data, UAV images and Very High Resolution (VHR) satellite imagery classified with OBIA. The GIS is useful for agriculture in general and not only for vineyard management, and takes into account the geomorphology of the land, climatic conditions (wind, rain etc.) and moisture conditions of the soil for the crops. This system can provide alerts in case interventions are needed depending on crop water stress.

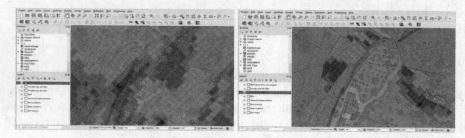

Fig. 7. GIS, VHR image: green = NDVI high; yellow = NDVI medium; red = NDVI low. (Color figure online)

Our analysis of satellite imagery at decametric resolution revealed limitations in providing information on the conditions of vineyards: indeed crop information can be modified by inter-row soil which, as for row crops, could modify the assessment. In fact, we found a strong correspondence between $NDVI_{sat}$ satellite map and $NDVI_{int}$ map obtained from UAV images depicting just inter-row pixels (table on Pearson's correlation coefficients above 0.6 over 65% of the map pairs and never below 0.52). In addition, we found a poor relationship among $NDVI_{sat}$ satellite map and $NDVI_{vin}$ map, that in UAV images considers only pixels of he vine canopies. More than 87% of the Pearson $R_{sat}/_{vin}$ correlation coefficients were equal to or less than 0.42 (Table 4).

This analysis shows that, in the presence of crops in which paths and inter-row surfaces cover a significant part of cultivated land, as vineyards, we see that the information by the satellite platforms with sensor of decameter spatial resolution is not sufficient to correctly assess the condition of the crops and their variability. The inter-row area may be bare soil, or covered by grass, by other crops for integrated pest control, according to the crop choices made. Thus, vineyard vigor may not match that of the inter-row areas, leading to biased assessments of vineyard vigor from decameter spatial resolution images. We verified the efficacy of $NDVI_{vin}$ and $NDVI_{sat}$ maps in identifying plant vigor, in accordance with expert field assessment, using statistical techniques based on analysis of variance method. The results show that, in crops where is inter-row ground, the information acquired from satellite platforms at decametric resolution do not allow to correctly assess the state and variability of the crops, which instead is possible and accurate through the use of sensors from UAV [34, 35]. This additional verification confirmed the most important result of the analysis performed, demonstrating that, when crops have inter-row areas covering a significant portion of the cultivated land, such as vineyards, satellite-acquired radiometric information may have difficulty in correctly assessing crop condition and variability. In these scenarios, to properly evaluate variation inside and between vines, high-resolution images are needed.

4   Conclusions

Our article introduces an in-depth analysis with a comparing of multispectral vineyard imagery acquired from satellite platforms as Sentinel-2 [36], at decameter resolution, and ultra-high resolution, low altitude UAV platforms. We evaluated the effectiveness of the specified satellite images and those from UAVs based on NDVI defining vineyard vigor. A farmland located in Bova Superiore (Calabria, Southern Italy) was selected as experimental site for the realization of four imaging campaigns scheduled according to the main phenological stages of the grapevine.

The outcomes demonstrate that in vineyards the data captured by satellite systems at decametric resolution are not adequate to correctly assess the condition and variability of crops. In fact, on the basis of Sentinel-2 images, vineyard vigor could be in discordance with inter-row zones obtaining an erroneous assessments of vineyard vigor. This was demonstrated by an in-depth analysis of the contribute of the various components within the cultivated land by determining three distinct NDVI indices from the high-resolution UAV images, considering: (i) the entire cropland area; (ii) only the vine canopy; and (iii) only the soil pixels between the rows. The satellite-based NDVI maps were shown to be better. correlated to NDVI maps calculated from high-resolution UAV imagery relating only to inter-row surfaces, whereas NDVI from UAV imagery relating only to pixels representing vine canopies better describes vineyard vigor. The proposed approach can be extended to other types of crops grown with substantial inter-row spaces.

The GIS realized for monitoring and managing agricultural land with Remote Sensing with UAV images and VHR satellite imagery classified with OBIA is very useful for agricultural management, producing also alerts in case of crop stress.

References

1. Arnó, J., Martínez-Casasnovas, J.A., Ribes-Dasi, M., Rosell, J.R.: Review, precision viticulture, research topics, challenges and opportunities in site-specific vineyard management. Span. J. Agric. Res. **7**, 779–790 (2009)
2. Silvestroni, O., Lanari, V., Lattanzi, T.: Canopy management strategies to control yield and grape composition of Montepulciano grapevines. Aust. J. Grape Wine Res **25**, 30–42 (2018)
3. Bramley, R.G.V., Hamilton, R.P.: Understanding variability in winegrape production systems. Aust. J. Grape Wine Res **10**, 32–45 (2004)
4. Song, J., et al.: Pinot Noir wine composition from different vine vigour zones classified by remote imaging technology. Food Chem **153**, 52–59 (2014)
5. Khaliq, A., Comba, L., Biglia, A., Ricauda Aimonino, D., Chiaberge, M., Gay, P.: Comparison of satellite and UAV-based multispectral imagery for vineyard variability assessment. Remote Sensing. **11**, 436 (2019)
6. Primicerio, J., Gay, P., Ricauda Aimonino, D., Comba, L., Matese, A., Di Gennaro, S.F.: NDVI-based vigour maps production using automatic detection of vine rows in ultra-high resolution aerial images. In: Proceedings of the 10th European Conference on Precision Agriculture, Israel, pp. 465–470 (2015)
7. Hall, A., Lamb, D.W., Holzapfel, B., Louis, J.: Optical remote sensing applications in viticulture - a review. Aust. J. Grape Wine Res **8**, 36–47 (2002)
8. Lanjeri, S., Melia, J., Segarra, D.: A multi-temporal masking classification method for vineyard monitoring in central Spain. Int. J. Remote Sens **22**, 3167–3186 (2001)
9. Bramley, R., Proffitt, A.P.B.: Managing variability in viticultural production. Grapegrow. Winemak **427**, 11–16 (1999)
10. Enenkel, M., et al.: What rainfall does not tell us—enhancing financial instruments with satellite-derived soil moisture and evaporative stress. Remote Sens. **10**, 1819 (2018)
11. Romero, M., Luo, Y., Su, B., Fuentes, S.: Vineyard water status estimation using multispectral imagery from an UAV platform and machine learning algorithms for irrigation scheduling management. Comput. Electron. Agric **147**, 109–117 (2018)
12. Comba, L., Biglia, A., Ricauda Aimonino, D., Gay, P.: Unsupervised detection of vineyards by 3D point-cloud UAV photogrammetry for precision agriculture. Comput. Electron. Agric **155**, 84–95 (2018)
13. Dobrowski, S.Z., Ustin, S.L., Wolpert, J.A.: Remote estimation of vine canopy density in vertically shoot-positioned vineyards: determining optimal vegetation indices. Aust. J. Grape Wine Res **8**, 117–125 (2002)
14. Sun, L., et al.: Daily mapping of 30 m LAI and NDVI for grape yield prediction in California vineyards. Remote Sens **9**, 317 (2017)
15. Johnson, L.F.: Temporal stability of an NDVI-LAI relationship in a Napa Valley vineyard. Aust. J. Grape Wine Res **9**, 96–101 (2003)
16. Johnson, L.F., Bosch, D.F., Williams, D.C., Lobitz, B.M.: Remote sensing of vineyard management zones: Implications for wine quality. Appl. Eng. Agric **17**, 557–560 (2001)
17. Barrile, V., Candela, G., Fotia, A., Bernardo, E.: UAV survey of bridges and viaduct: workflow and application. In: Misra, S., et al. (eds.) ICCSA 2019. LNCS, vol. 11622, pp. 269–284. Springer, Cham (2019). https://doi.org/10.1007/978-3-030-24305-0_21
18. Barrile, V., Fotia, A., Bernardo, E.: The submerged heritage: a virtual journey in our seabed. ISPRS Ann. Photogramm. Remote Sens. Spat. Inf. Sci. **42**(2/W10), 17–24 (2019)
19. Robinson, N.P., et al.: A dynamic landsat derived normalized difference vegetation index (NDVI) product for the conterminous United States. Remote Sens. **9**, 863 (2017)
20. Barrile, V., Bilotta. G.: An application of remote sensing: object oriented analysis of satellite data. Int. Arch. Photogramm. Remote Sens. Spatial Inf. Sci. 37, 107–114 (2008)

21. Johnson, L.F., Roczen, D.E., Youkhana, S.K., Nemani, R.R., Bosch, D.F.: Mapping vineyard leaf area with multispectral satellite imagery. Comput. Electron. Agric **38**, 33–44 (2003)
22. Sentinel-2A Processing Baseline (02.04). https://sentinel.esa.int/web/sentinel/missions/sentinel-2/news/-/article/new-processing-baseline-02-04-for-sentinel-2a-products, Accessed 11 Jan 2020
23. Borgogno-Mondino, E., Lessio, A., Tarricone, L., Novello, V., de Palma, L.: A comparison between multispectral aerial and satellite imagery in precision viticulture. Prec. Agric. **19**(2), 195–217 (2017). https://doi.org/10.1007/s11119-017-9510-0
24. Senthilnath, J., Kandukuri, M., Dokania, A., Ramesh, K.N.: Application of UAV imaging platform for vegetation analysis based on spectral-spatial methods. Comput. Electron. Agric. **140**, 8–24 (2017)
25. Peña, J.M., Torres-Sánchez, J., de Castro, A.I., Kelly, M., López-Granados, F.: Weed mapping in early-season maize fields using object-based analysis of unmanned aerial vehicle (UAV) images. PLoS ONE **8**, e77151 (2013)
26. Comba, L., Gay, P., Primicerio, J., Ricauda Aimonino, D.: Vineyard detection from unmanned aerial systems images. Comput. Electron. Agric. **114**, 78–87 (2015)
27. Barrile, V., Bilotta, G., Fotia, A., Bernardo, E.: Road extraction for emergencies from satellite imagery. In: Gervasi, O., et al. (eds.) ICCSA 2020. LNCS, vol. 12252, pp. 767–781. Springer, Cham (2020). https://doi.org/10.1007/978-3-030-58811-3_55
28. Barrile, V., Bilotta, G., Fotia, A., Bernardo, E.: Integrated GIS system for post-fire hazard assessments with remote sensing. Int. Arch. Photogramm. Remote Sens. Spatial Inf. Sci. **XLIV**, 13-20 (2020)
29. Deng, L., Mao, Z., Li, X., Zhuowei, H., Duan, F., Yan, Y.: UAV-based multispectral remote sensing for precision agriculture: a comparison between different cameras. ISPRS J. Photogramm Remote Sens. **146**, 124–136 (2018). https://doi.org/10.1016/j.isprsjprs.2018.09.008
30. Navia, J., Mondragon I., Patino, D., Colorado, J.: Multispectral mapping in agriculture: Terrain mosaic using an autonomous quadcopter UAV. In: 2016 International Conference on Unmanned Aircraft Systems (ICUAS), pp. 1351–1358 (2018)
31. Hall, A., Louis, J., Lamb, D.W.: A method for extracting detailed information from high resolution multispectral images of vineyards. CiteSeerx 10M (2001)
32. Barrile, V., Bernardo, E., Candela, G., Bilotta, G., Modafferi, A., Fotia, A.: Road infrastructure heritage: from scan to infrabim. WSEAS Trans. Environ. Dev. **16**, 633–642 (2020). https://doi.org/10.37394/232015.2020.16.65
33. Reza, M.N., Na, I.S., Baek, S.W., Lee, K.-H.: Rice yield estimation based on K-means clustering with graph-cut segmentation using low-altitude UAV images. Biosyst. Eng. **177**, 109–121 (2018)
34. Albetis, J., et al.: Detection of Flavescence dorée grapevine disease using unmanned aerial vehicle (UAV) multispectral imagery. Remote Sens. **9**, 308 (2017)
35. Barrile, V., Fotia, A., Candela, G., Bernardo, E.: Integration of 3D model from UAV survey in BIM environment. ISPRS Ann. Photogramm. Remote Sens. Spatial Inf. Sci. **42**(2/W11), 195–199 (2019)
36. ESA Earth Online. https://earth.esa.int/documents/247904/685211/Sentinel-2_User_Handbook, Accessed 25 Nov 2019
37. Ducati, J.R., Bombassaro, M.G., Fachel, J.M.G.: Classifying vineyards from satellite images: a case study on burgundy's côte d'or. Oeno One **48**, 247–260 (2014)
38. Copernicus Open Access Hub. https://scihub.copernicus.eu/dhus/#/home, Accessed 11 Jan 2020
39. Louis, J., Charantonis, A., Berthelot, B.: Cloud detection for sentinel-2. In: Proceedings of the ESA Living Planet Symposium, Bergen, Norway (2010)

40. Agisoft©. https://www.agisoft.com, Accessed 11 Jan 2020
41. Parrot   Drones©.   https://www.parrot.com/business-solutions-us/agriculture#agriculture, Accessed 11 Jan 2020
42. MicaSense.   https://www.micasense.com/accessories/#!/Calibrated-Reflectance-Panel, Accessed 11 Jan 2020
43. Jiang, R., et al.: Assessing the operation parameters of a low-altitude UAV for the collection of NDVI values over a paddy rice field. Remote Sens. **12**, 1850 (2020)
44. DatiMeteo. https://datimeteo.it, Accessed 11 Aug 2020

A Proposal for Crop Damage Assessment by Floods Based on an Integrated Approach Relying on Copernicus Sentinel Data and DTMs

F. Ghilardi[✉], S. De Petris, F. Sarvia, and E. Borgogno-Mondino

Department of Agricultural, Forest and Food Sciences - DISAFA - Università di Torino,
L.go Braccini 2, 10095 Grugliasco, TO, Italy
{federica.ghilardi,samuele.depetris,filippo.sarvia,
enrico.borgogno}@unito.it

Abstract. Flood-damages on crops are related to several factors concerning both flood event and crops characteristics. In particular, flooded area size and water level are critical parameters while assessing yield loss and damages related to agricultural infrastructure and irrigation systems. With reference to the Sesia river (North-Western Italy) flood, occurred on 3rd October 2020, a methodology to detect flooded areas and estimate water level above ground was proposed based on Sentinel-1 (S1) data and Digital Terrain Model (DTM). S1 imagery was collected and processed by GEE. In particular, S1 VV image difference (pre- post-event) was analyzed by Otsu's method to define a threshold able to map flooded pixels. A watershed segmentation was performed on DTM to locate terrain depressions patches that, once coupled with flooded areas map, made possible to get an estimate of water level and map it. Agricultural crops were recognized based on the CORINE Land Cover 2018 level 3 map. A Normalized Difference Vegetation Index map from Sentinel-2 data was also obtained to describe crop activity before the event and associated to crops. This made possible to investigate which "active" crops were flooded and get an estimate of the water level that affected each area. This issue, together with water time persistence, strictly influences the degree of damage that a crop can suffer from. With these premised, the proposed methodology could be intended as a useful tool to support agricultural-related damages models generating a preliminary and rapid map of flooded crops taking care of the local topography.

Keywords: SAR; flood mapping; crop damage mapping · Water level estimation · Otsu's thresholding

1 Introduction

Exceptional and heavy rains often result in floods impacting many sectors of human activity, including agriculture. Flood-related damages on crops depends on factors concerning both flood (water speed, lasting of the event, etc.) and crop (cultivar, soil type,

F. Ghilardi—Private author.

E. Borgogno-Mondino and P. Zamperlin (Eds.): ASITA 2021, CCIS 1507, pp. 43–54, 2022.
https://doi.org/10.1007/978-3-030-94426-1_4

stage of the growing season, etc.). The same water mass associated to a flood can generate a different intensity of damage to crop depending on its phenological stage and structural features [1]. Moreover, superficial and/or ground water stagnation during floods can both affect plants biomass and root edaphic conditions. Vegetation is known to play an important role in hydraulic models. In particular, soil erosion, flood energy and sediments dynamics are strictly related to vegetation cover. Flood extension and water level are fundamental while assessing agricultural-related damages (i.e. yield loss, agricultural infrastructure and irrigation systems damages). Also flooded water height above ground (WH) is a key parameter in damage assessment, since it can harm plants according to phenological stage. In fact, small WH may improve crop condition by depositing nutrients, or water, in the very early phenological stages; differently, high WH occurring during growing season late stages may compromise yield. Currently, WH estimation methods are mainly based on hydraulic models (e.g. HEC-RAS; MIKE 21, TUFLOW) [2]. These models estimate floods, WH, flood velocity and duration simulating water flow [3] by models requiring several hydrometric data and assumptions. Ordinary, in the agricultural context, hydrometric data are not available or obtainable in short times. Differently, data from Earth Observation (EO) satellites are widely known in literature to be a good tool for monitoring of catastrophic events affecting agriculture and forest [4–8]. Satellite remote sensing offers timely information for monitoring and mapping flood damage without requiring field inspections, saving up time and guaranteeing a synoptic evaluation of the event [9]. In this work, a methodology to detect flooded areas, mapping WH and relating its effects to phenologically active crops was proposed based on the integration of Copernicus Sentinel-1 (S1) and Sentinel-2 imagery, topographic data from a Digital Terrain Model (DTM) and CORINE land cover map. With these premised, the proposed methodology could be intended as a useful tool to support agricultural-related damages models generating a preliminary and rapid map of flooded crops taking care of the local topography.

2   Material and Methods

2.1   Study Area

On 3rd October 2020, more than 450 mm of rain were recorded in Northern Italy. This extreme rainfall event resulted in the flooding of the Sesia river, with significant damages to the agricultural sector in the Piemonte and Lombardia regions. The event occurred during the rice harvesting period impacting the income of many farmers. For this work an area of interest (AOI) including the municipalities of Pezzana, Caresana, Rosasco and Langosco was identified, sizing about 7689 ha (Fig. 1).

2.2   Available Data

Satellite Imagery
Satellite imagery (bot SAR and multispectral) was collected and processed by GEE with the aim of mapping and qualifying flooded areas. GEE provides pre-processed satellite imagery (from both geometric and radiometric point of view), allowing immediate

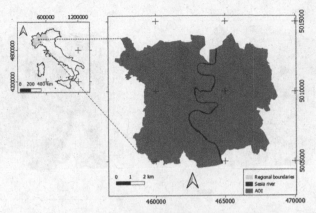

Fig. 1. Study area location (NW Italy) (Reference frame: WGS84 UTM32N).

interpretation of data and focus on the expected application. S1 ground range detected (GRDH) image collection was used having a nominal geometric resolution of 10 m and georeferenced into the WGS84 UTM 32N reference system. GRDH collection is made of images mapping the backscatter coefficient ($\sigma°$ [dB]) for VV and VH polarizations. Two VV-polarized images, one pre- and one post-event, were selected and processed within GEE. The pre-event reference image (RI) was acquired on 28th September 2020; the post-event image was acquired on 3rd October 2020 (Fig. 2). A Sentinel-2 (S2) multispectral image was also used to detect and map active vegetation in AOI at the date of the event. For this task a S2 acquisition of 28th September 2020 was used. The image was preventively orthoprojected into the WGS84 UTM 32N reference frame and calibrated into surface reflectance. With reference to the calibrated red (band 4) and NIR (band 8) bands the correspondent Normalized Difference Vegetation Index (NDVI) was calculated, having a GSD (Ground Sampling Distance) of 10 m.

Auxiliary Data

Two DTMs (GSD = 5 m) were obtained for free from the Piemonte and Lombardia geoportals (https://www.geoportale.piemonte.it/cms/; http://www.geoportale.reg ione.lombardia.it/) and mosaicked to generate a single $DTM(x,y)$ covering the whole AOI. DTM from Piemonte Region is updated at 2011 and have a height accuracy of ± 60 cm [10]. DTM from Lombardia Region is updated at 2015 and have a height accuracy of ± 30 cm [11]. In addition, the Corine Land Cover 2018 (CLC2018) level 3 map was used to map local agricultural classes. This level includes in the same class those patches have more than 75% of the characteristics of a given class. Agricultural classes and associated CLC2018 codes used for this work are reported in Table 1. CLC2018 can be obtained for free by the Land Monitoring Service Copernicus (https://land.cop ernicus.eu/pan-european/corine-land-cover).

Two vector layers mapping roads and rivers were also obtained by the above mentioned regional geoportals having a nominal scale of 1:10000, updated 2020 and georeferenced in the WGS84 UTM 32N reference frame. These data were used to filter out abrupt height changes due to man-made elements in DTM.

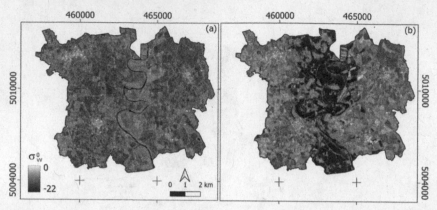

Fig. 2. Backscattering coefficient images for VV polarization in (a) 28th September 2020; (c) 3rd October 2020.

Table 1. Classes encoded by CLC2018 level 3 on the study area

Code class CLC2018 level-3	Code meaning
211	Not-irrigated arable land
213	Rice fields
231	Pastures
242	Complex cultivation patterns
243	Land principally occupied by agriculture, with significant areas of natural vegetation

Reference Data

The reference dataset (4 areas, Fig. 3), needed to validate results, was obtained through interviews with farmers and concerned verifications about the state of damage to crops and the estimate of water level above ground within flooded fields.

In particular, at this preliminary stage of investigation, only 4 fields were used and assumed as representatives of a wider area where similar conditions were observed. Among reference fields, 2 were damaged with different water heights and 2 unharmed. Author are aware that the reference dataset is too small to represent a robust and suitable statistic sample. Nevertheless, especially concerning information about water height after the flood, it is objectively difficult to gather records from farmers, since the most of them do not access flooded fields immediately after the event. With these clear limitations, the features of the reference dataset are reported in Table 2.

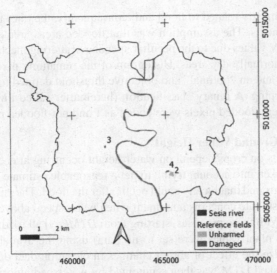

Fig. 3. Areas where reference fields were located (Reference frame: WGS84 UTM32N).

Table 2. Technical features of reference data.

Field ID	Municipality	Field status	Average WH (m)	Area (ha)	Number of 5 × 5 m pixels
1	Langosco	Unharmed	0	0.24	96
2	Langosco	Unharmed	0	4.96	1984
3	Caresana	Damaged	2	1.12	448
4	Langosco	Damaged	0.5	1.59	636
		Total		7.91	3164

2.3 Data Processing

Flooded Area Mapping

Several works reports usefulness of S1 data to map flooded areas [12, 13]. In fact, water surfaces generate a strong specular reflection of SAR signal resulting in dark pixels showing low intensity in all polarizations. Based on this assumption, many methods have been proposed to map flooded areas, the most of them based on image thresholding working on statistical distribution of pixel values [14]. In this work, the Otsu's method [15] was selected to automatically find an objective threshold able to separate flooded and not-flooded pixels. The method relies on the maximization of the separability of the compared classes in pixel values domain. Otsu's method was applied within GEE to generate a binary classification from the image difference (hereinafter called ΔVV) of pre- (VV_{pre}) and post- (VV_{post}) event VV acquisitions. The adopted procedure preliminarily masked out all $\Delta VV = VV_{post} - VV_{pre}$ pixels showing a value > 0. Negative changes were found to be mostly related to flood and, consequently, the ones to be thresholded for further refinements. The assumption was that flooded areas area expected to show very negative ΔVV values due to the peculiar specular scattering mechanism caused by flooded water in normally dry areas. Histogram of the remaining pixels was analyzed by Otsu's method and an "optimal" and objective threshold defined to further improve flooded pixel mapping. A binary classification (hereinafter called FM, Flooded Map) was generated where flooded pixels were coded as 1 and not-flooded pixels as 0.

Mapping Above Ground Water Height

Since flood impacts on crops depend on water height occurring at each position, local topography was taken into account trying to get a reasonable estimate of the maximum water level above ground that locally could occur after the flood. The underlying hypothesis was that the estimate concerns a moment when water speed above ground came to 0 after the event. With these premises, starting from $DTM(x,y)$ all roads and rivers were masked out (local pixel values were set to no data) using the available vector layers in order to minimize the effect of abrupt changes in elevation data during the following steps. The masked DTM was then segmented by watershed algorithm available in SAGA GIS 7.9.0. Tessellation was carried out to define local terrain depressions reasonably filled by water during flood. Segmentation was performed setting the following parameters: method = maxima; join segments on saddle difference using a threshold = 0.8. Resulting polygons represent patches (Depression Patches, DPs) defined by local watershed and, therefore, hydraulically separated by neighbour ones. With reference to mapped patches of DPs, the 5th and 95th percentiles of height local values (from $DTM(x,y)$) statistical distribution were calculated by zonal statistics. They were interpreted as good estimates of the local minimum and maximum height of the considered depression, able to overcome extreme values singularities possibly related to DTM accuracy or to the presence of residual anomalies related to buildings, roads or riverbanks. Percentiles were recorded as new attributes in the table associated with the vector layer representing DP. According to these values two raster layers were generated, with the same GSD as $DTM(x,y)$, representing local minima and maxima (at patch level). They were then compared by grid differencing to map the local maximum water level that could be found within the considered patch. Finally, WH was defined at pixel level by Eq. 1:

$$WH(x, y) = \left(DTM^i_{95th} - DTM^i_{5th}\right) - \left(DTM(x, y) - DTM^i_{5th}\right) \qquad (1)$$

where DTM^i_{95th} and DTM^i_{5th} correspond to the local maxima and minima DTM values within the generic i^{th} DP.

Mapping Active Crops

Since damages can vary according to local land cover and crops phenology a preliminary classification of active crops at the date of the event was mandatory. It is worth to remind that, depending on the stage of the growing season, damage to crop could be greatly varying; for example, already harvested crops have no consequence in terms of yearly yield and crops at their earlier stages could be possibly absorb the most of the impact. To take care about this, a vegetation mask was generated mapping active crops in the area.

All active vegetated areas were recognized and mapped by thresholding of the above mentioned NDVI map obtained from S2 data within GEE. To further separate crops from other vegetation classes, CLC2018 level-3 was used. Finally a comprehensive representation of active crops falling within the flooded area as mapped by FM was obtained intersecting all these information.

2.4 Validation

Accuracy of FM was verified at pixel level according to the reference dataset. All pixels falling into the 4 reference fields were correctly classified for both the flooded and unharmed ones. Similarly, WH was tested by computation of the mean absolute error (MAE, Eq. 2) of the local (pixel level) differences between the estimated value of water height and the one declared by farmers [16]:

$$MAE = \frac{\sum_{i=1}^{n} |x_i^r - x_i^o|}{n} \tag{2}$$

where x_i^r is reference WH value in the i-th pixels of RD, x_i^o is the observed WH resulted by applying the proposed method. This metric could be a little bit misleading being the compared values slightly different if referred to WH or to farmers' declared values. In fact, farmers communicated a single average value for the whole field that, in our computation, was replicated for each 5×5 m pixel of the field itself. Differently, WH contains a different WH estimate for each 5×5 m pixel of the patch depending on DTM.

3 Results and Discussions

3.1 Flooded Area Mapping

ΔVV histogram (Fig. 4a) was analysed by Otsu's method finding a threshold value = -6.94. Consequently, only those ΔVV pixels having values <-6.94 were labelled as flooded (FM code = 1). FM Is reported in Fig. 4b. Flooded areas, as mapped on 3rd October 2020 by S1, proved to be about 1071 ha. Almost 942 ha out of 1071 ha were associated to agricultural classes as mapped by CLC2018 level-3. The most affected CLC2018 class was rice (213), while pastures (231) and complex cultivation patterns (242) were not affected at all (Table 3).

All the pixels belonging to the reference dataset were correctly mapped for both flooded and unharmed fields.

Comparing VM (Fig. 5) and CLC2018, 3917 ha of rice resulted to be still harvested in the area. The 8% of these were mapped as flooded. This value correspond to about 313 ha. Differently, almost 630 ha of flooded fields labelled as crops (but different from rice), were assumed as not-damaged since, at the time of the event, hosted crop was absent, for evident phenological motivations. Specifically, flooded areas of classes 211 and 243, even if indicated as actively vegetated by VM, were assumed as not occupied by crops since agronomic calendars of local crops excluded this situation. Active vegetation in these areas were retained associated to weed species and, consequently, not interesting

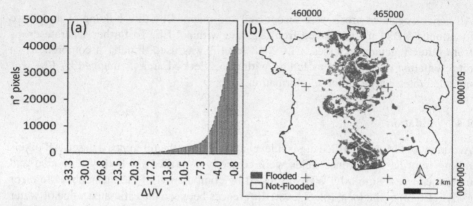

Fig. 4. (a) ΔVV image pixel distribution, red line indicates the threshold value determined by the Otsu's method. (b) Detected flooded areas (Reference frame: WGS84 UTM 32N). (Color figure online)

Table 3. Flooded areas of agricultural classes as mapped by CLC2018 level3.

	Not-irrigated arable land (211)	Rice fields (213)	Pastures (231)	Complex cultivation patterns (242)	Land principally occupied by agriculture, with significant areas of natural vegetation (243)
Active vegetated area (ha)	91.09	3917.79	24.99	27.84	154.45
Flooded area (ha)	58.84	786.46	0.00	0.00	97.25
Active crops affected by flood (ha)	8.70	312.99	0.00	0.00	55.22

from a yield damage assessment point of view. Nevertheless, they could present structural damages related to the irrigation network, soil composition (contaminants could have been deposed by flooded water) and/or soil washout. These damages could be interesting when a more general damage assessment is done. For this study these types of damage were not taken into consideration.

Previous experiences concerning past flooding events occurring about the harvest time, have taught to farmers that a complete abandonment of flooded crops is preferable with respect to a partial harvest. This is mainly related to the high probability that sand/clay, deposited over plants during the flood, could greatly damage harvesting machines making not profitable the harvest. In this context one can assume that all flooded rice areas will be not harvested. Consequently, an immediate estimate of the economic loss can be given once known the average yield that rice has in the area. This can be assumed equal to 7 ton·ha^{-1} [17] while a local rice price was equal to 340 €·ton^{-1} [18]. Consequently, the estimated economic loss can be estimated in 313 ha resulting in about 744940 €.

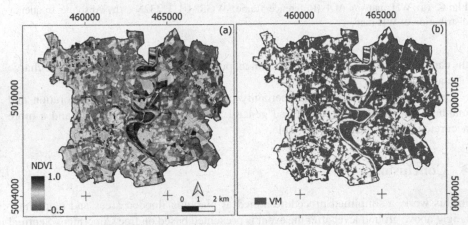

Fig. 5. (a) Pre-event NDVI map (8th September 2020); (b) Map of active vegetation obtained by thresholding NDVI map (NDVI > 0.4) (Reference frame: WGS84 UTM 32N).

3.2 Mapping and Validation WH

WH is reported in Fig. 6. According to Eq. 2, MAE of WH map was found to be equal to 0.58 m. This result is consistent with DTM accuracy (0.6 m). Given the great geometric regularity of soil surface in rice chambers, MAE value encourage to admit that WH variation within a chamber (possibly associated to one patch of DP) is negligible and mostly due to the random nature of the accidental error typical of all measures. It is worth to remind that rice average height at the mature stage in AOI is about 0.80 m [19]. Consequently, given the estimated MAE, WH estimates make possible to appreciate if the rice in a field was completely drown or not.

Given the above mentioned strategy from farmers concerning flood events over rice about the harvesting date, one could conclude that WH mapping is not important, since crop is abandoned whatever is the water level. This is probably true for the specific event we investigated. Nevertheless the possibility of mapping WH assume a crucial role when flood occurs in the initial or intermediate stages of the growing season, since the recovery or abandon strategy strictly depends on it (and on the water lasting). The present work has therefore to be intended as a possible answer to a more general problem:

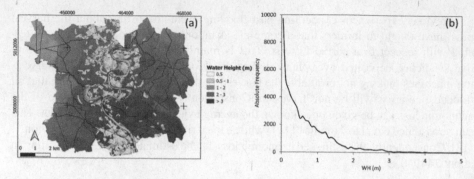

Fig. 6. (a) WH map in AOI (Reference frame: WGS84 UTM32N); (b) Absolute frequency distribution of WH map.

the early dam-age (to agriculture) assessment potentially supporting authorities in charge of managing rivers.

Future developments will be certainly addressed to deepen this exploration and making deductions more robust and general. A wider statistical sample and a more accurate DTM are certainly desirable.

4 Conclusions

In this work, a simplified procedure aimed at mapping flooded areas and map water height above ground level after the event is presented based on free Copernicus Sentinel 1 and Sentinel 2 data and DTMs. The expected operational context is the one related to the assessment and quantification of the damage to the agricultural compart. The main idea is that, prioritarily, for such a goal only fields where crop is active at the time of the event must be considered. Once the area impacted by flood is known, within active fields, water height is expected to play an important role in determining the level of damage especially if properly coupled with the phenological stage of the crop itself. The procedure was exemplified with reference to the flood event occurred on 3rd October 2020 in NW Italy along the Sesia river. The proposed method uses S1 data to detect and map flooded areas. In the meantime, it uses DTM to get an estimate, within the flooded areas, of the water level above ground. Auxiliary data from free sources, like CLC2018 level-3 dataset and S2 multispectral data, were used to classify crop types and testing their phenological activity. Even if working with a reduced and, probably, badly conditioned sample of test fields, some preliminary evaluations could have been done: classification accuracy of flooded areas by S1 was excellent; WH accuracy (measured by MAE) was found to be 0.58 m, a value that is consistent with DTM accuracy. It is worth to highlight that several methods are present in literature concerning WH estimation along river or water basins from satellite data, but very few [20–22] focus on crops. Authors tried to fill this gap pro-posing a first trial for the estimation of flood effects on crops. In AOI, 942 ha of crops were flooded but only the 40% was characterized by active vegetation, thereby yield was probably compromised. In conclusion, the authors presented a possible methodology able to support hydrologic models and crop dam-ages models where WH estimation is required. Results proved to be an effective tool to detect, map and monitor flooded areas and quantify crops damaged.

Acknowledgements. We would like to thank Dr. Sara Martinengo for providing reference data information useful to reach the results presented in this work.

References

1. Setiawan, M.A.: Integrated soil erosion risk management in the upper Serayu watershed, Wonosobo District, Central Java Province, Indonesia (2012)
2. Syme, W.J.: Modelling of bends and hydraulic structures in a two-dimensional scheme. In: 6th Conference on Hydraulics in Civil Engineering: The State of Hydraulics, Proceedings, p. 127. Institution of Engineers, Australia (2001)
3. Ezzine, A., Saidi, S., Hermassi, T., Kammessi, I., Darragi, F., Rajhi, H.: Flood mapping using hydraulic modeling and Sentinel-1 image: case study of Medjerda Basin, northern Tunisia. Egypt. J. Remote Sens. Space Sci. **23**, 303–310 (2020)
4. Sarvia, F., De Petris, S., Borgogno-Mondino, E.: Remotely sensed data to support insurance strategies in agriculture. In: Remote Sensing for Agriculture, Ecosystems, and Hydrology XXI. p. 111491H. International Society for Optics and Photonics (2019)
5. Borgogno-Mondino, E., Sarvia, F., Gomarasca, M.A.: Supporting insurance strategies in agriculture by remote sensing: a possible approach at regional level. In: Misra, S., et al. (eds.) ICCSA 2019. LNCS, vol. 11622, pp. 186–199. Springer, Cham (2019). https://doi.org/10.1007/978-3-030-24305-0_15
6. De Petris, S., Sarvia, F., Borgogno-Mondino, E.: A new index for assessing tree vigour decline based on sentinel-2 multitemporal data. Appl. Tree Fail. Risk Manag. Remote Sens. Lett. **12**, 58–67 (2020)
7. Sarvia, F., Xausa, E., De Petris, S.D., Cantamessa, G., Borgogno-Mondino, E.: A possible role of copernicus sentinel-2 data to support common agricultural policy controls in agriculture. Agronomy **10** (2021). https://doi.org/10.3390/agronomy11010110
8. Sarvia, F., De Petris, S., Borgogno-Mondino, E.: A methodological proposal to support estimation of damages from hailstorms based on copernicus sentinel 2 data times series. In: Gervasi, O., et al. (eds.) ICCSA 2020. LNCS, vol. 12252, pp. 737–751. Springer, Cham (2020). https://doi.org/10.1007/978-3-030-58811-3_53
9. Psomiadis, E., Diakakis, M., Soulis, K.X.: Combining SAR and optical earth observation with hydraulic simulation for flood mapping and impact assessment. Remote Sens. **12**, 3980 (2020)
10. Borgogno Mondino, E., Fissore, V., Lessio, A., Motta, R.: Are the new gridded DSM/DTMs of the Piemonte region (Italy) proper for forestry? a fast and simple approach for a posteriori metric assessment. iForest – Biogeosci. Forest. **9**, 901–909 (2016). https://doi.org/10.3832/ifor1992-009
11. Biagi, L., Carcano, L., Lucchese, A., Negretti, M.: Creation of a multiresolution and multi-accuracy DTM: problems and solutions for HELI-DEM case study. Int. Arch. Photogramm. Remote Sens. **XL-5 W.3** (2013)
12. Twele, A., Cao, W., Plank, S., Martinis, S.: Sentinel-1-based flood mapping: a fully automated processing chain. Int. J. Remote Sens. **37**, 2990–3004 (2016)
13. Bioresita, F., Puissant, A., Stumpf, A., Malet, J.-P.: A method for automatic and rapid mapping of water surfaces from sentinel-1 imagery. Remote Sens. **10**, 217 (2018)

14. Manavalan, R.: SAR image analysis techniques for flood area mapping-literature survey. Earth Sci. Inf. **10**, 1–14 (2017)

15. Otsu, N.: A threshold selection method from gray-level histograms. IEEE Trans. Syst. Man Cybern. **9**, 62–66 (1979)

16. Bui, D.T., Pradhan, B., Nampak, H., Bui, Q.-T., Tran, Q.-A., Nguyen, Q.-P.: Hybrid artificial intelligence approach based on neural fuzzy inference model and metaheuristic optimization for flood susceptibilitgy modeling in a high-frequency tropical cyclone area using GIS. J. Hydrol. **540**, 317–330 (2016)

17. Tesio, F., Tabacchi, M., Cerioli, S., Follis, F.: Sustainable hybrid rice cultivation in Italy. A review. Agron. Sustain. Dev. **34**, 93–102 (2014)

18. ISMEA: Riso - News mercati. Il settimanale Ismea di informazione sui prodotti agricoli e agroalimentari. http://www.ismeamercati.it

19. Fogliatto, S., Vidotto, F., Ferrero, A.: Morphological characterisation of Italian weedy rice (Oryza sativa) populations. Weed Res. **52**, 60–69 (2012)

20. Bremond, P.: Caractérisation et évaluation économique de la vulnérabilité des exploitations agricoles aux inondations (2011)

21. Förster, S., Kuhlmann, B., Lindenschmidt, K.-E., Bronstert, A.: Assessing flood risk for a rural detention area. Nat. Hazard. **8**, 311–322 (2008)

22. De Petris, S., Sarvia, F., Borgogno-Mondino, E.: Multi-temporal mapping of flood damage to crops using sentinel-1 imagery: a case study of the Sesia River. Remote Sens. Lett. **12**, 459–469 (2021). https://doi.org/10.1080/2150704X.2021.1890262

Satellite Data and Epidemic Cartography: A Study of the Relationship Between the Concentration of NO$_2$ and the COVID-19 Epidemic

Gianmarco Pignocchino⬮, Alessandro Pezzoli⬮, and Angelo Besana$^{(\boxtimes)}$⬮

Interuniversity Department of Regional and Urban Studies and Planning, Politecnico and University of Turin, Turin, Italy

gianmarco.pignocchin@edu.unito.it, alessandro.pezzoli@polito.it, angelo.besana@unito.it

Abstract. Satellite data are widely used to study the spatial component of epidemics: to monitor their evolution, to create epidemiological risk maps and predictive models. The improvement of data quality, not only in technical terms but also of scientific relevance and robustness, represents in this context one of the most important aspects for health information technology that can make further significant and useful progress in monitoring and managing epidemics. In this regard, this paper intends to address an issue that is not always adequately considered in the use of satellite data for the creation of maps and spatial models of epidemics, namely the preliminary verification of the level of spatial correlation between remote sensing environmental variables and epidemics. Specifically, we intend to evaluate the contribution of exposure to the pollutant nitrogen dioxide (NO$_2$) on the spatial spread of the virus and the severity of the current COVID infection.

Keywords: Satellite data · Nitrogen dioxide (NO$_2$) · COVID-19

1 Introduction

Satellite data, due to their capacity to guarantee constant and increasingly detailed observation, have long been permanently used to monitor and study spatial patterns and the spread of epidemics, in particular with respect to those variables that are believed to determine or favor the emergence and development of diseases, such as environmental conditions, distribution of causative agents and socio-demographic characteristics of human populations [8, 18, 20, 43]. In particular, the combination of derived field data, statistical variables and satellite data is a fundamental element for building epidemiological risk maps and predictive models [1, 25]. Moreover, the current pandemic emergency has highlighted the need to develop and implement such tools not only in the so-called developing countries, as has prevailed so far, but also in the more advanced

E. Borgogno-Mondino and P. Zamperlin (Eds.): ASITA 2021, CCIS 1507, pp. 55–67, 2022.
https://doi.org/10.1007/978-3-030-94426-1_5

countries, which have found themselves completely fragile with respect to such calamities and unprepared in the prevention and response measures, although such a danger was somewhat predictable [24, 42].

In the context of epidemic cartography, this contribution intends to deal in operational terms with an issue not always adequately considered in the use of satellite data for the creation of maps and spatial models of epidemics, i.e. the preliminary verification of the level of spatial correlation between remote sensing environmental variables and epidemics [19, 37]. More precisely, we intend to evaluate the contribution of exposure to the pollutant nitrogen dioxide (NO_2) on the spatial spread of the virus and on the severity of the current COVID-19 infection, in order to confirm the operational validity of the use of this environmental variable in the related epidemic cartography. The improvement of data quality, not only in technical terms but also of scientific relevance and robustness, is in fact one of the most important aspects for health information technology that can make further significant and useful progress in monitoring and managing epidemics [20, 39].

As it is known, Northern Italy was the area most affected by the first wave of the COVID-19 epidemic. The great speed and intensity with which COVID-19 disease has spread to these regions has prompted the hypothesis, in some preliminary studies, that high levels of pollution may play a role in viral transmission and in determining the severity of the infection [4, 6, 28, 35, 38, 40]. In fact, Northern Italy is considered as one of the most heavily polluted area in Europe in terms of smog and air pollution [2, 26, 33] because it is characterized by a high concentration of densely populated urban areas, as well as by a strong presence of industrial activities. In addition, the particular closed geomorphological conformation of Po Valley prevents pollutants re-circulation and release with their consequent stagnation due to the low ventilation [16].

2 Materials and Methods

We worked on data from the Northwest regions and the first wave of the epidemic.

2.1 Environmental Data

Pollution data on average concentrations of nitrogen dioxide (NO_2) expressed in $\mu mol/m^2$ were obtained using information provided by the space satellite Sentinel 5 Precursor (S5P), managed by the European Space Agency (ESA) and the European Commission under the *Copernicus* program [9].

The periods analyzed refer to one baseline period identified before the spread of the epidemic in Italy (February 1 - 24) and to the following weeks (February 24 - March 8, March 8 - 22, March 22 - April 5 and April 5 - 19).

For this study, it was considered the tropospheric vertical column of NO_2 reported by ESA Sentinel-5P and made available through high resolution offline (OFFL) image processing of nitrogen dioxide concentrations, obtainable approximately 5 days after detection time [10]. The satellite data therefore comes from the Sentinel-5P OFFL NO_2 dataset [15] of the Google Earth Engine API platform [17] through the use of Area of

Interest (AOI) tools and a simple Python programming code. We obtained a single satellite image defined by the mean of the NO_2 concentrations expressed in $\mu mol/m^2$, for each of the periods considered. The satellite images were downloaded in raster (Geotiff) format, georeferenced according to the World Geodetic System (WGS-1984) and then a population-weighted average was made for the year 2020 of the NO_2 values for each individual provinces and regions through the QGIS software. The population data used were obtained from the Gridded Population of the World - Fourth Version (GPWv4) dataset provided by the Center for International Earth Science Information Network (CIESIN) which models the distribution of the global human population consistent with national censuses and population registers, for the years 2000, 2005, 2010, 2015 and 2020 on grid cells of about 1 km [3]. In addition, we retrieved vertical air flows (omega) at 850 mb (about 1,5 km above sea level) that define the atmospheric capacity to disperse the gas, in order to obtain a better understanding of NO_2 concentrations during the period of the event considered. In regions where positive omega is observed, the atmosphere forces the polluted NO_2 to remain close to the surface, resulting in increased exposure to the risk factor for the population. On the contrary, in regions with negative omega, atmospheric conditions allow the dispersion of the gas further away and at higher altitudes. Therefore, in these regions there is a lower exposure of the population to air pollution and associated health risks [30]. Data were provided by the NOAA/OAR/ESRL PSD, Boulder, Colorado, USA [29].

2.2 Epidemiological Data

The trend data on the number of total positive cases of SARS-CoV-2 infection at regional and provincial level, corresponding respectively to levels 2 and 3 of the Nomenclature of territorial units for statistics (NUTS), were available on the website of the Civil Protection Department [7]. Considering the number of positive cases of COVID-19, prevalence rates per 100.000 inhabitants were obtained using the most up-to-date population data on January 1, 2019, available from the Italian National Institute of Statistic [22]. Prevalence rates were calculated as the ratio of the number of SARS-CoV-2 positive subjects to the total number of individuals in the population during the lock down (as of March 8, March 22, April 5 and April 19 2020).

Finally, in this research an analysis of excess mortality (in percentage values) was carried out, in order to indirectly evaluate the effect of COVID-19 epidemic on total deaths observed during the study period.

The excess mortality data defines the percentage change in deaths at the provincial level recorded in 2020 compared to the average of the previous five years (2015–2019). Clearly, positive values indicate an increase in deaths compared to the previous period considered. Deaths data were available from the European Statistical Office dataset [11], aggregated weekly at provincial level (NUTS 3).

For this analysis, it was chosen the period between the 10th week and the 16th week (March 2 – April 19 2020) because the first COVID-19 deaths in this regions occurred from March 3 to 5 respectively for Liguria and Piemonte, while the Valle d'Aosta has encountered the first deaths only later on March 11 [7].

2.3 Statistical Analysis

First, an exploratory and descriptive analysis of the dataset used was carried out, which made it possible to investigate the distribution of each variable and the presence of any anomalous values identifiable as outliers.

Second, the relationships between the average levels of NO_2 prior to the onset of the Italian epidemic (February 1–24) and the prevalence rates of SARS-CoV-2 infection in the periods March 8 and 22 March, April 5 and 19, 2020 were examined using Spearman's correlation coefficient (ρ). This non-parametric index calculates the relation based not on the values of the two variables but on their ordinal position (ranks). This allows to obtain an index value much less affected by outliers than the Pearson's linear coefficient. Similar to the latter, the Spearman's coefficient provides values between -1 and $+1$; the closer the index is to zero, the weaker the relationship will be, the closer it gets to -1 or $+1$ the stronger the relationship will be negative or positive.

Spearman's correlation coefficient was also useful for investigating the association between the average levels of NO_2 before February 24 and excess mortality data calculated for the period March 2 - April 19, 2020.

Once the functional relationships between the variables under consideration have been established, subsequent exploratory analyses have been carried out with Poisson regression model. Since evidence of overdispersion was observed, we applied quasi-Poisson multivariate models. These ones are a generalization of the Poisson regression and they allow to take into account the overdispersion of the data, adjusting the variance according to a specific dispersion parameter [36].

Within the models, some possible confounding factors were considered such as the percentage of the population over the age of 65 and the ratio of females to males, as the incidence of COVID-19 has proven to be higher among men and people 65 years of age or older [21]. In addition, another possible confounding factor taken into account was population density (population/km^2); in fact, one would expect the most densely populated provinces to be among the most polluted, due to the social and economic spatial concentration, but also the places where the contagion could have spread more easily with a potential greater impact on the exposed population. These data used were available from the Italian National Institute of Statistic (ISTAT), updated on January 1, 2019 [22].

The estimated coefficients, obtained from quasi-Poisson multivariate regression models, define the size of the variation in the dependent variable (prevalence rates or excess mortality) for a unit increase of the independent variable (defined as a $10 \, \mu mol/m^2$ increase in the average concentration of NO_2 before February 24).

The data of each variable was collected and organized in table format through Microsoft Excel program and then processed in statistical analysis using RStudio software.

3 Results

3.1 Analysis of Tropospheric NO$_2$ Concentrations

Figure 1 shows the geographical distribution at provincial level of the average concentrations of NO$_2$ tropospheric in μmol/m^2 weighted on the population for the five periods analyzed, corresponding to before and after the spread of the Italian epidemic.

The average concentrations of NO$_2$ had high values in the first period before the outbreak (February 1 to 24). They were particularly high in the Metropolitan City of Torino (119 μmol/m^2) and in the province of Novara (118 μmol/m^2). While, in the following weeks during the spread of the epidemic, there was a drastic reduction in concentrations of polluted, less than 90 μmol/m^2, in all the provinces analyzed. This reduction is attributable to the containment measures implemented by the government against the spread of COVID-19 disease, which led to a consequent sharp reduction in transportation-related emissions, as well as the decrease in industrial activities and electricity production.

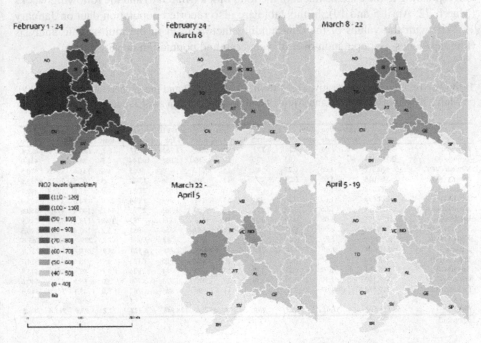

Fig. 1. Study area of North-Western Italy showing the average concentrations of tropospheric NO$_2$ (μmol/m^2) weighted on the population for the five periods considered in the analysis.

Key to abbreviations/provinces:

AL	Alessandria	CN	Cuneo	NO	Novara	TO	Torino
AO	Aosta	GE	Genova	SP	La Spezia	VB	Verbano C.O
AT	Asti	IM	Imperia	SV	Savona	VC	Vercelli
BI	Biella						

These concentrations of nitrogen dioxide, for the whole event considered, were also accompanied by vertical downward air flows (positive omega between 0 and 0,02 Pa/s) which prevented the dispersion of the pollutant and increased exposure and risk factors for the population.

3.2 Relationship Between NO_2 Pollution and Prevalence Rates

Table 1 shows the total number of SARS-CoV-2 positive cases and prevalence rates (per 100.000) calculated over the four time periods considered in the study, i.e. the one corresponding to the establishment of the total block (March 8) and the following weeks (March 22, April 5 and 19). In this table are also reported population data on January 1, 2019 with the values of the confounding factors used in the multivariate analysis (females/males, % population over 65 years old and population density).

Table 1. Total number of positive cases from SARS-CoV-2 and prevalence rates (per 100.000) on March 8, March 22, April 5 and April 19 and population data as of January 1, 2019.

	total	population (2019) female/male	over 65%	density*	total cases of COVID-19 08-mar	22-mar	05-apr	19-apr	prevalence rates (per 100.000) 08-mar	22-mar	05-apr	19-apr
Piemonte	*4.356.406*	*1,06*	*0,26*	*171*	*360*	*4.420*	*12.362*	*21.057*	*8,3*	*101,5*	*283,8*	*483,4*
Torino (TO)	2.259.523	1,07	0,25	330	89	1.989	5.985	10.144	3,9	88,0	264,9	448,9
Vercelli (VC)	170.911	1,06	0,27	82	15	242	605	975	8,8	141,6	354,0	570,5
Novara (NO)	369.018	1,05	0,24	275	13	398	986	1.987	3,5	107,9	267,2	538,5
Cuneo (CN)	587.098	1,03	0,24	85	5	303	1.071	2.053	0,9	51,6	182,4	349,7
Asti (AT)	214.638	1,04	0,26	141	58	181	596	1.064	27,0	84,3	277,7	495,7
Alessandria (AL)	421.284	1,06	0,28	118	60	760	1.763	2.783	14,2	180,4	418,5	660,6
Biella (BI)	175.585	1,08	0,29	191	19	243	571	783	10,8	138,4	325,2	445,9
Verbano C.O. (VB)	158.349	1,06	0,27	70	13	159	556	935	8,2	100,4	351,1	590,5
Valle d'Aosta	*125.666*	*1,05*	*0,24*	*38*	*9*	*364*	*782*	*1.088*	*7,2*	*289,7*	*622,3*	*865,8*
Liguria	*1.550.640*	*1,09*	*0,28*	*285*	*78*	*1.665*	*4.449*	*6.528*	*5,0*	*107,4*	*286,9*	*421,0*
Imperia (IM)	213.840	1,07	0,28	185	10	168	586	1.122	4,7	78,6	274,0	524,7
Savona (SV)	276.064	1,09	0,29	177	25	175	734	926	9,1	63,4	265,9	335,4
Genova (GE)	841.180	1,10	0,29	456	25	677	1.924	3.706	3,0	80,5	228,7	440,6
La Spezia (SP)	219.556	1,07	0,27	249	11	99	445	767	5,0	45,1	202,7	349,3
Italia	*60.359.546*	*1,05*	*0,23*	*199*	*7.375*	*59.138*	*128.948*	*178.972*	*12,2*	*98,0*	*213,6*	*296,5*

* pop/km2

The preliminary exploratory analysis of prevalence rates showed very high values that were numerically distant from the rest of the data collected, identifiable as outliers and corresponding to the Valle d'Aosta region. Therefore, the latter was excluded from the subsequent correlation analysis.

The variables have a positive monotone relationship for the periods March 22, April 5, and April 19, as evidenced by the regression lines in the scatter plots in Fig. 2.

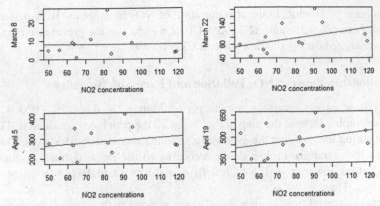

Fig. 2. Scatterplot of correlations between mean NO$_2$ levels before February 24 and prevalence rates (TP).

Sperman's coefficients showed positive correlations between NO$_2$ concentrations before February 24 and prevalence rates for the periods of March 22, April 5 and 19 (ρ = 0,65, p-value < 0,05; ρ = 0,21 and ρ = 0,40, p-value > 0,05, respectively). While a weak negative correlation for the period March 8 (ρ = −0,07, p-value > 0,05) may probably depend on the slowdown in cumulative positive cases of SARS-CoV-2 infection in the studied territories, until that day.

The results of estimates prevalence rate ratio of quasi-Poisson regression models are summarized on a logarithmic scale in the following Table 2 together with the corresponding standard error (*se*) for the four different periods considered (March 8 and 22, April 5 and 19).

Table 2. Estimates of prevalence rate ratio and the corresponding standard error (se) of quasi-Poisson regression models over the four periods considered.

		NO$_2$ concentrations	females /males	% pop over65	population density
March 8	estimated	1,9e-02	-4,4e+01	5,7e+01	-3,9e-04
	(se)	1,2e-02	3,1e+01	2,5e+01	3,6e-03
March 22	estimated	2,0e-02***	-1,6e+01	3,0e+01**	-9,6e-04
	(se)	2,8e-03	7,2e+00	5,7e+00	8,0e-04
April 5	estimated	1,1e-02***	-2,0e+00	1,3e+01**	-0,2e-02*
	(se)	1,8e-03	4,7e+00	3,8e+00	5,1e-04
April 19	estimated	9,0e-03*	-1,2e+01	1,6e+01*	1,8e-05
	(se)	2,6e-03	7,2e+00	5,8e+00	7,9e-04

***p < 0,001; **p < 0,01; *p < 0,05

An increase of 10 units in the concentration of NO_2 in $\mu mol/m^2$ is associated with an increase between 9.5% and 22% (95% CI: -2.6 ÷ 55) on the prevalence rates in the territories analyzed during the first wave of COVID-19.

3.3 Relationship Between NO_2 Pollution and Excess of Mortality

The analysis of excess mortality for the period March 2 – April 19, 2020 is shown spatially in graphic form in the map in Fig. 3, for all the provinces considered. The map was made taking into account the average (μ) and the standard deviation (σ). Therefore the classes identified are broken down according to the range defined by these two statistical values: lower ($x < \mu - \sigma$), low ($\mu - \sigma \leq x < \mu$), high ($\mu \leq x < \mu + \sigma$) and higher ($x \geq \mu + \sigma$).

The excess mortality is evident in all three regions with a significant increase in deaths in the provinces of Alessandria, Vercelli and Biella, respectively with 103% for the first two and 101% for the third one. The least affected provinces appear to be Cuneo and Savona, despite an increase in mortality between 43% and 47%.

Even there, the statistical analysis returned a positive correlation between pollution from NO_2 before February 24 and data on excess mortality for the period March 2 - April 19, 2020 ($\rho = 0,44$, p-value > 0,05), as also evidenced by the regression line of the scatterplot graph in Fig. 4.

The quasi-Poisson multivariate regression model returned the rate ratio estimated (RR) that are shown in the Table 3 with the corresponding standard error (se) values. An increase of 10 units in the concentration of NO_2 in $\mu mol/m^2$ has an estimated association of 4,7% (95%CI: 1,8 ÷ 7,9) on excess mortality over the period March 2 to April 19, 2020.

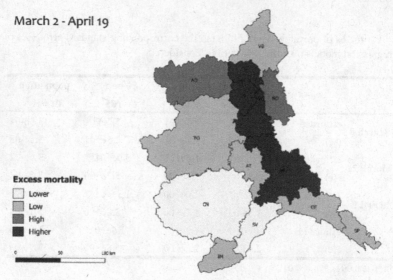

Fig. 3. Excess mortality recorded in the provinces of North-West Italy

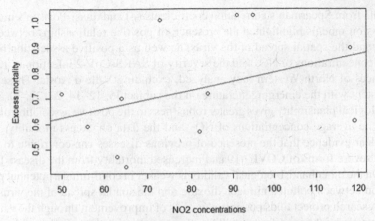

Fig. 4. Scatterplot of correlation between NO_2 levels before February 24 and excess mortality.

Table 3. Results of estimates rate ratio and the corresponding standard error (se) of quasi-Poisson regression model for excess mortality data.

	NO_2 concentrations	females /males	% pop over65	population density
estimated	4,685e-03*	-6,74e+00	1,023e+01*	8,2e-05
(se)	1,496e-03	-4,09e+00	3,309e+00	4,383e-04

*p < 0,05

4 Conclusion

The processing of satellite information showed high levels of nitrogen dioxide in $\mu mol/m^2$ in the pre-epidemic period and a consequent drastic reduction in pollution in the following weeks. In all the provinces considered, this reduction revealed an overall average of -43%, following the national containment and mitigation measures implemented by the government to deal with the spread of the SARS-CoV-2 virus.

The statistical analysis carried out in this research has allowed to obtain good evidence of the relationship between exposure to nitrogen dioxide (NO_2) and the COVID-19 epidemic. The relationships turn out to be positive but not significant, as also reflected in the wide confidence intervals (95%CI) because the dataset considered has low number and the statistical analysis was carried out with data at aggregate levels that do not allow to consider all the possible confounding factors that influenced the disease epidemic. With reference to the estimates obtained from the multivariate models of quasi-Poisson regression and the confounding factors, no effect related to the relationship between females and males is observed. Whereas it is noted that provinces with a higher share of the population aged 65 and over and with a higher population density were the most affected during the epidemic, as was likely.

Results from Spearman's correlation coefficients (ρ) and quasi-Poisson's multivariate regression models highlighted the presence of positive relationships between NO_2 pollution and the spatial spread of the virus, as well as a positive association between the same concentrations of NO_2 and the severity of SARS-CoV-2 infection in 12 of the 13 provinces of North-Western Italy analyzed, excluding Valle d'Aosta. These results are consistent with the emerging literature on the subject [5, 12–14, 23, 27, 30, 32, 44], while biological plausibility gives greater robustness to the positive association observed between the average concentrations of NO_2 and the data on excess mortality. In fact, there is clear evidence that the presence of previous diseases can contribute to a more clinically severe forms of COVID-19 and increased mortality from the disease [21, 31, 34, 41]. On the other hand, biological validity is weaker in confirming a potential positive association between polluted nitrogen dioxide and the spatial spread of the virus.

This research project finds possible elements of improvement through the validation of concentrations obtained from satellite information with those collected by ground monitoring stations; analyses carried out with other polluted such as atmospheric particulate matter (PM2,5 and PM10) or tropospheric ozone (O_3) to investigate their reduction in the period corresponding to lock-down but also to assess their possible contribution to the COVID-19 epidemic; analysis at more detailed scales, referring to individual urban areas or areas defined on mobility data (e.g. local labour systems - SLL); and finally, studies carried out with individual data that consider the individual risk factors that influenced SARS-CoV-2 infection. This allows regression models to be adjusted for all potential confusing factors, so that more robust and important statistical and biological validity can be achieved than those obtained here.

In conclusion, relationships obtained in this research confirm the hypothesis of an important contribution of chronic exposure to air pollution of nitrogen dioxide on the spatial spread and lethality of the SARS-CoV-2 virus. However, there is an awareness that a correlation study at the aggregate level and at the regional and provincial scale cannot identify a real causal link between an exposure and an outcome, but it only suggests a potential association. Therefore, the present work has addressed only a small part of this complex problem and it is appropriate to proceed with further analyzes to better clarify the role of air pollution during the COVID-19 pandemic, which may be useful to activate prevention plans for future health emergencies and encourage and promote sustainable environmental policies.

Acknowledgments. Here we want to thank Giovenale Moirano (MD-PhD, University of Turin) for the precious scientific contribution he has provided us.

References

1. Bergquist, R., Manda, S.: The world in your hands: GeoHealth then and now. Geospatial Health **14**(799), 3–16 (2019). https://doi.org/10.4081/gh.2019.779
2. Carugno, M., Consonni, D., Randi, G., Catelan, D., et al.: Air pollution exposure, cause-specific deaths and hospitalizations in a highly polluted Italian region. Environ. Res. **147** (2016). https://doi.org/10.1016/j.envres.2016.03.003

3. CIESIN. Center for International Earth Science Information Network - Columbia University. Gridded Population of the World, Version 4 (GPWv4): Population Count, Revision 11. Palisades, NY: NASA Socioeconomic Data and Applications Center (SEDAC) (2019). Accessed 18 June 2020. https://doi.org/10.7927/H4JW8BX5

4. Coccia, M.: Factors determining the diffusion of COVID-19 and suggested strategy to prevent future accelerated viral infectivity similar to COVID. Sci. Total Environ. **729** (2020). https://doi.org/10.1016/j.scitotenv.2020.138474

5. Coker, E.S., et al.: The effects of air pollution on COVID-19 related mortality in Northern Italy. Environ. Resource Econ. **76**(4), 611–634 (2020). https://doi.org/10.1007/s10640-020-00486-1

6. Conticini, E., Frediani, B., Caro, D.: Can atmospheric pollution be considered a cofactor in extremely high level of SARS-CoV-2 lethality in Northern Italy? Environ. Pollution **261** (2020). https://doi.org/10.1016/j.envpol.2020.114465

7. CPD, Civil Protection Department - official data on COVID-19. https://github.com/pcmdpc/COVID-19. Accessed 14 July 2020

8. Dlamini, S.N., Beloconi, A., Mabaso, S., Vounatsou, P., Impouma, B., Fall, I.S.: Review of remotely sensed data products for disease mapping and epidemiology. Remote Sensing Appl. Soc. Environ. **14**, 108–118 (2019). https://doi.org/10.1016/j.rsase.2019.02.005

9. ESA, European Space Agency - Sentinel-5P information. https://sentinel.esa.int/web/sentinel/missions/sentinel-5p. Accessed 15 June 2020

10. Eskes, H., van Geffen, J., Boersma, F., et al.: Sentinel-5 Precursor/TROPOMI Level 2 Product User Manual Nitrogen dioxide. Royal Netherlands Meteorological Institute (Ed.) (2019)

11. EUROSTAT, European Statistical Office - dataset. https://ec.europa.eu/eurostat/data/database. Accessed 3 Aug 2020

12. Fattorini, D., Regoli, F.: Role of the chronic air pollution levels in the Covid-19 outbreak risk in Italy. Environ. Pollution **264** (2020). https://doi.org/10.1016/j.envpol.2020.114732

13. Filippini, T., et al.: Associations between mortality from COVID-19 in two Italian regions and outdoor air pollution as assessed through tropospheric nitrogen dioxide. Sci. Total Environ. (2020). https://doi.org/10.1016/j.scitotenv.2020.143355

14. Filippini, T., Rothman, K.J., Goffi, A., Ferrari, F., Maffeis, G., Orsini, N., Vinceti, M.: Satellite-detected tropospheric nitrogen dioxide and spread of SARS-CoV-2 infection in Northern Italy. Sci. Total Environ. **739** (2020). https://doi.org/10.1016/j.sci-totenv.2020.140278

15. GEE, Google Earth Engine - Sentinel-5P OFFL NO_2 dataset. https://developers.google.com/earth-engine/datasets/catalog/COPERNICUS_S5P_OFFL_L3_NO2. Accessed 15 June 2020

16. Giulianelli, L., et al.: Fog occurrence and chemical composition in the Po valley over the last twenty years. Atmos. Environ. **98**, 394–401 (2014). https://doi.org/10.1016/j.atmosenv.2014.08.080

17. Gorelick, N., Hancher, M., Dixon, M., Ilyushchenko, S., Thau, D., Moore, R.: Google earth engine: planetary-scale geospatial analysis for everyone. Remote Sens. Environ. **202**, 18–27 (2017). https://doi.org/10.1016/j.rse.2017.06.031

18. Hay, S.I., Randolph, S., Rogers, D.: Remote sensing and geographical information systems in epidemiology. Advances in Parasitology (47). Academic Press (2000)

19. Hay, S.I., Battle, K.E., Pigott, D.M., Smith, D.L., Moyes, C.L., Bhatt, S., et al.: Global mapping of infectious disease. Philosophical Trans. Roy. Soc. B Biol. Sci. **368**(1614) (2013). https://doi.org/10.1098/rstb.2012.0250

20. Herbreteau, V., Salem, G., Souris, M., Hugot, J.-P., Gonzalez, J.-P.: Thirty years of use and improvement of remote sensing, applied to epidemiology: from early promises to lasting frustration. Health Place **13**(2), 400–403 (2007). https://doi.org/10.1016/j.healthplace.2006.03.003

21. ISS, Italian National Institute of Health - Characteristics of patients who died positive for SARS-CoV-2 infection in Italy. Data on 20 March 2020. https://www.epicentro.iss.it/corona virus/sars-cov-2-decessi-italia. Accessed 2 Nov 2020
22. ISTAT, Italian National Institute of Statistic - official data. https://www.istat.it/it/popolazione-e-famiglie. Accessed 15 July 2020
23. Jiang, F., Deng, L., Zhang, L., Cai, Y., Cheung, C.W., Xia, Z.: Review of the clinical characteristics of coronavirus disease 2019 (COVID-19). J. Gen. Intern. Med. **35**(5), 1545–1549 (2020). https://doi.org/10.1007/s11606-020-05762-w
24. Jones, K.E., et al.: Global trends in emerging infectious diseases. Nature **451**(7181), 990–993 (2008). https://doi.org/10.1038/nature06536
25. Kraemer, M.U.G., Hay, S.I., Pigott, D.M., Smith, D.L., Wint, G.R.W., Golding, N.: Progress and challenges in infectious disease cartography. Trends Parasitol. **32**(1), 19–29 (2016). https://doi.org/10.1016/j.pt.2015.09.006
26. Larsen, B., Gilardoni, S., Stenström, K., Niedzialek, J., Jimenez, J., Belis, C.: Sources for PM air pollution in the Po Plain, Italy: II. Probabilistic uncertainty characterization and sensitivity analysis of secondary and primary sources. Atmospheric Environ. **50**, 203–213 (2012). https://doi.org/10.1016/j.atmosenv.2011.12.038
27. Li, H., Xu, X.-L., Dai, D.-W., Huang, Z.-Y., Ma, Z., Guan, Y.-J.: Air pollution and temperature are associated with increased COVID-19 incidence: a time series study. Int. J. Infect. **97**, 278–282 (2020). https://doi.org/10.1016/j.ijid.2020.05.076
28. Martelletti, L., Martelletti, P.: Air pollution and the novel Covid-19 disease: a putative disease risk factor. SN Compr. Clin. Med. **2**(4), 383–387 (2020). https://doi.org/10.1007/s42399-020-00274-4
29. NOAA, National Oceanic and Atmospheric Administration - Physical Sciences Laboratory (PSL) dataset. http://www.esrl.noaa.gov/psd/. Accessed 23 July 2020
30. Ogen, Y.: Assessing nitrogen dioxide (NO_2) levels as a contributing factor to coronavirus (COVID-19) fatality. Science of The Total Environment, 7269 (2020). https://doi.org/10.1016/j.scitotenv.2020.138605
31. Onder, G., Rezza, G., Brusaferro, S.: Case-fatality rate and characteristics of patients dying in relation to COVID-19 in Italy. JAMA **323**, 1775–1776 (2020). https://doi.org/10.1001/jama.2020.4683
32. Pansini, R., Fornacca, D.: COVID-19 higher induced mortality in Chinese regions with lower air quality. medRxiv (2020). https://doi.org/10.1101/2020.04.04.20053595
33. Pozzer, A., Bacer, S., Sappadina, S.D.Z., Predicatori, F., Caleffi, A.: Long-term concentrations of fine particulate matter and impact on human health in Verona. Italy. Atmospheric Pollution Res. **10**, 731–738 (2019). https://doi.org/10.1016/j.apr.2018.11.012
34. Reilev, M., et al.: Characteristics and predictors of hospitalization and death in the first 11.122 cases with a positive RT-PCR test for SARS-CoV-2 in Denmark: a nationwide cohort. Int. J. Epidemiology (2020). https://doi.org/10.1093/ije/dyaa140
35. RIAS, Rete Italiana Ambiente e Salute - Inquinamento atmosferico e COVID-19. Accessed date: 18 October 2020. https://www.scienzainrete.it/articolo/inquinamento-atmosferico-e-covid-19/reteitaliana-ambiente-e-salute/2020-04-13
36. Richard, B., MacDonald, J.M.: Overdispersion and poisson regression. J. Quant. Criminol. **24**, 269–284 (2008). https://doi.org/10.1007/s10940-008-9048-4
37. Schneider, M.C., Machado, G.: Environmental and socioeconomic drivers in infectious disease. Lancet Planet. Health **2**(5), 198–199 (2018). https://doi.org/10.1016/S2542-519 6(18)30069-X
38. Setti, L., Passarini, F., Gennaro, G.D., et al.: Potential role of particulate matter in the spreading of COVID-19 in Northern Italy: first observational study based on initial epidemic diffusion. BMJ J. **10** (2020). https://doi.org/10.1136/bmjopen-2020-039338

39. Shaw, N., McGuire, S.: Understanding the use of geographical information systems (GIS) in health informatics research: a review. J. Innov. Health Inf. **24**(2), 228–233 (2017). https://doi.org/10.14236/jhi.v24i2.940

40. SIMA, Società Italiana di Medicina Ambientale: Particulate matter and COVID-19 - Position paper, (2020). http://www.simaonlus.it/wpsima/wp-content/uploads/2020/03/COVID_19_position-paper_ENG.pdf. Accessed 18 Oct 2020

41. Ssentongo, P., Ssentongo, A.E., Heilbrunn, E.S., Ba, D.M., Chinchilli, V.M.: Association of cardiovascular disease and 10 other pre-existing comorbidities with COVID-19 mortality: a systematic review and meta-analysis. PLoS One **15** (2020). https://doi.org/10.1371/journal.pone.0238215

42. Suk, J.E., Semenza, J.C.: Future infectious disease threats to Europe. Am. J. Public Health **101**(11), 2068–2079 (2011). https://doi.org/10.2105/AJPH.2011.300181

43. Viana, J., et al.: Remote sensing in human health: a 10-year bibliometric analysis. Remote Sens. **9**(12), 1225 (2017). https://doi.org/10.3390/rs9121225

44. Zoran, M.A., Savastru, R.S., Savastru, D.M., Tautan, M.N.: Assessing the relationship between ground levels of ozone (O_3) and nitrogen dioxide (NO_2) with coronavirus (COVID-19) in Milan, Italy. Sci. Total Environ. **740** (2020). https://doi.org/10.1016/j.scitotenv.2020.140005

Geomatics and Natural Hazards

Arno Riverbed Survey in Florence 1935 - 2019: From the Integrated Survey to the Geomatic Monitoring

Paolo Aminti(✉), Valentina Bonora[iD], Francesco Mugnai[iD], and Grazia Tucci[iD]

Department of Civil and Environmental Engineering, University of Florence, Florence, Italy
{paolo.aminti,valentina.bonora,francesco.mugnai,
grazia.tucci}@unfi.it

Abstract. On the 50th anniversary of the 1966 flood, the University of Florence, together with many other institutions, promoted the "Florence 2016 Project" by collecting materials, launching new research activities, supporting projects and events to obtain tangible results for the prevention of future disasters and identify good practices for the protection of people and of cultural, economic and environmental heritage. The paper aims to review how the Arno Hydrographic Office surveyed the river during World War Two by photogrammetry and classical topography and to compare the old surveys with the recent activities carried out as part of the Florence 2016 Project. By considering past and more recent surveys, it is possible to identify methodological approaches that retain their validity and to highlight the potentialities of innovative technologies that offer new perspectives for investigation and analysis.

In particular, GNSS (Global Navigation Satellite Systems) techniques offer an easy solution to survey georeferencing, with an evident advantage in repeatability and comparison of results, but a high precision survey needs a critical approach, so to aim at effective monitoring.

Keywords: Hydrographic risk · Classical topography · Aerial photogrammetry · Mobile mapping systems · Bathymetric survey · 3D modelling · Geomatics · Monitoring

1 Introduction

On the 50th anniversary of the 1966 flood, the University of Florence, together with many other institutions, has promoted the "Florence 2016 Project" by collecting materials, launching new research activities, supporting projects and events in order to obtain tangible results for the prevention of future disasters and to identify good practices for the protection of people, and of cultural, economic and environmental heritage [1].

The project was founded by the Municipality of Florence, the Consorzio di Bonifica Medio Valdarno, the Autorità Idrica Toscana, and Publiacqua. Many researchers from the Department of Civil and Environmental Engineering were involved, each contributing with his/her specific background – as well-known complex problems benefit from multidisciplinary approaches [2].

© Springer Nature Switzerland AG 2022
E. Borgogno-Mondino and P. Zamperlin (Eds.): ASITA 2021, CCIS 1507, pp. 71–82, 2022.
https://doi.org/10.1007/978-3-030-94426-1_6

One of the activities carried out as part of the project is the survey of a stretch of about 18 km of the Arno riverbed and its immediate surroundings, from Varlungo to the mouth of the Bisenzio River. A Mobile Mapping System (MMS), mounted on a rubber boat, integrates different sensors: a multi-beam echo sounder (MBES) for the riverbed documentation, a terrestrial laser scanner (TLS), in profiler mode, for the simultaneous survey of banks and architectural structures, and a series of valuable sensor for georeferencing 3D data acquired, contemporary, over and under the water.

The paper reviews how the Arno River was surveyed in the past, then presents some cutting edge techniques offered by geomatics to acquire, manage, and examine spatial data, and describes the specific case of the section of Arno under investigation. Lastly, it concludes with some remarks and perspectives about new studies we carried out recently in the west branch of the Arno, in Signa and Lastra a Signa.

2   The Survey Campaign 1935–1961

In 1935 the Arno Hydrographic Office started to survey the river, but they did not complete the work due to the Second World War, which destroyed most of the documents already completed. In the '50s, the same Office started to survey the river, starting from its mouth.

The results were published in 1954 (the first section of about 42 km) [3] and 1956 (the second section of 40 km more) [4]. In 1960–61 the survey was further extended in the urban stretch of the river (see Fig. 1) [5], then proceeding towards the river mouth in the later years. The following section provides some details about how, at that time, data was acquired to better make a comparison later with the new surveys.

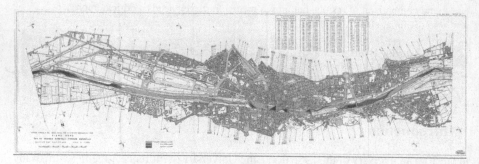

Fig. 1. River Arno plan in the Florentine urban area – cross-sections locations are visible

2.1   Classical Survey Techniques: Topography and Photogrammetry

An aerial photogrammetry survey was performed, and data that was not derivable from the aerial images, as the ground under the vegetation, and the riverbed, were measured by tacheometry and bathymetry. A Wild RC5 camera was mounted on an airplane, taking several images on 230 × 230 mm high film slides. Thanks to the stereoscopic observations of photogrammetric models (Fig. 2), the operator plotted all the relevant details, including urban areas facing the river. Integration of so many different survey techniques and instruments (triangulation, traverses, tacheometry, levelling, aerial photogrammetry), induces to define this approach as "ante litteram" geomatic.

Several traverses connected benchmarks, some of those already used in the 1935–36 survey, and some trigonometric points from the Italian Geographic Military Institute (IGMI) and Cadaster. A precise levelling was performed on the left bank, that served as a base for the levelling lines on the right bank, connected to principal line benchmarks with loop circuits. Cross-sections have been surveyed using tacheometers so as floodplain areas in order to allow a 25 cm contouring.

Therefore, we can say that the "state of the art" in mapping was applied to document the river, and it sounds clear that it has been a demanding work, considering technologies, the required time, and costs.

Fig. 2. Analogue stereo plotter (Galileo-Santoni Stereosimplex III)

2.2 Traditional Graphical Outputs

Conventional rules were well established for plotting traditional surveys: e.g., the plan view represents the outline of the right and left riverbanks, with the river's length in a smaller graphical scale than its breadth. The maximum depth line, or Thalweg line, the tributary waterways, and the bridges are also plotted. The profile stresses the elevations on a scale of 1:200, whilst the length of the whole river is on a scale of 1:50.000 (Fig. 3). In addition to the ground representation, the low-water and high-water levels are taken into account.

For the section of the Arno passing through Florence, 243 transversal sections describe bridges and weirs (Fig. 4). They were measured by tacheometry and levelling. Finally, contours lines, with a contour line distance of 25 cm, were plotted based on a tacheometric riverbanks survey with a resolution never lower than 10 points in a hectare.

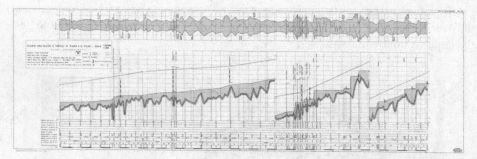

Fig. 3. River Arno longitudinal profile – scales: 1:50.000/1:200

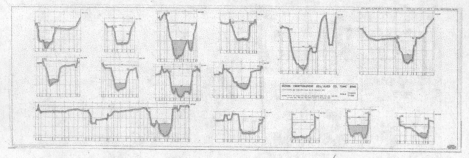

Fig. 4. River Arno cross-sections – scales: 1:2.500/1:250

2.3 Comments and Remarks

The report of the survey works done in the field at that time sounds fascinating to us, and we can appreciate the thorough description of the instruments and adopted methods, the precision declared, the admirable drawings. A massive amount of data was measured, computed, elaborated, and finally plotted to describe the river meticulously. Despite this, the river's description, with its banks, the bridges, the buildings close to it, is "discrete" or, as we would say nowadays, it has a "low resolution": in fact, the shape description of the riverbed is weak from the point of view of continuity, and only along cross-sections it is satisfactory.

3   The Contemporary Survey

A survey, even the best-done survey, is something valid at the moment when it is performed. Moreover, a river changes over time, even without considering exceptional events, like floods. Therefore, the "Firenze 2016" project gave the chance to perform a new survey of the Arno river urban section. Each survey documents the land portion, the built heritage, or the river that is under study, and the technologies and the advances in the know-how of its time. In the broader project aimed at monitoring the Arno River and at building an updated and effective hydraulic modelling, a 3D survey was performed from Varlungo Bridge to the Bisenzio river mouth in Signa.

Compared to what happened in the past, the instruments used nowadays are more complex, and several sensors are frequently integrated to record information of different nature simultaneously [6]. The time required in the field has been greatly reduced, thanks to the instruments' operating speed and the possibility of adopting automatisms. On the other hand, the need to plan the survey in a rigorous way remains unchanged, as well the need to adopt measurement methods that allow to certify the quality of the collected data, and to document exhaustively all that is done, to guarantee the possibility to evaluate, to continue, and to integrate the work previously done.

Fluvial studies require high quality topographic and bathymetric data. While Sect. 2 represents state of the art at that time, subsequently tacheometric [7], satellite positioning [8], and aerial photogrammetry techniques [9] have been widely used to produce digital terrain models with increasing accuracy and resolution. In this field of studies, the increasing speed at which geometric data are recorded today seems to be, however, more favourable from an operational point of view - it allows the time spent in the field to be limited - than for exploiting the high resolution that can be obtained [10, 11]. In the case of the project presented here, the realisation of an integrated survey was also aimed at - at least preliminary - documentation of the bridges, whose state of conservation must be carefully inspected and monitored [12, 13]. The short time that needs to be devoted to on-site acquisition operations also makes it possible to carry out multi-temporal surveys [14], thus providing valuable insights into fluvial morpho-dynamics. Detailed high-resolution maps of the river site can be rapidly and efficiently generated by boat-based MMS, which integrates various navigational and data acquisition sensors on a rigid and moving platform: GPS receivers and IMU (Inertial Measurement Unit) record the system trajectory, and laser scanners and digital cameras or videos record information from the surroundings of the river [15]. Integrating the MMS with a multi-beam echo sounder allows also reconstructing the submerged riverbed [16].

3.1   The Adopted Mobile Mapping System

The river survey was divided into seven areas, each characterised by shipping continuity and provided with a landing stage (see Fig. 5). An MMS was mounted on a rubber boat, integrating different sensors:

- a multi-beam echo sounder system,
- a 3D laser scanner, in profiler mode,

- moreover, a series of sensors for georeferencing 3D data acquired, contemporary, over and under the water.

During data acquisition, the onboard control system shows real-time info about the navigation and positioning, and data recorded by the multi-beam (underwater) and by the laser scanner (over the water). A subsampled view of 3D data is also visible on the screen. Figure 6 shows an example of the data recorded in the Sects. 2 and 3 of the river, where the Arno crosses the city centre, and Fig. 7 highlights that 3D data has a very high resolution.

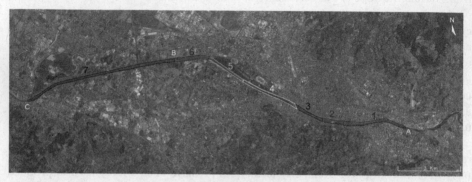

Fig. 5. The entire stretch of the river under consideration has been partitioned into continuously navigable segments

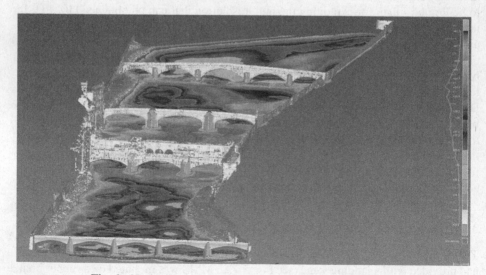

Fig. 6. 3D data recorded where the Arno crosses the city centre

Fig. 7. 3D data has a very high resolution, which also allows to check and monitor the piers of bridges

3.2 3D Data Georeferencing

To correctly georeference 3D data, the control network plays a key role, consisting of fixed points measured with great accuracy and therefore positioned in a specific reference system. Reaching high accuracy is an expensive task; that is why it is essential to plan the control network carefully, balance the need to have available reference points all along the river, and that of limit the resources that have to be employed to do it.

The Datum Choice. The official geodetic datum in Italy is the European system ETRS89 - ETRF2000 updated to 2008.0. However, for technical purposes, a cartographic projection must be defined but still considering deformations - of course, if and when they are relevant concerning the expected accuracy. Given the extent of the survey, neglecting these deformations would lead to an error of about 50 cm, much higher than the one resulting from position measurements, both satellite and topographic. Therefore, a local system was explicitly defined to limit deformation effects and to compute and adjust topographic measurements. The orthometric height was considered to support the hydraulic modelling correctly for elevations.

In order to improve interoperability - that is a relevant aspect in such an interdisciplinary project - all the benchmark's coordinates are computed both in UTM32 and in Gauss Boaga cartographic reference systems.

The Control Network - GNSS. In this case, a robust geodetic framework was defined by GNSS measurements, based on some permanent stations near the survey area: IGMI and PRAT (by EUREF network), CALA and EMNS (by ItalPoS network). Observations collected by high precision total station integrate the control network.

Control network vertices have been fixed on all bridges (except on Ponte Vecchio, where buildings blocked most of the satellites signals) and along the banks in obstacle-free zones to acquire satellite data with a strong geometry.

The Control Network – TS. TS measurements started from GNSS (static) determined fix points positioned on the bridges, banks, or both. Precision in benchmark (each suitable as station point) position is about ± 1–2 cm (planimetric). For height measurements, five IGMI high precision levelling network benchmarks were employed and tied to the local TS network; University-Military Geographical Institute synergy gave excellent results; in fact, the accuracy in local network fix points elevations was better than ±1 cm.

Ground Control Points. As ground control points, black and white targets were fixed on the riversides and measured by a total station (TS). They were later used to control the georeferencing of all the data acquired by TLS (out of the water) and MBES (underwater).

Through the same topographic instruments (TS Leica TCRP1201), 3D positions of about 100 ground control points (GCP) – targets placed along the river' section considered from time to time - were determined with a precision better than ±1 dm.

The entire mobile mapping survey was, at first, directly geo-referenced based on the onboard sensor observations (GNSS and inertial navigation system). Accuracy checks provided satisfactory results, showing differences between points measured by topography and the same recorded on the point model of about ± 1–3 dm, compliant with the survey purposes.

Considerations Concerning Accuracy and Resolution. Some studies about the hydraulic model's sensitivity to different topographic inputs demonstrated that the watercourse geometry and the inundation area are crucial elements to hydraulic models [17]. Given this, in the sections passing through the historical city centre, 3D data georeferencing was improved: by forcing GCP to correspond to topographic coordinates, sub-sets of laser scanner data were considered, and an adjustment was performed to enhance the survey accuracy and reliability globally. After that, the GCP root mean square errors are about ± 4 cm (planimetry) and ± 1 cm in height. Random checks on the point model showed that the actual accuracy is always compliant with the requests since never planimetric errors are worse than 10 cm and 5 cm in height.

Therefore, the new survey of the Arno is an accurate «digital twin» of the natural river. Graphical representation such as Digital Elevation Models (DEM), vertical sections, surface models, can be extracted from the available database, depending on the project's need, focusing on a long section or a small detail on a bridge's pier as well. Multi-beam resolution ranges from 1 to 5 cm, depending on the water depth and on some sensor parameters. Laser scanning resolution varies according to the scanned surfaces' position for the instrument path, with average values comparable to that of the multi-beam system. If a higher resolution is needed – for structures out of the water, of course - a terrestrial laser scanner can profitably be applied, thus allowing to resolve about half a centimetre – as shown in Fig. 8, about the 3D survey of Ponte Vecchio GeCo Lab did in 2012.

Fig. 8. Ponte Vecchio point model, TLS survey by GeCo Lab, 2012

4 Forthcoming Studies

In 2019, the Arno River survey extended for about 400 m towards the West (in the town of Signa and Lastra a Signa) in a research project aimed at the structural analysis of two bridges located in this area (Fig. 9). Accuracy requirements were stricter than those needed for the previous survey because of the new study's different purposes, mainly related to the structural analysis of bridges. Therefore, a laser scanning survey complemented the mobile mapping survey; a control network was designed to reach a precision of ± 1–2 mm and have GCP 3D positions defined in a ± 5–10 mm range. All the vertices were permanently fixed on stones on top of banks; temporary black and white targets were distributed along riverbanks to be used as GCP.

The control network was defined by combining GNSS and TS measurements, thus requiring a pre-calibrated mounting for the antenna to refer all the observations to the same point, both planimetrically and altimetrically. Apart from the increase in accuracy required by the new survey, the instruments and methods are the same as those used in 2015–2016, as is the reference system; by doing so, it will be possible to carry out new measurements that are entirely comparable with the current ones, even in the future.

Fig. 9. The road bridge crossing the Arno between the towns of Lastra and Lastra a Signa

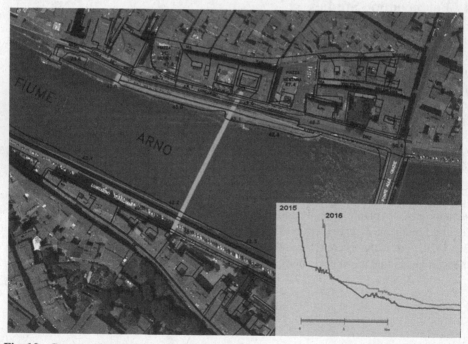

Fig. 10. Cross-sections in Lungarno Torrigiani before and after the wall collapse. (Color figure online)

5 Conclusions

The diachronic analysis of river Arno surveys executed along the last century highlights the evolution of instruments and methods for survey and representation of reality, also allowing to identify the aspects of continuity concerning the past:

- the relevance of the preliminary design of the field operations,
- the approach based on the integration of different techniques,
- the methodological rigour with which measurements and computations are carried out,
- the research of effective ways to represent the river and its surrounding area as exhaustively as possible.

Considering the survey activities concerning the time when they were carried out also allows to highlight which changes may have occurred in the area and to assess their entity: Fig. 10 shows a blue profile acquired in 2015 - during the survey campaign described above - and a red profile, recorded immediately after the collapse of the wall supporting the left bank in April 2016 in Lungarno Torrigiani, in the Florence city centre [18].

Acknowledgements. The coordination committee of the project "Firenze 2016" consists of a long list of public and private bodies (https://www.sba.unifi.it/p1612.html) as members or partners. Dario Nardella and Enrico Rossi served as Co-Presidents, Prof. Giorgio Valentino Federici as Secretary.

The Italian Geographic Military Institute kindly made available to the project precious resources to support data georeferencing.

Daniele Ostuni participated in field survey campaigns.

References

1. Bartolozzi, D., Caciolli, A., Castaldi, M., Paris, E., Solari, L.: L'Arno e il progetto Firenze 2016. Progettandoing **IX**(4), 19–28 (2016)
2. Peruzzi, C., Castaldi, M., Francalanci, S., Solari, L.: Three-dimensional hydraulic characterisation of the Arno River in Florence. J. Flood Risk Manage. **12**(S1), e12490 (2018)
3. Ufficio Idrografico dell'Arno: Arno: dalla foce alla confluenza con l'Era. Rilievi dell'Alveo dei corsi d'acqua (1954)
4. Ufficio Idrografico dell'Arno: Arno: dalla confluenza con l'Era a Montelupo. Rilievi dell'alveo dei corsi d'acqua (1956)
5. Ufficio Idrografico dell'Arno: Arno: da Montelupo a Nave Martelli. Rilievi dell'alveo dei corsi d'acqua (1962)
6. Mugnai, F., Ridolfi, A., Bianchi, M., Franchi, M., Tucci, G.: Developing affordable bathymetric analysis techniques using non-conventional payload for cultural heritage inspections. In: ISPRS International Archives of the Photogrammetry, Remote Sensing and Spatial Information Sciences, pp. 807–811 (2019)
7. Chappel, G.H., Fuller, I., Large, A., Milan, D.: Geostatistical analysis of ground-survey elevation data to elucidate spatial and temporal river channel change. Earth Surf. Process. Land. **28**, 349–370 (2003)

8. Higgitt, D., Warburton, J.: Applications of differential GPS in upland fluvial geomorphology. Geomorphology **29**(1–2), 121–134 (1999)
9. Heritage, G., Fuller, I., Charlton, M., Brewer, P., Passmore, D.: CDW photogrammetry of low relief fluvial features: accuracy and implications for reach-scale sediment budgeting. Earth Surf. Proc. Land. **23**(13), 1219–1233 (1999)
10. Hardy, R., Bates, P., Anderson, M.: The importance of spatial resolution in hydraulic models for floodplain environments. J. Hydrol. **216**(1–2), 124–136 (1999)
11. Alho, P., Hyyppa, H., Hyyppa, J.: Consequence of DTM precision for flood hazard mapping: a case study in SW Finland. Nordic J. Surveying Real Estate Res. **6**(1), 21–39 (2009)
12. Abudayyeh, O., Al Bataineh, M., Abdel-Qader, I.: An imaging data model for concrete bridge inspection. Adv. Eng. Softw. **35**, 473–480 (2004)
13. Mugnai, F., Lombardi, L., Tucci, G., Nocentini, M.G.G., Fanti, R.: Geomatics in bridge structural healt monitoring, integrating terrestrial laser scanning techniqies and geotechnical inspections on high value cultural heritage. International Archives of the Photogrammetry, Remote Sensing and Spatial Information Sciences, vols. 11, pp. 895–900 (2019)
14. Ozcan, O., Ozcan, O.: Multi-temporal UAV based repeat monitoring of rivers sensitive to flood. J. Maps **16**, 1–8 (2020)
15. Alho, P., Kukko, A., Hyyppa, H., Kaartinen, H., Hyyppa, J., Jaakkola, A.: Application of boat-based laser scanning for river survey. Earth Surf. Proc. Land. **34**, 1831–1838 (2009)
16. Federici, N.C., Ferrando, I., Sguerso, D., Lucarelli, A., Guida, S., Brandolini, P.: Remote sensing techniques applied to geomorphological mapping of rocky coast: the case study of Gallinara Island (Western Liguria, Italy). Europ. J. Remote Sens. **52**(sup4), 123–136 (2019). From Space to Land Management
17. Reil, C., Skoulikaris, T.A. Roub, R.: Evaluation of riverbed representation methods for one-dimensional flood hydraulics model. J. Flood Risk Manage. **11**, 169–179 (2018)
18. Bartolozzi, A., Caciolli, M., Castaldi, E.P., Solari, L.: Idrodinamica del fiume Arno in corrispondenza del fenomeno erosivo al ponte Amerigo Vespucc. Progettando Ing **XI**(4), 19–28 (2016)

Implementation of the Digital Inland Water Smart Strategy Using Geomatics Instruments and the Big Data SmartRiver Platform

Ernesto Bernardo[1]([⊠]) [ID], Stefano Bonfa[2], and Jesse Anderson[3]

[1] DICEAM - Department of Civil, Energy, Environment and Materials Engineering, Mediterranea University of Reggio Calabria, via Graziella, Feo di Vito, 89128 Reggio Calabria, Italy
ernesto.bernardo@unirc.it

[2] United Kingdom Economic Interest Grouping (UKEIG) OSDE, 87 Hungerdown, Chingford, London E4 6QJ, UK

[3] Bigdata Institute, Reno Ave., Reno, Nevada 89509, USA

Abstract. This research concerns an innovative method for land monitoring using data provided by geomatics instruments (images from ESA's earth observation satellites; images from UAVs; climatic data provided by Copernicus satellites), integrated with socio-economic data and geophysical data, in combination with the use of Artificial Intelligence and Analytics and integrating the data obtained within a cloud containing a Data Cube that acts as an Analytic-Ready-Data (ARD) data-lake storage; a GIS web application that allows the visualization of data and facilitates the involvement of stakeholders relevant to the river/water basin. Specifically, thanks to the use of the SmartRiver Platform implemented by us, using large amounts of data (Big Data) appropriately selected and processed, through Artificial and Analytical Intelligence we are able to provide knowledge and assistance in the development and forecasting the risks of climatic impacts on the territory (useful for the management/planning of projects by the bodies in charge). In the specific case, these forecasts will be useful both in the safety sector (allowing to foresee possible floods, and consequently allowing to plan the possible construction of dams, canals, embankments, etc.), and in the sector of management of water resources. It is possible with a view to an adaptation strategy in the management of resources according to climate change, allowing for drought periods to be foreseen, the bodies in charge will be able to evaluate in advance the best strategies to be implemented to contain any risks due to the lack of water in the agricultural and energy production sectors.

Keywords: Geomatics · Artificial Intelligence · Data analytics · Big data · GIS

1 Introduction

Although we are aware that understanding the process of climate change is complex and not yet fully understood, we believe that a key challenge for research is the creation of

© Springer Nature Switzerland AG 2022
E. Borgogno-Mondino and P. Zamperlin (Eds.): ASITA 2021, CCIS 1507, pp. 83–94, 2022.
https://doi.org/10.1007/978-3-030-94426-1_7

a system that helps develop actions to minimize the damage due to climate change and help countries and agencies to develop the best strategies in advance to minimize the impacts of these changes on the population and economy.

To solve these problems, it is clear that it is necessary to use large amounts of data of different types (thus clashing/necessarily having to deal with big data [1–3] and the rules that govern them).

Big Data. The real value associated with the great availability of data lies not only in the quantity, but in the ability to use them to process, analyze and find objective evidence and correlations between various sectors, in the specific example in favor of monitoring hydrogeological phenomena through big data.

Big Data therefore means the range of opportunities for analyzing the correlations on the data associated with this aspect, to be used for research, management and generation of new business value applications. To manage large amounts of data, basic technologies and specific technologies are required. In this article we want to describe a solution (the SmartRiver platform) able to enable the monitoring of hydrogeological phenomena thanks to the use of big data.

We have recently had a huge increase in all three main dimensions of big data: volume, speed and variety. This increase involves an enormous amount of new developments related to big data in many fields and made possible thanks to new technologies and new hardware and software developments, multi-temporal data analysis, data management and information extraction technologies [4–7].

Furthermore, also recently, we have had a momentum in the field of Big Data from space, thanks to the recent multiplication of open access initiatives that offer new opportunities to researchers and companies. In particular for the Space Science and Earth Observation data with the release to the public of the complete Landsat data archive by the United States Geological Survey and the European program Copernicus, whose Sentinel missions managed by the European Space Agency will provide free access and open to global data in the microwave and optical/infrared ranges.

The first one, Sentinel-1A, launched on April 3, 2014, and the second, Sentinel-1B, launched on April 25, 2016, are delivering high-resolution Synthetic Aperture Radar (SAR) global data every 12 days at a daily rate of 2.5 TB. The Sentinel-2A acquires optical data with high revisit frequency, coverage, timeliness and reliability with MSI Spectral Bands span from the Visible and the Near Infra-Red to the Short Wave Infra-Red: 4 bands at 10 m, 6 bands at 20 m, 3 bands at 60 m. It operates in a reference sun-synchronous orbit with a repeat cycle of 10 days for the overall duration of the mis-sion. Sentinel-2B in 2017 will be in the same orbit, allowing a ground-track revisit frequency of 5 days for the dual-spacecraft constellation.

In this research we used images from earth observation satellites; images from UAVs; GPS surveys, climatic data provided by Copernicus satellites; socioeconomic data; geophysical and geognostic data (ISPRA) [8], maps of the PAI (Piano di Assetto Idreogeologico) - hydrogeological plan, pluviometric data (Arpacal and meteorological satellites), various hydrological data calculated on the basis of pluviometric data, basin permeability coefficient, Horton order; Corrivation time, Digital Elevation Model - DEM (derivability parameters: average and median height), Socio-economic data (ISTAT) [9], combined with Artificial Intelligence and Analytics techniques, which integrate the data obtained within a Data Cube in order to create a SmartRiver platform for obtain forecasts on any periods of flooding/drought.

To exploit the value of data by looking at greater resilience with respect to natural risks over time, the platform aims to allow the monitoring of hydrogeological phenomena, thanks to a processing system based on forecasting models for rivers, streams and reservoirs and integrated with a geographic information system (GIS). End users (citizens, data scientists of public and private organizations, institutional decision makers), mainly belonging to river communities, but not only, can interact with the platform thanks to a web application built on GIS technology.

The SmartRiver platform combines tools from Geomatics, Artificial Intelligence and Analytics, in combination with a Data Cube to create an innovative solution in the management of risks due to climate impacts on the territory.

The experimental pilot project was carried out in the Stilo area, on the Ionian coast in the province of Reggio Calabria. The platform will therefore allow the interaction of interested parties related to river management.

2 Materials and Methods

SmartRiver is a platform capable of processing large amounts of data (Big Data) by providing climate forecast models [10–13] thanks to Artificial Intelligence and, thanks to the end-user APIs (Application Programming Interface), to allow the participation of people from River Communities through a WebGIS graphic interface, or "Big Data Living Labs". This platform allows for the interaction of stakeholders related to river management, together with the transfer of knowledge between river communities.

The SmartRiver platform consists of three main pillars:

(i)   The Open Data Cube cloud platform, which acts as a data-lake for ARD data (storage) and allows data processing and the creation of forecast models with algorithms and Artificial Intelligence (processing).

(ii)   An intermediate level of data services organization to interface Open Data Cube with the end-user APIs (interaction between storage and visualization).

(iii)   The APIs displayed on WebGIS for the end user to be implemented for the "Big Data Living Labs" case study for river communities (end-users view).

Specifically, as show in Fig. 1, the operation of the platform includes the following modules: 1) Open Data Cube, 2) Global Models Library 3) AI enabled services or Artificial intelligence living lab, and 4) the WebGIS application.

The process takes place in 5 stages:

1)   The Open Data Cube works as a multidimensional value matrix ("nD") to manage arrays, data warehouses of multiple terabytes/petabytes and time series of image data, thus acting as a storage data lake: the CEOS platform Open Data Cube [14], automatically and strategically (depending on the case study) acquires data from ESA's DIAS (services provided on access to data from Copernicus satellites).

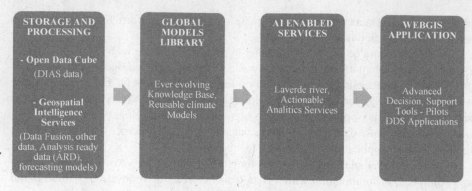

Fig. 1. Platform explanation

2) Geospatial Intelligence Services: the data is merged and integrated into the CEOS Open Data Cube and implemented with other data provided by the geomatics tools, loaded manually on the platform, creating an Analysis Ready Data (ARD). Specifically, the Artificial Intelligence creates the forecast model (for example on precipitations, flooding of the river, on subsidence or displacements of the land, etc.). Through the combined use of Earth Observation (EO) datasets and data acquired in the field in the pilot areas, the ARD enables complex automated workflows that use climate, hydrological models, etc. allowing us to extract information from multiple sources and concatenate them into a single source in order to be able to provide a single set of data that can be subsequently manipulated to extract and compare a greater number of better-quality information.

3) Global Models Library: the forecast models generated are loaded into this library (here the creation of the forecast models ends).

4) AI enabled services: once the models have been obtained, the operators (citizens or administrators) interrogate the library thanks to tools that allow them to query the forecast model or to extrapolate the information that best meets their needs. In our specific case, the information on the floods of the study on the Laverde river.

5) WebGIS: the WebGIS application created, allows end users, data scientists, citizens and managers, respectively to:

   a) Upload (additional input) land mapping data and simulate scenarios, for example of floods using artificial intelligence forecasting models, exploiting shared data made available both locally and globally.

   b) Enter data and opinions through targeted surveys, so that the various stakeholders can participate in the policy making process relating to rivers/basins.

   c) View the set of scenarios simulated by the data scientists on the ad-hoc dashboard based on the data made available by citizens, for a data-based decision-making process. When you use the APIs to retrieve responses to user queries, they will already contain the specific information you need in a particular format, and you will be able to execute HTTP requests whenever you need new ones. open data. Such open data can be processed and displayed in different ways, for example as text or on an interactive map, on the website, in the mobile application or in the software that is being developed.

3 Case Study

The experimental pilot project was carried out in the Stilo area, on the Ionian coast in the province of Reggio Calabria. The area is affected by the Laverde river that crosses the municipalities of Samo and Africo (Fig.2).

Fig. 2. Case study, Laverde river, crosses the municipalities of Samo and Africo, Calabria.

Storage

With reference to points 1–2 described above, the CEOS Open Data Cube platform has been programmed to be able to retrieve the enormous amount of data from the DIAS (services provided on access to data from Copernicus satellites) of ESA (Fig. 3).

Fig. 3. DIAS, services provided on access to Copernicus data

Once the automatic storage phase inside the Data Cube is completed, the satellite data [15–18] are merged and integrated into the CEOS Open Data Cube and implemented with other geomatic, hydrological, socio-economic, geophysical and geognostic data [19–26] (see following list) and loaded manually on the platform, creating an Analysis Ready Data (ARD).

More specifically, the following data were used:

– Satellite data (Landsat, Sentinel-1 and Sentinel-2 and therefore optical data, metric and optical SAR data) with all classifications, segmentations and temporal displays determination of settlements and displacements.

- Images (multispectral and thermal RGB) from UAV (Mavic2Pro e Matrice).
- GPS surveys (for calculation of settlements and displacements).
- Geophysical and geognostic data (ISPRA).
- PAI hydrogeological plan.
- Pluviometric data (Arpacal and meteorological satellites).
- Various hydrological data calculated as a function of rainfall data, basin permeability coefficient, Horton order, corrivation time.
- DEM (differentiability parameters: average and median height).
- Socio-economic data (ISTAT).

By way of example, we report below some data entered and used on the platform (see Fig. 4).

Creation of Forecast Models
Subsequently, through artificial intelligence techniques present within the Data Cube, the forecast model is created (in our case flooding of the river, periods of drought and socio-economic impact): through the combined use of Earth Observation data sets and data acquired in the field in the study areas, and other data, the ARD enables complex automated workflows that employ climate, hydrological models, etc. allowing us to extract information from multiple sources and link them into a single source in order to provide a single set of data that can be subsequently manipulated to extract and compare a greater number of better quality information. Specifically, for our application case, the "CREST" (Coupled Routing and Excess Storage) is used as a forecasting model for rivers, a distributed hydrological model developed to simulate the spatial and temporal variation of the earth's surface, underground water flows, etc.

The CREST model [27, 28] is a raster-based distributed hydrological model developed by the NASA SERVIR Project Team [29] and the University of Oklahoma [30]. It aims to simulate the spatio-temporal variation of water fluxes and storages on regular grid cells of arbitrary user-defined resolution [31]. The model accounts for main processes of water balance, i.e., runoff generation and infiltration. The mechanism of CREST model is briefly summarized as: (1) Use a variable infiltration curve [32] to represent the soil moisture storage capacity and to calculate runoff generation composition; (2) Use multi-linear reservoirs to simulate sub-grid cells routing of surface and subsurface runoff respectively; and (3) Couple the runoff generation and cell to cell routing components via feedback mechanisms to simulate the processes for water budget. This coupling allows the model to be applied at global, national and regional scales to make hydrological analysis.

The forecast models generated are then loaded into the Global Models Library [33–40].

Forecasting Models Obtained
Once the models have been obtained, the operators (citizens or administrators) are able to consult the Global Models Library thanks to tools that allow them to query the forecast model that interests them most through a WebGIS application.

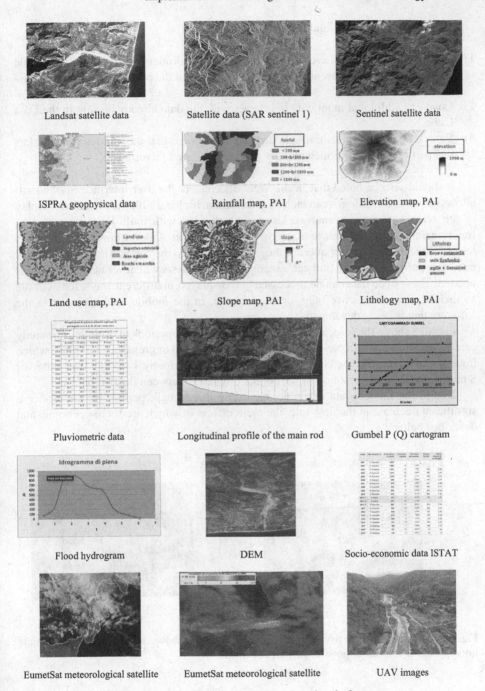

Fig. 4. Some data entered and used on the platform

This application allows end users to:

1) View the floods of the Laverde river, the periods of drought and the socio-economic impact that these two events bring to agriculture and the population affected by the river.
2) Load any additional input data to interact with the data already present in the Data Cube.
3) Enter data and opinions through targeted surveys, so that the various stakeholders can participate in the policy making process relating to river/basin.

It should also be noted that in the WebGIS created, the user interface (dashboard) allows customizations (eg. it can include information for local authorities) and the display of the set of simulated scenarios. Users are provided with multi-layer visualization functionalities, loading of earth mapping data, simulation of algorithms. By using APIs to retrieve responses to user queries, they already contain the specific information users need in a particular format and can execute HTTP requests whenever new open data is needed. These open data can be processed and displayed in different ways, for example as text or on an interactive map, on the website, in the mobile application or in the software that is being developed.

Figure 5 shows the forecast models of possible floods/periods of drought. The study carried out shows how in periods of flooding a transport of aggregates takes place which involves an increase in the coast at the mouth of the stream by 1 m (in a time range of 8 months) and the interruption of the connecting roads between the two banks.

Due to the limited data available, regarding the drought period, we can notice a significant decrease in the flow rate, the main effects of which are socio-economic and described below.

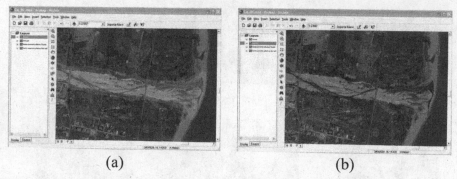

(a)   (b)

Fig. 5. Case study, Laverde river. The software implemented shows: a) the forecasts of possible flooding; b) the forecast of possible periods of drought.

The images contained in Fig. 6 show the forecast models of the socio-economic effects that the territories affected by possible floods/periods of drought of the Laverde river could have. To create these models, ISTAT socio-economic data on the resident population and satellite images were used for the identification of agricultural areas.

The socio-economic effects of periods of flooding lead to an overflow of the river-bank, mainly affecting the agricultural areas adjacent to the river and some houses, also leading to the interruption of the road that serves the population living between the two banks. As we can see from the images, the greatest socioeconomic effects occur during the drought period. During this period, in fact, the sector that is usually the first to be affected is the agricultural sector due to its strong dependence on the water content of the soil.

A short-term drought that persists for three to six months can have small and medium impacts (direct and indirect) on these sectors. Direct impacts: Reduction of crops, pastures and forest productivity; increased risk of fire; reduction of water levels; increase in the mortality rate of livestock and protected species. Indirect: reduced profits for farmers and the agri-food industry, unemployment, reduced tax revenues, foreclosures, devaluation of neighboring residential properties, emigration, disaster assistance programs, etc.

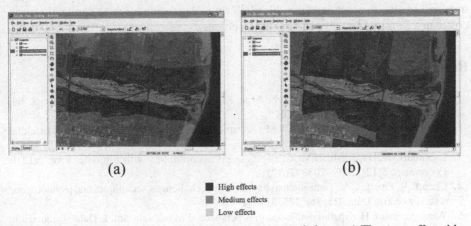

(a)   (b)

■ High effects
■ Medium effects
▢ Low effects

Fig. 6. Case study, Laverde river. The software implemented shows: a) The areas affected by the effects (socio-economic on the territory) of the flooding periods. b) The areas affected by the (socio-economic on the territory) effects of periods of drought.

4 Conclusion

The level of awareness of the effects of climate change is high among many countries. Investments in institutions, structures and policy development are high, with considerable international support. Having services that provide local predictive models that can go beyond just abstract data collection for analysis would provide significant benefits to local populations. This will support better policymaking on water management and the development of better climate adaptation strategies. Furthermore, this research represents a unique opportunity to support the existing agricultural industrial sector as well, which should result in an increase in production and trade. SmartRiver can enable governments, agencies and farmers to benefit from more effective and realistic information that facilitates greater adaptive capacity and climate resilience through the use of resources, especially in preparing for climate change. For governments/people the value of this project is very significant above all because it can be replicated in areas with water scarcity and if extended throughout the territory it would entail the following advantages:

- It would allow the country to become more resilient to climate change and be able to benefit from climate increases (around 5% of GDP).
- Production of small farmers would increase (10–20% increase).
- It would improve preparedness for climate shocks (around 5% of GDP).

Commercial enterprises in many countries will be able to improve their existing services (such as agriculture or energy) through better information and support additional services, especially in sectors with low water resources. Furthermore, start-ups in countries will be able to access and use this platform to develop innovative applications and create new jobs and foster economic development.

References

1. Gandomi, A., Haider, M.: Beyond the hype: Big data concepts, methods, and analytics. Int. J. Inf. Manage. **35**(2), 137–144 (2015)
2. De Mauro, A., Greco, M., Grimaldi, M.: A formal definition of Big Data based on its essential features. Libr. Rev. **65**(3), 122–135 (2016)
3. Labrinidis, A., Jagadish, H.V.: Challenges and opportunities with big data. Proc. VLDB Endowment **5**(12), 2032–2033 (2012)
4. Chen, C.P., Zhang, C.Y.: Data-intensive applications, challenges, techniques and technologies: a survey on Big Data. Inf. Sci. **275**, 314–347 (2014)
5. Wang, S., Yuan, H.: Spatial data mining: A perspective of big data. Int. J. Data Warehousing Mining (IJDWM) **10**(4), 50–70 (2014)
6. Bello-Orgaz, G., Jung, J.J., Camacho, D.: Social big data: recent achievements and new challenges. Inf. Fusion **28**, 45–59 (2016)
7. Jin, X., Wah, B.W., Cheng, X., Wang, Y.: Significance and challenges of big data research. Big Data Res. **2**(2), 59–64 (2015)
8. ISPRA Homepage. https://www.isprambiente.gov.it/it. Accessed 31 May 2021
9. ISTAT Homepage. https://www.istat.it. Accessed 31 May 2021
10. Chen, H., Chiang, R.H., Storey, V.C.: Business intelligence and analytics: from big data to big impact. MIS Q. **36**(4), 1165–1188 (2012)
11. Demchenko, Y., Zhao, Z., Grosso, P., Wibisono, A., De Laat, C.: Addressing big data challenges for scientific data infrastructure. In: 2012 IEEE 4th International Conference on Cloud Computing Technology and Science (CloudCom), pp. 614–617. IEEE (2012)
12. Inglis, M.: December. In: Inglis, M. (ed.) Patrick Moore's Observer's Year: 366 Nights of the Universe. TPMPAS, pp. 343–369. Springer, Cham (2015). https://doi.org/10.1007/978-3-319-18678-8_12
13. Wang, Y.M., Yang, J.B., Xu, D.L.: Environmental impact assessment using the evidential reasoning approach. Eur. J. Oper. Res. **174**(3), 1885–1913 (2006)
14. CEOS Open Data Cube. https://www.opendatacube.org/ceos. Accessed 31 May 2021

15. Jongman, B., Wagemaker, J., Romero, B.R., de Perez, E.C.: Early flood detection for rapid humanitarian response: harnessing near real-time satellite and Twitter signals. ISPRS Int. J. Geo-Information **4**(4), 2246–2266 (2015)

16. Tellman, B., Schwarz, B., Burns, R., Adams, C.: UN Development Report 2015 Chapter Disaster Risk Reduction Big Data in the Disaster Cycle: Overview of use of big data and satellite imaging in monitoring risk and impact of disasters

17. Aires, F., Miolane, L., Prigent, C., et al.: A global dynamic long-term inundation extent dataset at high spatial resolution derived through downscaling of satellite observations. J. Hydrometeor. **18**, 1305–1325 (2017). https://doi.org/10.1175/JHM-D-16-0155.1

18. Andreadis K.M., Schumann GJ-P.: Estimating the impact of satellite observations on the predictability of large-scale hydraulic models. Adv. Water Resour. **73**, 44–54 (2014). https://doi.org/10.1016/j.advwatres.2014.06.006

19. Barrile, V., Candela, G., Fotia, A., Bernardo, E.: UAV survey of bridges and viaduct: workflow and application. In: Misra, S., et al. (eds.) ICCSA 2019. LNCS, vol. 11622, pp. 269–284. Springer, Cham (2019). https://doi.org/10.1007/978-3-030-24305-0_21

20. Barrile, V., Bilotta, G., D'Amore, E., Meduri, G.M., Trovato, S.: Structural modeling of a historic castle using close range photogrammetry. Int. J. Math. Comput. Simul. **10**, 370–380 (2016)

21. Postorino, M.N., Barrile, V., Cotroneo, F.: Surface movement ground control by means of a GPS-GIS system. J. Air Transp. Manage. **12**(6), 375–381 (2006)

22. Barrile, V., Meduri, G., Bilotta, G.: Laser scanner surveying techniques aiming to the study and the spreading of recent architectural structures. In: Proceedings of the 9th WSEAS International Conference on Signal, Speech and Image Processing, SSIP '09, Proc. 9th WSEAS Int. Conf. Multimedia, Internet and Video Technologies, MIV 2009, pp. 92–95 (2009)

23. Bernardo, E., Bilotta, G.: Monumental Arc 3D model reconstruction through BIM technology. In: Bevilacqua, C., Calabrò, F., Della Spina, L. (eds.) NMP 2020. SIST, vol. 178, pp. 1581–1589. Springer, Cham (2021). https://doi.org/10.1007/978-3-030-48279-4_148

24. Bernardo, E., Musolino, M., Maesano, M.: San Pietro di Deca: from knowledge to restoration. studies and geomatics investigations for conservation, redevelopment and promotion. In: Bevilacqua, C., Calabrò, F., Della Spina, L. (eds.) NMP 2020. SIST, vol. 178, pp. 1572–1580. Springer, Cham (2021). https://doi.org/10.1007/978-3-030-48279-4_147

25. Bernardo, E., Barrile, V., Fotia, A.: Innovative UAV methods for intelligent landslide monitoring. In: Conference Proceedings, International Conference of Young Professionals «GeoTerrace-2020», Dec 2020, Volume 2020, 1, pp. 1–5 (2020). European Association of Geoscientists & Engineers. https://doi.org/10.3997/2214-4609.20205713. https://www.earthdoc.org/content/papers/10.3997/2214-4609.20205713, ISSN = "2214-4609"

26. Fotia, A., Pucinotti, R.: Applying 3D and photogrammetric scanning systems to the case of cultural heritage. In: Bevilacqua, C., Calabrò, F., Della Spina, L. (eds.) NMP 2020. SIST, vol. 178, pp. 1532–1540. Springer, Cham (2021). https://doi.org/10.1007/978-3-030-48279-4_143

27. Wang, J., Hong, Y., Li, L., et al.: The coupled routing and excess storage (CREST) distributed hydrological model. Hydrol. Sci. J. **56**(1), 84–98 (2011)

28. Khan, S.I., Hong, J., Yilmaz, K.K., et al.: Satellite remote sensing and hydrologic modeling for flood inundation mapping in Lake Victoria basin: Implications for hydrologic prediction in ungauged basins. IEEE Trans. Geosci. Remote Sens. **49**(1), 85–95 (2011)

29. SERVIR Homepage. http://www.servir.net. Accessed 31 May 2021

30. CREST Homepage. http://hydro.ou.edu/research/crest/. Accessed 31 May 2021

31. Khan, S.I., Adhikari, P., Hong, Y., et al.: Hydroclimatology of Lake Victoria region using hydrologic model and satellite remote sensing data. Hydrol. Earth Syst. Sci. **15**, 107–117 (2011)

32. Zhao, R.J., Zhang, Y.L., Fang, L.R., et al.: The Xinanjiang model. Proc. Hydrol. Forecast., 351–356 (1980)
33. Abelen, S., Seitz, F., Abarca-del-Rio, R., Güntner, A.: Droughts and floods in the La Plata Basin in soil moisture data and GRACE. Remote Sens. **7**, 7324–7349 (2015). Doi: https://doi.org/10.3390/rs70607324
34. Morita, M.: Flood risk impact factor for comparatively evaluating the main causes that contribute to flood risk in urban drainage areas. Water **6**(2), 253–270 (2014)
35. Kezia, S.P., Mary, A.V.A.: Prediction of rapid floods from big data using map reduce technique. Global J. Pure Appl. Math. **12**(1), 369–373 (2016)
36. Bernardo, E., Barrile, V., Fotia, A., Bilotta, G.: Landslide susceptibility mapping with fuzzy methodology. In: Conference Proceedings, International Conference of Young Professionals «GeoTerrace-2020», Dec 2020, vol. 2020, 1, pp. 1–5 (2020). European Association of Geoscientists & Engineers. https://doi.org/10.3997/2214-4609.20205712. https://www.earthdoc.org/content/papers/10.3997/2214-4609.20205712, ISSN = "2214-4609"
37. Barbaro, G., Fiamma, V., Barrile, V., Foti, G., Ielo, G.: Analysis of the shoreline changes of Reggio Calabria (Italy). Int. J. Civil Eng. Technol. **8**(10), 1777–1791 (2017)
38. Barrile, V., Bilotta, G., Fotia, A.: Analysis of hydraulic risk territories: comparison between LIDAR and other different techniques for 3D modeling. WSEAS Trans. Environ. Dev. **14**, 45–52 (2018)
39. Yusoff, A., Din, N.M., Yussof, S., Khan, S.U.: Big data analytics for Flood information management in Kelantan, Malaysia. In: 2015 IEEE Student Conference on Research and Development (SCOReD), pp. 311–316. IEEE (2015)
40. Pyayt, A.L., Mokhov, I.I., Lang, B., Krzhizhanovskaya, V.V., Meijer, R.J.: Machine learning methods for environmental monitoring and flood protection. World Acad. Sci. Eng. Technol. **78**, 118–123 (2011)

The WRF-ERDS Workflow in the November 2020 Calabria Flood Event

Paola Mazzoglio[1]([✉]) [iD], Andrea Ajmar[1] [iD], Antonio Parodi[2] [iD], Lorenza Bovio[3],
Andrea Parodi[2], Paolo Pasquali[3], and Jan Martinovic[4] [iD]

[1] Politecnico di Torino, 10125 Turin, Italy
paola.mazzoglio@polito.it
[2] CIMA Research Foundation, 17100 Savona, Italy
[3] ITHACA, 10138 Turin, Italy
[4] IT4Innovations, VSB – Technical University of Ostrava, 708 00 Ostrava, Czech Republic

Abstract. The LEXIS (Large-scale EXecution for Industry & Society) H2020 project is building an advanced engineering platform taking advantage of HPC, Cloud solutions and Big Data, leveraging existing HPC infrastructures. In the framework of the LEXIS project, CIMA Research Foundation is running a three nested domain WRF Model with European coverage and radar data assimilation over Italy. WRF data is then processed by ITHACA Extreme Rainfall Detection System (ERDS), an early warning system developed for the monitoring of heavy rainfall events. The WRF-ERDS workflow has been applied to the heavy rainfall event that affected Southern Italy, in particular Calabria Region, at the end of November 2020. Rainfall depths obtained using global-scale rainfall datasets and WRF data have been compared both with rain gauge data and with the daily bulletins issued by the Italian Civil Protection Department. The data obtained by running the WRF-ERDS workflow shows as an advanced engineering platform based on HPC and cloud solutions can provide more detailed forecasts to an early warning system like ERDS.

Keywords: Calabria · Flood · Early warning · HPC · WRF model

1 Introduction

The increasing amount of data created by modern industrial and business processes, as well as by socio-economic applications dealing with environmental themes (flood, forest fire, air quality, agriculture), represents a great challenge for all organizations seeking to use them. Organizations can potentially gain large advantages by making use of these data, but this requires a sequence of complex processes of generation, transformation and sharing of data across system, locations and organizations.

A possible solution to this problem comes from the combination of High Performance Computing (HPC) technologies and Big Data provided through cloud services into an advanced engineering platform. Accessing them has been quite difficult for Small and Medium-size Enterprises in the past due to both technical and financial reasons, but

E. Borgogno-Mondino and P. Zamperlin (Eds.): ASITA 2021, CCIS 1507, pp. 95–105, 2022.
https://doi.org/10.1007/978-3-030-94426-1_8

nowadays lowering the barrier to entry in HPC, Big Data and cloud computing services is possible.

The LEXIS (Large-scale Execution for Industry & Society) H2020 project is currently developing an advanced system for Big Data analytics that takes advantage of interacting large-scale geographically-distributed HPC infrastructure and cloud services [1]. This prototype is currently being tested and validated within three targeted pilot test-beds in industrial and scientific sectors: Aeronautics, Weather and Climate, Earthquake and Tsunami. The Weather and Climate Large-scale Pilot is related to hydro-meteorological applications of interest for Civil Protection, agriculture, air quality and renewable energy predictions. The Weather & Climate Use Case is mainly focused on a complex cloud computing system, able to provide a various set of weather-related computational models to improve the prediction of water-food-energy nexus phenomena and their associated socio-economic impacts.

In the framework of the Weather & Climate pilot, CIMA Research Foundation is running the Weather Research and Forecasting (WRF) model over Europe. WRF data is then processed by ITHACA Extreme Rainfall Detection System (ERDS), an early warning system developed to monitor and detect heavy rainfall events. Preliminary results obtained by applying the WRF-ERDS workflow to a case study are presented here, together with the description of the entire setup.

2 The WRF-ERDS Workflow

2.1 The WRF Model

The atmospheric model WRF (Weather Research and Forecasting) is an open source code conceived and developed since the mid 90's by the National Center for Atmospheric Research (NCAR), the National Oceanic and Atmospheric Administration (NOAA), the U.S. Air Force, the Naval Research Laboratory, the University of Oklahoma, and the Federal Aviation Administration. WRF is a mesoscale forecasting system designed for both research and operational applications, capable of operating at spatial resolutions from hundreds of meters to hundreds of kilometers.

The WRF simulations are produced in two phases: the first to configure the model domain(s) and prepare the initial and boundary conditions; the second one to execute the predictive model including the dynamic solver as well as the physics packages for atmospheric processes (for example, microphysics, radiative processes, planetary boundary layer).

The WRF model is also inclusive of a 3DVAR and 4DVAR variational assimilation package. In the framework of LEXIS project, the WRF configuration with 3DVAR variational assimilation pertains three domains, two-way nested, respectively with spatial resolution 22.5, 7.5 and 2.5 km with 50 vertical levels (Fig. 1). The analysis data and boundary conditions (with tri-hourly frequency) are obtained from the Global Forecast System (GFS) model at 0.25° of resolution and 3 h temporal resolution. The assimilation scheme is performed as it follows. WRF-2.5 km is initialized with the GFS model of the 18 UTC, whose analysis is integrated, by means of 3DVAR, by radar remote sensing data of the Italian Civil Protection Department. The WRF model is thus executed for 3 h until 21 UTC, when a second 3DVAR assimilation cycle is applied. Finally, the WRF model is executed until 00 UTC when the final assimilation cycle is performed. The simulation is then carried out for a further 48 h starting from 00 UTC in order to have 2 complete days of forecasting.

This forecast is currently performed on computing resources at the CIMA Foundation, it is available operationally within 8:00 UTC and it has been validated in a significant number of case studies [2–4]. In the near future, these modelling experiments will be executed on the LEXIS computing and data management platform with novel Orchestration Service and Distributed Data Infrastructure, and it is expected to assimilate in situ weather stations from the Italian Civil Protection Department in Italy and from Weather Underground in Europe.

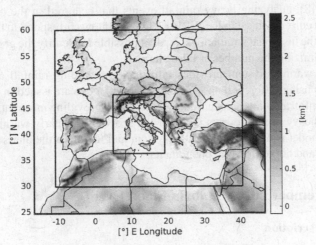

Fig. 1. WRF domains (outermost domain at 22.5 km, middle one at 7.5 km, and innermost at 2.5 km). The colormap refers to the elevation.

2.2 The Extreme Rainfall Detection System

The Extreme Rainfall Detection System (ERDS) is a service for the monitoring and forecasting of rainfall events developed by ITHACA [5]. The hydrometeorological information is provided through a WebGIS application developed in an open source environment [6].

Two different global-scale datasets are currently used to provide information about rainfall amounts. The near real-time rainfall monitoring is performed using the Global Precipitation Measurement (GPM) Integrated Multi-satellitE Retrievals for GPM (IMERG) Early run data [7], made available with a 4 h latency, a 0.1° spatial resolution and a 30 min temporal resolution. The data are downloaded by ERDS every hour to update the rainfall amount measured over the past 12, 24, 48, 72 and 96 h. Short-term rainfall predictions are instead obtained thanks to the GFS, that provides data with 0.25° spatial resolution every 6 h. Data produced by the 00 and 12 UTC model runs are processed by ERDS to provide forecasts for the following 12, 24, 48, 72 and 96 h.

With the aim of increasing the accuracy of the information related to rainfall forecasts, WRF data are now included in ERDS. Thanks to the work carried out in the framework of LEXIS project, CIMA Research Foundation is now providing 48-h forecasts at 7.5 km resolution, hourly temporal resolution, and daily updates (00 UTC).

Rainfall information reported in the accumulated rainfall maps are then processed to detect the presence of areas affected by intense rainfall events. The extreme rainfall identification currently implemented in ERDS is based on threshold values: an alert is provided if the accumulated rainfall is higher than a specific threshold [8]. Threshold values vary from place to place (i.e., thresholds have the same resolution of the precipitation data) and increase as the aggregation interval increases (longer intervals are characterized by higher thresholds). These values have been calculated using an empirical approach [8], analyzing heavy rainfall events that occurred in the past 10 years. The thresholds currently used in the WRF-ERDS workflow correspond to the thresholds which, during the historical simulations, made it possible to identify the greatest number of events, minimizing the number of false alarms.

This early warning system provides information regarding rainfall amounts with hourly updates using different datasets. Heavy rainfall alerts are issued in places where exceptional rainfall amounts are recorded. At this stage, providing information regarding the impact of heavy rainfall events is out of the scope of this early warning system: a hydrological model is not included in the system and therefore the alerts are linked to rainfall events and not to flooding phenomena.

3 The November 2020 Calabria Flood Event

3.1 Event Description

An intense meteorological event affected the Calabria region between 21st and 23rd November 2020. Persistent and localized rainfall events affected the Ionian coastal areas and significant rainfall depths (greater than 300 mm) were recorded by most of the rain gauges located in Crotone province [9]. Table 1 contains the highest rainfall depths recorded by rain gauges in that area during the entire event [9].

The analysis carried out by the Regional Agency for the Protection of the Environmental (ARPACAL), that acts as Decentralized Functional Centre of Civil Protection, pointed out that this event can be considered as "exceptional". Despite the rainfall time series of the Crotone rain gauge is one of the longest among those available, the daily precipitation recorded by the station on 21st November is the highest ever since 1916, the year the instrument was installed [9].

Table 1. Rainfall depth recorded by rain gauges during the event.

Rain gauge name	Rainfall depth (mm)
Cirò Marina – Punta Alice	414.8
Cirò Superiore	384.6
Crucoli	362.6
Crotone – Salica	339.8
Crotone	338.6
Cropalati	291.8
Crotone – Papanice	271.0
San Nicola dell'Alto	261.6
Rossano	239.4
Corigliano Calabro	225.2
Cutro	205.2

Figure 2 shows the Surface Rainfall Total (SRT) produced by the Italian Civil Protection Department, accessed through the MyDewetra platform. SRT represents the accumulated rainfall (in this case, recorded in 24 consecutive hours) and is obtained by integrating the radar network data with in-situ measurements.

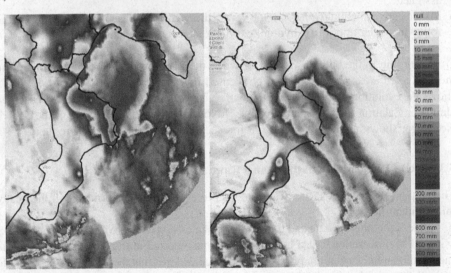

Fig. 2. 24 h SRT, acquired during the 21th (left) and the 22th (right) of November. Image derived from MyDewetra platform, courtesy of the Italian Civil Protection Department.

3.2   Alert Bulletins of the Department of Civil Protection

The national alert bulletin contains the alerts issued by the Decentralized Functional Centers of Civil Protection. The alerts evaluation is performed in an independent manner for three risk (hydrogeological risk, thunderstorm risk and hydraulic risk) and each risk has four severity levels [10]:

- absence of criticalities - no alerts;
- ordinary criticality - yellow alert;
- moderate criticality - orange alert;
- high criticality - red alert.

The only exception is the thunderstorm risk, that does not have the high critical-ity - red alert level because these phenomena are associated with intense and often widespread perturbed weather conditions that already characterize the red alert of the hydrogeological scenario [10].

Within the civil protection framework, the Italian territory is divided into several alert zones. Each zone is a homogeneous area with respect to the type and intensity of the weather phenomena that typically occur and their effect on the territory. Regarding the maps included in these bulletins:

- if there are no criticalities the area is marked as absence of criticality - no alert;
- if there are criticalities, the area is represented with the highest alert among those assigned;
- if there are criticalities of the same level, the area is represented according to the following order of priority: hydraulic, thunderstorms, hydrogeological.

According to the bulletins issued between the 21th and the 23rd of November, the most affected areas are expected to be located in the east coast of Calabria. Figure 3 shows the evolution of the alerts issued by the Department of Civil Protection. The last alert over Calabria was issued on the 23th of November: the daily bulletin of the 24th of November shows absence of significant foreseeable phenomena over the region.

3.3   ERDS Performance in the Heavy Rainfall Identification

The output produced by ERDS was analyzed to evaluate its performance in the heavy rainfall identification.

Table 2 contains the date and time of the first alerts provided over Calabria by ERDS using GPM observational data as input. The time reported in the table is related to the "acquisition time". In this analysis, it should be considered that the GPM data is available with a latency of the order of 4 h and, therefore, this latency should be added to the date reported in the table for obtaining the publication time.

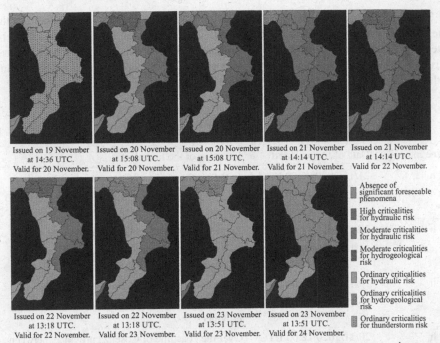

Issued on 19 November at 14:36 UTC. Valid for 20 November.

Issued on 20 November at 15:08 UTC. Valid for 20 November.

Issued on 20 November at 15:08 UTC. Valid for 21 November.

Issued on 21 November at 14:14 UTC. Valid for 21 November.

Issued on 21 November at 14:14 UTC. Valid for 22 November.

Issued on 22 November at 13:18 UTC. Valid for 22 November.

Issued on 22 November at 13:18 UTC. Valid for 23 November.

Issued on 23 November at 13:51 UTC. Valid for 23 November.

Issued on 23 November at 13:51 UTC. Valid for 24 November.

Absence of significant foreseeable phenomena

High criticalities for hydraulic risk

Moderate criticalities for hydraulic risk

Moderate criticalities for hydrogeological risk

Ordinary criticalities for hydraulic risk

Ordinary criticalities for hydrogeological risk

Ordinary criticalities for thunderstorm risk

Fig. 3. Daily bulletins issued by the Department of Civil Protection between 19th and 23rd November 2020.

ERDS provided timely alerts in the coastal areas of Crotone province between Cariati and Capo Rizzuto. Despite considerable rainfall amounts (greater than 200 mm) have been recorded by several rain gauges located in the eastern areas of Cosenza province (e.g., Cropalati, Rossano, Corigliano Calabro), ERDS was not able to provide alerts in this part of Calabria region due to an underestimation of the rainfall rates in the GPM data. During the entire event, from 20th November 2020 23:00 UTC until 23rd November 2020 23:00 UTC, GPM data estimated between 20 and 60 mm of rainfall in that area.

Table 2. Date and time of the first alerts provided by ERDS using GPM data as input.

Time interval	Date of the first alert	Location of the first alert
12 h	21/11/2020 04:00 UTC	Over the coastline near Crotone
24 h	21/11/2020 05:00 UTC	Over the coastline near Crotone
48 h	21/11/2020 06:00 UTC	Over the sea, between Crotone and Cirò Marina
72 h	21/11/2020 07:00 UTC	Over the sea, between Crotone and Cirò Marina
96 h	21/11/2020 07:00 UTC	Over the sea, between Crotone and Cirò Marina

The same analysis was also performed using GFS data as input. Table 3 contains the date of the first alerts provided by ERDS using GFS data. Even in this case it should be noted that the data are available with a 6 h latency. ERDS was able to provide the first alert over the most affected areas in the afternoon of 20th November (Cirò Marina) and in the morning of 21st November (Crotone).

Table 3. Date and time of the first alerts provided by ERDS using GFS data as input.

Time interval	Date of the first alert	Location of the first alert
12 h	21/11/2020 00:00 UTC	In the northern part of Cosenza province
	21/11/2020 12:00 UTC	Over the coastline of Crotone province, near Cirò Marina
24 h	20/11/2020 12:00 UTC	In the northern part of Cosenza province
	21/11/2020 00:00 UTC	Over the coastline of Cosenza and Crotone provinces
48 h	20/11/2020 00:00 UTC	In the northern part of Cosenza province
	20/11/2020 12:00 UTC	Over the coastline of Cosenza and Crotone provinces
72 h	20/11/2020 12:00 UTC	Over the coastline of Cosenza province, between Rossano and Cirò Marina
96 h	No alert	–

3.4   WRF-ERDS Performance in the Heavy Rainfall Identification

An analysis has been carried out also using WRF data. Figure 4 shows the rainfall depths forecasted by the WRF model while Fig. 5 shows the spatial and temporal distribution of the alerts issued on the basis of these predictions. The first alert over Calabria was provided with the 48-h forecasts produced during the 19th of November. However, in this case, only the alerts over the eastern part of Cosenza province were properly issued while no alerts are present over Crotone. Proper alerts were issued the following day, the 20th of November. According to WRF-ERDS output, the most affected areas are located in the east coast of Calabria. This evidence is also reported in the bulletins issued by the Italian Civil Protection Department.

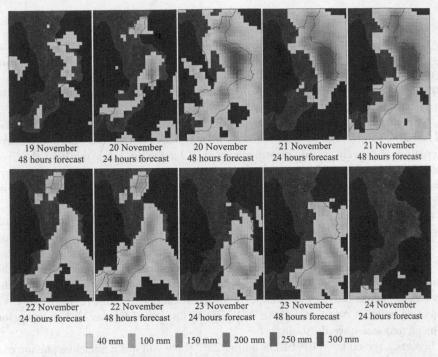

Fig. 4. Rainfall depths forecasted by WRF model between 19th and 24th November 2020.

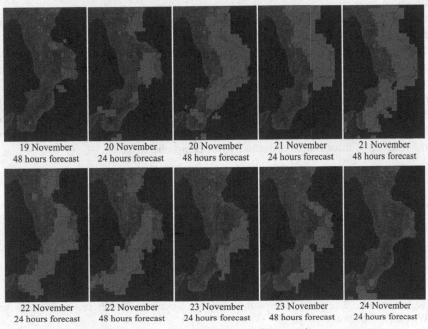

Fig. 5. WRF-ERDS alerts issued between 19th and 24th November 2020.

4 Conclusions

The capacity to compare the Civil Protection bulletins with WRF-ERDS alerts is partially affected by the way the two products are delivered: the Civil Protection bulletins aggregate alerts by regions while WRF-ERDS analysis and output is pixel-based. Whilst keeping this aspect into adequate consideration, the comparison of the outputs of the two systems provides few relevant insights (Fig. 6).

WRF-ERDS first alerts were identified on 19th November 2021 with 48 h forecast, and therefore valid for the 19th–20th of November: few areas on the Northern and Western Sila plateau cliffs were already identified as critical. On the same day (the 19th), the Civil Protection bulletin valid for the 20th mentioned ordinary criticalities for thunderstorm risk over the whole region: moderate hydraulic risk alerts were firstly issued only one day later, with the bulletin issued on the 20th and valid for the same day.

Forecasts issued by WRF-ERDS on the 20th and on the 21st fits quite well with corresponding forecasts issued the same day by the Civil Protection, at least in identifying the most critical geographical areas. In particular, comparing the products issued on the 20th, both systems clearly depicted the intensification of the meteorological event on the Eastern part of the region. The products issued on the 21st substantially differ from the previous for an increment of the alert level for the Western part of the region in the Civil Protection bulletin. Additionally, the WRF-ERDS forecasted for the 22nd an extension of the alerted area towards South.

Forecasts issued by WRF-ERDS on the 22nd show still quite intensive phenomena for the same and next day compared to the Civil Protection ones indicating a general alert level attenuation. The trend of WRF-ERDS in alerting the southern part of the region continues.

On the 23rd both systems clearly forecasted an attenuation of the alerts, with a tendency to concentrate in the southern part of the region.

Overall WRF-ERDS seems to have a longer forecast capacity, without losing so much in accuracy. Additional validation includes a comparison with the registered impact of the event: unfortunately, this kind of information is difficult to retrieve from authoritative sources in a form suitable for this validation. In this case, the disaster report drawn up by ARPACAL [9] focuses only on the meteorological reconstruction of the event. Information regarding the impact was not included. Several media news were retrieved but those kinds of information are usually not comprehensive.

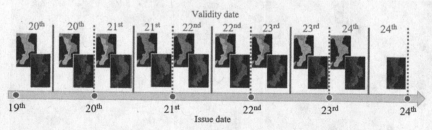

Fig. 6. November 2020 event timeline with a comparison between Civil Protection bulletins (top) and WRF-ERDS outputs (bottom).

Acknowledgments. The authors acknowledge the funding support provided by European Union's Horizon 2020 research and innovation programme through the project "LEXIS" (Large-scale EXecution for Industry & Society) under grant agreement n° 825532.

The authors also acknowledge the use of imagery from the NASA Worldview application (https://worldview.earthdata.nasa.gov/), part of the NASA Earth Observing System Data and Information System (EOSDIS).

References

1. Parodi, A., et al.: LEXIS weather and climate large-scale pilot. In: Barolli, L., Poniszewska-Maranda, A., Enokido, T. (eds.) CISIS 2020. AISC, vol. 1194, pp. 267–277. Springer, Cham (2021). https://doi.org/10.1007/978-3-030-50454-0_25
2. Lagasio, M., Parodi, A., Pulvirenti, L., Meroni, A.N., Boni, G., Pierdicca, N., et al.: A synergistic use of a high-resolution numerical weather prediction model and high-resolution earth observation products to improve precipitation forecast. Remote Sens. **11**(20), 2387 (2019)
3. Lagasio, M., Silvestro, F., Campo, L., Parodi, A.: Predictive capability of a high-resolution hydrometeorological forecasting framework coupling WRF cycling 3DVAR and Continuum. J. Hydrometeorol. **20**(7), 1307–1337 (2019)
4. Burlando, M., Romanic, D., Boni, G., Lagasio, M., Parodi, A.: Investigation of the weather conditions during the collapse of the Morandi Bridge in Genoa on 14 August 2018 using field observations and WRF model. Atmosphere **11**(7), 724 (2020)
5. ITHACA – Information Technology for Humanitarian Assistance, Cooperation and Action. https://www.ithacaweb.org. Accessed 09 Jan 2021
6. Extreme Rainfall Detection System. http://erds.ithacaweb.org. Accessed 09 Jan 2021
7. Huffman, G.J., et al.: NASA Global Precipitation Measurement (GPM) Integrated Multi-satellitE Retrievals for GPM (IMERG) Algorithm Theoretical Basis Document (ATBD) Version 06 (2020). https://gpm.nasa.gov/sites/default/files/2020-05/IMERG_ATBD_V06.3.pdf. Accessed 09 Jan 2021
8. Mazzoglio, P., Laio, F., Balbo, S., Boccardo, P., Disabato, F.: Improving an extreme rainfall detection system with GPM IMERG data. Remote Sens. **11**(6), 677 (2019)
9. Arcuri, S., Fusto, F., Marsico, L., Rotundo, R.: Evento pluviometrico del 21–23 novembre 2020. Rapporto di evento. https://www.cfd.calabria.it//DatiVari/Pubblicazioni/rapporto%20evento%2021-23%20novembre_2020_finale.pdf. Accessed 09 Jan 2021
10. Department of Civil Protection: Guida alla consultazione del bollettino di criticità nazionale/allerta. http://www.protezionecivile.gov.it/documents/20195/1002389/GUIDA_6_3_def.pdf/8ec519e6-14f1-41a4-badd-09e0f2915f7e. Accessed 30 Jan 2021

The Subsurface Database of the Torino Area (Western Po Plain): From the Design of the Conceptual Scheme to 3D Modeling

Igor Marcelli[1]([✉]) [iD], Andrea Irace[1]([✉]), Gianfranco Fioraso[1]([✉]), Giulio Masetti[2]([✉]), Elisa Brussolo[3]([✉]), Brunella Raco[2]([✉]), Matia Menichini[2]([✉]), Gianna Vivaldo[2]([✉]), Marco Doveri[2]([✉]), Rocco Pispico[4]([✉]), and Stefano Cozzula[4]([✉])

[1] CNR-IGG (Consiglio Nazionale delle Ricerche, Istituto di Geoscienze e Georisorse - Sede Distaccata di Torino), Via Valperga Caluso, 35, 10125 Torino, Italia
`{andrea.irace,gianfranco.fioraso}@cnr.it`
[2] CNR-IGG (Sede di Pisa), Via G. Moruzzi, 1, 56124 Pisa, Italia
`{giulio.masetti,brunella.raco,matia.menichini,gianna.vivaldo,`
`marco.doveri}@cnr.it`
[3] SMAT (Società Metropolitana Acque Torino, Centro Ricerche), Viale Maestri del Lavoro, 4, 10127 Torino, Italia
`elisa.brussolo@smatorino.it`
[4] Arpa Piemonte (Agenzia Regionale Per la Protezione Ambientale), Via Pio VII, 9, 10135 Torino, Italia
`{rocco.pispico,stefano.cozzula}@arpa.piemonte.it`

Abstract. Geological models, and related geo-databases, derived from the integration of multiple datasets, are important tools for land planning and management of underground resources. This contribution describes a geo-database structure designed to manage a large amount of geo-environmental data used for setting up a subsurface 3D model of the Torino area, at the western termination of the Po Plain. An innovative dataset structure, founded on an explicit conceptual model, was designed to provide a reliable representation of the distribution of well and boreholes data along x, y and z axes, as well as their integration with surface geology. This framework allowed the elaboration of 3D a geological-hydrostratigraphic model, portraying the distribution and geometry of the subsurface sedimentary successions, and those of the aquifer systems and permeability barriers.

Some issues related to the representation of well data and boreholes in the z axis (QGIS), as well as their conversion and transfer to 3D software (GMS - Groundwater Modeling System) were also discussed.

Keywords: Subsurface database · 3D modeling · Geological mapping

1 Introduction

The development of subsurface database is essential for the creation of geological models useful to ensure a better territorial planning, on the surface, and a more correct

© Springer Nature Switzerland AG 2022
E. Borgogno-Mondino and P. Zamperlin (Eds.): ASITA 2021, CCIS 1507, pp. 106–119, 2022.
https://doi.org/10.1007/978-3-030-94426-1_9

management of geo-resources, in depth. In fact, geo-databases, and geological models of the subsurface are the starting point for addressing specialized research on specific and strategic issues: from the estimate of the geo-environmental hazard connected to the anthropic impact on the territory (great engineering infrastructures), to the assessment of seismic hazard, up to the analysis and use of groundwater and geothermal resources.

In the past, subsurface geo-databases made available by the Piemonte Public Administrations were mostly conceived as repositories for practical information about subsoil, concerning borehole, well log and/or piezometric data (Geotechnical Database of Arpa Piemonte [2] and Arpa Piemonte Regional Monitoring Network [16]). By representing the basic information for lithotecnical characterization, as well surface water, and groundwater monitoring, querying and use of such databases have been consistently increasing in the last years by both the research and professional commuinities. However, the interpretation of open environmental data is frequently hampered as they still need to be integrated with correlative geologic attributes.

In recent times, the growing demand for operational consultation tools, combined with the great progress of information technology has seen the widespread production of spatial databases and three-dimensional underground models (e.g., 3D geological modeling and visualization from the digital Geological map of Piemonte [12]).

In this paper we present the Subsurface Database of the Torino Area (SDTA), a new original geological database that is first of all aimed at constraining the 2D (see Fig. 1.a) and 3D (see Fig. 1.c) geological modeling of the Pliocene-Quaternary successions and main tectonic structures buried under the western part of the Po alluvial Plain. Consistently, it is also aimed at providing a reference data infrastructure, useful for different thematic research with applied purposes.

In particular, the present paper illustrates the framework of the SDTA data model and presents a first example of its direct application to the "hydrostratigraphic" characterization of the underground successions. This was developed in the frame of a research project between Società Metropolitana Acque Torino (SMAT) and the Institute of Geosciences and Georesources of the National Research Council of Italy (CNR-IGG), aimed at improving a sustainable utilization and safeguard of the aquifers in the Torino area.

The set-up of the SDTA and related 3D "hydrostratigraphic" model was articulated into three different operational phases.

The "PHASE 1" consisted in the construction of the conceptual scheme of the GIS geo-database, in order to store and manage the different types of available subsurface and surface geological data. These are represented by i) about 700 stratigraphic logs of water-wells and boreholes (on average depth of 200 m) collected from different institutions (CARG project dataset of the CNR-IGG [1, 5]; SMAT archive; geotechnical database of Arpa Piemonte [2]), ii) some geological maps [1, 4, 5, 9, 13] at various scales and seismic images [3, 6, 8, 11], which were critically reviewed.

The "PHASE 2" consisted in the compilation of the GIS geo-database and in the lithostratigraphic classification of selected stratigraphic logs through i) their correlation with the surface geology of the adjoining hilly and Alpine sectors and ii) the analysis of the lithological, sedimentological, compositional, and paleontological characteristics of the stratigraphic logs.

The "PHASE 3" concerned the 3D geological-hydrostratigraphic modeling based on integration of the GIS geo-database multiple datasets and the GMS ("Groundwater Modeling System") 3D modeling software as you can see in the chapter 3 (see Fig. 1c).

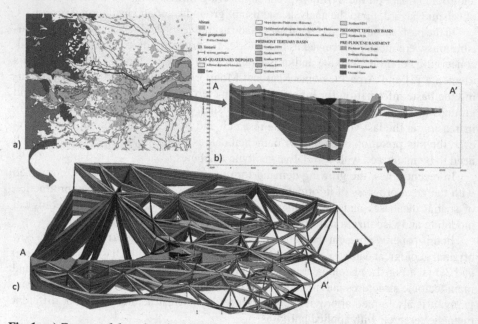

Fig. 1. a) Excerpt of the subsurface database of the Torino area (SDTA) taken from the QGIS project. **b)** Hydrostratigraphic section A-A' extracted from the three-dimensional model of Fig. 1-c; the light- and dark-coloured levels refer respectively to permeable and impermeable levels of the succession. **c)** 3D hydrostratigraphic model of the Torino subsurface consisting of a network of geological cross-sections designed and processed in GMS [7]. (Color figure online)

2   SDTA Infrastructure

The wide range and heterogeneity of surface and subsurface input datasets implied the construction of a geo-database capable of storing, managing, and analyzing sedimento-logical, stratigraphic, structural and hydrogeological data through a single information system. The SDTA was designed for the study of the Torino subsurface area, but its structure is suitable for any geological context in which a (hydro) stratigraphic charac-terization should be needed. The SDTA subsurface is based on a conceptual model (see Fig. 2), created for the project, and processed in the GIS system. With reference to the introduction chapter, the construction of the database involved the first two phases ("1" and "2") of the workflow.

Available data are reported in layer (containing specific features as points, lines, and polygons) for which original "Input/Output" masks were built to facilitate management and visualization of the stored geo-environmental data.

The Open-Source platform QGIS (version 3.4_Madeira, [14]) was used for the design of the SDTA, in order to ensure greater accessibility and sharing of data.

The multidisciplinary datasets in the project provide the constraints on which the geo-hydrogeological model was built, according to the guidelines carried out by CNR-IGG_Pisa for the definition of the groundwater resources of the Toscana region [10]. Particular attention was paid to the design of the "WATER-WELLS_&_BOREHOLES" dataset since 3D geological models rely on the accurate georeferencing and the in-depth projection of the stratigraphic contacts.

The stratigraphic columns have been gathered in the punctual dataset "WATER-WELLS_&_BOREHOLES" (see "Level I" in Fig. 2), which encloses all the general information and constrains the position of the logs in the space. All the stratigraphies have been digitized in a dbf table called "HYDROLAYER" (see "Level II" in Fig. 2) directly associated with the punctual dataset through a n: 1 relation (see Fig. 2).

The relationship (orange arrow in Fig. 2), explained in the data management mask (Input/Output) of the punctual shapefile "WATER-WELLS_&_BOREHOLES" (see chapter 2.1) allows georeferencing and in depth projection (according to a progressive Z) of all the horizons described in the stratigraphic logs (selected for quality and reliability). Each horizon has been classified according to the sedimentological-textural and paleontological characteristics and to the reference geological units, which the horizons belong to. The geological units correspond with the "Geo-Units" of the Geo-Piemonte Map [13] and constitute the fundamental "tools" for stratigraphic correlations subsurface.

The complete version of the conceptual diagram contains as many blocks of "Level II" as the number of horizons composing the stratigraphic log. However, for the sake of space, only an excerpt of the conceptual scheme is here reported (see Fig. 2). This illustrates that a single "Level II" dataset is related only to the one layer (the 2nd one, below ground surface) of the stratigraphic log record 1000001083 (actually composed by 19 horizons). This conceptual model clarifies the relationships between the attributes of the "WATER-WELLS_&_BOREHOLES" and "HYDROLAYER" datasets, expressed in the form of classes (yellow boxes), with their relative properties (or instances; gray boxes) that constrain their choices. These attributes are grouped into two hierarchical levels, one for each dataset, related (as made explicit by the orange link) by the borehole identifier (B.hole_ID) common to both datasets. The relationship between the two datasets is 1: n and this indicates that for each point element occurring in the shapefile "WATER-WELLS_&_BOREHOLES", there are "n" stratigraphic horizons associated with the single stratigraphy (single point element of the shapefile).

2.1 Description of the Attributes of the Datasets "WATER-WELLS_&_BOREHOLES" and "HYDROLAYER"

The most important and common attribute of both datasets is given by the Borehole identification code (B.hole_ID): it identifies the record and allows the unique relationship with the horizons indicated in the dbf.

The Level I contains the attributes of the "WATER-WELLS_&_BOREHOLES" shapefile and is dedicated to general information like the identifying terms (name, borehole identification code, CARG code), the data source (source and notes), its spatial position (X, Y, Z coordinates), the well or borehole features (ground elevation, depth),

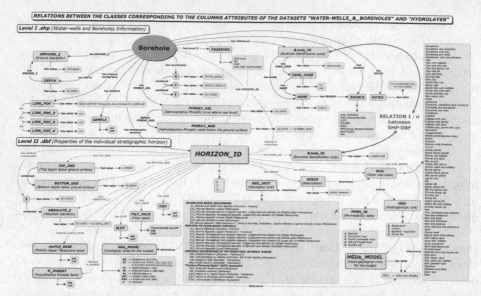

Fig. 2. Conceptual scheme describing the links between the attribute of the punctual shapefile (WATER-WELLS_&_BOREHOLES) and his dbf reference table "HYDROLAYER". For this purpose the record 1000001083 has been taken as an example; in red are indicated the values. The yellow boxes indicate the attributes, the gray ones group the related instances. The instances preceded by the link "is" are bound to the choices shown in the gray box; those preceded by the link "has value" can be filled in. The yellow boxes with the red border intrinsically have values subject to errors depending on the degree of experience of the operator who digitizes the stratigraphic log (possible different interpretation). The green links define the relationships between the general characteristics of the Borehole (attributes of the "WATER-WELLS_&_BOREHOLES" shapefile), while the blue links define the relationships between the properties of the individual stratigraphic horizons (attributes of the "HYDROLAYER" table). The black links express the relationship between the attribute and its own instances, whereas the dotted ones indicate the relationships of existence between attributes (there is no child attribute without the parent one). The 1: n relationship that links the shapefile "WATER-WELLS_&_ BOREHOLES" (Level I) with the table "HYDROLAYER" (Level II) is made explicit by the link in orange. (Color figure online)

the elevation and depth of the phreatic level (above sea level and below ground surface, respectively), the links to the original pdf file of the stratigraphic log, digitized in the dbf "HYDROLAYER" table and if a water sample was collected.

The Level II contains the attributes of the "HYDROLAYER" dbf table used to digitize and classify each single horizon of the stratigraphic logs. For each stratigraphic horizon (HORIZON_ID) it reports both descriptive information (see left part of the Level II in Fig. 2) and geological and hydrostratigraphic data (central and right part). The descriptive side includes information about the relative and absolute elevation (bottom and top depth below ground surface, absolute elevation), the conditions of the well for that specific horizon (presence of water, drainage, filtered section), if it indicates levels (i.e. base of the Middle-Upper Pleistocene fluvial sediments) and its description. The other side includes the horizon's geological unit, its characterizations (grain size class, hydrogeological unit, permeability class) and the resulting units necessary for 3D modeling (geological and hydrogeological units).

Identifying Terms (Level I). NAME and CARG_CODE are the original identifying terms derived from other databases [1, 5]. They were preserved despite the new identification codes (B.hole_ID) because they often constitute the only reference to the original documentation on boreholes and water wells.

Data Source (Level I). SOURCE of the stratigraphic log permits tracing of the origin and purpose of data and, in part, also their reliability. The NOTE field is used to indicate any observations or inconsistencies, as for those circumstances in which the same log was unsuitably recycled, in the past, to portray the stratigraphic records of different far apart locations (see the example "One stratigraphic log for two records" in the upper right part of Fig. 2).

Spatial Position (Level I). X and Y represent the coordinates according to the local conventional reference system WGS 84/UTM zone 32N EPSG: 32632. The Z represents the absolute elevation of the head of the borehole point in m a.s.l., extracted from the GRID of the DTM_5m (Regione Piemonte, DTM capture ICE 2009–2011 tile size 5 m, [15]) to guarantee a homogeneous vertical reference system in the export of data in GMS.

The Elevation of the Phreatic Surface (Level I). PHREAT_ASL and PHREAT_BGS, respectively, indicate the absolute elevation above sea level (m a.s.l.) and relative depth from the ground level (m b.g.s.) of the "Administrative" Phreatic surface [4].

Links to the Original pdf file (Level I). LINK_PDF and the others, report the links to the path of the original stratigraphic log in pdf format. From the data management interface "Input/Output" mask, the pdf can be directly opened through the "Run Actions" command (see Fig. 4).

Water Sample Collected (Level I). Indicated by the existence field "yes" or "null", the SAMPLE item shows if water samples have been collected to be analyzed during the sampling campaigns.

HORIZON_ID (Level II). Placed in the center of the conceptual diagram, the HORIZON_ID play a "pivotal" role in the relation among all attributes. They refer to the individual stratigraphic horizons (horizon 1, 2, n...) and are essential to maintain the depositional stacking within the "Input/Output" data management mask as shown in Fig. 4.

Horizon Z (Level II). TOP_DGS and BOTTOM_DGS report the relative depth (m b.g.s.) of the top and bottom for each horizon. The ABSOLUTE_Z, expressed in m a.s.l., refers to the absolute elevation (as to sea level) of the horizon's bottom and is obtained by the difference between Z (taken from the "WATER-WELLS_&_BOREHOLES" shapefile) and BOTTOM_DGS. X and Y coordinates of boreholes and ABSOLUTE_Z, which the HORIZON_IDs are associated to, allows 3D georeferencing, suitable for modeling.

Completion of Well (Level II). The H2O and SLOT are descriptive fields that can be compiled, horizon by horizon, in order to show and manage additional data about well completion logs in the "Input/Output" management mask. For these fields, a "yes" or a "null" value is envisaged, thus indicating i) if water does or does not occur and ii) if the well is or is not fenestrated. The item FILT_PACK indicates, where present, the characteristics of the cavity outside the well casing piezometer such as the presence impermeable backfill (bentonite, cementation…) or filter pack (sand, gravel). This kind of information is very important for identifying inefficiency of wells completion (e.g., continuous drainage) as a possible cause of mixing processes among shallower and deeper aquifers.

Concerning the SLOT and FILT_PACK, the values entered in the boxes do not correspond to those of the instances in the conceptual model but are made explicit by means of dedicated symbols (see example in Fig. 4).

Base of the Phreatic Aquifer (Level II). The H_PHREAT field highlights the horizon's bottom that likely corresponds to the base of the "hypothetical" phreatic level, inferred from the lithostratigraphic log. In the dataset it is indicated by the field "yes" or "null", but similarly to SLOT and FILT_PACK is explicit in the "Input/Output" management mask by a dedicated symbol (see example in Fig. 4).

Description and Characterizations (Level II). The DESCR attribute includes all facies features (i.e., lithology, sedimentology, composition, fossil content, colour) described in the original document of a stratigraphic log. These information are essential for classifying horizons and horizon-sets in accordance with the GEO_UNITs (see after). The DESCR field binds the instance of SOIL attribute that simplifies the original description of the horizon into a few lithological and textural terms (see right part of Fig. 2), for sake of uniformity and for attributing the permeability degree. In this respect, PERM_ID and HGU depend on the value of SOIL. The PERM_ID defines the expected permeability class of the horizon according to 5 reference instances 1. Bedrock ($K < 10^{-12}$ m/s), 2. Permeable layer ($K > 10^{-4}$ m/s), 3. Poorly permeable layer ($10^{-7} < K < 10^{-5}$ m/s), 4. Not permeable layer ($K < 10^{-8}$ m/s), 5. Surface soil. The HGU indicates the hydrogeological unit (i.e., the expected hydrogeologic role) of the horizon according to 4 instances: S. Substratum ($K < 10^{-12}$ m/s), A. Aquifer ($K > 10^{-4}$ m/s), I. Aquitard – aquiclude ($K < 10^{-5}$ m/s), C. Cover soil) (see example in Fig. 4).

Base of the Terraced Quaternary Fluvial Deposits (Level II). The muPLE-BASE allows to point to the horizon's bottom, likely corresponding to the base of Middle-Upper Pleistocene alluvial deposits, inferred for each stratigraphic log.

Units for 3D Modeling (Level II). GEO_UNIT, GU_MODEL and HGU_MODEL are the result of the combination of different values and indices.

The GEO_UNIT is a key attribute indicating the (field-equivalent) lithostratigraphic units of the Geo Piemonte map legend [13], which the horizons of the stratigraphic logs have been referred to. Twenty-two GEO_UNITs of the Geo Piemonte have been distinguished in the Torino area (see Fig. 2). They have been grouped into eight main GEO_UNITs, defined as GEO UNITs_MODEL (GUs_MODEL), allowing a feasible identification of the sedimentary units and geological contacts within the stratigraphic logs. The eight GUs_MODEL are directly linked to a GEO_UNIT of Geo-Piemonte Map and they have been defined on the basis of the bounding surfaces and vertical facies organization, pointed out by the log descriptions. They have been correlated both in the subsurface and outcrops, through the integrated analysis of field geology, borehole and well stratigraphic logs (DESCR field) and geophysical images (see chapter 3). It has been assumed that, due to its peculiar stratigraphic features, each GUs_ MODEL will present homogeneous hydrostratigraphic properties (e.g., grain-size, unconfined or semi-confined to confined framework). In this sense, the GUs_ MODEL represents the fundamental hydrostratigraphic unit.

Each GU_ MODEL can be characterized by a single or a combination of the four main typologies of HGU. These will present a peculiar and distinctive instance in each single GU_ MODEL. Consequently, the GUs_ MODEL can be subdivided into lower rank hydrogeologic units, here defined as HYDROGEOLOGIC UNITs_MODEL (HGUs_MODEL). The HGU-GU_ MODEL concatenation allows identifying, for each layer, the HGU_MODEL.

GU_ MODEL and HGU_MODEL are essential attributes for 3D hydrostratigraphic modeling.

2.2 Property of the Dataset "WATER-WELLS_&_BOREHOLES"

The SDTA structure allows to connect countless thematic datasets using the common denominator borehole identification code (B.hole_ID), by which the data model can be easily implemented. The resulting conceptual scheme structure could be assimilated to a pyramid with the main dataset "WATER-WELLS_&_BOREHOLES" at the top and the secondary dataset on opposite sides, connected through a 1: 1 relationship. In this representation, each face of the pyramid expresses a 1: 1 relationship that can be summarized by a defined conceptual scheme (see Fig. 3).

For example, the SDTA was implemented with a "Geochemical_Dataset" (Level III), including the results of the chemical and isotopic analyses performed on the sampled waters (see Fig. 3 and 5).

2.3 Data Management GIS Interface

To facilitate data entry and search, an "Input/Output Data Management Mask" has been designed. This mask graphically represents in the GIS environment, through direct correspondence, the data stored in the attribute tables of the described datasets (see Fig. 4). This interface makes both data management and visualization easier, allowing the end user to consult simultaneously different typologies of datasets and to extract their economic and social implications (e.g., data processing in the field of aquifer analysis for forecasting and environmental protection purposes).

Following the hierarchical criteria of the conceptual model (see Fig. 2), the information in the mask is separated into two groups. Using the borehole identification code (B.hole_ID) common to both datasets ("WATER-WELLS_&_BOREHOLES" and "HYDROLAYER"), a unique 1: n relationship was set up, thus allowing to associate and

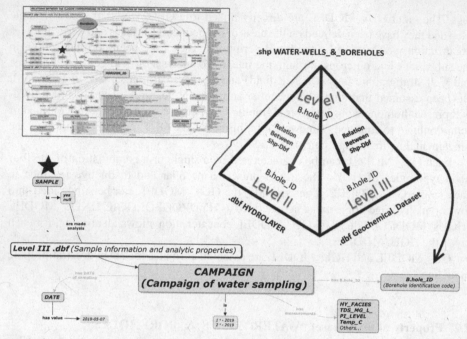

Fig. 3. The pyramid images the implementable structure of the database that uses the common denominator borehole identification code (B.hole_ID) to link "n" minor datasets to the main dataset "WATER-WELLS_&_BOREHOLES". The left face summarizes the diagram of Fig. 2. The right face instead summarized the relation between the main dataset "WATER-WELLS_&_BOREHOLES" and the minor "Geochemical_Dataset" explained by the conceptual scheme on the bottom. It is present subject to the presence of the sample (see "yes" value, green star). (Color figure online)

display both the general characteristics of the borehole (see green box of Fig. 4) and all the properties of the single stratigraphic horizons (see blue box of Fig. 4).

This compilation process guarantees a reduction in errors, a better transparency of the data entered, and a continuous updating with new data or new datasets that can be associated (e.g., additional masks with new piezometric and geochemical data).

The box "Geochemical_Dataset" of the Level III has been associated with the general characteristics of Level I. It is dedicated to collecting and making explicit data on the campaigns of water sampling and analysis (see Fig. 5).

Within it, the values of HYDROCHEMICAL FACIES (HY_FACIES), those of the concentration of TOTAL DISSOLVED SALTS in MG/L (TDS_MG_L_) and the PIEZO-METRIC LEVEL (PI_LEVEL) are reported (see Fig. 5, center part). By selecting the "table" symbol on the right part, the entire data string consisting of 60 attributes (look some in Fig. 5, lower part) can be viewed and consulted.

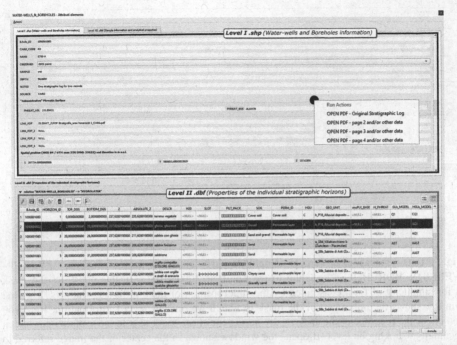

Fig. 4. Data management mask (Input/Output) of the point shapefile "WATER-WELLS_&_BOREHOLES" relating to the borehole 1000001083. The information of the borehole (GIS attributes or classes of the datasets) is separated into three groups, here visible only two. The level I group (green box) contains the general attributes of the record present within the "WATER-WELLS_&_BOREHOLES" shapefile. The level II group (blue box, which can be activated by clicking on the attribute table symbol on the right of the function bar), contains all the properties of the individual digitized stratigraphic horizons in the dbf "HYDROLAYER" table. The box at the top right of the "Run Actions" command (which can be activated with the right mouse button), contains the links to view additional information relating to the selected function (for example the original stratigraphic log). The active links are those that present the paths to the folders in the "LINK" items on the left. (Color figure online)

3 Physical-Geological-Hydrostratigraphic Model

The reconstruction of the physical 2D–3D hydrostratigraphic model in the Torino area, through the aid of the GMS modeling software, was part of the operational phase "3" of the workflow (see "Introduction" – chapter 1). This activity relied on the subsurface stratigraphic correlation of logs, through the construction of a dense network of 2D stratigraphic panels that cover the entire study area (approximately 800 km^2) and a maximum investigation depth of 410 m below ground surface (on average 200 m b.g.s.). Fence diagram construction also benefited of robust constraints, coming from the knowledge of surface geology and seismic-scale architectures and unconformities. These data allowed to better define the genetic relationships of sedimentary bodies and tectonic structures, thus increasing the reliability of the model. The integrated approach permitted to portray,

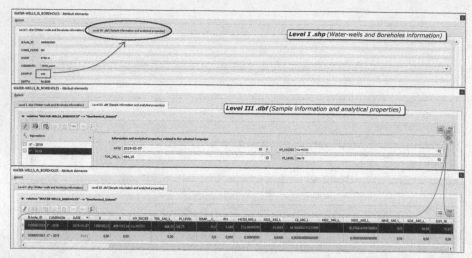

Fig. 5. Data management mask (Input/Output) of the point shapefile "WATER-WELLS_&_BOREHOLES" relating to the borehole 1000001083. In this construct the mask is for simplicity of form constituted by the superposition of three different windows. The first window shows the upper part of the mask in which we find the level I information. Here you can check the presence of the analyzes by noting the check mark next to the sample item (green rectangle). Clicking on level III opens the window shown in the center of the image referred to the "Geochemical_Dataset". Here you can read some of the values that have been highlighted such as the sampling date (DATE), the values of HYDROCHEMICAL FACIES (HY_FACIES), those of the concentration of TOTAL DISSOLVED SALTS per MG/L (TDS_MG_L_) and the PIEZOMETRIC LEVEL (PI_LEVEL). For a more complete analysis, clicking on the table symbol on the right (highlighted by yellow dots) opens the third window on the bottom in which all 60 attribute fields are found. (Color figure online)

also in those areas with scarce wells data, the geometry and architecture of aquifer systems and permeability barriers belonging to the main Pliocene-Pleistocene successions characterizing the Torino subsurface.

More specifically, the hydrostratigraphic modeling of the study area can be summarized in three steps (see Fig. 6).

The first step concerned the importing into GMS software of digitized boreholes and well data, classified according to the GEO UNITs_MODEL (GUs_MODEL) and HYDROGEOLOGIC UNITs_MODEL (HGUs_MODEL) (see "Units for 3D modeling" at chapter 2.1).

The second step consisted in the construction of a mesh of 2D reference cross-section with a preferred orientation (i.e., mainly perpendicular, and parallel to main tectonic structures), by taking advantage of deepest and more reliable well/borehole logs. This activity was aimed at a preliminary "1st level" model building. It led to delineate the geometry of the Pliocene-Pleistocene GEO UNITs_MODEL (GUs_MODEL), which are the higher rank hydrostratigraphic units, and the relationships they have with undifferentiated pre-Pliocene bedrock.

Fig. 6. Schematic model of the solid construction of the multilayer architecture of an aquifer using the images extracted from the 3D model processed in GMS. **a)** Cloud of boreholes imported from the SDTA. **b)** 1st step physical model consisting of the main sections. **c)** 2nd step physical model with triangulation of all boreholes.

The third step was dedicated to the thickening of the network of sections, by using triangle meshes, in order to complete correlations and increase the detail degree. This step yielded a "2nd level" model building, which portrayed the comprehensive architecture of both the main GUs_MODEL and the lower rank "hydrostratigraphic horizons" (i.e., aquifer vs aquitard/aquiclude systems) within them. "Hydrostratigraphic horizons" derived from the detailed correlation of permeable (HGU type A: Aquifer) or impermeable (HGU type I: Aquitard/Aquiclude) intervals i) that have been identified in the water-wells/borehole stratigraphic logs and ii) that have been defined as HYDROGEO-LOGIC UNITs_MODEL (HGUs_MODEL) i.e., HYDROGEOLOGIC UNITs peculiar to the GUs_MODEL, they belong to.

Main GUs_MODEL and their bounding surfaces represented the reference tools for constraining the distribution of the "hydrostratigraphic horizons" and their mutual relationships. By this way, mapping of "hydrostratigraphic horizons" was improved by the preliminary 3D framework of GUs_MODEL, the use of which significantly limited mismatches in the correlation of the HGUs_MODEL.

To the "hydrostratigraphic horizons" have been assigned a progressive and unique reference number on the scale of the survey area which considers the geometric constraints, given by the GEO UNITs_MODEL to which they belong, and the depositional order. This process also makes it possible to avoid correlation in the space of different horizons. The numbering of the horizons is gradually increasing, passing from the oldest and stratigraphically lower GEO UNIT_MODEL to the younger one. Each GEO UNIT_MODEL includes its own specific "stacking" of horizons, having a distinct numbering range with respect to the horizons of the underlying and overlying Geo-Unit. The amount of total and partial horizons (within each single GEO UNIT_MODEL) and the minimum and maximum numerical values were defined through the completion of the triangulation process, which provided a definitive overview.

4   Concluding Remarks and Future Developments

The large amount and heterogeneity of geo-environmental data (mainly borehole and water well logs) available for the Torino area required the creation of a suitable GIS geo-database. The construction of a Subsurface Database has been possible for the first time in northwestern Italy. The new Subsurface Database of the Torino Area (SDTA) is based on an explicit conceptual model that facilitates the storage, management, and correlation of different types of surface and subsurface (i.e., stratigraphic, structural, geophysical, and hydrogeological) data. The proposed data model ensures a continuous updating of included datasets, as well as the database implementation with new thematic datasets. Moreover, its structure can be applied to many comparable geological contexts.

A 3D model (set up on GMS modeling software) was coupled with the GIS SDTA, allowing detailed reconstruction of the geological setting of the Pliocene-Pleistocene of the study area. The definition of the 3D geological model, as well as the identification of the data model structure were favored by the mutual calibration of the multidisciplinary information stored in the geo-database.

The coupling between GIS SDTA and geological model provides the basis for a 3D hydrostratigraphic application, which is still in progress, in the frame of a better understanding of the complex hydrogeology of the Torino area (research collaboration with Società Metropolitana Acque Torino - SMAT SpA). In particular, the elaborated 3D hydrostratigraphic model represents the starting point for the future development of a conceptual model of groundwater circulation and a numerical flow model.

The presented case study highlights that the large amount of geo-environmental data provided for groundwater research and management should be adequately managed by setting up a dedicated GIS geo-database structure, based on an explicit logical model and feasible to support the conversion between GIS and 3D modeling systems.

In conclusion, future work should focus on: i) study and modeling of adjoining sectors, to the north and south of the study area and ii) data model adjustment to the INSPIRE international standards.

In addition, the methodical and orderly organization is potentially ready for loading on a dedicated WebGIS WMS System, guaranteeing a service for the society and a tool for territorial and resource planning.

Acknowledgments. This research was developed during a two-year scholarship, made possible by the CNR-Istituto di Geoscienze e Georisorse (CNR-IGG), in the framework of the Executive Project "Gronda di Genova" (ASPI - Autostrade per l'Italia, Roma), commissioned by Spea Engineering spa (Milano), and the Project "MINIDROSA" commissioned by Società Metropolitana Acque Torino SMAT SpA (Torino). Special thanks to Dr. Luigi Leardi (SMAT SpA, Torino) for his fruitful discussions on wells completion and hydrostratigraphic model.

References

1. Balestro, G., et al.: Carta Geologica d'Italia alla scala 1:50:000, Foglio 155 Torino Ovest. ISPRA, Istituto Superiore per la Protezione e la Ricerca Ambientale, Roma (2009)
2. Banca Dati Geotecnica Arpa Homepage. http://webGIS.arpa.piemonte.it/geoportale/index.php/notizie-mob/16-geologia-e-dissesto/375-banca-dati-geotecnica. Accessed 05 Jan 2021
3. D'Ambrogi, C., et al.: 3D geological model of the Po Plain subsurface: an example of open geological base data for basin analysis. In: EGU General Assembly 2020, Online, 4–8 May 2020, EGU2020-9889. https://doi.org/10.5194/egusphere-egu2020-9889 (2020)
4. De Luca D., Ossella, L.: Assetto idrogeologico della Città di Torino e del suo hinterland. Geologia dell'Ambiente, 1 (suppl.), pp. 10–15 (2014)
5. Festa, A., et al.: Carta Geologica d'Italia alla scala 1: 50.000. Foglio 156 "Torino Est". ISPRA - Istituto Superiore per la Protezione e la Ricerca Ambientale, Roma (2009)

6. Ghielmi, M., Rogledi, S., Vigna, B., Violanti, D.: La successione messiniana e plio-pleistocenica del Bacino di Savigliano (settore occidentale del Bacino Terziario Piemontese) - Italia. Geol. Insubr. **13**(1), 141 (2019)

7. GMS Homepage. https://www.aquaveo.com/software/gms-groundwater-modeling-system-introduction. Accessed 05 Jan 2021

8. Irace A., et al.: Geologia e idrostratigrafia profonda della Pianura Padana Occidentale. La Nuova Lito, Firenze (2009)

9. Lucchesi, S.: Sintesi preliminare dei dati di sottosuolo della pianura piemontese centrale. GEAM **103**, 115–121 (2001)

10. Masetti, G.: Modello logico e fisico dei dati – Dizionario degli attributi delle classi. Banca Dati dei Corpi Idrici Sotterranei della Regione Toscana – Adeguamento alla DGRT 939/2009, Technical Report, intervento, vol. 6, 21p. (2016)

11. Mosca, P., Polino, R., Rogledi, S., Rossi, M.: New data for the kinematic interpretation of the alps-Apennines junction (Nordwestern Italy). Int. J. Earth Sci. (Geol Rundsch), 99, 833–849 (2010). https://doi.org/10.1007/s00531-009-0428-2

12. Morelli, M., Mallen, L., Nicolò, G., Cozzula, S., Irace, A., Piana, F.: 3D geological modeling and visualization of the subsurface data of the Piemonte plains derived from the geodatabase of digital Geological map of Piemonte. Rendiconti Online Società Geologica Italiana **42**, 90–93 (2017)

13. Piana F., et al.: Geology of Piemonte region (NW Italy, Alps-Apennines interference zone). J. Maps **13**(2), 395–405 (2017)

14. QGIS Homepage. https://www.qgis.org/it/site/. Accessed 25 May 2021

15. Regione Piemonte, DTM capture ICE 2009–2011 tile size 5 m, metadata at the link. http://www.geoportale.piemonte.it/geonetworkrp/srv/ita/metadata.show?id=2552. Accessed 25 May 2021

16. Rete di Monitoraggio Acque Sotterranee Homepage. http://webgis.arpa.piemonte.it/monitoraggio_qualita_acque_mapseries/monitoraggio_qualita_acque_webapp/. Accessed 25 May 2021

Artificial Intelligence for a Multi-temporal Classification of Fluvial Geomorphic Units of the River Isonzo: A Comparison of Different Techniques

Filippo Tonion[1,2]([⊠]) [iD] and Francesco Pirotti[1] [iD]

[1] TESAF Department and CIRGEO Interdepartmental Research Center in Geomatics,
University of Padova, Viale dell'Università 16, PD 35020 Legnaro, Italy
[2] T.E.R.R.A. S.r.l., Galleria Progresso, 5, VE 30027 San Donà di Piave, Italy
f.tonion@terrasrl.com

Abstract. The pressure of human activities is particularly relevant on fluvial ecosystems, where activity such hydroelectric energy production can change natural dynamics. For this reason it is important to monitor, with a systematic approach, river geomorphic units distribution and their evolution over time. In particular this work consists of an application of different AI techniques to process Sentinel-2 optical data to acquire a multitemporal classification of fluvial geomorphic units (Channels, Pools, Bars, Island, Vegetation) on a study area of the river Isonzo in Friuli Venezia Giulia (Italy). Results showed that all the AI methods tested allow to perform accurate classification, with best results obtained by Random Forest, that reach an overall accuracy of 0.986, and the most confusion between Bars and Island classes with F-measure of 0.931 and 0.961 respectively.

Keywords: Machine Learning · Sentinel-2 · Geomorphic units classification

1 Introduction

The pressure of human activities on ecosystems and their connection is particularly relevant that lead different authors to speak about the geological era called "Anthropocene" [1–3]. The pressure factors of human activities influence ecosystems in different ways, such as soil erosion, species loss and fragmentation. Pressure factors are particularly relevant in fluvial ecosystems, where human activities, along with natural influences such as flood events and climate trends, represent drivers for change in fluvial geomorphology [4].

A systematic approach to the classification of fluvial geomorphic units is fundamental to have a better understanding of the evolution scheme of river ecosystems. To do this there are different consolidated approaches, that take in consideration different surveying techniques and different kinds of river [5–8]. If classification methodologies are consolidated, their practical application can be difficult over large study areas. In fact the execution of topographic surveys or in situ measurements on large areas can

© Springer Nature Switzerland AG 2022
E. Borgogno-Mondino and P. Zamperlin (Eds.): ASITA 2021, CCIS 1507, pp. 120–132, 2022.
https://doi.org/10.1007/978-3-030-94426-1_10

be highly expensive; this fact consistently reduces the possibility of studying temporal evolution of geomorphic units distribution.

Remote sensing techniques become increasingly more consolidated, due to the improvement of satellite data quality and to the introduction of Artificial Intelligence (AI). In particular AI gives a strong contribution in the acquisition of a better understanding of earth surface dynamics at a large scale. The application of AI techniques is consolidated in different fields, like for example land use monitoring [9, 10], crop optimization [11, 12], pollution analysis [13, 14] and coastal erosion monitoring [15, 16]. This approach to data analysis can be the basis for the creation of highly automated systems, capable of continuous monitoring of environmental phenomena and earth surface processes.

Within the ensemble of AI techniques, some Machine Learning (ML) methods are particularly useful to classify land dynamics with high precision. In particular for classification problems three commonly used models are Support Vector Machines (SVM), Random Forest (RF) and Neural Networks (NN); in particular good results in the analysis of satellite data using these methods are shown by different authors [17–19].

The present work consists of an application of AI techniques to acquire a multitemporal classification of geomorphic units of an area of interest in the Isonzo river. The aim of the work is the test of three different ML methods (RF, SVM and NN) to define the most precise approach to the multitemporal monitoring of the river Isonzo.

2 Materials and Methods

2.1 Study Area

The study area (shown with the red line in Fig. 1) is situated in Friuli Venezia Giulia (IT), within the Province of Gorizia (GO), and it consists of a part of the riverbed of the River Isonzo; the geospatial grid of the following picture (Fig. 1) is based on WGS 84 Coordinate Reference Sistem (EPSG 4326).

In detail the study area includes the riverbed from the fluvial traverse of Sagrado to the bridge of Pieris. This area extends approximately 6.72 km^2, distributed around a longitudinal axis, long 13.2 km. The above described study area has been selected because it is particularly affected by antropic influences, due to hidraulic management of the river Isonzo. In particular the main influences derive from the Salcano dam, which was built in order to produce hydroelectric energy. The Salcano dam is situated near the city of Salcano in Slovenia and it is approximately 16km from the study area. The main effect of hydroelectric energy production of the Salcano dam is the sudden variation of water volumes discharge, that can vary from extremely low water amounts to extremely high one in hours. This pattern of flow is particularly problematic for ecological connection of the river, for agriculture and for end users. Considering all these aspects, the selected study area is particularly vocated to a multitemporal monitoring of geomorphic units evolution.

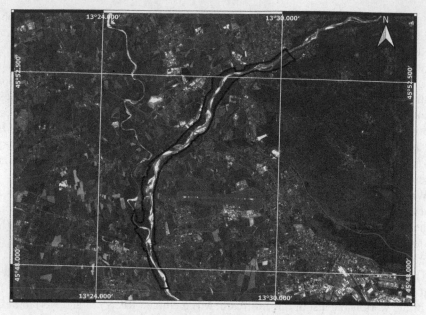

Fig. 1. Study area on the River Isonzo.

2.2 Satellite Data

Considering the aim of this work, it was decided to acquire satellite data from a single platform, in order to have the possibility of reprocessing satellite data faster and to perform an efficient multi-temporal monitoring of the area of interest. Based on the needs of the highest spatial resolution (ground sample distance - GSD) available as open-data, it was decided to use data from the Sentinel-2 platform. In the following table (Table 1) a description of the bands of Sentinel-2 selected for the classification of geomorphic units on the study area of the river Isonzo is provided.

Table 1. Bands of Sentinel-2 used for the study of geomorphic units' evolution.

ID	Sentinel-2 bands	Central wavelength (μ m)	Resolution (m)
B02	Band 2	0.490	10
B03	Band 3	0.560	10
B04	Band 4	0.665	10
B08	Band 8	0.842	10
B11	Band 11	1.610	20
B12	Band 12	2.190	20

The selection of which satellite data comprehend in the analysis, among those available in the entire year 2020, was based on the following criteria:

- Meteorological conditions. During the acquisition of satellite data only those pictures without clouds or hazes inside the area of analysis were considered.
- Water discharge conditions. Having the availability of half-hourly measurement of water discharge at traverse of Gradisca d'Isonzo for the entire year 2020 (situated approximately at 1 km of distance from the area of interest), it was decided to select only satellite data collected in period with water discharge lower than 65 m^3; this assumption allow to focus on the critical situation, when there is low water connection on the river bed (far from a bankfull discharge situation).
- Temporal representativity. During the selection among satellite images collected in different dates, in compliance with previous criteria, it was attempted to select images representative of the entire year.

Based on the previously described criteria, the selected images included Sentinel-2 data of 13 different days of the year 2020; both Sentinel-2A and Sentinel-2B data were acquired, assuming no differences between different platforms of Sentinel mission. The following table (Table 2) provides a description of selected images and of the condition of water discharge at Gradisca d'Isonzo.

Table 2. Sentinel-2 images selected and condition of water discharge (WD) at Gradisca d'Isonzo station.

ID	Day	WD (m3)	ID	Day	WD (m3)
1	05/02/2020	32.2	7	07/07/2020	31.4
2	16/03/2020	48.8	8	14/07/2020	44.0
3	15/04/2020	16.9	9	29/07/2020	10.0
4	23/04/2020	15.3	10	13/08/2020	14.8
5	03/05/2020	44.4	11	05/09/2020	43.3
6	27/06/2020	63.6	12	20/09/2020	7.43
			13	24/11/2020	20.9

All the selected data were acquired in the Sentinel-2 level 2A product which is already processed for atmospheric corrections and does not require further pre-processings. Each of the selected images was then processed in order to extract predictors for the following analysis with AI models. In particular predictors were calculated by combining different Sentinel-2 bands to obtain different indexes, commonly used in land monitoring and classification; to do this raster data from bands 11 and 12 of the Sentinel-2 were resampled to a 10 m × 10 m ground sample distance. The following table (Table 3) contains all the details of calculated indexes and the formula used during calculation.

Table 3. Index calculated as predictors.

Index	Formula
NDVI [20]	(B08-B04)/(B08 + B04)
NDWI [21]	(B03-B08)/(B03 + B08)
MNDWI [22]	(B03-B11)/(B03 + B11)
AWEI1 [23]	(4*(B03-B11)*(0.25*B08 + 2.75*B12))/(B03 + B11 + B12)
AWEI 2 [24]	B02 + 2.5*B03–1.5*(B08 + B11)-0.25*B12

In the following paragraph a description is provided of the approach to the classification of geomorphic units, that are the variables targeted in the AI models.

The calculation of above mentioned indexes was achieved using the software R Studio.

2.3 Building of Training and Validation Datasets

The choice of a systematic approach to the classification of fluvial geomorphic units was the starting point for the construction of the training and validation datasets. In particular the methodology adopted was those defined in the Manual of the italian Istituto Superiore per la Protezione e la Ricerca Ambientale (ISPRA), published in 2015 [25]. The manual in particular identifies the typical geomorphic units of different kinds of river, considering different factors, like for example the degree of river confinement, the riverbed shape and riverbed slope. Considering the characteristics of the selected study area we selected the following morphologic units, which in our work are the classes to be predicted:

1) Channels. This class includes the area with low water depth in condition of low water discharge.
2) Pools. This class includes those areas of the riverbed characterized by higher water depth, even if water discharge conditions are low.
3) Bars. This class includes the areas of the riverbed characterised by the presence of mobile stones (i.e. sediments that can change their position due to bankfull discharge effects).
4) Islands. This class includes areas with consolidated sediments; these areas are higher than normal water level and are less affected by water induced changes.
5) Vegetation. This class includes all the areas of the riverbed covered by vegetation.

The choice of the previous classes was done considering also the approach to river morphologic units classification adopted in this work, which is based on spectral information from satellite imagery. In particular, it is worth noting that with the spatial resolution of Sentinel-2 data (10 m in the visible area of the spectral range), some geomorphological units can't be detected. This is the reason because some geomorphic units, such as channels without water and single logs in the river, were not considered.

The approach to the classification was supervised. For each date, i.e. thirteen satellite images (see Table 2), different polygons over different regions of each class were created. The polygons did not cover the entire area of analysis, but only well-defined areas of each class.

During the creation of polygons, all the data and the information available for the study area were considered. For example, the aerial photography of the area of analysis collected in 2018 was considered in order to have a better understanding of the distribution of islands and consolidated vegetation. Moreover, the material of project "Camis", project "Nexus" and those of "Laboratorio Isonzo", supported and promoted by Regione Friuli Venezia Giulia, were studied in order to acquire an historical view of the evolution of morphology of the study area.

After the creation, the polygons were splitted randomly in two parts, in order to create completely independent training and validation datasets. After this division, for each polygon in it was created a grid of points of size 10 m (equal to the GSD of Sentinel-2 in the visible bands); for each point it was extracted the information of the geomorphic unit class, derived from the polygon. The result of this operation was a training and a validation dataset completely independent and representative of each satellite acquisition date; in the following table (Table 4) it is provided an overall analysis of training and validation datasets composition.

Table 4. Training and validation dataset composition - number of observations.

Class ID	Class	Train	Test
1	Channels	269	253
2	Pools	164	123
3	Bars	183	238
4	Island	184	425
5	Vegetation	523	650

As represented in the previous table the overall numerosity of the training and the validation datasets was 1323 and 1689 respectively; the numerosity of each class was very similar and balanced. Eventually to complete the two datasets, for each point of both training and validation dataset the values of predictors, described in the previous paragraph (i.e. NDVI, NDWI, MNDWI, AWEI1 and AWEI2) were extracted.

All the operations described were achieved using the software R Studio.

2.4 Artificial Intelligence Processing

In order to acquire the best multi-temporal classification of geomorphic units different AI algorithms were used; the algorithms were developed and tested using R Studio software. The selected ML algorithms were Random Forest (RF), Support Vector Machines (SVM) and Artificial Neural Networks (NNs). All these algorithms were trained on the training dataset with an automated process, developed in order to acquire the best computational asset in terms of overall accuracy. A complete evaluation of each algorithm's best configuration was achieved by computing the confusion matrix, considering reference and predicted class on the test dataset and calculating all the conventional metrics (overall accuracy, accuracy by classes and k index). In the following chapters a description of the tuning process developed for the different algorithms used is provided.

Random Forest (RF). RF tuning procedures kept in consideration the parameters "ntree" and "mtry". The "ntree" parameters represent the number of decision trees built by the model. The "ntree" variation range varied from 100 to 1500 trees, by 100. The "mtry" parameter represents the number of variables to be split during to build each tree. The "mtry" variation range assumed varied from 1 to 5.

Support Vector Machines (SVM). SVM setting procedures dealt with the kind of kernel used to pre-process data. The parameter "Kernel" represents the kind of transformation function that substitutes the scalar product of predictors. The main kinds of SVM kernel functions are linear, radial, polynomial and sigmoid. During the model tuning it was observed that radial kernel function was not applicable due to the introduction of NA values. Considering this result only linear, polynomial and sigmoid kernels were tested for the classification. The scale factor was maintained constant and equal to the default value (1).

Neural Network. Among all possible configurations of NN structure it was decided to adopt the Feed Forward Neural Networks (FFNN), without any convolution or recursion. The decision of considering only FFNN was based on the fact that this kind of NN structure gives the possibility of a fast automation of the tuning process compared to other kinds of NN. In fact the tuning procedure was developed focusing only on the number of hidden layers (HL) and on the number of neurons of each HL. About the number of HL, three different NN configurations were tested, that are: 3,4 and 5 HL. For each of the previous configurations, models were tested with a different number of neurons in each HL; in particular the following points provide a description of the ranges of variation of neurons number for each HL in the different configuration adopted.

- 3 hidden layers. Neurons layer 1 from 4 to 10, neurons layer 2 from 4 to 8 and neurons layer from 3 to 8.
- 4 hidden layers. Neurons layer 1 from 5 to 10, neurons layer 2 from 5 to 10, neurons layer 3 from 4 to 7 and neurons layer 4 from 4 to 7.
- 5 hidden layers. Neurons layer 1 from 6 to 10, neurons layer 2 from 6 to 10, neurons layer 3 from 4 to 7, neurons layer 4 from 4 to 7 and neurons layer 5 from 4 to 6.

Within these ranges of variation all possible combinations of FFNN structure were tested.

3 Results

The automated tuning procedure showed that the best classification performances of SVM were obtained with "linear" kernel function; in particular the overall accuracy of SVM classification was equal to 0.976, while the others function tested lead to estimation with overall accuracy lower than 0.90.

The following plot (Fig. 2) represents RF performances, with values ranging from 0 to 1 that represent respectively minimum and maximum values of RF accuracy. About the tuning process of RF it was found that the best performances in terms of overall accuracy were achieved with 600 trees and with mtry value equal to 1; with this configuration the overall accuracy was equal to 0.986. However in general RF performances were particularly accurate, considering that the minimum value of overall accuracy was equal to 0.979.

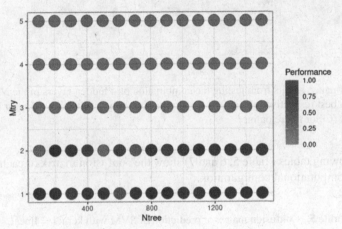

Fig. 2. Performance results from combining variables in random forest - rescaled from worse to best respectively from 0 to 1.

The NN tuning procedure showed in general that an increasing number of HL lead to higher accuracy. In fact, the maximum values of overall accuracy with different numbers of HL were equal to 0.969 with 3 HL, 0.972 with 4 HL and 0.979 with 5 HL. The lowest accuracy values were similar for all numbers of HL considered, with an overall accuracy near to 0.5. The following plot gives a representation of the variation of overall accuracy performances with all the FFNN structure combinations tested (Fig. 3).

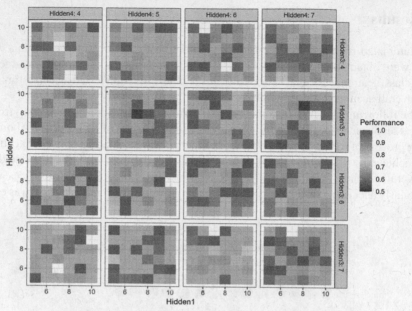

Fig. 3. Performance results from testing the combination of 4 hidden layers in the NN- rescaled from worse to best respectively from 0 to 1 and reporting only results above 0.5 for better color interpretation. (Color figure online)

The following tables (Table 5, 6 and 7) show the confusion matrix of each AI model in the best computational configuration.

Table 5. Confusion matrix of prediction of SVM with kernel = linear.

	Channels	Pools	Bars	Island	Vegetation	F measure
Channels	253	8	0	0	0	0.984
Pools	0	115	0	0	0	0.966
Bars	0	0	224	19	0	0.931
Island	0	0	14	406	0	0.961
Vegetation	0	0	0	0	650	1.000

The following picture (Fig. 4) shows a prediction of three best models over a small area inside the study areas.

Table 6. Confusion matrix of prediction of RF with Ntree = 600 and Mtry = 1.

	Channels	Pools	Bars	Island	Vegetation	F measure
Channels	253	0	0	0	0	1.000
Pools	0	123	0	1	0	0.996
Bars	0	0	221	6	0	0.951
Island	0	0	17	418	0	0.972
Vegetation	0	0	0	0	650	1.000

Table 7. Confusion matrix of prediction of NN with 5 hidden layer and a 8, 10, 6, 5, 6 neurons configuration

	Channels	Pools	Bars	Island	Vegetation	F Measure
Channels	252	2	0	1	0	0.994
Pools	1	121	0	0	0	0.980
Bars	0	0	218	11	0	0.934
Island	0	0	20	412	0	0.961
Vegetation	0	0	0	0	650	1.000

4 Discussion

The present work was focused on a comparison of three AI methods (SVM, RF and FFNN). The parameters tuning phase of these methods was different. In fact, if for SVM and RF the tuning procedures were quite fast, FFNN required a bigger computational effort; the individuation of the best FFNN configuration was based on the test of 1986 different FFNNs, with different number of hidden layers and with different neurons per each hidden layer. In particular the computational time for the test of each FFNN with an Intel Xeon processor (3.60 GHz) was approximately 30 s per FFNN tested.

The best performances with all the metrics considered in the previous chapter were achieved with RF with a 600 trees and mtry values equal to 1 configuration. About SVM and FFN the performances compared were very similar, except for the extreme quickness of SVM computational time. However, as it is possible to notice from the examination of the previous Fig. 4, the predictions adopted with all three different models show a good response in comparison with the true color image. The goodness of the prediction is particularly relevant if considering the fact that the training and validation datasets are comprehensive of satellite data collected over different times of the year. This means that the models created are capable of effectively classifying fluvial geomorphic units, even if considering the possible variations of geomorphic units characteristics during the year (for example water turbidity, water color and vegetation characteristics).

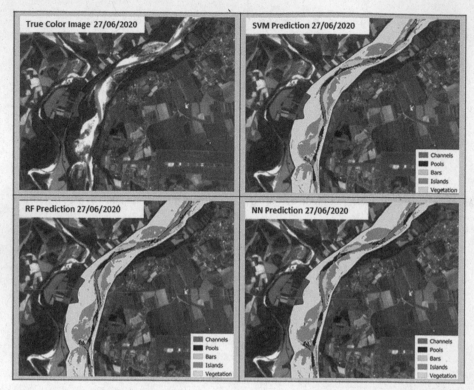

Fig. 4. Prediction of the three tested models over the Sentinel-2 data collected on 27/06/2020.

5   Conclusions

The study has compared three different AI models' performance in the classification of river geomorphic units on a study area of the river Isonzo. Results showed that RF performance was higher than SVM and FFNN; SVM and FFNN precision in classification of river geomorphic units were similar, except for the higher computational time required to achieve the best computational configuration of FFNN. All the models considered showed a good response and the possibility to be adopted in a multitemporal monitoring of riverbed geomorphic evolution.

5.1   Further Development

In future this work continue trying to test improvement in the following aspects:

- AI approach to data analysis. In future it will be interesting to test different Machine Learning models or to investigate Deep Learning potentiality to improve precision in classification of geomorphic units.
- In field survey. In order to acquire a more detailed feedback on classification performances of the proposed method it would be important to conduct an in field survey to verify the classification satellite based.

References

1. Ruddiman, W.F.: The Anthropocene. Annu. Rev. Earth Planet. Sci. **41**, 45–68 (2013). https://doi.org/10.1146/annurev-earth-050212-123944
2. Lewis, S.L., Maslin, M.A.: Defining the Anthropocene. Nature **519**, 171–180 (2015). https://doi.org/10.1038/nature14258
3. Zalasiewicz, J., Waters, C., Williams, M.: The Anthropocene. In: Geologic Time Scale 2020. pp. 1257–1280. Elsevier (2020). https://doi.org/10.1016/B978-0-12-824360-2.00031-0
4. Downs, P.W., Piégay, H.: Catchment-scale cumulative impact of human activities on river channels in the late Anthropocene: implications, limitations, prospect. Geomorphology **338**, 88–104 (2019). https://doi.org/10.1016/j.geomorph.2019.03.021
5. Belletti, B., et al.: Characterising physical habitats and fluvial hydromorphology: a new system for the survey and classification of river geomorphic units. Geomorphology **283**, 143–157 (2017). https://doi.org/10.1016/j.geomorph.2017.01.032
6. Rinaldi, M., Surian, N., Comiti, F., Bussettini, M.: A method for the assessment and analysis of the hydromorphological condition of Italian streams: The morphological quality index (MQI). Geomorphology **180–181**, 96–108 (2013). https://doi.org/10.1016/j.geomorph.2012.09.009
7. Wheaton, J.M., Fryirs, K.A., Brierley, G., Bangen, S.G., Bouwes, N., O'Brien, G.: Geomorphic mapping and taxonomy of fluvial landforms. Geomorphology **248**, 273–295 (2015). https://doi.org/10.1016/j.geomorph.2015.07.010
8. Fryirs, K.A., Brierley, G.J.: What's in a name? A naming convention for geomorphic river types using the river styles framework. PLoS ONE **13**, e0201909 (2018). https://doi.org/10.1371/journal.pone.0201909
9. Whyte, A., Ferentinos, K.P., Petropoulos, G.P.: A new synergistic approach for monitoring wetlands using sentinels -1 and 2 data with object-based machine learning algorithms. Environ. Model. Softw. **104**, 40–54 (2018). https://doi.org/10.1016/j.envsoft.2018.01.023
10. Jamali, A.: Evaluation and comparison of eight machine learning models in land use/land cover mapping using Landsat 8 OLI: a case study of the northern region of Iran. SN Appl. Sci. **1**(11), 1–11 (2019). https://doi.org/10.1007/s42452-019-1527-8
11. Talaviya, T., Shah, D., Patel, N., Yagnik, H., Shah, M.: Implementation of artificial intelligence in agriculture for optimisation of irrigation and application of pesticides and herbicides. Artif. Intell. Agric. **4**, 58–73 (2020). https://doi.org/10.1016/j.aiia.2020.04.002
12. Maimaitijiang, M., Sagan, V., Sidike, P., Daloye, A.M., Erkbol, H., Fritschi, F.B.: Crop monitoring using satellite/UAV data fusion and machine learning. Remote Sens. **12**, 1357 (2020). https://doi.org/10.3390/rs12091357
13. Danesh Yazdi, M., et al.: Predicting fine particulate matter (PM2.5) in the greater London Area: an ensemble approach using machine learning methods. Remote Sens. **12**, 914 (2020). https://doi.org/10.3390/rs12060914
14. Just, A.C., Arfer, K.B., Rush, J., Dorman, M., Shtein, A., Lyapustin, A., Kloog, I.: Advancing methodologies for applying machine learning and evaluating spatiotemporal models of fine particulate matter (PM2.5) using satellite data over large regions. Atmos. Environ. **239**, 117649 (2020). https://doi.org/10.1016/j.atmosenv.2020.117649
15. Tonion, F., Pirotti, F., Faina, G., Paltrinieri, D.: A machine learning approach to multispectral satellite derived bathymetry. ISPRS Ann. Photogramm. Remote Sens. Spat. Inf. Sci. **V-3-2020**, 565–570 (2020). https://doi.org/10.5194/isprs-annals-V-3-2020-565-2020
16. Ghorbanidehno, H., Lee, J., Farthing, M., Hesser, T., Darve, E.F., Kitanidis, P.K.: Deep learning technique for fast inference of large-scale riverine bathymetry. Adv. Water Resour. **147**, 103715 (2021). https://doi.org/10.1016/j.advwatres.2020.103715

17. Pirotti, F., Sunar, F., Piragnolo, M.: Benchmark of machine learning methods for classification of a sentineL-2 image. ISPRS - Int. Arch. Photogramm. Remote Sens. Spat. Inf. Sci. **XLI-B7**, 335–340 (2016). https://doi.org/10.5194/isprsarchives-XLI-B7-335-2016

18. Qiu, C., Mou, L., Schmitt, M., Zhu, X.X.: Local climate zone-based urban land cover classification from multi-seasonal sentinel-2 images with a recurrent residual network. ISPRS J. Photogramm. Remote Sens. **154**, 151–162 (2019). https://doi.org/10.1016/j.isprsjprs.2019.05.004

19. Thanh Noi, P., Kappas, M.: Comparison of random forest, k-nearest neighbor, and support vector machine classifiers for land cover classification using sentinel-2 imagery. Sensors. **18**, 18 (2017). https://doi.org/10.3390/s18010018

20. Goward, S.N., Markham, B., Dye, D.G., Dulaney, W., Yang, J.: Normalized difference vegetation index measurements from the advanced very high resolution radiometer. Remote Sens. Environ. **35**, 257–277 (1991)

21. Gao, B.-C.: NDWI—a normalized difference water index for remote sensing of vegetation liquid water from space. Remote Sens. Environ. **58**, 257–266 (1996)

22. Han-Qiu, X.: A study on information extraction of water body with the modified normalized difference water index (MNDWI). J. Remote Sens. **5**, 589–595 (2005)

23. Fisher, A., Flood, N., Danaher, T.: Comparing landsat water index methods for automated water classification in eastern Australia. Remote Sens. Environ. **175**, 167–182 (2016)

24. Feyisa, G.L., Meilby, H., Fensholt, R., Proud, S.R.: Automated Water Extraction index: a new technique for surface water mapping using Landsat imagery. Remote Sens. Environ. **140**, 23–35 (2014)

25. Rinaldi, M., Belletti, B., Comiti, F., Nardi, L., Mao, L., Bussettini, M.: Sistema di rilevamento e classificazione delle Unità Morfologiche dei corsi d'acqua (SUM). ISPRA – Settore Editoria, Roma (2015)

Geomatics for Terrain's Deformation Monitoring: The H2020 LiquefACT Field Trial in Pieve di Cento, Italy

Vittorio Casella[ID] and Marica Franzini[✉][ID]

Department of Civil Engineering and Architecture, University of Pavia, Pavia, Italy
{vittorio.casella,marica.franzini}@unipv.it

Abstract. The paper presents a case study on the application of Geomatics to terrain's deformation monitoring. Within the EU H2020 LiquefACT project, the Laboratory of Geomatics of the University of Pavia (Italy) was appointed to quantify the subsidence suffered by the terrain due to some trials conducted in the test site of Pieve di Cento, Northern Italy. Geomatics has long been used for deformation monitoring, but present paper deals with two peculiar elements: the constraints given by the test field, its layout, the allowed and forbidden actions, that forced the surveyors to elaborate an unconventional surveying design, and the use of a state-of-the-art instrument, the Trimble SX10. It mainly is a high-level topographic total station; being robotized, it has interesting laser scanning capabilities. In the paper, the survey design will be illustrated and discussed, and a selection of the obtained results will be presented. They highlight how much geomatics can be flexible and adaptable and, at the same time, precise and accurate.

Keywords: Geomatics · Topographic survey · Laser scanner · Deformation monitoring · Accuracy · Precision

1 Introduction

Geomatics can be defined as a systemic, multidisciplinary, integrated approach to select the instruments and the appropriate techniques for collecting, storing, integrating, modelling, analysing, retrieving at will, transforming, displaying and distributing spatially georeferenced data from different sources with well-defined accuracy characteristics, continuity and in a digital format [1]. Geomatics includes several disciplines such as geodesy, surveying, global navigation satellite systems, photogrammetry, lidar, cartography, GIS, theory of errors. Most often, they are used in an integrated way, as it happened in the described experiment. One distinguishing feature of geomatics is the capability of performing high precision measurements in a controlled way. This means that not only unknowns, such as distances and coordinates, are measured, but their statistical uncertainty is also assessed.

E. Borgogno-Mondino and P. Zamperlin (Eds.): ASITA 2021, CCIS 1507, pp. 133–147, 2022.
https://doi.org/10.1007/978-3-030-94426-1_11

Thanks to this versatility, geomatics has always had several areas of application such as cultural heritage [2, 3], urban and regional planning [4–6] and natural hazard management [7, 8] and forensic sciences [9, 10] and monitoring. Geomatics supports monitoring with a variety of instruments and techniques but, in this introduction, only a quick overview will be given on those used inside this contribution which means total station and terrestrial laser scanner.

Total Station (TS) is the more traditional instruments and has numerous advantages [11] that include the high accuracy, the capability to perform indoor and in urban canyon measurements [12] and, with new generations of instruments completely robotized, the automation of targets recognition and observation [13, 14]. Among disadvantages, there could be limitation due to adverse weather conditions [15] and the necessity to have a clear line of sight between TS and the prisms. There are several applications fields; here are some examples: [16] shows the use of TS for bridge vibrations monitoring in a lab simulation and in a field experiment in Graz (Austria); [17] has used four TS to estimate the displacements suffered by a metro tunnel in Lisbon (Portugal) cause by a mud flooding; [18] reports an experience on the use of TS for the monitoring of an earthfill dam in southern California obtaining good results when atmospheric refraction correction has been taken into consideration.

Terrestrial Laser Scanner (TLS) is widely used in monitoring and there is abundance of articles on its use in literature. TLS has advantages and disadvantages too [19]: thank to the high density of the collected points, it allows to perform a continuous 3D analysis in a quick and completely autonomous way; however, it is more expensive, requires clear line of sight, as for TS, and is less reliable in time series when a stable setting up is not guarantee [20, 21]. It was used for several application such as landslide displacements studies [21–23], glaciers [24], bridges [25–27] and dams [28, 29]. The reported experiences agree in arguing that TLS monitoring gives important contribution to the deformation analysis thanks to high density data [20]; moreover, the obtained accuracies satisfy the quality requirements [30] even if the survey geometry must be carefully planned [31].

As with almost every research area, the field of surveying and its equipment evolve with the technological innovations leading to ever faster, more accurate and more versatile devices. The recent Trimble SX10 scanning total station [32] belongs to this category of multi-sensor systems. The system is, at the same time, a topographical total station, capable to carry out high quality topographic measurements, and a terrestrial laser scanner; besides, it has three calibrated cameras able to acquire oriented images, if necessary. In literature, a few experiences are available on its use such as [33] that has tested the instrument in several contexts comparing results with those obtained from traditional systems; the paper also reports a technical properties review.

2 Introduction to the Experiment of Pieve di Cento

The EU H2020 LiquefACT project sets out to achieve a comprehensive understanding of Earthquake Induced Liquefaction Disasters (EILDs), the applications of the mitigation techniques, and the development of more appropriate techniques tailored to each specific scenario, for both European and worldwide situations (http://www.liquefact.eu/). A test

trial was organized in Pieve di Cento (BO), Northern Italy (Fig. 1b), to test some mitigation methods. Tests lasted two days, 22nd and 23rd October 2018. In that occasion, the
Laboratory of Geomatics of the University of Pavia was appointed to perform geomatic
surveying and to quantify subsidence induced by the experiment (Fig. 1).

(a)   (b)

                            (c)

Fig. 1. An overview of the Pieve di Cento test field and the Megashaker vehicle: (a) The four
test areas outline on the background of the orthophoto generated by UAV-acquired data; (b) The
excerpt from the Google Satellite Data (MapData@2019Google); (c) The Megashaker vehicle
used to simulate earthquakes.

The test field was a large dig where four test areas were prepared, which were
characterized by different mitigation methods for soil liquefaction. Figure 2a shows
a site overview together with the test area outlines: Area1 had virgin soil because no
mitigation techniques were applied, Area2 and Area3 were treated with horizontal drains
having different section shape, while the Induced Partial Saturation (IPS) method was
applied to Area4. In each area, several simulated earthquake shocks were applied by a
special vehicle which is capable to simulate an earthquake (Fig. 2c). The shaking actions
are produced by a hydraulic system acting on two plates, once for each side of the vehicle,
which are laid on the ground and transmit vibrations to the terrain, at a defined frequency;
noticeably, the machine can produce P- and S-waves. The described vehicle is called
megashaker in the documents of the LiquefACT project and we will adopt that name
since now. The typical sequence of the experiment was: the megashaker was moved to
one of the four areas and plates were laid on the terrain. Some time was waited so that
terrain strains were dissipated. A first shake was performed having planned duration
and frequency and activities were stopped for an appropriate time; then, another shake

was applied with same or different parameters. After a certain number of shakes in the same area, the vehicle was moved to another one according to the initial plan and to the on-the-fly decisions taken by the management team. The Laboratory of Geomatics was appointed to perform geomatic surveying and to quantify subsidence induced by these experiments.

3 The Geomatic Surveying Performed in Pieve di Cento

To effectively design a topographic survey, it is necessary to know the goals, in terms of resolution and precision. The scientists who organized the experiment did not have a sharp idea of the expected size of induced subsidence; they considered desirable the capability of detecting movements of a few millimetres and wanted to be sure to detect those of 1 cm and up. Therefore, a high-quality survey was planned, which had nevertheless to cope with the many constraints posed by the field test, as it will be explained in the following. Two techniques were taken into consideration: topographic surveying and terrestrial laser scanning.

Topographic surveying is based on the use of topographic total station instruments, which measure horizonal and vertical angles and slope distance. Typically, measurements are taken from a stable point of known coordinates; specific target points are observed, and their coordinates are calculated. Topographic surveying is very precise, and coordinates can be determined with an uncertainty of 0.5 mm, if site has limited size and particular care is taken.

Terrestrial laser scanning is performed by instruments measuring the same quantities as total stations. Difference is that they automatically and quickly scan the selected scene thus producing a dense point cloud. Point clouds are very attractive as they seem a sort of a continuous model, including all the details of reality. An often-underestimated issue is that point density is highly variable as decreases as the distance from the instrument increases. Anyway, the major disadvantage of such technique is, for the considered scenario, that a single scan can take from several minutes to hours. Dedicated laser scanning can be performed with dedicated instruments, which are capable to acquire between 10^5 and 10^6 points per second.

In the Pieve di Cento site, Trimble SX10 scanning total station was used instead, for both types of surveying. It is a state-of-the-art multi-sensor systems since the it is, at the same time, a topographical total station, capable to carry out high quality topographic measurements, and a terrestrial laser scanner.

3.1 Topographic Survey

The integrated Trimble SX10 instrument was adopted which is, first, a topographic total station of the highest quality, being able to measure angles with a precision of 1 arcsec and distances with a precision of 1 mm plus 1.5 ppm [32]. Before discussing the survey schema, it is worth mentioning that the general design of the Pieve di Cento experiment was performed long time before and dealt with several aspects such as the paths followed by the megashaker and the position of all other geotechnics instruments.

Geomatics monitoring was not planned and therefore, when it was designed, it was mandatory to cope with the constraints coming from other features of the site.

It was not easy to monitor terrain's subsidence in the described framework, because the part of the terrain that suffered the major sinking was hidden by the vehicle; moreover, it was not easy to ascertain whether superficial shape modifications simply pointed out shifting of the gravel or an actual deformation. We concluded that, targeting the shown plate, was the most reliable way to monitor the terrain underneath.

The shaking actions were produced by the vehicle thanks to hydraulic mechanisms and transmitted to the terrain through the plates lying on it. Plates can be considered integral to the terrain itself because of its significant weight and because wheels were unloaded from the megashaker weight, during the shake; therefore, each displacement measured on the plates can be reasonably connected to a subsidence suffered by the terrain. To quantify these displacements, several topographic targets were placed on the plate, on the side visible from the instrument. Figure 2a shows the targets fixed on a plate of the vehicle; each marker, Fig. 2b, was identified with a letter that also indicates the measuring order. Section 4 will illustrate the results obtained from targets' measurements.

   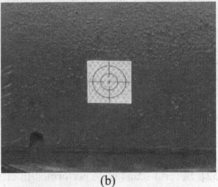

(a)   (b)

Fig. 2. The reflective markers fixed on one plate of the vehicle: (a) Overview; (b) Detail.

The inaccessibility to some areas of the yard had as main consequence that only one setup point per day was allowed. Figure 3a and Fig. 3b show the schemas followed in the two days, where red points are the reference framework which will be illustrated ahead, blue points are the setup locations and points in magenta symbolize the markers on the plate; yellow lines represent topographic measurements. Setup location was moved, from S1 to S2, according to megashaker position and orientation (fundamental for markers visibility); for first day, shaking tests were performed in the first three areas, whereas, the day after, the experiments were conducted in Area4. Since there was only one setup point and it necessarily was very close to the operation area, this schema had two main consequences: first, most of the surveying was iso-determined, as markers on the plate have not been surveyed in a redundant way; secondly, stability of the setup point over the time could not be assumed, as the terrain at the setup location, could have experienced a minor sink effect, due to shacking actions.

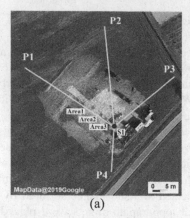

(a)   (b)

Fig. 3. Design of topographic measurements; the image shown is a merge: the large background image is from Google, while the central and detailed part is from our detailed orthophoto: (a) Day 1, October 22nd, 2018; (b) Day 2, October 23rd, 2018. (Color figure online)

To overcome this problem, four benchmarks were created, which are visible in Fig. 3, having names P1–P4. According to the judgement of the geotechnical engineers involved, they were created far enough from the shaking area in order not to perceive vibrations and therefore to be stable. They represented the reference frame of the measurements and were observed before each measurement cycle following the Bessel's rule (target points were observed twice, in the so-called direct and reverse position).

3.2   Terrestrial Laser Scanning Survey

Trimble SX10 is also a laser scanner, having a range accuracy of about 1.5 mm at a 50 m distance and is capable to acquire the remarkable amount of $2.7 \cdot 10^4$ points per second [32]. Several scans were performed in an integrated way with the topographic survey. When a cycle of topographic measurements was started, its orientation could also be used to perform one or more scans; this gave us the advantage of a perfect co-registration between the different measurements acquired.

At the Pieve di Cento site three types of scans were performed, which are listed in Table 1. Panoramic scans are 360° horizon tours acquired at a moderate resolution. They are useful to capture the whole context of the survey: point linear spacing is 40 cm at 200 m and completion time is around 12 min. High resolution scans are focused on the strict operation zone, where are the four test areas. Point spacing is 4.5 cm at a 50 m distance, being the maximum range achieved while it is much smaller in the parts closer to the instrument, down to 2 mm at 3 m. Presented figures clearly demonstrates that point clouds produced by laser scanning do not have a uniform density; acquiring the whole dig at high resolution took around 30 min, which was incompatible with the experiment's schedule. High resolution partial scans were also acquired, embracing only one of the test areas: point density is the same, while acquisition time was around 8 min.

Periodically acquired laser scans can be used to form the differences between them and thus to detect variations; this was done and is illustrated in the Sect. 4.

Table 1. Characteristics of performed scans.

Acronym	Explanation	Linear spacing of the point cloud	Time required
PANORAMIC	360° scan of the whole area	1 cm at 3 m; 40 cm at 200 m	12 min
HRES_WHOLE	High resolution scan of the whole dig area	2 mm at 3 m; 4.5 cm at 50 m	30 min
HRES_DETAIL	High resolution scan of one test area, out of four	Same as above	8 min

4 Results for Terrain Subsidence

Section will report only a selection of the obtained results even if topographic and laser surveys were conducted on all areas and for all the 12 performed shaking tests. Indeed, the focus of present paper is on methodology, rather than on systematic illustration of subsidence induced by the experiments. To carry out analysis and prepare the shown figures, specifically written Matlab scripts and functions were coded.

4.1 Area 3

Area3 is characterized by horizontal drains and was involved in the shaking tests #6 and #7, in late afternoon of October 22nd. Six targets, whose names range from 'a' to 'f', were placed on the megashaker plate and theirs positions were measured three times, when plates were placed on the ground and just after the two shaking tests (Fig. 2a). Table 2 shows the time series of the events concerned.

Table 2. Description of Area3 measurements temporal sequence.

# Area	Date	Time	Description
3	22nd October	16:52	Targets' measurement after plates were placed on the ground
		16:57	#6 shaking test
		17:05	Targets' measurement after the shaking
		17:11	#7 shaking test
		17:19	Targets' measurement after the shaking

For each measurement cycle, we determined the coordinates of markers a-f with respect to the same reference system. We then point-wise subtracted the coordinates determined at the 16:52 cycle from all the set of coordinates. Differences in x and y are negligible and are not reported here, where only the z component is illustrated, showing significant variations. Table 3 reports such differences: they are null for the 16:52 row by construction; for the other measurement cycles (17:05 and 17:19) differences highlight displacements. For the sake of clarity, point a, had a first downward shift of 11.4 cm, after test #6, and a further one of 7.7 cm, after test #7; the total displacement is then 19.1 cm.

Table 3. Vertical displacements in Area3 due to shaking tests #6 and #7.

Time	ΔZ [m]					
	a	b	c	d	e	f
16:52	0.000	0.000	0.000	0.000	0.000	0.000
16:57	#6 shaking test					
17:05	−0.114	−0.122	−0.133	−0.141	−0.139	−0.139
17:11	#7 shaking test					
17:19	−0.191	−0.212	−0.239	−0.259	−0.222	−0.224

Results obtained for the targets positioned in the lower part of the plate (from 'a' to 'd') and in the upper one ('e' and 'f') must be discussed separately (Fig. 2a) since the lower part can be considered integral to the ground as the plate is lying on it by gravity; the upper part is instead separated by a hydraulic system. In principle, the displacements measured for such targets cannot be directly attributed to the terrain. Problem is that, in some cases, there had been a very large subsidence of the land and the lower part of the device was totally buried, thus preventing us from taking any measurement. Observing the first four targets, the vertical displacement ranges between 19 to 26 cm showing a significant tilt of the plate; the last two targets show instead substantially equal values of about 22 cm.

Figure 4a and Fig. 4b give a graphical representation of vertical displacements as a function of time for the lower and upper parts of the plate, respectively. Dots represent the shift values obtained at each measurement epoch while the black vertical lines report the time of the two shaking events (#6 and #7). As no hypothesis can be done about the shifts of the targets between two measurements, dots were connected with horizontal dashed lines; they are dashed to underline their arbitrariness. Figure also shows the rotation suffered by the lower part of the plate; in the left part of the graphical, only one dot is visible because all the four markers considered have the same height, in the representation considered and explained before. In the central part four dots are visible because they no longer have the same height, meaning that their height variations have been odd; and, of course, they are all lower than the left dot, meaning that the plate has lowered on average. The same phenomenon, with even a major spread of the dots and inclination of the plate, happens in the right part. As previously observed, markers placed in the upper part of the shaking device, named 'e' and 'f', behave in a different way and remain almost horizontal.

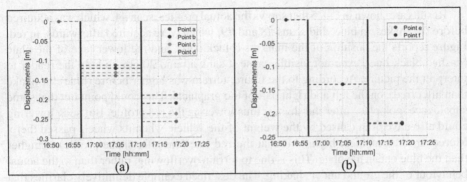

Fig. 4. Vertical displacements, for Area3, as a function of time; (a) Results for the four lower targets; (b) Results for the two upper ones. Black vertical lines represent the shaking events. (Color figure online)

The subsidence suffered by the terrain was also investigated by laser data: in principle, by comparing a point cloud acquired after a shake and another one surveyed before, the effects of the simulated earthquake should be delineated. Unfortunately, for the quite long time needed for acquisition, laser scans are not as dense in time as topographic surveys. Therefore, it is not guaranteed that there is a point cloud acquired just before one shaking event and another one surveyed just after. Nevertheless, for Area 3 it was possible to find a scan performed at the beginning of the day and another one acquired after shaking test #7. Indeed, the latter was acquired in two steps, due to the presence of people near the megashaker, which obliged us to stop acquisition and to start a new one, after the area was cleared, to survey the missing part. Table 4 shows time series of the events involved.

Table 4. Time series of laser scans and shaking events for Area3.

# Area	Date	Time	Description
3	22ⁿᵈ October	09:10	scan#4 - HRES_WHOLE
		16:57	#6 shaking test
		17:11	#7 shaking test
		17:21	scan#8 and scan #9 - Area3 HRES_DETAIL

To simplify the analysis, a significant profile was considered. A neighbourhood was generated for each point cloud; it is defined by the plane passing through the external and vertical face of the megashaker plate and has a depth of 15 cm forward and backward. All the points belonging to the neighbourhood were orthogonally projected onto the generating plane.

Results are shown in Fig. 5 that shows the actual profiles: scan #4, which was acquired before the shakes, in blue, and scans #8 and #9, which were acquired afterwards, in red. Figure reports the position of the markers (black dots), and the lower face of the plate (dashed black line), even not visible cause it sank around 20 cm, to help the reader to interpret the picture. According to the figure, terrain was higher before (blue) the shake than after (red), on the left and right part of the graphical. This could point out that some subsidence took place after the shakes, thus lowering the red profile. But such lowering could also have been caused by the weight of the vehicle when its wheels passed there. Moreover, the graphical highlights that the red line (the after-shake profile) is higher than the blue one in the plate. This is due to terrain overflowing, rather than to the actual behaviour of the ground under shaking. The described example definitively clarifies that point clouds were not a good source for this study (Fig. 5).

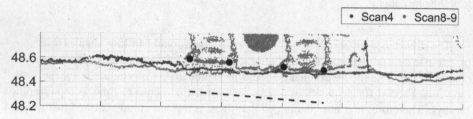

Fig. 5. Comparison between point clouds acquired by terrestrial laser scanning for Area4.

4.2 Area4

Area4 is characterized by the IPS mitigation technique and was involved in several tests. The present section only focuses on tests #8 and #9 performed in the late morning of 23rd October. The second day, seven targets were applied to the vehicle: five in the lower part, named a-e, and two in the upper part, named f-g. Differently from Area3, some time has passed after the plates were laid on the terrain and before the shakes, to leave the terrain, dissipate internal strains (Table 5); this gave us the opportunity to perform two measurement cycles before the shakes. Data processing was carried out in the same way of Area 3; tables and graphical shown can be interpreted exactly in the same way.

Table 6 shows the displacements observed in Area4 due to the two shaking tests. Taking point 'a' as an example, the marker has subsided 0.7 cm during the dissipation phase, 13.3 cm after test #8, and another 6.5 cm, after test #8; the total displacement is then 20.5 cm. The first five targets, which are integral to the ground, have a vertical displacement ranging between 18 to 20 cm; the other two targets show instead substantially equal values of about 14 cm. Figure 6a and Fig. 6b give the graphical representation of vertical displacements as a function of time for the lower and the upper parts of the plate, respectively. Dots represent the shift values obtained at each measurement epoch while the black vertical lines report the two shaking events (#8 and #9). The first two measurements relate to continuous line suggesting a linear-in-time displacement between them, while across the shaking events, the connections are represented by horizontal dashed lines. Figure once again shows the rotation suffered by the lower part of the plate while the upper part remains substantially horizontal.

Table 5. Description of Area4 measurements temporal sequence.

# Area	Date	Time	Description
4	23rd October	12:19	Targets measurement after plates were placed on the ground
		12:32	Targets measurements after the dissipation of terrain strains
		12:40	#8 shaking test
		12:47	Targets measurement after the shaking
		13:08	#9 shaking test
		13:16	Targets measurement after the shaking

Table 6. Vertical displacements in Area4 due to shaking tests #8 and #9.

Time	ΔZ [m]						
	a	b	c	d	e	f	g
12:19	0.000	0.000	0.000	0.000	0.000	0.000	0.000
12:32	−0.007	−0.004	−0.004	−0.004	−0.003	−0.002	−0.002
12:40	#8 shaking test						
12:47	−0.140	−0.136	−0.132	−0.126	−0.122	−0.075	−0.072
13:08	#9 shaking test						
13:16	−0.205	−0.199	−0.196	−0.183	−0.177	−0.143	−0.141

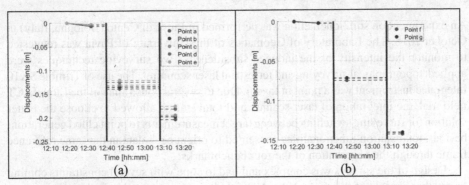

Fig. 6. Vertical displacements, for Area4, as a function of time; (a) Results for the five lower targets; (b) Results for the two upper ones. Black vertical lines represent the shaking events.

Table 7. Time series of laser scans and shaking events for Area4.

# Area	Date	Time	Description
4	23rd October	08.32	scan#12 - HRES_WHOLE
		12:40	#8 shaking test
		13:08	#9 shaking test
		13:13	scan#18 - Area4 HRES_DETAIL

For Area4 it was possible, once again, to find two laser scans acquired before and after scans #8 and #9: they are listed in Table 7. They were processed in the same way described before and Fig. 7 was produced. Once again, the post-shake profile, shown in red, is at the same level of the blue profile or higher, as it seems to be in the area of the plate. As the plate significantly sinks, the surrounding terrain overflows: this might be interesting for geotechnics studies in general, but not to quantify the amount of the land subsidence (Fig. 7).

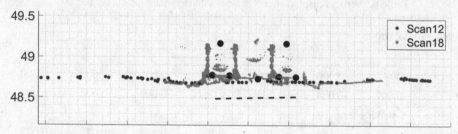

Fig. 7. Comparison between point clouds acquired by terrestrial laser scanning for Area4.

5   Conclusion and Further Activities

An experiment on soil liquefaction was performed in Pieve di Cento (Bologna, Italy) in October 2018. The Laboratory of Geomatics of the University of Pavia was requested to monitor the intensity of the induced subsidence. Two surveying techniques were applied: topographical surveying and terrestrial laser scanning. The use of Trimble SX10 integrated instrument was a point in favour. Due to several constraints of the LiquefACT field trial, the integration of laser scanner and total station allowed to choose the better solution for surveying switching between target measurements to point cluod generation; besides, total station functionalities consented to orient each data in the same reference frame through the observation of the four benchmarks.

Design of the surveys was complex and had to cope with several constraints coming from other aspects of the experiment. Nevertheless, it was possible to design a surveying schema which is sufficiently controlled and produced very precise measurements. We have been able to quantify sinking of the megashaker plate at each epoch of the experiment and before and after each shake.

Geomatics proved to be very flexible and capable to adapt to varied scenarios and, at the same time, rigorous and highly precise. Trimble SX10 follows a modern concept of integrated topographical instrument and proved to be precise and adaptable; it seems particularly suited for monitoring applications.

The described project highlights that, to produce the expected results in demanding situations, the tools available to Geomatics must be used in appropriate and sometimes unconventional ways: to properly do so, a deep knowledge of the discipline and of its background is required. This seems in contrast with the ease of use of current instruments: it is easy to setup them and to take measurements on the field.

What is missing? Explicit evaluation of the accuracy of coordinates of plate's markers. This is due to a fundamental lack: we could not survey detail points from two setup positions, due to the constrains of the site. It will not be possible to fully overcome this limitation, but something can probably be done. We will introduce in the adjustment distance constraints, as it is reasonable to suppose that the distance between markers remained unchanged all along the day. This should allow us to come out with not only coordinates of markers, but also their precision.

Acknowledgements. Trimble-Italy is acknowledged here for lending us the SX10 instrument. This research has been carried out within the framework of the European LIQUEFACT project. The LIQUEFACT project has received funding from the European Union's Horizon 2020 Research and Innovation Programme under Grant Agreement No. 700748. This support is gratefully acknowledged by the authors.

References

1. Gomarasca, M.A.: Geomatics. In: Gomarasca, M.A. (ed.) Basics of Geomatics. pp. 1–17. Springer, Netherlands (2009). https://link.springer.com/article/10.1007/s12518-010-0029-6
2. Chiabrando, F., Donadio, E., Rinaudo, F.: SfM for orthophoto generation: A winning approach for cultural heritage knowledge. Int. Arch. Photogramm. Remote Sens. Spatial Inf. Sci. **XL-5/W7**, 91–98 (2015). http://dx.doi.org/10.5194/isprsarchives-XL-5-W7-91-2015
3. Xiao, W., Mills, J., Guidi, G., Rodríguez-Gonzálvez, P., Gonizzi Barsanti, S., González-Aguilera, D.: Geoinformatics for the conservation and promotion of cultural heritage in support of the UN sustainable development goals. ISPRS J. Photogramm. Remote Sens. **142**, 389–406 (2018). https://doi.org/10.1016/j.isprsjprs.2018.01.001
4. Holmberg, S.C.: Geoinformatics for urban and regional planning. Environ. Plan. B Plan. Des. **21**, 5–19 (1994). https://doi.org/10.1068/b210005
5. Bhatta, B.: Modelling of urban growth boundary using geoinformatics. Int. J. Digit. Earth. **2**, 359–381 (2009). https://doi.org/10.1080/17538940902971383
6. De Lotto, R., et al.: Estimating the biotope area factor (BAF) by means of existing digital maps and GIS technology. In: Gervasi, O., et al. (eds.) Computational Science and Its Applications -- ICCSA 2015. ICCSA 2015. Lecture Notes in Computer Science, vol. 9157, pp. 617–632. Springer, Cham (2015). https://doi.org/10.1007/978-3-319-21470-2_45
7. Casella, V., Franzini, M., Padova, B., Lingesso, L., Pappani, G., Gentili, G.: Leica ADS40 imagery for disaster management. Ital. J. Remote Sens. Riv. Ital. di Telerilevamento. **43**, 129–135 (2011). https://doi.org/10.5721/ItJRS201143210

8. Giordan, D., Manconi, A., Remondino, F., Nex, F.: Use of unmanned aerial vehicles in monitoring application and management of natural hazards. Geomatics Nat. Hazards Risk **8**(1), 1–4 (2017). https://www.tandfonline.com/action/journalInformation?journalCode=tgnh20

9. Gonzalez-Aguilera, D., Gomez-Lahoz, J.: Forensic terrestrial photogrammetry from a single image. J. Forensic Sci. **54**, 1376–1387 (2009). https://doi.org/10.1111/j.1556-4029.2009.01170.x

10. Pringle, J.K., et al.: The use of geoscience methods for terrestrial forensic searches. Earth-Sci. Rev. **114**(1-2), 108–123 (2012)

11. Cosser, E., Roberts, G.W., Meng, X., Dodson, A.H.: Measuring the dynamic deformation of bridges using a total station. In: Proceedings of 11th FIG symposium on deformation monitoring (2003)

12. Radovanovic, R.S., Teskey, W.F.: Dynamic monitoring of deforming structures : GPS versus robotic tacheometry systems. In: Proceeding the10th FIG International Symposium on Deformation Measurements, pp. 61–70 (2001)

13. Palazzo, D.R., et al.: Dynamic monitoring of structures using a robotic total station. In: Proceedings of the Shaping the Change XXIII FIG Congress (2006)

14. Woźniak, M.: Investigation of using total station with ATR system in monitoring of displacements. Reports Geod. z. **1**(76), 221–226 (2006)

15. Afeni, T.B., Cawood, F.T.: Slope monitoring using total station: what are the challenges and how should these be mitigated? South Afr. J. Geomatics. **2**, 41–53 (2013)

16. Lienhart, W., Ehrhart, M., Grick, M.: High frequent total station measurements for the monitoring of bridge vibrations. J. Appl. Geod. **11**, 1–8 (2017). https://doi.org/10.1515/jag-2016-0028

17. Berberan, A., Machado, M., Batista, S.: Automatic multi total station monitoring of a tunnel. Surv. Rev. **39**, 203–211 (2007). https://doi.org/10.1179/003962607X165177

18. Lutes, J.A.: Automated Dam Displacement Monitoring Using a Robotic Total Station. Engineering (2002)

19. Jaafar, H.A.: Detection and localisation of structural deformations using terrestrial laser scanning and generalised procrustes analysis (2017)

20. Alba, M., Fregonese, L., Prandi, F., Scaioni, M., Valgoi, P.: Structural monitoring of a large dam by terrestrial laser scanning. Int. Arch. Photogramm. Remote Sens. Spat. Inf. Sci. **36**, 6 (2006)

21. Prokop, A., Panholzer, H.: Assessing the capability of terrestrial laser scanning for monitoring slow moving landslides. Nat. Hazards Earth Syst. Sci. **9**, 1921–1928 (2009). https://doi.org/10.5194/nhess-9-1921-2009

22. Giussani, A., Scaioni, M.: Application of TLS to support landslides study: survey planning, operational issues and data processing. Int. Arch. Photogramm. Remote Sens. Spat. Inf. **36**, 318–323 (2004)

23. Travelletti, J., Oppikofer, T., Delacourt, C., Malet, J.-P., Jaboyedoff, M.: Monitoring landslide displacements during a controlled rain experiment using a long-range terrestrial laser scanning (TLS). In: International Archives of the Photogrammetry, Remote Sensing and Spatial Information Sciences - ISPRS Archives (2008)

24. Fischer, M., Huss, M., Kummert, M., Hoelzle, M.: Application and validation of long-range terrestrial laser scanning to monitor the mass balance of very small glaciers in the Swiss Alps. Cryosphere. **10**, 1279–1295 (2016). https://doi.org/10.5194/tc-10-1279-2016

25. Erdélyi, J., Kopáčik, A., Lipták, I., Kyrinovič, P.: Pedestrian bridge monitoring using terrestrial laser scanning. In: Advances and Trends in Engineering Sciences and Technologies - Proceedings of the International Conference on Engineering Sciences and Technologies, ESaT 2015, pp. 51–56 (2016)

26. Lõhmus, H., Ellmann, A., Märdla, S., Idnurm, S.: Terrestrial laser scanning for the monitoring of bridge load tests–two case studies. Surv. Rev. **50**, 270–284 (2018). https://doi.org/10.1080/00396265.2016.1266117

27. Gawronek, P., Makuch, M.: TLS measurement during static load testing of a railway bridge. ISPRS Int. J. Geo-Inf. **8**, 44 (2019). https://doi.org/10.3390/ijgi8010044

28. González-Aguilera, D., Gómez-Lahoz, J., Sánchez, J.: A new approach for structural monitoring of large dams with a three-dimensional laser scanner. Sensors **8**, 5866–5883 (2008). https://doi.org/10.3390/s8095866

29. Kalkan, Y.: Geodetic deformation monitoring of Ataturk dam in Turkey. Arab. J. Geosci. **7**(1), 397–405 (2012). https://doi.org/10.1007/s12517-012-0765-5

30. Medjkane, M., et al.: High-resolution monitoring of complex coastal morphology changes: cross-efficiency of SfM and TLS-based survey (Vaches-Noires cliffs, Normandy, France). Landslides **15**(6), 1097–1108 (2018). https://doi.org/10.1007/s10346-017-0942-4

31. Mill, T.: Simulation of terrestrial laser scanning errors occurring during deformation monitoring. In: 3rd Joint International Symposium on Deformation Monitoring (JISDM) (2016)

32. Trimbe SX10 Datasheet. https://geospatial.trimble.com/sites/geospatial.trimble.com/files/2019-10/Datasheet-SX10ScanningTotalStation-EnglishUSL-Screen.pdf

33. Lachat, E., Landes, T., Grussenmeyer, P.: Investigation of a combined surveying and scanning device: the trimble SX10 scanning total station. Sensors (Switzerland). **17**, 730 (2017). https://doi.org/10.3390/s17040730

Geomatics for Cultural Heritage and Natural Resources

The Early Cartography of Petroleum Resources in Italy (1866–1926)

Paolo Macini[1]([⊠]) [iD], Fabiana Console[2] [iD], and Marco Pantaloni[2] [iD]

[1] University of Bologna, Via U. Terracini 28, 40131 Bologna, Italy
paolo.macini@unibo.it
[2] ISPRA, Via V. Brancati 48, 00144 Rome, Italy

Abstract. The paper outlines the birth and development of petroleum resources mapping in Italy. Starting with the pioneering works of Antonio Stoppani, who in 1866 published the first map of petroleum zones of the Emilia region, thematic cartography went hand in hand with the preparation of the geological map of Italy, a project promoted by the government as early as 1861. Soon after the Italian unification, petroleum exploration kicked off in many areas of the country and generated the elaboration of technical and statistical reports carried out by the *Corpo Reale delle Miniere* (royal corps of mines) and the *Regio Ufficio Geologico* (royal geological survey), which began to rationalize the cartography of petroleum resources in 1891. The time limit of this study is set at 1926, coinciding with the unification of the mining laws and the foundation of AGIP, the Italian state-owned oil company in charge of the management of this strategic industrial sector for the years to come.

Keywords: Historical cartography · Petroleum resources · Geological mapping

1 Introduction

In 1815 William Smith published *A delineation of the strata of England and Wales, with part of Scotland* [1], to reproduce the sequence and extent of the rocky bodies in the British area, highlighting the coal resources which became the economic engine of the country. This milestone raised geology to the highest step of the podium among the applied sciences, which transformed the western world from peasant to industrial, contributing to one of the greatest changes in human history. In fact, the large availability of low-cost energy is the factor that best describes the complex dynamic of changes that shaped the world in the past 200 years.

Although the modern petroleum industry was born in the mid-1800s, oily substances and natural gas oozing from the ground attracted the attention of scientific investigators since ancient times. After 1859, following the successful discovery of Edwin Laurentine Drake, frenetic activity of production, refining and export of petroleum products developed in North America: the "oil rush", which can be considered the first example of commercial globalization. In a few years, numerous companies dealing with oil and gas exploration actively operated in Italy, also nourished by the long national historical

© Springer Nature Switzerland AG 2022
E. Borgogno-Mondino and P. Zamperlin (Eds.): ASITA 2021, CCIS 1507, pp. 151–162, 2022.
https://doi.org/10.1007/978-3-030-94426-1_12

and scientific memory, as well as by the centuries-old handcraft practices of collecting and selling the *olio di sasso* (rock oil). This activity was originally centered in the Emilia region (provinces of Piacenza, Parma and Modena), and extended to Abruzzi (Pescara Valley, between Tocco da Casauria and Lettomanoppello), Lazio (former region of Terra di Lavoro, between Ripi and San Giovanni Incarico) and Sicily [2–5].

Soon after the Italian Unification (1861), the exploration of domestic petroleum resources supported efforts and enthusiasm to promote a modern and efficient national industrial development, based on the models of Northern European countries. Today we know that the scientific and industrial progress of the second half of the 19th century has fully unfolded thanks to the development of new metallurgical processes (iron, cast iron and steel), based on the availability of abundant and low-cost energy sources (coal and steam). However, we also know that Italy was a country poor in minerals, iron ores, and even more so in coal and technology.

Throughout the 19th century, and still today, the endemic shortage of domestic energy sources marked the main developments of the Italian heavy industry, almost entirely dependent on coal and oil imports from abroad. Thus, after 1860, the advent of new fuels on the market attracted the attention of Italian prospectors, geologists and mining engineers.

2   The Geological Map of Italy

For the Italian Government, the need to improve and rationalize the knowledge of the territory of the newly enlarged Kingdom, including underground resources, was very clear. Therefore, soon after the unification, the mining sector was immediately reorganized. In the Sardinian Kingdom, Carlo Felice had established the *Corpo Reale delle Miniere* (royal corps of mines) in 1822. With the Royal Decree of 22 August 1848, the corps shifted from the control of the Ministry of the Interior to that of the Ministry of Agriculture. After the annexation of Lombardy to the Kingdom of Sardinia, Italian Law n° 3755 issued on 20 November 1859 reshaped the corps. Subsequently, the Royal Decree of 7 May 1860 entrusted the mining services to the Ministry of Agriculture, Industry and Trade, and organized the offices in eight regional districts. The creation of a centralized bureaucracy took place gradually, slowly reshaping the inhomogeneous mining legislation and technical bodies already present in the Pre-Unitarian States.

These years marked the transition from speculative geology to "geology at the service of industry". Having identified the prerogatives offered by the geological knowledge of the territory, the most advanced European countries implemented their administrative bodies with technical structures with the task of studying, creating and updating the basic geological cartography. The first national "geological services" were established in Great Britain, France and Austria. In this context, even in Italy, the importance of mapping was conceived as an activity no longer merely obedient to military purposes, but as an essential tool for administrative and cadastral purposes, as well as an instrument for economic development promotion. Already in 1861 Quintino Sella, Minister of Finance and he himself a mining engineer, supported and encouraged by Antonio Stoppani and Felice Giordano [6, 7], promoted the constitution of a National Committee in charge of "discussing the methods and establishing the rules for the formation of the geological map of the Kingdom of Italy" (Royal Decree n° 139 of 28 July 1861). Royal Decree n° 408-*octies* was issued a few months later, on 12 December 1861, and "ordered the formation of a geological map of the Kingdom of Italy".

In addition to the launch of this ambitious cartographic project, the creation of a more homogeneous corps of mines was also discussed, with the purpose to collect the experiences of: the *ingegneri di miniera* of the Kingdom of Sardinia; the *commissarii montanistici* of the Lombardo-Venetian Kingdom; the Tuscan *consultori di miniera*; and the Sicilian *ispettori di solfare e calchere*, all local terms indicating mining engineers and mining officials responsible for safety and administration.

However, the *Reale Comitato Geologico* (royal geological committee) was established in 1867, and began the publication of its Bulletin in 1870. The Geological Section of the corps of mines was established in 1873, and later became the *Regio Ufficio Geologico* (royal geological survey), with the task of creating and publishing the geological map of Italy. Its operative activity was entrusted to the personnel of the corps of mines under the technical and disciplinary control of the Chief Inspector of the corps and the scientific direction of the royal geological committee. The systematic field survey, however, only started in 1877, also thanks to the availability of the new topographic maps of the Italian Military Geographical Institute and the achievement of a high degree of technical-scientific training and specialization of the staff of geologists and engineers at the royal geological survey [8–11].

The geological map of Italy remained closely intertwined with the mining services, according to organizational contiguity between the mining and geological institutions that characterized the sector of natural resources until recently, in 1987, when the geological survey moved from the control of the Ministry of Industry to that of the Ministry of the Environment.

3 The Early Italian Petroleum Resource Mapping

Antonio Stoppani, one of the founders of Italian geology, clearly stated that all geological expertise had to be aimed at the benefit of industry, creating a mutual enrichment for the well-being of the Country and the advancement of science and technology. "We would thus have an application of geology to industry that is no less important, and perhaps more relevant to Italy, than those concerning fossil fuels, which every information gathered so far attests we are short" [12] (Authors' translation).

Undoubtedly, Stoppani was the first Italian scholar to take an interest in petroleum geology from a national perspective, and he wrote a long dissertation dealing with the nature, distribution and origin of crude oil and natural gas [12]. His work is not only limited to the analysis of the promising Italian petroleum potential, but the author also broadened his view worldwide, with a keen eye on the recently discovered oilfields of the Russian Empire, Canada, and the United States of America. Stoppani developed avant-garde geological insights for his time, demonstrating an in-depth knowledge of recent American technical literature, in particular the studies of Thomas Sterry Hunt [13], which paved the way for the development of the tectonics of anticlines.

In addition to the above dissertation [12], Stoppani also dealt with petroleum sciences in a number of articles published in the Italian Journal *Il Politecnico* [14]. Here, he described the Italian oil fields, resulting from personal visits and surveys made between 1864 and 1866 (Abruzzi, Piacenza area, Parma area, Reggio Emilia area, Modena area, Bologna area, Imola area, and Sicily, the latter not visited personally). The map annexed to the article *Il petrolio nel Piacentino* (petroleum in the Piacenza area), a small-scale map entitled *Carta della zona petroleifera dell'Emilia* (map of the petroleum zones in the Emilia region, Fig. 1), is of particular interest. It represents the Northern Apennine ridge from Bobbio to Faenza. This was the first regional thematic map concerning the distribution of the Italian petroleum resources known at that time.

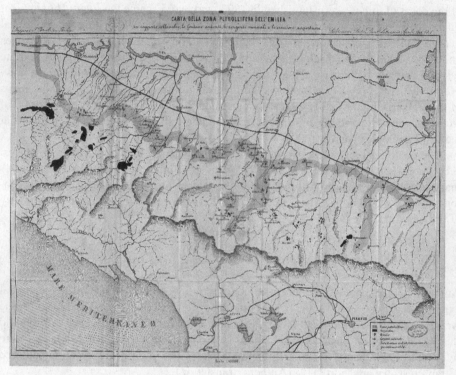

Fig. 1. Map of the petroleum zones in the Emilia region (1866), on a scale of 1:400,000. Gray shaded areas indicate the petroleum zones; dark black spots show the principal outcrops of ophiolitic rocks. The map locates oil springs, active oil wells, mineral springs, mud volcanoes, and gas seepages [14].

This map is not a true geological map (although it shows the main outcrops of ophiolitic rocks, indeed very detailed especially in the Western part of the area), but rather it is conceived for the petroleum zoning of the territory. The map is the result of an independent elaboration, and it does not fit into the project of the geological map of Italy, due to its topographical base, probably a railway map.

In the same years, Emilio Stöhr, Massimiliano Calegari, and Giovanni Canestrini studied the oil springs and the mud volcanoes of Modena, making observations and field surveys [15]. In particular, Stöhr carried out technical and mining studies, and in 1867 elaborated a map of the petroleum zones of Montegibbio (Fig. 2), in the Apennine foothills of Modena [16].

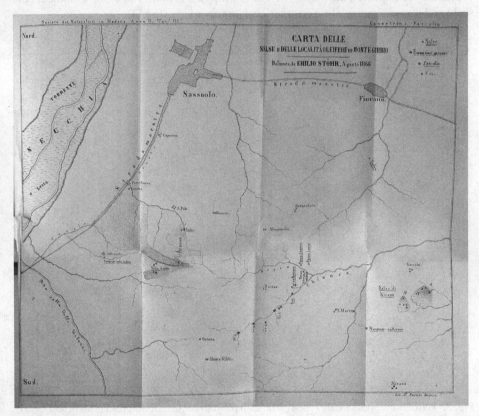

Fig. 2. Map of the petroleum zones of Montegibbio (1867), on a scale of 1:14,400. It reports mud volcanoes, salt water with gas springs, oil wells, and mineral water springs [16].

The topographical base map relies on the triangulation sheets on a scale of 1:14,400 of the *Kriegskarte*, the war map surveyed by the Austrian Ministry of Defense General Staff of the former Duchy of Modena. The author states that "the map serves as a basis for a geological map, which I have already begun, of the surroundings of Montegibbio" [16], which unfortunately has not been recovered so far.

In 1868 Edward Fairman published *A treatise on the petroleum zones of Italy* [17]. The volume collects observations, comments and auspices on the newborn petroleum industry. Fairman was well informed about the developments of the oil industry in North America, which had not yet turned 10 years from Drake's discovery, and his treatise was aimed at inspiring the interest of investors in this industrial sector. Fairman himself purchased plots of land encompassing petroleum seepages in the Modena area, and attempted some exploratory activity. The work is written in a modern and accurate language, in terms of both style and terminology, and contrasts with the studies of the Italian scholars of the time, still tied to an academic language and a stylistic inspiration that recalls 18th century literary prose. The volume contains a map of the "Petroleum zones of Italy", indeed circumscribed to the Emilia region only. The publishing house copied and re-engraved the map from that of Stoppani (1866), forgetting to indicate the scale and introducing spelling errors in certain toponyms (Fig. 3).

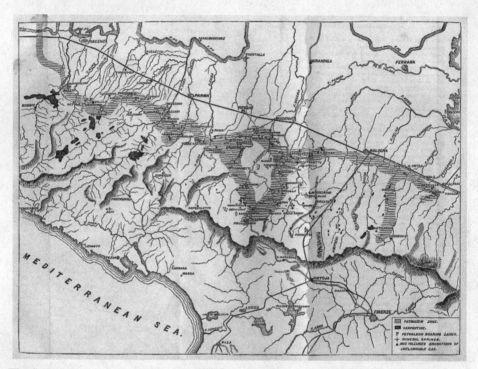

Fig. 3. Petroleum zones of Italy (1868). The map plagiarizes that of Stoppani (1866), and clearly shows the same petroleum zones; the scale of the map is not reported [17].

4 The Official Cartography of the Corps of Mines and the Royal Geological Survey

In 1891 the corps of mines published a general report entitled *Notizie sulla produzione di petrolio in Italia* (news on oil production in Italy) and a list of oil wells and oil fields which illustrates the developments of the works carried out in the various concessions during the previous 25 years [18]. The report contains a large-format folded map, showing the location of oil wells, petroleum processing plants, and boundaries of the petroleum concessions in force in the Emilia region (Fig. 4).

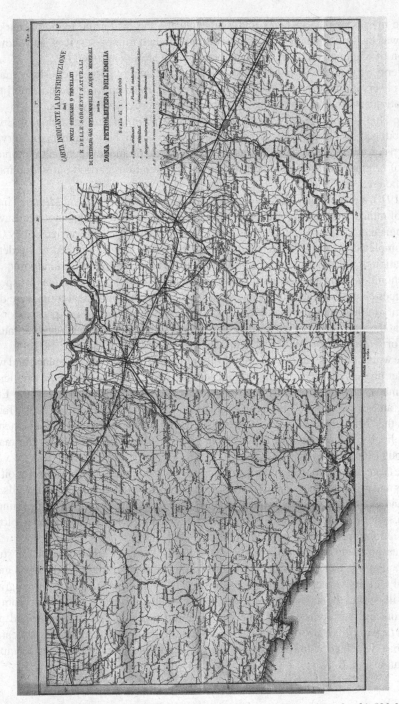

Fig. 4. Map of oil wells and oil, gas, and mineral water springs (1891), on a scale of 1:500,000. The map also locates both the petroleum processing plants and the boundaries of petroleum concession areas in force in the Emilia region [18].

The map is printed in black and white, but the targets on the map are marked in red. It was the first thematic map prepared by the Italian mining services, and shows the location of 65 items, numbered and analyzed in the aforementioned list.

Twenty years later, in 1911, the royal geological survey published a study that collected observations, original geological interpretations and information related to the exploration activities in Emilia that took place in the previous fifty years.

The study, entitled *I giacimenti petroleiferi dell'Emilia* (the oil fields of Emilia), was produced by Enrico Camerana and Bartolomeo Galdi, both engineers in service at the corps of mines in Bologna. It was the first systematic monograph on this topic, the result of original field surveys and geological interpretations carried out with a modern scientific method [19].

In 1910, a preliminary study was presented to the *Ispettorato delle Miniere* (inspectorate of mines) in Rome. However, as the royal geological survey had not yet drawn up a geological map of the Emilia region, new "tectonic" surveys were carried out by Galdi, who completed the final version of the study. His work was also aimed at the detailed localization of petroleum seepages, also from a detailed cartographic standpoint.

It should be remembered that in those years there were no geophysical prospecting techniques capable of identifying hydrocarbon deposits. Geophysical tools were developed only in the following two decades, and therefore the attention of prospectors was aimed at the study of outcrops, morphology of geological formations, regional faulting, unconformities, etc., possibly scaled up close to oil and gas seepages.

The work contains 127 figures, numerous tables and 16 large maps in black and white, the latter properly folded and bound in a separate atlas that completes the publication. These maps, drawn up on different scales, describe the major oil fields of the Emilia region, and are completed by geological cross-sections. In the above atlas, Table 1 depicts the "Map of the oil fields of Emilia, showing the main tectonic lines", extending longitudinally from Faenza to Bobbio (Fig. 5), the same area covered by the map by Stoppani (1866, Fig. 1).

The targets on the map include: mining concessions (namely, concessions for oil, natural gas and mineral waters), petroleum seepages, oil wells and clusters of oil wells, saltwater and gas springs, mineral water springs (sulphurous waters containing bromine and iodine), synclines and anticlines. Many other large-scale geological maps and geological cross-sections are included directly in the text [19].

After the tragic and catastrophic years of World War I, the Italian petroleum studies were soon reorganized: by then, the strategic importance of crude oil and natural gas for national security was clear. A volume published in 1926, consisting of 13 monographic papers, illustrates the state-of-the-art of geologic studies carried out in the most promising Italian oil and gas areas [20]. Camerana prepared a robust and well informed paper entitled *Le manifestazioni di idrocarburi nell'Emilia* (the manifestations of hydrocarbons in Emilia), which contains an accurate map bound in the separate atlas that completes the volume (Fig. 6).

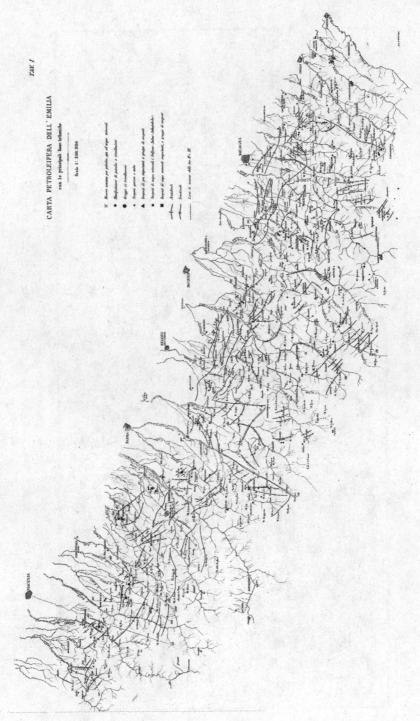

Fig. 5. Map of the oil fields of Emilia (1911), on a scale of 1:200,000 [19].

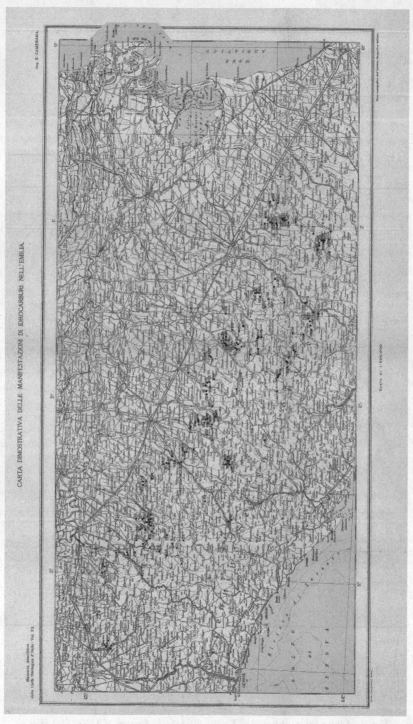

Fig. 6. Map of the hydrocarbon manifestations of Emilia (1926), on a scale of 1:500,000 [20].

The map as in Fig. 6 locates 213 sites, a very high number, which testifies to intense petroleum exploration activity carried out in Italy in the early 1900s. However, the number of productive wells in Emilia was much larger: in the *Velleja* "mine" (i.e., the petroleum concession area) there were about 300 wells, while in the *Montechino* mine there were almost 200, some of them drilled to more than 1000 m deep.

In the meantime, the Inspectorate of Mines promoted the creation of the *Carta mineraria d'Italia* (mining map of Italy) [21], on a scale of 1:500,000. As far as the oil fields of the Emilia region are concerned, the map illustrating the Mining District of Bologna (in charge of the Emilia area), dated 25 March 1927, shows in less detail the information already contained in the above-reported map as in Fig. 6 (1926).

5 Conclusions

In 1866 Antonio Stoppani published a map of the petroleum zones of the Emilia region, marking the beginning of petroleum resource cartography in Italy. Soon after the Italian unification, petroleum exploration kicked off in many areas of the Country. This generated the elaboration of technical and statistical reports, although the rationalization of official mapping of petroleum resources only began in 1891. In this context, early petroleum resource mapping concerned only the most productive and developed oilfields – i.e., the Apenninic areas of some provinces of the Emilia region, carefully studied, surveyed and mapped by Camerana and Galdi in 1911.

After World War I, the studies of geologists and engineers of the corps of mines and of the royal geological survey continued rapidly, and in 1926 a systematic study on domestic petroleum resources was published, which updated the knowledge of the territory from the standpoint of both topographical mapping and geological cartography. As for of the other small petroleum areas known until 1930s and located outside the Emilia region (Lazio and Abruzzi, with discontinuous and negligible production), no official cartography was ever published.

The time limit for this study was set at 1926, coinciding with the unitization of mining laws, mining rights and underground ownership, together with the foundation of AGIP (*Agenzia Generale Italiana Petroli*, the Italian state-owned oil company). In particular, this latter act marked the takeover and control of the Mussolini government in the strategic activities concerning petroleum resources. In the following years, the Italian oil industry and the related geological studies shifted almost entirely into the hands of AGIP (also as an instrument of political propaganda which peaked in the autarchy era), the national company in charge of managing this strategic industrial sector, in Italy and abroad, for the years to come.

References

1. Smith, W.: A Delineation of the Strata of England and Wales, with Part of Scotland. John Cary, London (1815)
2. Yergin, D.: The Prize: The Epic Quest for Oil, Money, and Power. Simon & Schuster, New York (1990)

3. Macini, P., Mesini, E., Gerali, F.: Historical study on geosciences and engineering in the oil fields of Emilia Romagna region in the socio-economic context of the post-Unitarian Italy (1861–1914). In: Craig, J., Gerali, F., MacAulay, F., Sorkhabi, R. (eds.), History of the European Oil and Gas Industry, Geological Society of London, Special Publications 465, pp. 305–332, London (2018). https://doi.org/10.1144/SP465.21
4. Brighenti, G., Macini, P.: History of the Upstream Industry. Encyclopedia of Hydrocarbons, Istituto della Enciclopedia Italiana Treccani, vol. 5, pp. 525–548, Rome (2008)
5. Novelli, L., Sella, M.: Il petrolio, una storia antica. Silvana Editoriale, Cinisello Balsamo (2009)
6. De Stefani, C.: Osservazioni sulla Carta Geologica d'Italia pubblicata in occasione del Congresso di Bologna. Bollettino Società Geologica Italiana 1, 165–182 (1882)
7. Pantaloni, M.: La carta geologica d'Italia alla scala di 1:1.000.000: una pietra miliare nel percorso della conoscenza geologica. Geologia Tecnica e Ambientale 2–3, 88–99 (2011)
8. Baldacci, L.: La Carta geologica d'Italia. Bollettino Regio Comitato Geologico d'Italia 42(2), 99–169 (1911)
9. Giarratana, A.: La Carta geologica d'Italia. Rivista italiana del petrolio e delle altre fonti di energia 1, 8–10 (1965)
10. Pantaloni, M., Galluzzo, F., Marino, M.: Gli aspetti scientifici della Carta geologica d'Italia alla scala 1:100.000. Memorie descrittive della carta geologica d'Italia 100, 106–121 (2016)
11. Pantaloni, M.: La carta geologica d'Italia alla scala di 1:1.000.000 dal 1881 al 2011. Memorie descrittive della carta geologica d'Italia 100, 74–78 (2016)
12. Stoppani, A.: Saggio di una storia naturale dei petrolii. Il Politecnico 23(100–101), 5–94 (1864)
13. Sterry Hunt, T.: Notes on the history of petroleum or rock oil. Annual Report of the Board of Regents of the Smithsonian Institution, showing the operations, expenditures, and condition of the Institution for the year 1861, House of Representatives, Miscellaneous Document 77, 37th Congress, 2nd Session, Washington D.C., pp. 319–329 (1862)
14. Stoppani, A.: I petrolii in Italia. Il Politecnico I (1866)
15. Calegari, M., Canestrini, G.: Storia della salsa di sopra presso Sassuolo, della sorgente della Salvarola e dei pozzi oleiferi di Montegibio. Annuario della Società dei Naturalisti in Modena 2, 147–168 (1867)
16. Stöhr, E.: Schiarimenti intorno alla carta delle salse e delle località oleifere di Monte Gibio. Annuario della Società dei Naturalisti in Modena 2, 169–178 (1867)
17. Fairman, E.: A Treatise on the Petroleum Zones of Italy. E. & F.N. Spon, London (1868)
18. Ministero Agricoltura, Industria e Commercio: Annali di Agricoltura 1891. Rivista del Servizio Minerario nel 1890, Barbera, Firenze (1891)
19. Camerana, E., Galdi, B.: I giacimenti petroleiferi dell'Emilia. Memorie descrittive della carta geologica d'Italia 14, Stabilimento Poligrafico Emiliano, Bologna (1911)
20. Regio Ufficio Geologico: Studi geologici per la ricerca del petrolio in Italia, con Atlante. Memorie descrittive della Carta Geologica d'Italia 20, Provveditorato Generale dello Stato, Roma (1926)
21. Corpo Reale delle Miniere: Carta mineraria d'Italia, Scala 1:500.000, 1 carta in 13 fogli a colori e nota illustrativa, Roma (1926–1935?)

Methodological Report on Emergency Surveys for Cultural Heritage

Sara Gagliolo(✉) ⓘ, Bianca Federici ⓘ, Ilaria Ferrando ⓘ, Daniele Passoni ⓘ, and Domenico Sguerso ⓘ

Laboratory of Geodesy, Geomatics and GIS, Department of Civil, Chemical and Environmental Engineering (DICCA), University of Genoa, via Montallegro 1, 16145 Genoa, Italy
`sara.gagliolo@edu.unige.it`

Abstract. The management of emergency scenario is a very complex issue, due to the risk of recurrence of the calamity itself. The present work is intended as a methodological report based on the gained professional and scientific experience of the authors, involved in the survey of several Cultural Heritage buildings hit by the earthquakes that afflicted Central Italy in 2016. The examined structures include the Civic Tower in Norcia, the co-cathedral Santa Maria Argentea and the San Salvatore church in Campi di Norcia. The survey campaigns were performed immediately after the aftershocks occurred in the end of October, on behalf of the Italian Ministry that at the time was called of Cultural Heritage and Activities and Tourism (MiBACT), in order to ease the securing of the sites and their restoration. Because of the necessity to provide the survey products as quickly as possible, typical in an emergency situation, particular attention was paid to optimize both the on-site and the post-processing phases, with respect to the required accuracy. In this regard, U.Ph.O. (Unmanned Photogrammetric Office), a tool developed during the Ph.D. thesis work of one of the authors, is particularly useful for the a priori evaluation of the realistic accuracy obtainable during a photogrammetric survey. In the present work, this tool was applied to the San Salvatore Church, taken as case study to check the influence on the photogrammetric products of two of the main planning parameters: the image overlapping and the accuracy in Unmanned Aerial Vehicle (UAV) positioning.

Keywords: Survey and processing optimization · Realistic planning simulation · Accuracy · Cultural Heritage · Central Italy earthquake · Emergency · Unmanned Aerial Vehicle (UAV)

1 Introduction

In the last decade, the Italian mainland has been afflicted by several catastrophic earthquakes, which devastated entire villages and caused hundreds of victims. The high frequency and the gravity of these natural disasters sensitized the scientific community to contribute to the improvement of efficiency in emergency procedures management.

© Springer Nature Switzerland AG 2022
E. Borgogno-Mondino and P. Zamperlin (Eds.): ASITA 2021, CCIS 1507, pp. 163–181, 2022.
https://doi.org/10.1007/978-3-030-94426-1_13

Geomatics has the task of providing a geometrically correct and accurate vision, which is fundamental for planning and prioritizing safety operations, for investigating the state of repair of structures, including those belonging to the Cultural Heritage, and for planning the strengthening and restoration of structures and infrastructures.

One of the most recent severe earthquakes in the Italian peninsula happened in 2016 and involved a wide territory including three regions of Central Italy: Marche, Umbria and Lazio. The first shockwave took place in August 2016. After the initial phase of the emergency, which was dedicated to the rescue of people, the so-called "red zones" have been created to delineate the areas where the structural damages of buildings and infrastructures were so huge that the access was not permitted to the population.

In this scenario, the necessity of surveys to plan the securing, the restoration and the material disposal arose in the numerous sites involved. The situation became even more critical as a consequence of the aftershocks in the end of October 2016.

The survey activities of our research group started in this period, mainly focusing on churches and Cultural Heritage buildings in general, with the support of a structural engineers' team from Genoa. In parallel, other experts in structural engineering deepened more in detail different topics, including schools and strategic buildings [1, 2], complying with priorities and guidelines decided by the Ministries.

The peculiar aim of each survey campaign was established according to the state of preservation of the examined structure. The first data acquisition took place on 3rd November 2016 to survey the Civic Tower of Norcia and the co-cathedral of Santa Maria Argentea in the same place. In that case, in particular, the purpose of the survey was to support the planning of the controlled dismantling of the structure in order to avoid its collapse, and the design of the structural reinforcements. In the following weeks, the attention was focused on the San Salvatore Church in Campi di Norcia, with the participation of the students of the course *Geomatics applied to Construction*, offered at the Master's Degree in Building Engineering-Architecture.

The operating conditions in which the surveys were conducted made necessary the permanent supervision of the fire-fighters, in charge of the post-event securing procedures. In such scenario, Unmanned Aerial Vehicle (UAV) photogrammetry was identified as the most suitable survey technique, taking into account both the on-site safety and the results requirements [3–6].

The main challenges during the survey campaigns were related to the number of images and Ground Control Points (GCPs) positioning. The first one must balance the proper quantity and location to obtain a complete survey and allow a quick post-processing, the latter one was strongly conditioned by the inaccessibility of the unsafe areas.

The present work is intended to summarize the phases of the whole operating chain, giving a critical description of the carried out work and its achievements. An important contribution during the survey planning is given by the tool U.Ph.O. (Unmanned Photogrammetric Office), developed during the Ph.D. thesis work of one of the authors. The tool, here applied to the case study of the San Salvatore church, is based on a network simulation and conceived for the a priori evaluation of the realistic accuracy obtainable during the photogrammetric survey. It requires as input data the camera parameters, the site configuration represented by a Digital Surface Model (DSM), and the Ground

Control Points (GCPs) positioning. Several configurations are here tested, to understand the influence of and the overlapping, hence the number of images, and the accuracy of UAV positioning. Although U.Ph.O. automatically takes into account the obstructions related to the site complexity, a flat scenario was specifically chosen to highlight more distinctly the exclusive influences of the analyzed parameters.

The paper is organized as follows: the considered sites are described in Sect. 2, together with the respective survey campaigns instrumentation and procedures; in Sect. 3, the post-processing workflow is reported; Sect. 4 concerns the U.Ph.O. application to the case study; finally, Sect. 5 is dedicated to the conclusions and the lesson learnt from the mentioned experiences.

2   Description of Sites and Related Survey Campaigns

As already mentioned, different sites were analyzed, including the Civic Tower and the co-cathedral of Santa Maria Argentea church in San Benedetto square in Norcia, San Salvatore church in Campi di Norcia and others ones primarily handled by the survey equipe from Gter Ltd, Innovation in Geomatics, GNSS and GIS (hereafter Gter), a spin-off company of the Genoa University. Each survey campaign was planned to comply with the context and the state of the buildings. In facts, two diametrically opposite situations occurred: a simpler situation, where the object of the survey was located in a wide and clear area, and a more complex condition, in which the structure was surrounded by other buildings. The first scenario is well represented by the operating conditions found during the survey of San Salvatore church in Campi di Norcia. It was located in a flat and isolated area in the countryside, surrounded by a wide field, a parking area and adjacent to a cemetery. It was totally destroyed by the earthquake, so there was no risk of residual collapse of materials. A completely different operating scenario was found while surveying the Civic Tower of Norcia. Immediately after the shockwave, it was the building in the best state of conservation, in facts it was possible to dismantle the structure in a controlled way in order to reinforce and restore it. The criticality arose because the structure is surrounded by the complex of the historical center, such as San Benedetto Basilica and Santa Maria Argentea church, whose conditions were not safe and the possibility of collapses of materials could not be excluded. In those conditions, a different approach to the survey and different precautions were carried out.

The following subsections describe each structure, together with the conducted survey campaigns. All the UAV flights have been performed using a DJI© Inspire drone, with different models of embedded cameras according to the site condition and the pursued Ground Sample Distance (GSD).

2.1   Civic Tower, Norcia

The Civic Tower of Norcia (Fig. 1) is a bell-tower built in 1713 next to the City Hall Palace, arisen in the XIII century and restored several times because of the recurring earthquakes in the area.

The Tower is a masonry building with a square plan and a height of 25 m.

Fig. 1. The Civic Tower (on the left) and the façade of San Benedetto Basilica.

The survey campaign was performed in a single day on 3rd November 2016. The following day was dedicated to the photogrammetric post-processing, referring to the optimized criteria reported in [7, 8]. The resulting 3D model was used to design the reinforcing structures, which were installed on 5th November.

As already stated, the UAV employed for the operations is a DJI© Inspire, with an embedded Zenmuse X3 camera characterized by the following parameters: the focal length is 3.61 mm, and the sensor size is 4000 × 3000 pixels, with a pixel dimension of 1.56 μm. The flight was performed with a nadiral shooting geometry and a relative height of about 50 m, leading to a GSD of 22 mm and collecting 81 pictures. Further images of the Tower were acquired from the UAV through a frontal flight and from a terrestrial point of view.

A support survey was performed using a GNSS receiver in order to acquire the GCPs coordinates. The distribution and survey of the four GCPs targets were operated in safe conditions thanks to the fire-fighter's cooperation and support.

During this survey, and in all those that involved the structures located in San Benedetto square in Norcia (see Sect. 2.2 and 2.3), the fire-fighters had a fundamental role in guaranteeing the safety of operators and guiding us through the ruins, as imposed by the safety dispositions. With such strict conditions and rules, the timings of the survey campaign increased.

2.2 Santa Maria Argentea Church, Norcia

The co-cathedral of Santa Maria Argentea (Fig. 2) was built in the XVI century in Renaissance style, but it was restored several times because of the recurring earthquakes in the area, as already mentioned concerning the Civic Tower. From the III century, the site already held a temple dedicated to the goddess Fortuna Argentea, then converted to the Christian cult.

Fig. 2. Nadiral view of the Santa Maria Argentea church.

The building housed many remarkable works of art; their saving was the main purpose of the performed survey campaign, rather than the structure, which was completely collapsed except for the perimeter façades.

The UAV survey was realized on 24th November 2016, using the Zenmuse X5 camera characterized by the following parameters: a fixed focal length equal to 15 mm, a sensor size of 4608 × 3456 pixels with a pixel dimension of 3.76 μm. The flight was performed with a nadiral shooting geometry for the overall structure at a relative height of about 30 m, leading to a GSD of 8 mm.

A supplementary group of images was acquired with the camera tilted at a frontal view in order to fully reconstruct the bell-tower. Moreover, terrestrial imagery was added to cover the lateral and posterior façades, located in a narrow path.

Further than the mentioned datasets, a photogrammetric block focused on the whole context of San Benedetto square, including the homonym cathedral and the aforementioned Civic Tower, has been acquired, in order to obtain an overall vision of the site. This contribution eased the solution of the georeferencing issue: thanks to the reciprocal proximity of the buildings, it has been possible to employ the GCPs collected with a GNSS receiver during both the survey campaigns, 14 in total, 4 of which used as Check Points (CPs).

In Fig. 3, a nadiral view of the San Benedetto Square 3D model is depicted.

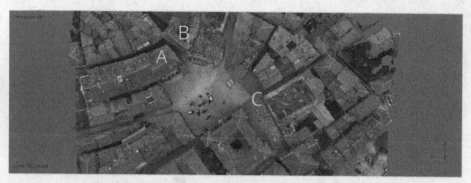

Fig. 3. Top view of the San Benedetto square point cloud, including the buildings: A. Civic Tower, B. San Benedetto Basilica and C. Santa Maria Argentea church (Agisoft Metashape© background).

2.3 San Salvatore Church, Campi di Norcia

The San Salvatore church was built in 1115 with the name of Pieve di Santa Maria in Campi di Norcia, in an area previously occupied by a pagan temple. Within the XIV and the XVI century, it was expanded with a new aisle and a bell-tower.

The building, which is actually completely destroyed (Fig. 4), housed many remarkable frescos, whose saving was the focus of the post-seismic operations.

The survey campaign was performed in a single day on 23rd November 2016, using the Zenmuse X5 camera for the UAV acquisition, as already described in Sect. 2.2. The amount of collected images is 110.

The flight was performed considering a nadiral attitude and a relative height of about 50 m, which leaded to a GSD of 13 mm. Further images were acquired both from oblique and terrestrial points of view.

A GNSS survey was performed to acquire the GCPs coordinates (9 in total).

Fig. 4. San Salvatore church ruins.

3 Data Post-processing and Fruition of Products

All the acquired datasets, consisting in several tens of images per each building were post-processed using the software package Agisoft Photoscan© (now Metashape©) [9] and hardware devices with at least 16 GB of RAM and 4 GB of GPU.

The quality for the Agisoft Photoscan© workflow operations was set to *High* for both the aerotriangulation and the dense cloud reconstruction, in order to obtain a point density corresponding to the double of the GSD dimension, i.e. in the order of few centimeters. In case of absolute urgency, as in the case of the Civic Tower, the processing was performed setting *Medium* quality to obtain preliminary results in a reasonable time, but with a lower accuracy and resolution. In facts, the downscaling factor applied to the images during the processing is quadrupled for each different quality step, producing sparser and lower-quality results.

Concerning the case of the Civic Tower of Norcia, even the lack and the bad distribution of the GCPs, due to the complex surrounding scenario, represented an obstacle, since it was not possible to choose among them any Check Points (CPs) to verify the quality of measurements. Moreover, sometimes the urgency of the operations forced the acquisition of images during evening hours, thus in not optimal light and shade conditions.

The case study of Santa Maria Argentea is remarkable because of the problems occurred in linking the datasets derived from different shooting geometries. In facts, the alignment of images coming from several points of view is prevented when the overlapping among the blocks is not sufficient, thus, i.e. when the transition from the initial to the final position is not gradual enough, as in moving from nadiral to terrestrial points of view. In particular, the lateral and posterior façades of the church were located in narrow paths, in which the operator was forced to take terrestrial images at a short distance from the structure, omitting the upper part of the walls that, conversely, was easily recognizable in the nadiral shots. Moreover, the attempt to add oblique images was not very useful, due to the shadow zones along the narrow paths. This issue was compensated pinpointing as GCPs some natural points deriving from the registered Terrestrial Laser Scanner (TLS) acquisitions, in order to locate the portions of the point cloud in the same Reference System.

The case study of San Salvatore church (Fig. 5 and 6) was characterized by less complex survey conditions, which are reflected in a faster survey campaign and post-processing phase, despite the bigger extension of the surveyed area. This was sadly due to the bad state of conservation of the structure, so that there was no distinction between internal and external portions. Moreover, the difference in height of the various blocks was not so relevant to create shadow areas.

The absence of unstable tall structures and the wide field around the church made this context safer for the operators employed in the survey and securing activities, thanks to the lower risk of sudden collapses. Taking advantage of these features, it was possible to acquire a good number of well distributed GCPs (nine) too, as shown in Fig. 5.

In spite of the described complications occurred in some scenarios, all the surveyed datasets are consistent and the outputs accuracy is within the expected range of a few centimeters. The produced outputs were mainly 3D point clouds and textured meshes.

Fig. 5. Target distribution around the San Salvatore site.

Fig. 6. Top view of the San Salvatore church point cloud (Agisoft Metashape© background).

Free access to the meshes can be made available to the general public, as well as to professionals, by means of an interactive Web publication. It was achieved by means of the tool 3D Heritage Online Presenter (3DHOP), developed by the Visual Computing Lab of ISTI-CNR (Pisa, Italy). 3DHOP is a free and open-source package, which provides ready-to-use components and functions for the interactive Web visualization of high-resolution meshes [13, 14]. It is based on multi-resolution data structure, which is generally composed by different chunks with different levels of detail. The multi-resolution approach makes the Web visualization faster, but it requires a pre-processing phase for the 3D models. Thanks to its open-source nature, 3DHOP web viewer is highly flexible and suitable for creating customized renderer with different levels of complexity, depending on the developer's programming skills.

Moreover, 3D point clouds can be shared by means of the tool Potree, a free open-source WebGL based point cloud renderer for large point clouds [15, 16].

Hence, the 3D models of the examined buildings have been provided at the public web page: https://www.gter.it/3dhosting/rilievi_terremoto/index.php (courtesy of Gter).

Visiting such web page, the user can view, measure and section the 3D models, obtaining metrical and reliable information without the necessity to download any data. In Fig. 7 and 8, the 3D mesh representing the Norcia Civic Tower and the 3D point cloud of Santa Maria Argentea church are depicted. The toolbar on the left allows to interact with the model, in particular operating measurements and sections.

Fig. 7. Example of 3DHOP web viewer to navigate the model of Norcia Civic Tower (courtesy of Gter).

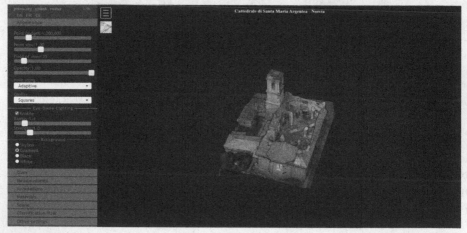

Fig. 8. Example of Potree web interface to navigate Santa Maria Argentea church model (courtesy of Gter).

4   U.Ph.O. Tool Applied to San Salvatore Church

In addition to the point clouds and textured meshes produced for all the examined sites, the Civic Tower of Norcia and the San Salvatore church in Campi di Norcia were further analyzed and used as case studies to test two photogrammetric tools conceived within the Geomatics Laboratory of University of Genoa: U.Ph.O. and MAGO [10]. U.Ph.O. was employed to simulate the operations planning applying a rigorous method [11, 17], while MAGO was used to produce orthophotos by means of an innovative procedure based on the reconstruction of a step-by-step adaptive mesh of the object [12, 18]. The peculiarity of these two buildings, for which they were selected among the others, consists in their clear distinction in terms of state of conservation and surrounding context. These differences led to dissimilarities in the final results in terms of both estimated accuracy by U.Ph.O. and orthophoto production by MAGO.

In previous experience the expected accuracy in several working scenarios, mainly influenced by site geometry, were compared applying U.Ph.O. In the present work further tests have been carried out to examine the variations in the estimated accuracy due to changes in the overlapping, hence the number of images, and in the accuracy of UAV positioning (shooting centers) for a given context. The analyzed case study is the destroyed San Salvatore Church, a site characterized by an almost homogeneous height. In this way the variations in elevation do not strongly affect the final results, allowing to highlight the specific contribution of the two parameters examined here.

Four configurations were employed for the simulation by means of U.Ph.O., considering alternately both the longitudinal and transversal overlapping set at 70% or 80% and a metric or centimetric accuracy of the UAV positioning, simulating the use of Stand-Alone or Real-Time Kinematic (RTK) GNSS positioning, respectively.

All the tests have been performed considering the four GCPs closest to the perimeter of the site and a supplementary one located approximately in the center of the area (indicated as 1, 3, 5, 8, and 7 in Fig. 5).

In Fig. 9, the flight planning and the ground coverage of a single frame are depicted in the case of 70% and 80% overlapping on the left and right respectively. The images are oriented so that their width is orthogonal to the longitudinal direction of the flight. Moreover, in Fig. 10 the source DSM used as input for all the configurations tested is shown.

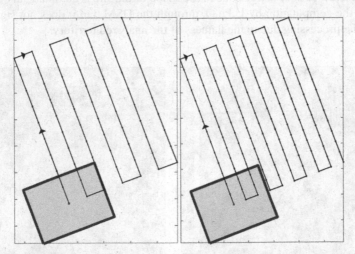

Fig. 9. Flight planning and footprint of a single frame in the configurations with 70% (left) or 80% (right) overlapping. The width of the picture is orthogonal to the longitudinal direction of the flight.

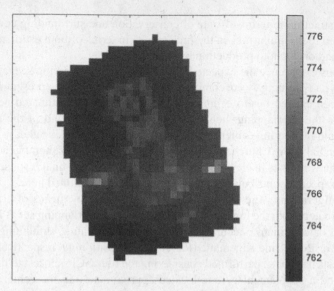

Fig. 10. Source DSM of the San Salvatore site (in meters).

Figure 11 shows the number of images covering each cell of the source DSM for the configuration with 70% (left) and 80% (right) overlapping, together with the distribution of the center of the images themselves (black dots).

The presence of obstructions due to the shape of the site is automatically taken into account in the computation by U.Ph.O. through the DSM, but it does not significantly influence the processing due to the flatness of the analyzed territory.

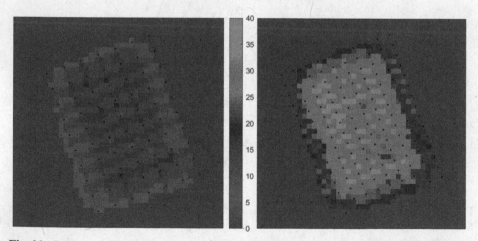

Fig. 11. Images number and camera positions for the combinations with both longitudinal and transversal overlapping at 70% (left) and 80% (right). Black dots indicate the image capture centers.

Figures 12, 13, 14, 15, 16 and 17 depict the expected accuracy along the planimetric coordinates X, Y, corresponding to the basis and the height of the figures themselves, and along the altitude direction Z for all the four combinations. Table 1 contains the maximum values of σ, hence the lower accuracy, for each diagram.

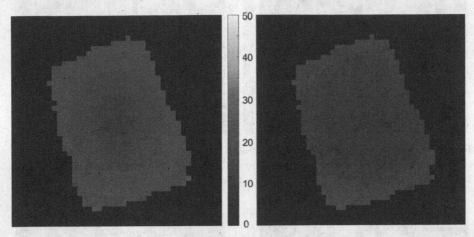

Fig. 12. Expected accuracy σ [mm] along X axis for the combinations with longitudinal and transversal overlapping at 70% and Stand-Alone (left) or RTK (right) positioning. Black dots indicate the GCPs.

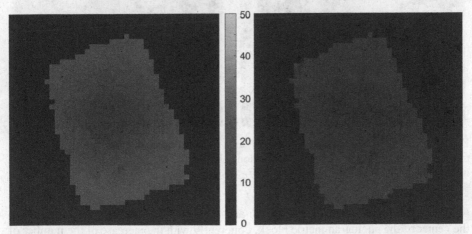

Fig. 13. Expected accuracy σ [mm] along X axis for the combinations with longitudinal and transversal overlapping at 80% and Stand-Alone (left) or RTK (right) positioning. Black dots indicate the GCPs.

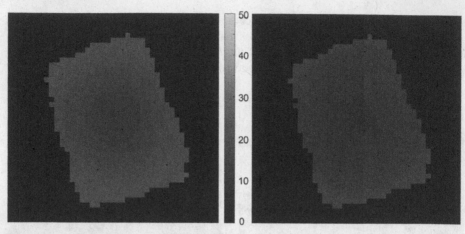

Fig. 14. Expected accuracy σ [mm] along Y axis for the combinations with longitudinal and transversal overlapping at 70% and Stand-Alone (left) or RTK (right) positioning. Black dots indicate the GCPs.

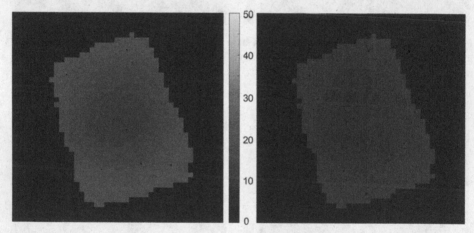

Fig. 15. Expected accuracy σ [mm] along Y axis for the combinations with longitudinal and transversal overlapping at 80% and Stand-Alone (left) or RTK (right) positioning. Black dots indicate the GCPs.

The previous Figs. 12, 13, 14, 15, 16 and 17 shows that the accuracy is higher in the center of the photogrammetric block, coherently with the increase of the number of images that cover this portion, as expected.

Comparing the four combinations along each direction, it results that RTK positioning is a predominant factor in achieving higher accuracy than increasing the overlapping ratio. In facts, the higher accuracy, that can be obtained for the shooting centers by means of RTK positioning, strengthens the photogrammetric block much more than the overlapping does. However, in the configurations with RTK positioning, a higher overlapping

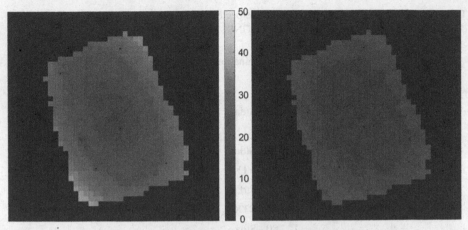

Fig. 16. Expected accuracy σ [mm] along Z axis for the combinations with longitudinal and transversal overlapping at 70% and Stand-Alone (left) or RTK (right) positioning. Black dots indicate the GCPs.

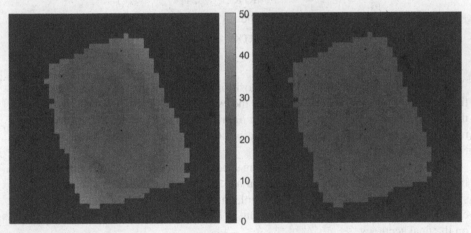

Fig. 17. Expected accuracy σ [mm] along Z axis for the combinations with longitudinal and transversal overlapping at 70% and Stand-Alone (left) or RTK (right) positioning. Black dots indicate the GCPs.

rate allows for further improvement in accuracy. On the other hand, the accuracy of the Stand-Alone solution is not significantly improved by increasing overlapping rate.

The reported outputs from U.Ph.O. procedure show that in all the proposed circumstances it is possible to obtain a survey with an expected accuracy in the order of few centimeters. As expected, the standard deviation along X and Y axes are fully comparable in each configuration, while in Z coordinate the standard deviation is slightly higher than in the planimetric components.

Table 1. Resume on the maximum values of expected accuracy σ for the evaluated combinations: (70–80)% with Stand-Alone (Stda) and RTK GNSS positioning of the UAV.

Reference axis	Combination	Maximum value σ [mm]
X	70 - Stda	25
	70 - RTK	18
	80 - Stda	25
	80 - RTK	14
Y	70 - Stda	25
	70 - RTK	17
	80 - Stda	25
	80 - RTK	14
Z	70 - Stda	39
	70 - RTK	24
	80 - Stda	37
	80 - RTK	17

Furthermore, the use of GNSS RTK positioning, to track the UAV during its navigation and shooting, significantly decreases the estimated standard deviation. In this case, the Z component experiences a significant improvement of 7 mm for higher overlapping rate. Instead, in the Stand-Alone combinations the standard deviation doesn't change as the overlapping rate varies.

As known, a reduction in overlapping leads to fewer images and consequently a faster post-processing, which is crucial in an emergency scenario. For this reason, the simulation obtained with the U.Ph.O. tool, in order to know in advance the realistic expected accuracy, is particularly important to assess the significance of the parameters on the final accuracy.

5 Conclusions

The management of emergency scenarios is a very complex issue, due to the wide spectrum of problems that need to be solved urgently because of the risk of recurrence of the calamity itself and the absolute necessity of the operators' safety. Our research group had the opportunity to face with this challenging working scenario in 2016, when it was involved in the survey of several collapsed Cultural Heritage buildings after the earthquakes that afflicted Central Italy.

The survey campaigns aim is to obtain metrical information in order to support the following steps: planning and prioritizing the securing operations, designing the strengthening and the restoration of structures and infrastructures, investigating the state of repair of the Cultural Heritage, evaluating the volume of the ruins to dispose of.

In such emergency scenario, the most suitable survey technique was identified in UAV Photogrammetry, combined with the use of GNSS to acquire the coordinates of some GCPs. Indeed, the use of UAV allows the execution of the operations in safe conditions, compatibly with the necessity of fast and high-quality results, with respect to the required level of accuracy.

The majority of the examined sites are located in historical centers; this condition makes even more relevant the analysis of possible obstructions and the choice of an adequate shooting geometry for image acquisition. The case of San Salvatore church in Campi di Norcia represents an exception, since both the main building and the surrounding structures were isolated and barely raised vertically, because completely destroyed.

Because of the necessity to produce the survey products as quickly as possible, particular attention was paid to optimize both the on-site and the post-processing phases without compromising the expected accuracy. An important instrument to optimize the planning phase is U.Ph.O., a tool that allows to predict the expected accuracy resulting from the survey parameters and conditions. In facts, it permits to obtain a realistic evaluation of the accuracy on each DSM cell of the surveyed object, allowing, if needed, to mainly focus on the areas which deserve a higher attention.

The San Salvatore Church was chosen among the others as a case study to investigate the accuracy variations due to the accuracy of UAV positioning and image overlapping, neglecting the possible effects caused by obstructions, which are anyway automatically taken into account by U.Ph.O. tool. According to the performed tests, the accuracy in the UAV positioning results to be the most influent on the final quality of the survey. In facts, the expected accuracy is significantly higher for the combination with the use of RTK positioning, even if it implicates higher costs for the employed instrumentation.

The simulations performed using U.Ph.O. prove that its contribution is significant and incisive in planning surveys, especially in a complex scenario, leading to have higher control on the final quality of the results.

The obtained photogrammetric point clouds have GSD and expected accuracy in the order of few centimeters, satisfying the requirements for the various examined structures, i.e. designing reinforcements, saving valuables, and disposing of ruins. Starting from the supplied point clouds, other experts were allowed to reconstruct structural models or 2D representations.

In conclusion, the described experience was deeply constructive and useful in understanding the best management strategies in a complex emergency situation, e.g. following an earthquake. The lesson learnt concerns the necessity of optimization, reaching an effective compromise in order to conciliate the aspects of quickness, safety, and feasibility, without neglecting the final accuracy. All the workflow steps have to be faced balancing costs and benefits. On the one hand, a good planning is very useful to organize and accelerate the following procedures. On the other hand, the post-processing operations, which usually take the longest time, could be performed more efficiently privileging the best shooting geometry and the essential level of detail, focusing on the portion of interest. Improving the efficiency of emergency survey procedures is extremely important with respect to planning and securing operations, and investigating the vulnerability of the Cultural Heritage, whose preservation is a fundamental goal, not only for the mere proof of the past but also for the promotion of life quality in contemporary cities.

Acknowledgements. The authors wish to thank:

– MiBAC (Italian Ministry of Cultural Heritage and Activities), for the kind availability and cooperativeness;

– Gter Ltd, Innovation in Geomatics, GNSS and GIS, for the web publication of the obtained textured meshes and point clouds;

– Studio Giampaolo Grosso, for executing the surveys of the buildings on behalf of Gter with the cooperations of some of the authors;

– Prof. Stefano Podestà and Yellow Room Engineering Company, for the expertise in the retrofitting design.

References

1. Casapulla, C., Giresini, L., Argiento, L.U., Lagomarsino, S.: Incremental static and dynamic analyses of the out-of-plane response of a Masonry Church damaged by 2016–2017 central Italy earthquakes. In: Atti del XVII Convegno ANIDIS L'ingegneria Sismica in Italia, Pistoia, 17–21 September 2017, Pisa University Press (2017)
2. Ferrero, C., Barbosa, P., Calderini, C.: Nonlinear modeling of unreinforced masonry structures under seismic actions: validation using a building hit by the 2016 Central Italy earthquake. Frattura ed Integrità Strutturale **14**(51), 92–114 (2019)
3. Adams, S.M., Friedland, C.J.: A survey of Unmanned Aerial Vehicle (UAV) usage for imagery collection in disaster research and management. In: Proceedings of the Ninth International Workshop on Remote Sensing for Disaster Response, 15–16 September, Stanford, CA, USA (2011)
4. Achille, C., et al.: UAV-based photogrammetry and integrated technologies for architectural applications - Methodological strategies for the after-quake survey of vertical structures in Mantua (Italy). Sensors **15**(7), 15520–15539 (2015)
5. Meyer, D., Hess, M., Lo, E., Wittich, C.E., Hutchinson, T.C., Kuester, F.: UAV-based post disaster assessment of cultural heritage sites following the 2014 South Napa Earthquake. Digit. Heritage **2**, 421–424 (2015)
6. Nannei, V.M., Fassi, F., Mirabella Roberti, G.: Photogrammetry for quick survey in emergency conditions: the case of Villa Galvagnina. In: International Archives of the Photogrammetry, Remote Sensing and Spatial Information Sciences, vol. XLII-2/W15, pp. 835–842 (2019)
7. Gagliolo, S., et al.: Use of UAS for the conservation of historical buildings in case of emergencies. In: International Archives of the Photogrammetry, Remote Sensing and Spatial Information Sciences, vol. XLII-5/W1, pp. 81–88 (2017)
8. Gagliolo, S., et al.: Parameter optimization for creating reliable photogrammetric models in emergency scenarios. Appl. Geomat. **10**(4), 501–514 (2018). https://doi.org/10.1007/s12518-018-0224-4
9. Agisoft PhotoScan©. http://www.agisoft.com. Accessed 25 Mar 2019
10. Gagliolo, S., Passoni, D., Federici, B., Ferrando, I., Sguerso, D.: U.Ph.O and MAGO: two useful instruments in support of photogrammetric UAV survey. In: International Archives of the Photogrammetry, Remote Sensing and Spatial Information Sciences, vol. XLII-2/W13, pp. 289–296 (2019)

11. Passoni, D., Federici, B., Ferrando, I., Gagliolo, S., Sguerso, D.: The estimation of accuracy in the planning of UAS photogrammetric surveys. In: International Archives of the Photogrammetry, Remote Sensing and Spatial Information Sciences, vol. XLII-2, pp. 837–843 (2018)
12. Gagliolo, S., Federici, B., Ferrando, I., Sguerso, D.: MAGO: a new approach for orthophotos production based on adaptive mesh reconstruction. In: International Archives of the Photogrammetry, Remote Sensing and Spatial Information Sciences, vol. XLII-2/W11, 533–538 (2019)
13. Potenziani, M., Callieri, M., Dellepiane, M., Corsini, M., Ponchio, F., Scopigno, R.: 3DHOP: 3D Heritage Online Presenter. Comput. Graph. **52**, 129–141 (2015)
14. 3DHOP. http://vcg.isti.cnr.it/3dhop. Accessed 15 Jan 2018
15. Schuetz, M.: Potree: Rendering large point clouds in Web browser (2016)
16. Potree. http://potree.org/. Accessed 15 Jan 2018
17. Gagliolo, S., Callà, J., Cosso, T., Sguerso, D.: Comparison of UAV LiDAR and photogrammetry approaches for the survey of the Cultural Heritage in challenging conditions, Extended Abstract at GIS Ostrava 2020 (2020)
18. Gagliolo, S.: Ortofoto ad alta risoluzione per individuazione di lesioni strutturali con "MAGO" (High resolution orthophotos for the recognition of structural lesions with "MAGO"). In Bollettino SIFET n.1 – ANNO 2019. Abstract available in English (2019)

A BIM-GIS Integrated Database to Support Planned Maintenance Activities of Historical Built Heritage

Elisabetta Colucci[1] , Emmanuele Iacono[2] , Francesca Matrone[1]([✉]) ,
and Gianvito Marino Ventura[2]

[1] Department of Environmental, Land and Infrastructure Engineering (DIATI), Politecnico di Torino, C.so Duca degli Abruzzi 24, 10129 Turin, Italy
{elisabetta.colucci,francesca.matrone}@polito.it
[2] Department of Economics and Business Studies (DISEI), Università del Piemonte Orientale, via Duomo 6, 13100 Vercelli, Italy
{emmanuele.iacono,gianvito.ventura}@uniupo.it

Abstract. Planned maintenance represents a strategy to facilitate the conservation of architectural heritage, preventing invasive restoration activities. For this purpose, the management of a maintenance plan through the integration of BIM and GIS domains is here proposed. In particular, the first results of the Interreg Main.10.ance project are described, namely the definition of a unique spatial database divided into different Levels of Detail, compliant with geographical standards and user-friendly for the professionals involved. This integration is addressed through the use of Dynamo, which allows the dialogue between the BIM and GIS data in the PostgreSQL database.

Keywords: Spatial DB · Cultural heritage · Maintenance · HBIM · GIS · LoD · 3D model visualisation and querying

1 Introduction

The planned maintenance of cultural heritage (CH), in recent years, has been strongly supported by innovations in the digital field and, in particular, by digital models. In fact, the 3D representations of the architectural asset inserted into its context allow to understand the environmental conditions in which it is located, analyse and understand its behaviour and record the data of interventions or restoration activities performed. In this framework, BIM-GIS integration is currently a hot topic, and it is increasingly applied with different methodologies and approaches.

Starting from some previous works [1, 2], in this contribution, we combine the BIM-GIS domains not only by verifying the correctness of the information when the BIM models are imported into the GIS environment but rather by investigating the possibility to simultaneously query a unique database (DB) including information with different levels of detail. This DB is structured according to European cartographic standards and

E. Borgogno-Mondino and P. Zamperlin (Eds.): ASITA 2021, CCIS 1507, pp. 182–194, 2022.
https://doi.org/10.1007/978-3-030-94426-1_14

it points to the data of both domains. Thus, the main objective is to view the geometries, query them and, most of all, once the new data have been entered (planned maintenance records, history of activities, etc.), convey them into the DB structured according to the INSPIRE Directive (2007/2/EC, Infrastructure for spatial information in Europe) [3] or CityGML [4] standard with its Level of Detail – LoDs) for the GIS representation and IFC [5] for the BIM one. The Italian National Unification (UNI) norms have also been considered for the DB design. To do this, we had to overcome incompatibilities due to data formats, geometries, standards, diverse LoDs and software, since BIM and GIS were born for different purposes and scale of representation. In this project, the data of the two domains meet in a core database capable of managing dynamic and continuously updated data both of the building and urban-territorial components.

1.1 Case Study

The case study considered for the research is the "Sacred Mounts" (*Sacri Monti*) system in northern Italy, dating back to the 15th century. In particular, the site of Varallo has been chosen thanks to its multi-dimension in terms of the scale of representation (45 chapels distributed with an urban spatial dislocation), heritage variety, historical relevance, involved stakeholders and operators, as well as the related maintenance complexity [6]. In addition to these peculiarities, it is included in the Main.10.ance project funded by ERDF (European Regional Development Fund) within the Interreg programme. This is a research project (Interreg Italy-Switzerland "MAIN.10.ANCE", 2019–2021) [7] with the primary objective of creating a tool to support the planned maintenance of the Italian and Swiss *Sacri Monti*.

The chapels constituting the architectural complex are generally "semi-confined" environments, namely environments which, despite being closed, have a continuous and climatic exchange with the outdoor environment through wooden or metal grates. They are, in fact, spaces with sculptures, frescoes, stuccoes or local handicrafts (Fig. 1) freely opened to tourists.

The most common pathology at the *Sacro Monte di Varallo* is the presence of humidity that acts, most of the time, both through infiltrations from the roofs and capillary rising from the ground. It affects the state of conservation of the frescoes, sculptures and architecture itself. To this condition, it must also be considered the wooded environmental context and the presence of unfavourable climatic conditions.

Since it is not possible to keep all the chapels and the artefacts contained therein in an optimal state of conservation, given the large number, it is advisable to avoid at least their deterioration. To reach this, various classes of intervention have been foreseen:

- ordinary and extraordinary maintenance of the roof systems,
- inspection and routine maintenance of the indoor environments of the chapels,
- monitoring of the action of humidity.

Precisely for these reasons, many professional figures are involved in the maintenance plan of the *Sacri Monti* and their coordination with a unique and updated database would undoubtedly be beneficial.

Fig. 1. The indoor environment of two chapels at the Sacro Monte di Varallo.

1.2   Related Works

In this context, the integration of data with different levels of detail, which allow multi-scale analysis, becomes indispensable for managing the built heritage, such that of *Sacri Monti*, and the union of BIM and GIS domains can provide an adequate solution.

Their integration is not a novel idea [8–11], and it is subject of international benchmarks as GeoBIM [12, 13] where conversion procedures between IFC and CityGML have been investigated. The potentialities for smart cities [14], sustainable environment [15] or the construction industry [16] are just some of the manifold positive implications. However, relying on a unique standard-compliant database that combines the informative levels of both the environments constitutes a relatively new approach. Specifically, [17] proposed to merge BIM and GIS through ontologies in the ACTIVe3D project, but the use of a database constitutes, in this case, a drawback as it would limit the power of ontologies. A very similar project is Chimera [18], where GIS and BIM are organised and viewed in a single environment, with different scales of details and data query and updating is easily accessible.

Despite these various efforts above-mentioned, a lack of a complete workflow for HBIM-GIS integration based on a unique standard-compliant spatial database that store, edit and query information about historical built heritage at different scales for maintenance plans and analysis emerged.

Moreover, the adoption and the reuse of SDIs (Spatial Data Infrastructures), national and regional geoportals, WebGIS solution, spatial ontologies and standards, allow the fruition of information and knowledge in different domain through a user-friendly solution and thanks to standard structure and semantics. In this context, geographic information standards play a crucial role in the scenario of data models' integration. International standards to represent built heritage have been therefore investigated and applied.

The efforts made ten years ago by the Open Geospatial Web Services (OGC) for CAD-GIS-BIM integration are essential to mention among the BIM-GIS data format integration. It defined the requirements for linking the AEC world's data models and workflows with those of the geospatial community to make BIM objects available in both the IFC (Industry Foundation Classes) and CityGML (Geography Markup Language) standards. CityGML was developed in 2002, and it became ISO standard in 2008. It is an open data model for the storage and exchange of virtual 3D city models. The development of CityGML aims to reach a standard definition of the basic entities, attributes, and relations of a 3D city model. Several geometries can be associated with the same object to obtain a multi-representation based on time, different reconstruction hypotheses, or different detail levels. This last case is foreseen by the standard, which implements 5 levels of detail (LoD) for a multi-scale representation of cartographic objects. On the other side, the IFC data schema architecture, in the BIM domain, relies on a higher level of detail and defines different conceptual layers, where each schema is assigned to precisely one conceptual layer.

2 Methodology

The methodology described in this paper focuses on the structuring of the DB according to the different LoDs and geographic standards. This spatial databased (DB) has been designed with the free and open-source relational database management system PostgreSQL (with the spatial extension PostGIS) and it is connected to the data derived from the BIM models. In particular, the users involved need to analyse data at different levels: tourists should query only general data and information; the managing body must inspect all the specific entities and files, while the professionals and artisans only their relative parts and details. This multi-level structure is reflected in the database, organised according to the users' needs and specificities, where LoDs 0–2 are rather contextual

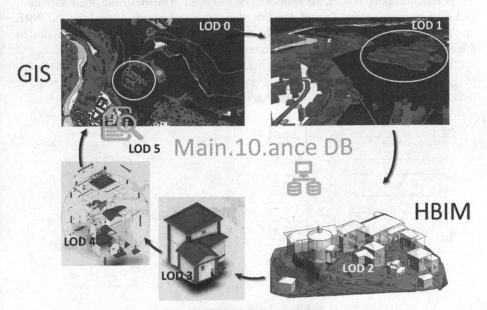

Fig. 2. Methodological workflow.

data and represents a urban scale, Lod 2–3 define the outdoor environment and architectural component, LoD 4 the indoor elements and LoD 5 the alphanumerical data about maintenance plans and the state of conservation (Fig. 2).

2.1 The Data Model and the Spatial Database Design

After the standards and data model analysis in geographic information, the spatial database has been designed with the free and open-source relational database management system PostgreSQL (version 13, with the graphical interface PgAdmin 4).

Hence, the database structure integrates standards' entities and properties, follows the CityGML LoDs subdivision and assimilates knowledge useful for restoration, preservation and conservation activities. Cartographic 2D data of the case study selected from the regional geoportal (BDTRE, Territorial Database) [19, 20] have been selected and stored in the DB platform. Subsequently, the BIM model database has been connected. Before the DB implementation, the preliminary phase of the database modelling aimed to choose an appropriate data model to manage the specific application domain data. Different information from many actors, stakeholders, and technicians have been collected to represent the historical building domain correctly and to structure the DB upon the users' necessities. The successive modelling phases followed the standard workflow with the definition of [21]:

- the external model;
- the conceptual model (identification of concepts and relations);
- the logical model for the implementation of the conceptual model;
- the internal model (or physical model) for system implementation.

In the conceptual model, the entities to be managed in the database, their attributes, and their associations are formal. For this step, our research considered the INSPIRE and the OGC CityGML data models. The Level of Details have been adopted to design the conceptual model for the spatial database creation.

These LoDs have been related to the macro-categories *Outdoor Environment, Building, Immovable* and *Movable assets* and are linked to LoD 5 containing alphanumeric data over maintenance activities of the Sacred Mounts (Fig. 3).

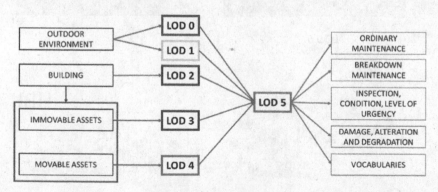

Fig. 3. LoDs subdivision.

The *IfcBuildingElement* connects, through the *mass/volumetric unit*, the urban data to the architectural ones, namely the CityGML with the IFC. Most of the GIS entities recall the BDTRE, which is INSPIRE compliant, while the data related to the status of conservation refers to UNI 11182:2006 and to a specific glossary elaborated by the partners and taking into account different Italian, Swiss and international terminologies (Fig. 4).

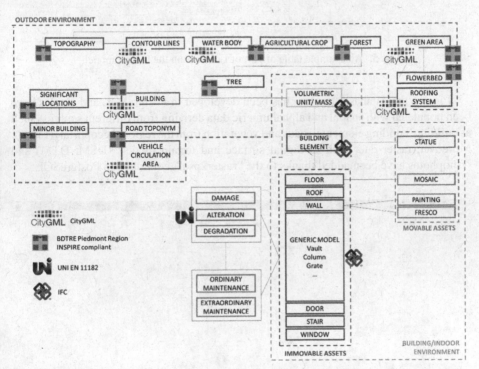

Fig. 4. Simplified schema of entities for each LoD and their relations. A specification of the standard they are derived from is also included.

The conceptual model is graphically represented with a diagram (usually a UML) illustrating the entity's name and the series of attributes associated. To better visualise the entities and their features, we reported a schematic view (Fig. 5) of the model. The logical model is adopted to express the conceptual model in a data structure readable by the machine. In this phase, we defined the connection among data and their values typologies. Depending on the type of data, storage takes place according to integers (Integer), floating-point numbers (Float), character strings (Character Varying) and a set of values to select from a list (Enumeration).

LOD 1					
CODICE	ENTITA'	n.	CAMPI	DESCRIZIONE DEI CAMPI	DATO
UN_VOL	1.1 Unità volumetrica	1	OID	Identificativo numerico dell'unità volumetrica	Integer
		2	UUID_unvol	Identificativo alfanumerico dell'unità volumetrica	Character Varying
		2	UUID_edi	Identificativo alfanumerico dell'edificio	Character Varying
		5	ENTE_PROD	Ente produttore del dato (proprietario del dato)	Character Varying
			MOD_ACQ	Modalità di acquisizione/rilevamento del dato	Enumeration
		13	UN_VOL_AV	Altezza volume	Float
		11	GEOM_poligono	Tipo di geometria del dato (poligono)	Geometry
		12	DATA_INS	Data di insetimento del dato	Character Varying
ORTOFOTO	1.2 Ortofoto	11	GEOM_raster (Raster)	Dato raster dell'ortofoto	Raster
		5	ENTE_PROD	Ente produttore del dato (proprietario del dato)	Character Varying
		7	SC_ACQ	Scala di acquisizione del dato	Character Varying
		12	DATA_INS	Data di inserimento del dato	Character Varying
DSM	1.3 DSM (Modello Digitale di Superficie)	11	GEOM_raster (Raster)	Dato raster del DSM	Raster

Fig. 5. An example table of part of LoD 1 from the logical model.

Finally, the database structure has been developed in PostgreSQL and classes have been populated with spatial and alphanumeric data deriving from different sources (such as building, building elements, roads and vegetation from the regional geoportal) (Fig. 6). Moreover, raster data such as digital surface and terrain models (DSM, DTM) and orthophotos have been added thanks to the "raster2psql" command in PostgreSQL.

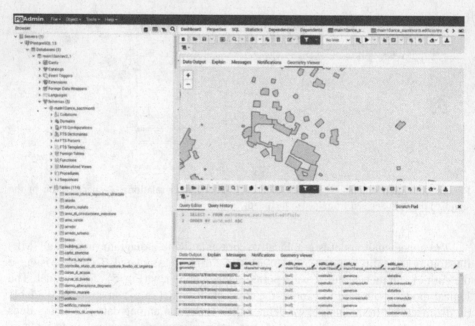

Fig. 6. Database tables and raws in PgAdmin.

2.2   The BIM Model and Its Relational Database

The realisation of a BIM model involves the automatic creation of a relational database structured according to the IFC standard, useful for the organisation, management and interoperability of AEC (Architecture Engineering Construction) data. The database can be exported and consulted in RDBMS (Relational Database Management System) by connecting to an external data source that uses ODBC (Open DataBase Connectivity) drivers. During ODBC export, through Autodesk Revit [22] it was possible to create tables and adds relations between them using primary keys and reference values. This can be done using the "Export" command or using Revit-DB-Link, a plugin whose advantage is the ability to maintain the correlation between three-dimensional objects and information by allowing bidirectionality of the data through the "Edit and Import" command. In both cases, any changes to the database structure will be overwritten at the next export. The BIM modelling of the Sacro Monte of Varallo has been carried out, in several phases, by different people who have collaborated in this project over time. Each building or portion of the building has been modelled separately, starting from groups of point clouds obtained from the surveys [6, 23]. However, since the objective was to create a database of the entire religious complex, one of the problems that emerged was that of reuniting in a single place, the scattered information regarding the various chapels. In concrete terms, this meant finding a solution to the fragmentation of data and models concerning the Sacro Monte. A possible solution was to resort to a federated model (Fig. 7), in which the entire complex would be recomposed through the combination of all the models, taking advantage of the fact that all of them had always been created from georeferenced point clouds and therefore their relative position in space was correct.

Fig. 7. Federated model into Revit.

This strategy turned out to be inadequate because the federation does not imply the possibility of accessing the informative part of the single models, nor therefore to its overall export. On the other hand, the export of individual databases can lead to inconsistencies arising from the potential for ID duplication of elements.

For all these reasons, we opted for an alternative way of BIM data management, given the need to record information within a database with a structure already set, useful to achieve the project objectives.

2.3 Working with VPL (Visual Programming Language)

In order to facilitate the automation of the process of data exchange between the BIM model and its database built in PostgreSQL, it was decided to use the Revit plugin called Dynamo. This tool's operative logic is that of VPL (Visual Programming Language), which allows, even without any knowledge of traditional programming, to create algorithms that perform specific operations not otherwise provided for in the standard commands of the software in use. This is concretely possible through a step-by-step procedure in which a series of "pre-programmed" elements are placed in sequence to perform a specific function and provided with particular inputs and outputs. Joining together these different elements through logical and operational links, it is possible to create an entirely new sequence of operations, made up of a combination of simple instructions concatenated between them, which has the ultimate goal of carrying out a specific task otherwise not achievable.

This approach has been used for the realisation of an algorithm as a bidirectional information bridge between the modelling software and PostgreSQL.

3   First Results

3.1   GIS Database Connection and Entities Visualisation and Querying

After the database population of objects and their attributes harmonisation, it was possible to connect the data structure in GIS.

Thanks to the open-source platform QGIS (version 3.16.1) and the spatial extension PotsGIS, the users can visualise, query and edit (with different level of permission) the data related to the Sacred Mount of Varallo.

Figure 8 shows examples of Chapels 14 and 26 queried; in this case, attributes of different tables connected to the "building" could be integrated and updated.

Fig. 8. QGIS visualisation of entities attributes and relations of the spatial database.

3.2 BIM Data Integration Through Dynamo

The bidirectional data bridge with the VPL methodology previously described is made of a series of Dynamo script, each with a specific function. A script allows the export, extracting from the BIM model a series of parameters related to information necessary for maintenance, such as dimensional data, materials, textual parameters containing information on the last maintenance operations carried out, notes on the peculiar characteristics of certain elements. This information is then used to populate the respective attributes within the database in PostgreSQL in tables previously created and related to the GIS ones. This data transfer is possible by using the "Get Parameter" and Python nodes which, given a series of variable Revit inputs, generates a matrix of commands in SQL (Structured Query Language) and sends it to the database via a connection string. This operation can be repeated to update the BIM data by running an additional script to overwrite the previous content. Finally, a script allows the data import, i.e. reading potential changes from the PostgresSQL database, directly into Dynamo through specific queries and transferring them to Revit parameters based on the proper correspondences, using the "Set Parameter" node (Fig. 9).

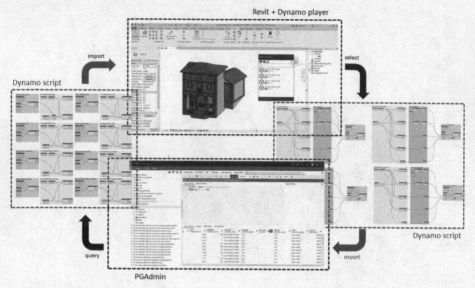

Fig. 9. PostgresSQL database connection of one of the BIM models through Dynamo.

The final result is a one-click action that the end user will start through Dynamo Player, then depending on the operation performed the output will just be a notice of operation occurred correctly. Through this application and the graphical client PgAdmin, the database administrator will be able to manage in a simplified way the PostgreSQL database and the integration of GIS-BIM data. This methodology allows the continuous updating of the data but, above all, it allows the bidirectionality of the information as Revit-DB-Link keeps unchanged the structure of the database, which is an essential requirement to achieve the project goals. Through the viewer, it is possible to edit the data of the models that will be automatically updated in the DB with time versioning. In fact, a specific field permits to store the date of data insertion and, depending on the kind of data, it will be replaced or simply stored. In particular, the data that must maintain a registration frequency for maintenance purposes would not be overwritten, otherwise the data substitution allows an easiest storage, lowering memory capacity, exploiting also the SQL option to make database backups, restoring a data history.

4 Conclusions and Future Developments

The present paper illustrates the first results of a three-year research project for planned cultural heritage maintenance (both movable and immovable). The project's first developments are essential to structure an integrated database, following geographic standards such as INSPIRE, CityGML and IFC and containing Sacred Mounts' data represented in different levels of detail. Hence, thanks to the LoDs subdivision, it is possible to describe and visualise both the architectural assets and the urban-territorial contexts. Moreover, the HBIM models and cartographic data visualised and queried in GIS derived from post-processed data of 3D metric survey performed.

The main innovation consists of creating a unique platform in which it is possible to visualise and query the HBIM model, GIS and acquired data and maintenance parameters. In this way, interoperability problems between DBs are avoided, and data management and updating are simplified. The GIS-BIM database integration has been achieved by using Dynamo, a visual programming language, which made it possible to create a script to connect the DB of the object-oriented software (Revit in this case) with the Developed DB (in PostgreSQL). The existing data from the parametric model are converted and inserted directly into the DB's table; moreover, BIM parameters could be updated from PostgreSQL.

Ongoing development of this project involves creating a viewer platform in which it could be possible to visualise, query and update all the data stored in the DB. This demonstrator should include a user-friendly dashboard to immediately understand complex and multi-scale data through graphs or charts and the option to modify only specific parameters according to the login type (with different level of permission of access according to different types of users, such as tourists, maintenance technicians, architects, restorers and artisans).

References

1. Matrone, F., Colucci, E., De Ruvo, V., Lingua, A., Spanò, A.: HBIM in a semantic 3D GIS database. Int. Arch. Photogramm. Remote Sens. Spat. Inf. Sci. **XLII-2/W11**, 857–865 (2019)
2. Colucci, E., De Ruvo, V., Lingua, A., Matrone, F., Rizzo, G.: HBIM-GIS integration: from IFC to CityGML standard for damaged cultural heritage in a multi-scale 3D GIS. Appl. Sci. **10**, 1356 (2020)
3. INSPIRE. https://inspire.ec.europa.eu/. Accessed 3 Feb 2021
4. CityGML. https://www.ogc.org/standards/citygml. Accessed 02 Feb 2021
5. IFC. https://www.buildingsmart.org/standards/bsi-standards/industry-foundation-classes/. Accessed 2 Feb 2021
6. Zerbinatti, M., Matrone, F., Lingua, A.: Planned maintenance for architectural heritage. Experiences in progress from 3D survey to intervention programmes through HBIM. TEMA Technol. Eng. Mater. Archit. **7**(21), 32–42 (2021)
7. MAIN.10.ANCE project. https://main10ance.eu/. Accessed 27 Mar 2021
8. El Meouche, R., Rezoug, M., Hijazi, I.: Integrating and managing BIM in GIS, software review. Int. Arch. Photogramm. Remote Sens. Spat. Inf. Sci. **XL-2/W2**, 31–34 (2013)
9. Del Giudice, M., Osello, A., Patti, E.: BIM and GIS for district modeling. In: 10th European Conference on Product and Process Modelling (ECPPM 2014), Vienna, Austria (2014)
10. Fosu, R.; Suprabhas, K.; Rathore, Z.; Cory, C.: Integration of Building Information Modeling (BIM) and Geographic Information Systems (GIS) – a literature review and future needs. In: Proceedings of 32nd CIB W78 Conference 2015, Eindhoven, The Netherlands (2015)
11. Amirebrahimi, S., Rajabifard, A., Mendis, P., Ngo, T.: A BIM-GIS integration method in support of the assessment and 3D visualisation of flood damage to a building. J. Spat. Sci. **61**(2), 317–350 (2016)

12. Noardo, F., et al.: GeoBIM benchmark 2019: design and initial results. Int. Arch. Photogramm. Remote Sens. Spat. Inf. Sci. **XLII-2/W13**, 1339–1346 (2019)

13. Noardo, F., et al.: GeoBIM benchmark 2019: intermediate results. Int. Arch. Photogramm. Remote Sens. Spat. Inf. Sci. **15**, 47–52 (2019)

14. Månsson, U.: BIM & GIS connectivity paves the way for really smart cities. Geoforum Perspektiv **14**(25), 19–24 (2015)

15. Wang, H., Pan, Y., Luo, X.: Integration of BIM and GIS in sustainable built environment: a review and bibliometric analysis. Autom. Constr. **103**, 41–52 (2019)

16. Song, Y., et al.: Trends and opportunities of BIM-GIS integration in the architecture, engineering and construction industry: a review from a spatio-temporal statistical perspective. ISPRS Int. J. Geo-Inf. **6**(12), 397 (2017)

17. Mignard, C., Nicolle, C.: Merging BIM and GIS using ontologies application to urban facility management in ACTIVe3D. Comput. Ind. **65**(9), 1276–1290 (2014)

18. Bruno, N., Rechichi, F., Achille, C., Zerbi, A., Roncella, R., Fassi, F.: Integration of historical GIS data in A HBIM system. ISPRS Int. Arch. Photogramm. Remote Sens. Spat. Inf. Sci. **XLIII-B4-2020**, 427–434 (2020)

19. BDTRE: La Base Dati Territoriale di Riferimento degli Enti piemontesi. https://www.geoportale.piemonte.it/cms/bdtre/bdtre-2. Accessed 25 May 2021

20. Catalogo dei dati territoriali, Specifiche di contenuto per i DataBase Geotopografici della Regione Piemonte. https://www.geoportale.piemonte.it/cms/images/bdtre_doc/Specifica2.0.pdf. Accessed 25 May 2021

21. Laurini, R., Thompson, D.: Fundamentals of Spatial Information Systems, vol. 37. Academic Press, London (1992)

22. Autodesk Revit. https://www.autodesk.com/products/revit/architecture. Accessed 25 May 2021

23. Del Giudice, M., Lingua, A., Matrone, F., Noardo, F., Sanna, S., Zerbinatti, M.: Rilevamento metrico 3D e modellazione HBIM per la manutenzione programmata del patrimonio architettonico. In: Atti conferenza ASITA 2017, pp. 356–364 (2017). ISBN 978–88–941232–8–9

"Bronzi di Riace" Geomatics Techniques in Augmented Reality for Cultural Heritage Dissemination

Vincenzo Barrile[iD], Ernesto Bernardo[✉][iD], Giuliana Bilotta[iD], and Antonino Fotia[iD]

Department of Civil, Energy, Environment and Materials Engineering (DICEAM), University of Mediterranea of Reggio Calabria, Via Graziella, Feo di Vito, 89128 Reggio Calabria, Italy
ernesto.bernardo@unirc.it

Abstract. In the National Archaeological Museum of Reggio Calabria (Southern Italy) are located two full-size bronzes cast around the 5th century BC: The "Bronzi di Riace". Thanks to their outstanding manufacture, they truly represent significant sculptural masterpieces of Greek art in the world. This paper describes the methodology used by the Geomatics Laboratory of the DICEAM of the Mediterranean University of Reggio Calabria to achieve a 3D model of the two sculptures. The 3D modelling is based on the use of imaging techniques, such as digital photogrammetry and computer vision. The achieved results demonstrate the effectiveness of the technique used in the cultural heritage field for the creation of a digital production and replication through 3D printing. Moreover, for tourism purposes in order to further valorize and disseminate archaeological heritage, we developed an app based on Augmented Reality (AR). There is a renewed interest in the context of international museological studies and AR innovation represents a new method for amplifying visitor numbers into museums, despite concerns over returns on investment. The enhancement of cultural heritage by 3D acquisition and modeling tools represents one of the fields of study that will see rapid development in the near future. The created app allows the users, in real time, to obtain additional information on the object of investigation, even allowing them to view the 3D model in AR. Moreover, the app combines AR and Virtual Reality (VR) technologies with the opportunities offered by 3D printing.

Keywords: 3D model · 3D printing · Virtual Reality · Augmented Reality

1 Introduction

The National Archaeological Museum of Reggio Calabria has been recognized among the most prestigious archaeological museums in Italy. There is a revaluation of the artistic and cultural heritage, which especially in recent years is no longer seen as an argument of interest only for specialists but also and above all as a tool for the socio-economic development of the territory. Therefore, we have taken into consideration the possibility of favoring the entry into the National Archaeological Museum of Reggio Calabria of new technological tools, such as Augmented Reality (AR) and Virtual Reality (VR). We want to encourage a modern approach to the use of cultural heritage by

© Springer Nature Switzerland AG 2022
E. Borgogno-Mondino and P. Zamperlin (Eds.): ASITA 2021, CCIS 1507, pp. 195–215, 2022.
https://doi.org/10.1007/978-3-030-94426-1_15

these new technologies, which are already successfully applied by other institutions and foundations such as the Musée d'Art et d'Histoire in Geneva or in Italy in Rome at the Terme di Diocleziano [1, 2].

The application of these technologies allows us to offer to users an extremely immersive experience; such an incredible experience is not offered by the classic visit to a museum. Thanks to VR it will be possible for users to visit the museum even before setting foot in it or to view works that for logistic reasons cannot be physically exposed. Using the AR it is possible for the museum to create references to the works on the territory present in the museum to increase engagement. To this effect, 3D scanners and computer graphics have proved to be very powerful tools for creating static or interactive models, through the creation of three-dimensional models that allow access to the general public to artworks that cannot be exhibited due to lack of space or that could otherwise be degraded or damaged.

The most valuable works in the National Archaeological Museum of Reggio Calabria are the "Bronzi di Riace" (Fig. 1), recovered in 1972 representing one of the most significant examples of classical Greek art. In fact, every physical contact, like casts, with works like the "Bronzi di Riace", necessarily leads to a degradation of the artwork. And it is for this reason that the creation of highly detailed three-dimensional models, whose survey occurs without requiring direct physical contact with the works, and the subsequent 3D printing of the created model, make it possible to guarantee the fruition of the work without affecting its duration in the time. With the use of technology at the base of 3D printing, it is possible to produce faithful copies, which allows us to use them for exposures subject to atmospheric or the other aggressive agents, allowing the use of works in places in which they are not exposed to and from which they cannot be moved without significant costs and risks during their transport. Furthermore, the three-dimensional models created could be implemented in apps that can be accessed from smartphones that allow museum visitors, through AR, to have access to an incredibly greater amount of information than they are commonly exposed to during the view of an artwork. Just think of the possibilities connected with the use of video or audio, during the visit, or the possibility of creating different thematic routes depending on the choices made by the user on the app. This visit thus offers a much more user-oriented experience who is no longer forced to follow paths predetermined by the museum curator. Likewise, by making use of VR, the user can access historical reconstructions of events or places linked to the works on display to be prepared to view them in an active and non-passive manner, as we are commonly accustomed to considering a visit to the museum.

For such reasons the Geomatics Laboratory of Reggio Calabria has decided to engage in the development of an app for tourist and academic purposes that allows taking advantage of the three-dimensional reconstruction of the goods present in the National Archaeological Museum of Reggio Calabria. If you want to view some works without physically accessing the structure it is possible thanks to VR. Furthermore, an app is being designed that offers the user the possibility of requesting the three-dimensional printing of some works or some of their reconstructions.

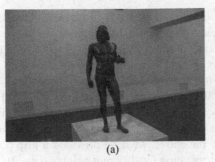 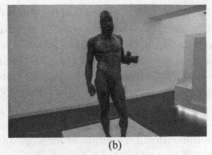

(a)   (b)

Fig. 1. Bronze statues located at the National Archaeological Museum of Reggio Calabria (Italy): (a) Bronze A; (b) Bronze B.

2 Materials and Methods

2.1 Survey and 3D Modeling

In the last decade, one of the technologies that has increasingly been affirming, especially for its relatively low cost compared to the quality of the results, is photogrammetry. This technique is based on the principle of "Structure from Motion" (SfM), which is the most widely used technique of range imaging in computer vision. Through photogrammetry to the theoretical principles of collinearity, intersection of projective rays, camera calibration, the typical algorithms of robotic vision are used, which allow to analyze and correlate digital images quickly and automatically.

The logic behind SfM is the following: by acquiring the image of an object from different perspectives, we are able to obtain a three-dimensional reproduction of the same, applying specific algorithms to the photos. In practice, with this software is exploited the principle of stereoscopic vision used by human eyes to return three-dimensional images. According to this principle, if we have two photographs of an object whose centers are placed at a sufficient distance between them, approximately between 1/10 and 1/5 of the distance between the camera and the object, it is possible to reconstruct a three-dimensional image of the object. Then, by taking a series of photos, you can create a three-dimensional digital model of the object captured by the lens.

The fundamental characteristic that the 3D digital model has to possess is to be metrically correct: this means that the model must be in the right scale and it should be possible to make precise measurements on it. A second important feature, although not fundamental, is that the color must be realistic: this condition is not always necessary and depends on the purpose for which the 3D model is created. In the case of a model that must be used on the web or on applications for tablets and smartphones, it is important that the color is realistic. This is not essential, in the case of a model created in function of a reproduction in 3D printing, being this technology not able to reproduce color. In order to obtain a good result, we must be secure that the adjacent digital images overlap each other for at least 80% laterally and at least 30% vertically. The final quality of the three-dimensional model depends directly on the resolution of the photos and therefore on the camera and the optics used for the survey campaign. The redundancy of the data depends on the survey campaign, as we have seen; the images must overlap, and thanks to this redundancy is guaranteed the complete and realistic reconstruction of the model. Finally, since the model we want to achieve must be metrically accurate, we will have to foresee the positioning and an accurate survey of the constraints [3–9]. For our major campaign, we used a Canon EOS 6D which is a 35 m Digital Single Lens Reflex (DSLR) full-frame. It features a 20.2 megapixel full-frame metal oxide semiconductor (CMOS) image sensor and an ISO range of 100–25,600, expandable to L: 50, H1: 51,200 and H2: 102,400, for higher quality image, even in poor lighting conditions. The effective pixel size is 26.2 megapixels, which are more than enough to achieve a high resolution of the three-dimensional model. In order to ensure the above, we have provided a grip point every 10° to cover a corner and repeated the operation for different heights (Fig. 2).

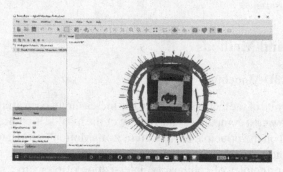

Fig. 2. Camera positions.

It can also be seen how markers were placed at the foot of the works that serve to ensure the dimensional correspondence between the digital model and the real work, actually acting as constraints, even if the software could still obtain correct dimensional results without requiring physical constraints (by entering in it the reference dimensions in length and height for scaling).

To make the three-dimensional model we used the commercial software Metashape produced by Agisoft. Through the elaboration of the photographs, the user is able to construct the texture of a three-dimensional model.

To do this it operates through three main phases:

1. Camera alignment. Metashape obtains common points on the photographs to obtain a scattered points cloud.
2. Dense point cloud construction. Metashape generates a point cloud denser and more detailed based on the estimated photos positions.
3. Mesh generation. Metashape merge the dense point cloud to reconstruct the surface of a 3D polygons.
4. Build Texture and 3D model. The generated mesh is corrected, and a texture is built.

In the alignment phase Metashape looks for common points between the various images and matches them; at the same time, it calculates the position of the camera for each image and perfects the calibration parameters of the same. It then outputs a scattered point cloud and the positions of the camera. This is because by deducing the position taken by the individual photographs it is possible to deduce by triangulation the position of the objects in them and from this position obtain the three-dimensional model of the objects. To deduce the position of the photos we use image-matching algorithms that identify key points, easily recognizable in three or more images: in fact, they are those constraints that serve to ensure a metric correspondence between model and real object.

Starting from the key points, through a procedure of photogrammetric triangulation with projective stars (better known as bundle adjustment), in an automatic way the camera is calibrated (internal orientation: calculation of the focal length and of the main point). The shooting position of the single photograph is rebuilt (external orientation: coordinates of the grip centers and frame rotations), and for each key point we obtained the real coordinates x, y, z, which are three-dimensionally materialized in a sparse points cloud, that is a cloud of points with low density (sparse reconstruction).

In the second phase, based on the positions of the points in the sparse point cloud, it is thickened to generate a dense point cloud; to do this, the coordinates of the points obtained in the first phase are used to estimate the position of the intermediate points in order to thicken the point cloud.

This dense point cloud can be interpreted as a raw data, which is nothing more than a series of coordinates (x, y, z) of the points.

After the creation of the dense point cloud, the software generates a continuous polygonal surface that is a 3D polygonal mesh. It represents the surface of the object we are detecting through a triangular mesh and each of these triangles has a vertex in one of the points of the cloud previously generated.

Once the mesh is generated, we can modify it in order to improve the final result, however this operation is limited. In fact, within Metashape, we are only allowed to delete polygons or repair any holes in the mesh, if we need to intervene more markedly, we must necessarily resort to third-part software.

The mesh originally has no color, so it must be assigned to the polygons. The color can be assigned to the polygons that make up the mesh in two different ways: by color-per-vertex or texture mapping.

The first is to mediate on each triangle of the mesh the color that each of its three points had originally in the dense point cloud, while the second involves the use of the starting images or being the same already oriented with respect to the model, their color is projected onto the latter and give rise to a square texture on the model.

The choice between the two depends mainly on the quality of the photos and their number, in fact with the second method the quality of the result is independent of the density of the dense point cloud but is influenced by the quality of the photos. In the case of the survey of museum artifacts, however it is good always use the texture mapping, as it is a result more adherent to the original model.

The generated three-dimensional model (Fig. 3) can then be exported in various formats that can be edited by different software, in our case it was exported in STL format (acronym for Standard Triangulation Language) and then used to create a physical model of the Bronzes printed in 3D.

In addition, as is well known, there are many methodologies for creating 3D models, and each has a different level of detail accuracy, depending on the instrumentation and methodology used in relation to the end use for which the work is intended.

(a)   (b)

Fig. 3. (a, b) 3D model.

In this case, because the didactic nature and the touristic finality of the application, the metric accuracy of the 3D model assumes a lower importance than the need to visualize its shape. For this reason, we decided to carry on the 3D survey of the National Archeological Museum, in an easier way, using directly a dataset obtainable from Google Earth, and then processed by classical photogrammetric techniques (Fig. 4).

Clearly, as we aspect, the precision between the model generated by this application has an accuracy lower than 3D model generated with laser scanner or UAV.

Fig. 4. Museum 3D model.

2.2 3D Printing

Rapid prototyping, or 3D printing from a digital model, enables the production of physical models at scale and with user-set definition.

Before the advent of this technology, it was necessary to resort to plaster casts of the object to obtain a physical model perfectly corresponding to the reality of an object, such as a work of artistic interest or an archaeological find. However, it was necessary to resort to plaster casts of the object, but this operation inevitably risked degrading the artwork in addition to the tangible risk of damaging it during surveying or handling operations. Furthermore, the objective impossibility of scaling the work necessarily led to the realization of copies in a 1:1 scale. This is desirable for surveys that served for the mere realization of a copy of the original but made it impossible for a whole series of possibilities that opens the reduction in scale of the original, such as the production of merchandising perfectly adherent to the original artwork.

Today it is instead possible to obtain the three-dimensional digital model of the artifact of interest through photogrammetry, without any physical contact between the artwork and the gripping tools, and then make a print of the artifact on the desired scale, which as seen was impossible with plaster casts, where the scale was necessarily 1:1. Obviously, the printing of large models is difficult and economically inconvenient.

3D printing can be based on two different CNC (Computer Numerical Control) applications:

- Subtractive printing: printing is by subsequent deletion, usually milling or selective laser, of layers or pieces of the material to be modeled; it represents the required choice to make elements in steel or aluminum. However, it allows the creation of prototypes with materials having a greater mechanical strength than those used in additive printing, but anyhow it has important limitations in the printing of elements with a complex geometry.
- Additive printing: it is a print in the strict sense, which is based on the subsequent overlapping of layers of extruded material that allows prototypes to be obtained, even with a very complex geometry, in a relatively short time, and if desired consisting of two or three different materials. Naturally, it prints with materials that can be extruded, such as clay, PLA, ABS, and alike, which therefore have a lower mechanical strength, although in recent years it has been possible to print the Nylon, thus overcoming this problem in part.

The applications of a similar technology in the field of cultural heritage are not limited to the production of realistic copies, but they are multiple applications, in fact, it can be used for:

- making copies to be exhibited temporarily or permanently, for example to temporarily replace a piece subjected to restoration or to definitively replace a work of historical or artistic interest that is undergoing excessive degradation due to exposure to atmospheric agents;
- we can think of support for blind people, who need to "touch" a work to be able to appreciate it, which otherwise would have no way of appreciating much of our artistic heritage;
- the mass production of merchandising that corresponds to the original work, so of certainly high quality as well as having a didactic value;
- installation of sensors, which if connected to the AR can offer visitors a more immersive and complete experience while visiting our artistic heritage;
- realization of exhibitions with 3D printed pieces; for example, with the display of works that for structural or conservation reasons cannot be exhibited or transported.

Furthermore, it is also possible to use this technology for the restoration of a previously damaged work. In fact, it is possible to digitally model a missing or damaged piece of the original work, print it with suitable material and then mount it on the original artwork with a final aesthetic effect that will depend exclusively on the materials and the definition chosen.

We verified that the print quality is such to allow the production of elements suitable for the production of merchandising and the possible application of the same technology for the temporary replacement of artworks [10–12].

The printer used to produce the scale model of the "Bronzi di Riace" is a "Bq Hephestos 2", which for the realization, or rather the printing, of the object exploits the subsequent deposition of layers of molten material or FDM (Fused Deposition Modeling).

It is possible to print with only a material of choice at time for a single-extruder printer. The material chosen to print the model was polylactic acid (PLA). It represents now a standard for printing through this technology, thanks to its relatively low temperature of fusion (starting from 180 °C), to its low retraction index, to the discrete mechanical properties, but mainly because, unlike the ABS, its predecessor and it does not release toxic fumes during the extrusion operations.

The software is Repetier-Host and it is used to translate the three-dimensional model into commands in G-Code, that is the programming language of the CNC (those codes and commands that position the extruder and start to execute the print). Hot-World GmbH & Co. KG, a German software house that distributes it as "free to use", produced it.

The first operation was to set the printing parameters (Table 1) and check the integrity of the three-dimensional model, namely the absence of damage and gaps or cuts in the mesh and above all its structural integrity.

Table 1. Printing parameters.

Quality	Layer height	0.2 mm
Shell	Wall thickness	1
	Upper/lower layer thickness	1 mm
Filling	Filling density	20%
	Fill configuration	Honeycomb
Material	Printing temperature	200 °C
	Type material	PLA
Speed	Filling speed	80 mm/s
	Support speed	60 mm/s
	Displacement speed	100 mm/s
	External/internal wall speed	40 mm/s
	Initial layer speed	30 mm/s
Support	Support positioning	In all necessary point
	Overhang angle of support	50°

The first is only a necessary verification (the object must be manifold) to obtain a model that can be printed without problems, an operation that the software automatically performs and could even solve by itself without excessively altering the result. This control is necessary because in the case in which the object we want to print is not manifold, the slicer is not able to design the printing path since it would be found with an open and not closed three-dimensional model, as it expected instead.

In this regard, we have verified that the repair carried out directly by the software is fine for minor imperfections, which are therefore not appreciable when the printing is completed, while for problems related to the closure of the relevant model, better results are obtained by performing the repair manually through third party software.

The second is usually solved by the software and concerns the need to create some supports for the suspended parts of the model (Fig. 5). These supports are indispensable since in FDM printing operations of a layer at a given height from the base is printed all at once, so if we must print a suspended piece, like the arm of Bronze A, the printer will extrude the filament on the void with the obvious consequences. Naturally, these supports will then be eliminated subsequently in a mechanical way through special pliers. In the case in which it is not possible to remove the supports, the best results are obtained with printers, equipped with double extruder, which can print the model in two different materials. For example, the model is printed in PLA and the supports in HIPS (High Impact Polystyrene) which is soluble in the D-Limonene, a volatile hydrocarbone, and then by immersing the model in the solvent the supports "melt" on their own.

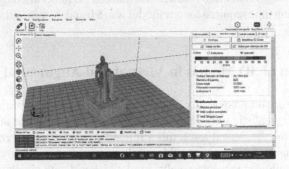

Fig. 5. 3D model to print.

Once the integrity of the model has been verified, it is possible to proceed with the Slicing that is with its subdivision into a series of "slices" (in English it is generally translated as "layer") horizontal planes, which will then be extruded one above the other, by depositing molten material from the printer extruder.

In the final object (Fig. 6) there will be the presence of a slight horizontal scoring that can be reduced by reducing the printing speed, in particular on the external perimeter. If we want to eliminate the height of the layers and the thickness of the hot-end, we can reduce it to a minimum already in the printing phase or we can proceed with the post-print abrasion of the PLA model using sandpaper.

Similarly, to what we saw for the external perimeter, we can define the type of Infill or filling of the model. Since there are no reasons to completely fill the extruded

Fig. 6. 3D print.

PLA model, it is used to fill with geometric motifs, so that the Infill directly affects the mechanical capacity of the final object. In our case, to get good mechanical skills we made use of an Infill Honeycomb that has excellent mechanical capabilities and does not go too far in prolonging printing times.

The software that allowed us to define the above is Slic3r; it is one of the internal slicers in Repetier Host, released with an Open Source license that effectively transforms the three-dimensional model into instructions that can be understood by the printer (G-Code). The printing time required for our model was 5 h and 30 min and we used 23.74 m of PLA.

3   Integration of 3D Models in Virtual and Augmented Reality

Virtual Reality (VR) simulates reality. The advancement of computer technologies allows navigating in photorealistic settings in real time, interacting with the objects present in them. Even if at the theoretical level, this simulated reality could interact with all five human senses contemporary; it is possible to use it on a large scale only for hearing and sight. The user is allowed in a completely simulated world with which it can interact, in the case of VR apps, via sensors or taps on the smartphone screen. The most interesting application of this technology, at least as regards cultural heritage, is the simulation of realistic environments such as a virtual tour inside a museum or a building of particular historical or architectural interest, perhaps with a guide that tells the story of the artworks on display as we move within the virtual environment. While for Augmented Reality (AR), or reality mediated by the computer, we mean the enrichment of human sensory perception by means of information, generally handled and conveyed electronically, which would not be perceptible with the five senses. Museums today play a particularly important role in modern society, as they preserve events of the past and present them in a way that can be understood and appreciated by a modern public. From this point of view, the AR represents a tool with great potential, given the fact that nowadays the visitor is no longer satisfied with an analogical experience but wants to accompany it with a digital experience that the AR can offer by representing a point of connection between the two experiences. To make use of this technology, the hardware, through specific sensors and algorithms, determines the position and orientation of the camera and the AR imposes 3D models on what the camera sees essentially imposing data or images on the real. And it is here that the real potential of this technology is captured, in fact through the AR we can observe a work, such as a painting or a sculpture, and see the same in motion or the artist who created the work explain to us why of a certain stylistic choice or tell us his story. Moreover, it navigates in a direction that many museums have understood how the use of AR and VR allows them to offer visitors a much more immersive experience than traditional and that places the user-visitor at the center (Fig. 7 and 8).

Fig. 7. View 3D model in augmented reality.

Fig. 8. View 3D model and details in augmented reality.

Of course, this brings the advantage of both actors in the game, in fact the visitors see themselves placed at the center of the visit. At the same time, the museum or the authority that takes care of the realization of the app increases engagement and at the same time obtains important information on user preferences by evaluating their interactions with the various exhibited works. Because of the potential inherent in these technologies, museums are proving to be one of the most interesting sectors in which to apply them, in fact through the integration of 3D models in Augmented Reality environments museums can offer a vision of history richer in information and much more interactive. In fact, through AR it is possible to add virtual elements to the physical reality. These elements are not limited in appearing on the screen but interacting with each other and with the user in real time, providing information on the artworks observed and providing the user with choices on how to continue the visit. Thanks to these virtual elements, they allow us to guarantee a much more formative and immersive experience for the user, but above all they place it at the center of the experience, in particular if they allow it to share the same through social media. The use of AR is not limited to museums but can be extended to the entire artistic heritage of the city, in fact, it is also possible to implement it on the external cultural heritage, perhaps with references to works present in the museum, and thus allow the visitor to do not end your experience once the visit is over. Furthermore, the use of VR, which as we have seen is the user's immersion in a digital world, can allow the fruition of the works inside the museum through the creation of a digital model of the same with three-dimensional models inside, captured through photogrammetric techniques, of the exhibited works and not only. In a physical structure, space is limited, in fact, most museums cannot exhibit all the artworks they own but must necessarily choose some, in a virtual structure we do not have this problem so that the entire collection owned by the museum can be exhibited. Thus, will increase the influx of visitors to the institution. Nevertheless, the possibilities offered by Virtual Reality also allow us to reconstruct environments of historical interest, regarding the exhibited works, which the user could visit in VR and receive information on them from an audio guide. In this regard, to favor the development of the territory it can be interesting to combine the AR and therefore push the visitor to go to the place where a certain event occurred and through the camera of their smartphone interact and watch particular micro-events or historical-artistic accurate reconstructions of an area or some historical events. One of the most interesting applications of this integration between AR and VR is the possibility to create events related not only to the space and to the place where the user is located, but also to the time [13–16].

Figure 9 shows the possibility of interacting in VR with the 3D model of the reconstruction of a bronze (reproduced, as it should have been originally, including the missing parts). The user can interact, add and subtract additional elements of the statue that are currently missing (spear, helmet and shield).

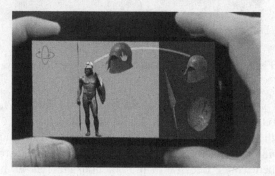

Fig. 9. View 3D model in virtual reality.

All these previously described functions have been implemented in a more complete app suitably created for the complete management and use of the museum.

4 The Developed App

Internet, social networks, apps are now the preferential information channel for art tourism, in fact it is through them that the travel is organized, museums and works to be visited are chosen and more and more often the tickets are purchased. And it is in this context that a tourist app for mobile devices (still under development and updating) has been created that allows the user, in real time, to view the 3D AR model of the object of interest, to have further information on the same and to buy a three-dimensional PLA print.

The app, in addition to exploiting the possibilities offered by AR and VR, wants to combine these technologies with the opportunities offered by 3D printing. It has been designed to allow visitors to request the printing of miniatures of 3D models of some works but not only. In effect, it is possible to reassemble the findings in Virtual Reality, to entirely reconstruct the missing parts, to view the original model and finally to modify, even with a certain freedom, the same and at the end to request the printing for each of the results offered by these possibilities. Obviously, in the classic meanings of VR, it allows you to take a virtual tour of the museum as a passive spectator or allow the visitor to be accompanied during the visit by a virtual guide that interacts with the surrounding environment. In order to develop tourism, in the city of Reggio Calabria, the Geomatics Laboratory of the Mediterranean University is implementing (with the Unity 3D platform) an application for tourism and educational purposes, for mobile devices, which allows users to take information, written and multimedia, concerning different points of interest in the city (squares, sculptures, churches and museums using AR technology). In particular, the app is currently being defined and allows users to access different services based on the choices previously made. In the future, we hope to add tags linked to the position to offer a series of services related to the place where you are [17–24]. In particular, in the National Archaeological Museum of Reggio Calabria, the app is able to:

- show different information, concerning the history of the artifact, depending on what the smartphone camera is capturing in that moment;
- display the multimedia content, such as video or audio, associated with the object framed by the user through their device;
- highlight the details of interest directly on the object that we are framing and of which we want to carry out a more detailed study, making learning easier and immediate;
- view the 3D model of the artifact, modify it or disassemble and rebuild it;
- making a virtual tour of the museum as a passive spectator, or take the same tour but as an active spectator interacting through the screen of your device;
- offer the user a virtual guide that accompanies him during the visit of the museum and relates to the surrounding environment;
- display the visitor's position in the museum's floor plans with the names of the rooms in which you are located;
- reconstruct and assemble (even imaginatively) one or more three-dimensional models and then book a 3D print.

The app we refereed before, is made with Unity 3D, and it is structured through a series of scenes. Precisely, we have an initial scene, a loading scene and an exploration scene, whose sequence depends on the choices made by the user. The two main scripts are the SceneManager that performs the initialization operations and the SceneLoader that loads the desired scene and controls the transition between one scene and another. Being the app, or rather its project, conceived as a series of scenes that follow one another over time, the first part of the work focuses on the creation of the basic elements of the virtual tour that is the main scene containing all the information on the immersive environment we want to create. At this point, it will be understood how the virtual tour is conceived as a sequence of scenes presented in succession during the passage of time, creating what is the sensation of movement. Motion tracking allows us to activate animations or videos based on the position and orientation of the device, move around an object and interact with it as if it were part of the environment and allows tracking the position of the device in relation to the surrounding environment. This type of tracking has already been implemented in our app. It allows the app to us to know when we are moving and consequently to react accordingly; in order to achieve this we must make use of ARCore, a software development kit made by Google that is implemented within the Unity environment to obtain the desired result. ARCore receives information from the room and from the inertial sensors present in the hardware on which we run our app. Through a process called Concurrent Odometry and Mapping (COM) is able to determine the position of the smartphone that moves in space and correctly render the three-dimensional model in AR in such a way that it looks realistic, autonomously defining plans and feature points to identify the appropriate constraints for the correct positioning of the object in space and with respect to the camera. In essence, it allows the smartphone to understand where it is in relation to the world around it, and once the location of the device is known, ARCore is able to position the objects in such a way that their interaction with the environment is realistic and the device. It is also able to observe the surrounding light and illuminate objects as if they were part of the environment. We performed the test on Unity 2019.2.13 and with ARCore SDK for Unity 1.13, to make use of this package we loaded it into the Unity environment, and we enabled its use from Player Settings > XR Settings > ARCore Supported and disabled the Auto Graphics API from Player Settings > Other Settings > Rendering. After that we imported the three-dimensional model inside the scene, defined the laying position (Center Eye). In order to obtain the desired effect inside the GameObject MainCamera, we added the components Track Pose Driver and ARCore Session, configured the same and finally defined the Background as an ARBackground to see the object inside the device as if interacting with the surrounding environment. As we want to make the experience as realistic as possible and at the same time increase the engagement of the user, we realized that the user may want to pause the experience and then resume it later, as putting the experience to rest and then resuming from scratch it can greatly reduce the user's interest. In order to achieve this, we can make use of ARCore's short native break, but for our purposes, we needed something different, so we tested the following script:

```
main.py                                              [ ]   (`   Run

897   using System.Collections;
898   using System.Collections.Generic;
899   using UnityEngine;
900   using GoogleARCore;
901 · public class PauseAR :
902   MonoBehaviour
903 · {
904   public ARCoreSession
905   SessionController;
906   private bool m_sessionPaused = false;
907   public void TooglePauseMode()
908 · {
909   if (SessionController == null)
910 · {
911   return;
912   }
913   SessionController.enabled = m_sessionPaused;
914   m_sessionPaused = !m_sessionPaused;
915   }
916   }
```

That makes an image appear full screen during the break and allows you to pick up where you left off. We have considered it necessary to proceed in this direction rather than making use of ARCore's native pauses because it forces the user to resume the reproduction of the entire scene from the beginning for a medium-long pause, as can be a phone call. Using a Remote Position Call (RPC) function, we are able, based on the contents of the buffer, to make the object in question perform an action defined for a predetermined event and this action is performed both on the object present in the client than on the one present in the server (Fig. 10).

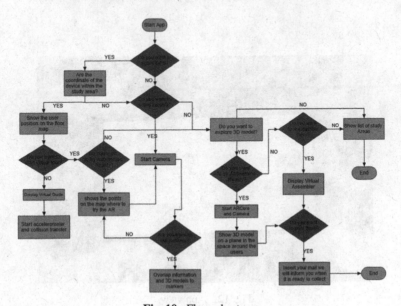

Fig. 10. Flow chart app.

Just as an example, we report some functions of the app:

- With the app it is possible to create an event that can be viewed through AR only if you are in a specific place at a specific time interval; of course, this type of operation is very marketing oriented and would mainly serve to push the interest of users of the museum towards particular places or events of historical interest.
- The app shows nearby places of interest and events (Fig. 11a). When a place of interest or an event is nearby, a notification arrives on the smartphone where the app is installed, and the closest route is calculated and displayed in AR (Fig. 11b).

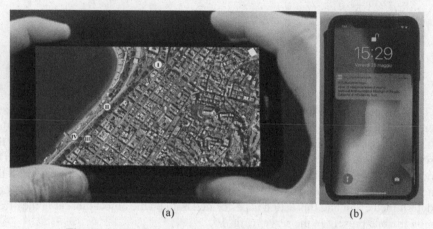

(a)   (b)

Fig. 11. (a) Place of interest into app map; (b) app notification.

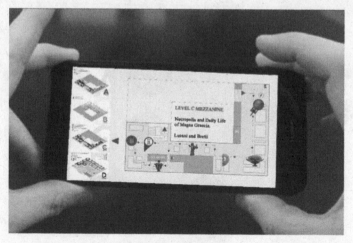

Fig. 12. App view.

Fig. 13. Booking mode 3D printing from the app.

Fig. 14. Video reconstructing one of "Bronzi di Riace".

- It is possible to visualize the visitor's position in the museum plans with the names of the rooms in which he is located (Fig. 12).
- It is possible to book a 3D reproduction (Fig. 13) with the possibility of printing an assembled and customized model.
- It is possible to view videos of the artefact contained in the museum (Fig. 14).

5 Upgrades Planned for the App

Currently we are developing some upgrades to be implemented within our app. The one of the immediate implementation and currently being studied is the possibility of offering to the user a choice of the material with which to print his model and we are evaluating the possibilities offered by:

- Metal Filaments: it is a mixed filament consisting of PLA and metallic powder, often of copper, which allows having a print with a metallic appearance, which is of a higher quality than plastic;
- Laywood: a filament made of 40% recycled wood that offers a final product with an appearance equivalent to that of a wooden product;
- ASA (Acrylonitrile Styrene Acrylate): whose structure makes it suitable for prints that are required to be exposed to atmospheric agents, to UV rays, require a certain thermal resistance and you want to keep the color over time;
- Clay: it is a print always based on the CNC but requires a special printer that is able to extrude directly the clay; of course, the result is more valuable than that obtainable with the classic print using thermoplastic polymers.

Another important upgrade concerns the implementation of 360° videos inside the VR in order to do this we are testing the shader produced by Toulouse de Margerie and uploaded on GitHub at the link https://github.com/Unity-Technologies/SkyboxPanoramicShader. By this shade, it is possible to make Unity support video at 180 and 360° in equiangular layouts (longitude and latitude) or cube map (6 frames). Of course, it will be necessary to make Skybox-PanoramicBeta.shader available in the project resources and inserting SkyboxPanoramicBetaShaderGUI.cs in a resource subfolder called "Editor". Conceptually we can make Unity process a 360° video through the following steps: 1. Set the Video Player to process the video file as Render Texture; 2. Set a Skybox Material to receive the Render Texture; 3. Set the scene that will use the Skybox Material. The part of the code that actually represents the heart of the shade is the following:

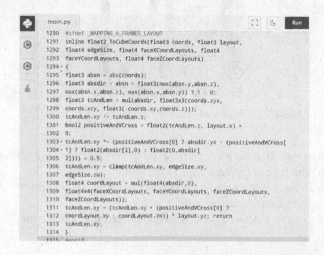

Finally, we are studying a way to use the motion tracking of ARCore to determine the position of the user in the space and therefore inside a building even without GPS. To do this, it is sufficient for us to define points of known coordinates, ideally the markers that activate the AR. Since ARCore calculates the distance between the object in AR and the user and the relative positions to give the sensation of movement and interaction of the object with the environment, we are implementing algorithms that allow us to use this distance to define the user's position within the museum (Fig. 15).

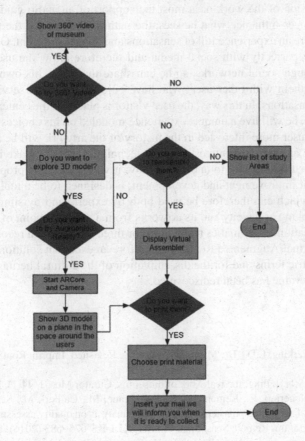

Fig. 15. Flow chart upgrades app.

6 Conclusion

The enhancement of cultural heritage by 3D acquisition and modeling tools represents one of the fields of study that will see rapid development in the near future. In fact, new technologies, such as AR or VR, allow us to further enhance our cultural heritage and at the same time completely change the experience of its use. In particular, they allow you to enjoy an experience that is developed on multiple levels. There will be the real level or the vision of the work inside the museum, but there will be one or more levels of use of the same provided by the AR that we allow access, by observing the work through a smartphone camera, to a quantity of information, through videos, audio or three-dimensional reconstructions, which it would not be possible to provide otherwise.

At the same time, VR allows us to reconstruct digitally entire works and environments, thus allowing museum visitors to view works that may not be displayed at the time of the visit. Therefore, the visitor passes from a passive user, who is limited to enjoying the vision of the work or at most the support of an audio guide, to an active user whose choices influence what he sees, the paths to follow and the type of use by offering therefore an experience full of sensations and always different. Of course, these technologies go perfectly with social media and therefore allow the user to share the experience through social networks, so he can share the paths, his own opinions and maybe discuss them with other users who have enjoyed the same service by sharing opinions and sensations. In this way, the user-visitor is placed at the center of the experience. Therefore, he will live a unique, experience modeled on his choices, and interests, consequently a user more interested in the history of the artwork will be able to deepen the same, while another user interested in the techniques used to make it can follow a different path that allows him to understand how it was made. The proposed app, still in the process of improvement and development, is designed to be a tool that moves in this direction, which can therefore be used both by experts and by simple enthusiasts interested in looking at the city and its artworks from a different point of view.

The combination of geomatics techniques for three-dimensional reconstruction, 3D printing and Virtual/Augmented Reality is therefore an excellent solution for conservation both in metric terms and for the dissemination of the cultural heritage of which in recent years the value has been rediscovered.

References

1. Falk, J.H., Dierking, L.D.: The Museum Experience Revisited. Imprint Routledge, New York (2013)
2. Bedford, L.: Storytelling: the real work of museums. Curator Mus. J. **44**(1), 27–34 (2001)
3. Menna, F., Nocerino, E., Remondino, F., Dellepiane, M., Callieri, M., Scopigno, R.: 3D Digitization of an heritage masterpiece - a critical analysis on quality assessment. ISPRS Int. Arch. Photogramm. Remote Sens. Spat. Inf. Sci. **XLI-B5**, 675–683 (2016)
4. Tucci, G., Bonora, V., Conti, A., Fiorini, L.: High-quality 3D models and their use in a cultural heritage conservation project. ISPRS Int. Arch. Photogramm. Remote Sens. Spat. Inf. Sci. **XLII-2/W5**, 687–693 (2017)
5. Apollonio, F.I., Ballabeni, M., Bertacchi, S., Fallavollita, F., Foschi, R., Gaiani, M.: From documentation images to restauration support tools: a path following the Neptune fountain in bologna design process. ISPRS Int. Arch. Photogramm. Remote Sens. Spat. Inf. Sci. **XLII-5/W1**, 329–336 (2017)
6. Micheletti, N., Kraus, K.: Photogrammetry–Geometry from Images and Laser Scans, pp. 47–125. Walter de Gruyter, Berlin (2007)
7. Green, S., Bevan, A., Shapland, M.: A comparative assessment of structure from motion methods for archaeological research. J. Archaeol. Sci. **46**, 173–181 (2014)

8. Barazzetti, L., Remondino, F., Scaioni, M.: Orientation and 3D modelling from markerless terrestrial images: combining accuracy with automation. Photogram. Record **25**(132), 356–381 (2010)
9. Chandler, J.H., Lane, S.N.: Structure from Motion (SFM) Photogrammetry. Geomorphological Techniques, Chap. 2, Sec. 2.2, pp. 1–12 (2015)
10. Bearman, D.: 3D Representations in museums. Curator Mus. J. **54**(1), 55–61 (2011)
11. Buehler, E., Kane, S.K., Hurst, A.: ABC and 3D: opportunities and obstacles to 3D printing in special education environments. In: Proceedings of the 16th International ACM SIGACCESS Conference on Computers and Accessibility, pp. 107–114, ASSETS '14. ACM: New York, NY, USA (2014)
12. Di Franco, P.D.G., Camporesi, C., Galeazzi, F., Kallmann, M.: 3D printing and immersive visualization for improved perception of ancient artifacts. Presence **24**(3), 243–264 (2015)
13. Bernardo, E., Bilotta, G.: Monumental arc 3D model reconstruction through BIM technology. In: Bevilacqua, C., Calabrò, F., Della Spina, L. (eds.) New Metropolitan Perspectives. NMP 2020. Smart Innovation, Systems and Technologies, 178 SIST, pp. 1581–1589. Springer, Cham (2021)
14. Barrile, V., Fotia, A., Bilotta, G., De Carlo, D.: Integration of geomatics methodologies and creation of a cultural heritage app using augmented reality. Virtual Archaeol. Rev. **10**(20), 40–51 (2019)
15. Barrile, V., Bilotta, G.: Computer vision in 3D modeling of cultural heritage: the Riace bronzes. ISPRS workshop on multi-dimensional & multi-scale spatial data modeling. Adv. Sci. Lett. **24**(1), 581–586 (2018)
16. Lowe, D.G.: Distinctive image features from scale-invariant keypoints. Int. J. Comput. Vision **60**(2), 91–110 (2004)
17. Caspani, S., Brumana, R., Oreni, D., Previtali, M.: Virtual museums as digital storytellers for dissemination of built environment: possible narratives and outlooks for appealing and rich encounters with the past. Int. Arch. Photogram. Remote Sens. Spat. Inform. Sci. **XLII-2/W5**, 113–119 (2017)
18. Redweik, P., Cláudio, A., Carmo, M., Naranjo, J., Sanjosé, J.: Digital preservation of cultural and scientific heritage: involving university students to raise awareness of its importance. Virtual Archaeol. Rev. **8**(16), 22–34 (2017)
19. Rinaudo, F., Bornaz, L., Ardissone, P.: 3D high accuracy survey and modelling for cultural heritage documentation and restoration. In: Vast 2007–Future Technologies to Empower Heritage Professionals, 26–29 Nov 2007, Brighton, UK, Archaeolingua Hun, pp. 19–23 (2007)
20. Bae, H., Golparvar-Fard, M., White, J.: High-precision vision-based mobile augmented reality system for context-aware architectural, engineering, construction and facility management (AEC/FM) applications. Visual. Eng. **1**(1), 1–13 (2013)
21. Barrile, V., Fotia, A., Bilotta, G.: Geomatics and augmented reality experiments for the cultural heritage. Appl. Geomatics **10**(4), 569–578 (2018)
22. Barrile, V., Fotia, A., Ponterio, R., Mollica Nardo, V., Giuffrida, D., Mastelloni, M.A.: A combined study of art works preserved in the archaeological museums: 3D survey, spectroscopic approach and augmented reality. Int. Arch. Photogramm. Remote Sens. Spatial Inf. Sci. **XLII-2/W11**, 201–207 (2019)
23. Bernardo, E., Musolino, M., Maesano, M.: San Pietro di Deca: from knowledge to restoration. Studies and geomatics investigations for conservation, redevelopment and promotion. In: Bevilacqua, C., Calabrò, F., Della Spina, L. (eds.) New Metropolitan Perspectives. NMP 2020. Smart Innovation, Systems and Technologies, vol. 178, pp. 1572–1580. Springer, Cham (2021)
24. Cuca, B., Brumana, R., Scaioni, M., Oreni, D.: Spatial data management of temporal map series for cultural and environmental heritage. Int. J. Spat. Data Infrastruct. Res. IJSDIR **6**, 1–31 (2011)

The New Geodatabase of the Municipality of Genoa: Innovative Aspects and Applications

Marco D'Orazi[1], Gabriele Garnero[2]([⊠]) [iD], Stefania Traverso[1], and Emilio Vertamy[1]

[1] Comune di Genova – Direzione Sistemi Informativi, Via di Francia 3, Genova, Italy
{mdorazi,stefaniatraverso,evertamy}@comune.genova.it
[2] Politecnico e Università degli Studi di Torino, Dip. DIST, Viale Mattioli 39, Turin, Italy
gabriele.garnero@unito.it

Abstract. This article presents methods underlying the accomplishment of the new topographic database [DBT] of the Municipality of Genoa.

This final product presents innovative aspects both for adopted methodologies and outputs, and therefore consists of a significant application of cartographic data model specifications in force at national level.

Here are also introduced some prototype studies based on DBT, still under development.

Keywords: DBT · 3D city model · Digital twin

1 Introduction

Within the National Operational Program for Metropolitan Cities PON METRO 2014–2020 - Axis 1 "Metropolitan Digital Agenda", co-financed using Community resources (European Structural and Investment Funds) and using national resources (Agency for Territorial Cohesion), the Municipality of Genoa started the modernization of its topographic database (DBT), with the aim of integrating all information related to its activities regarding territorial objects.

The project involves the creation of ICT services aimed to display and exploit information stored in various subsystems, including management, and related each other through unique certified identifiers based on the reengineered and updated DBT: the possible usages may span from managing emergency interventions to counteract hydrogeological risk to urban planning [1, 2].

The new production of DBT has been realized at the scale 1:1000 for urbanized areas and at the scale 1:2000 for extra-urban areas. It consists of an update of the existing topographic database of the Municipality of Genoa, previously already developed according the specifications of Ministerial Decree 10.11.2011 "Technical rules for the definition of the content specifications of the geotopographic databases" (Official Gazette no. 48 of 27/02/2012 - Ordinary Supplement no. 37) [8].

E. Borgogno-Mondino and P. Zamperlin (Eds.): ASITA 2021, CCIS 1507, pp. 216–229, 2022.
https://doi.org/10.1007/978-3-030-94426-1_16

2 Characteristics of the Production

Within the aforementioned national cartographic specifications, the work has been oriented to obtain valuable cartographic products, including some ones not strictly conventional: it seems that at the present time the Municipality of Genoa is the Italian territory with the most updated and innovative topographic database at national level.

The production was carried out by a Temporary Grouping of Companies consisting of Servizi di Informazione Territoriale S.r.l. (agent company, based in Noci - BA), Corvallis SpA (Padua), Arcadia Sistemi Informativi Territoriali S.r.l. (Milan) and Aerosigma S.r.l. (Grottaglie - TA).

2.1 Photogrammetric and LiDAR Aerial Photos

The specifications of the tender provided for photogrammetric images integrated by LiDAR. The latter is fundamental for the definition of a correct territorial modeling in vegetated areas, and it is strategic to generate detailed Digital Surface Model and Digital Terrain Model (DSM/DTM). These models are essential to advanced hydrogeological modeling, among the main purposes of the project due to local morphology and territorial characteristics [3, 4].

The aerial photos were performed with a Vexcel UltraCam Eagle Mark 3 photogrammetric camera aboard a Vulcanair P68 Victor B twin-engine and aimed at producing about 5000 RGBN frames with GSD at 5 cm for the 1:1000 scale and with GSD at 9 cm for the remainder territorial portion; the level of coverage is high (of the order of 80–90% in the longitudinal sense of 60% in the transversal sense) given the territorial conformation and the presence of a particularly large and dense urban center.

The LiDAR recording was carried out with a Riegl LMS-Q1560 sensor with a density of 55 pts/m^2 for urban areas and 40 pts/m^2 for the rest of the territory. The high quality sensors made it possible to achieve an accuracy on the Check Points of less than 10 cm, as regards photogrammetry, and of 5 cm as regards the residues in Z for the LiDAR strips: values are fully compatible with the requests of the tender and with standards indicated in international literature.

2.2 MMS Data

The particular territorial density led the municipal administration to request a Mobile Mapping System (MMS) data acquisition on all city streets. It has been carried out from a vehicle (Videocar) with LiDAR Riegl Vux1 sensor equipped with GNSS/IMU equipment with resulting acquisition density on the facades of the urban scenes estimated in the order of 4–5000 pts/m^2, that has been integrated with a spherical Ladybug camera (8000*3000 pixel sensor) for 360° photographic shots.

During the production, those devices have been integrated with more manageable ones due the particular morphology of the territory (pedestrian areas, local typical alleys 'caruggi,'...):

- the narrowest alleys have been detected with *Backpack type* equipment integrated by *Gexcel* company: using a SLAM technology, laser data with *Velodine* sensor and resulting resolutions of the order of 3–4,000 pts/m^2 have been acquired;

- in areas not accessible by *Videocar*, but where SLAM technology would not give optimal results given the distance from details to be detected, a Leica static scanner has been used with stationing points repeated every 20–30 m, resulting in resolutions around 20–30,000 pts/m^2, reduced for the final outputs. In order to acquire information for coloring the points cloud, a 20,000*10,000 pixels reflex has been paired to the campaign survey (Figs. 1 and 2).

Fig. 1. Main devices used for acquisitions: Videocar equipped with Vux1 + Ladybug camera (left) and Backpack Gexcel with LiDAR Velodine sensor (right)

Fig. 2. Traces of the acquisition trajectories from Videocar and example of one of them

3 Outputs

Advanced and integrated data processing led to the creation of topographic and tematic maps (Fig. 3):

- DBTs according to the shared specifications ex D.M. 10/11/2011;
- DSMs/DSMs level 6 for extra-urban areas and 7 for urbanized areas;
- True orthophoto.

Fig. 3. Orthophoto (left) and True Ortofoto (right) in correspondence with the Municipal building of "Matitone"

The aim of the paper is not the description of traditional products but rather in the analysis of innovative ones that are not yet widespread on national territory, except in prototypes, and which are instead widely applied to the territory of Municipality of Genoa.

3.1 Integration Between Aerial and Terrestrial LiDAR Point Clouds

The availability of point clouds acquired both by plane and vehicle makes it possible to have extremely detailed geometric descriptions and integrates the peculiarities of different acquisition points: on the one hand is aerial LIDAR, which allows optimal acquisition of road surfaces and roofs; while on the other is mobile LIDAR which, in addition to road surfaces, guarantees significant coverage of facades of buildings along streets and public spaces, thus excluding private areas and roofs.

The validation of integration between the two families of point clouds led to the following results, tested on significant samples and in different territorial portions (Figs. 4 and 5):

- planimetric mean of residuals between different Videocar acquisitions: ±2 cm;
- altimetric mean of residuals between different Videocar acquisitions: ±2 cm;
- altimetric mean of residuals between Videocar acquisitions and aerial LiDAR acquisitions: ±6 cm.

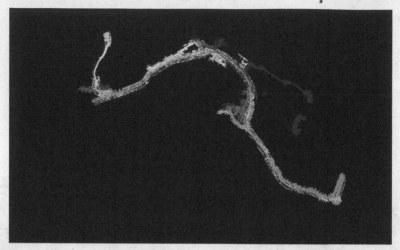

Fig. 4. Set of terrestrial shots, classified by acquisition mission: total of 21 shots - Porto Antico area

Fig. 5. Overlap of aerial (purple) and terrestrial (yellow) clouds - area of 'Sopraelevata road' (urban highway) in front of Galleon (top), in a section between buildings (bottom) (Color figure online)

3.2 Software for Displaying Terrestrial LiDAR Data Merged with Spherical Images (SmartCity3D)

This is a navigation system that allows integration between LiDAR data and photographic data, through an intuitive interface:

- the user can navigate on the cartographic support and identify the spherical images related to the area of interest;
- a spherical image which is geometrically consistent with the terrestrial LiDAR is displayed: it is selected through the correct georeferencing of the center of the images and the orientation of the camera;
- the user can then exploit the spherical image as a base to perform accurate measurements on the LiDAR cloud, thus making it possible to perform measures on the photographic support.

Through this tool, it is possible to have support from a measurable point of view taken at ground level, therefore from the ordinary point of view of users. It is an element that contributes to the creation of the so-called "digital twin" of the city, the virtual representation of complex physical entities such as urban systems. The digital component is connected with the physical one, with which can share data and information, both in synchronous and asynchronous mode (Fig. 6).

Fig. 6. Measurements on spherical photos, with the support of point clouds

Using this tool, the executing Company provided the Municipal Administration with a series of significant elements for administrative management, such as advertising installations, driveways and dehors.

To better appreciate the whole extent of the work, some numbers are listed:

- the database is made up of a total of 390640 360° orbital photos integrated by a complex of 947 ground laser acquisitions for a total of 1563 single extended (a total of 1953 km including vehicle overhauls), of which:

  o track acquired by MMS vehicle equal to: 1508 km (not including overhauls);
  o track acquired by walking operator with backpack: 12 km;
  o tracked by static laser scan footage: 43 km;

- through this tool, the Company proceeded to acquire the following assets:

  o 39498 driveways have been identified in the municipal area, of which 13818 have been correctly connected with the databases available in the current municipal archives (starting from the 15405 currently present in the municipal archives), while the remaining part will be subsequently worked to allow alignment between the detected situation and the management databases;
  o advertising systems: 39253 occurrences detected;
  o dehors: about 200 recorded occurrences.

In addition to correct object georeferencing, working environment also enables the acquisition of main typological and dimensional characteristics useful for tax purposes (width of driveways, surface of advertising systems,…), with tolerances in the order of 5 cm.

Fig. 7. Visualization of point clouds and their sections

It should be noted that this survey covers an area with extremely complex characteristics, due to the orographic situation and the high density of the urban center (Fig. 7).

4   First Exploits of the New Database

4.1   Event Scenarios for the Municipal Department for Civil Protection

As part of the PON METRO Project [Data Sheet 1.1.1-g - Digital model of rain and hydrometric level data] of the Municipality of Genoa, event scenarios relating to both floods and landslides have been developed through the usage of new products.

The company in charge (DHI Italia) of hydraulic studies for disaster scenarios on some specific hydrographic basins in the municipal territory, used the new DTM and DSM for the production of flood hazard maps, as in the following images (Fig. 8).

Fig. 8. Event scenarios related to floods

In addition, the company in charge (Art Ambiente s.r.l.) for geological studies developed some disaster scenario related to landslides. The digital survey of terrain was fundamental to study and define the morphometric characteristics for all hydrographic basins analyzed: the conditions of instability for slopes have been defined and maps of critical rainfall have been produced for specific scenarios (Fig. 9).

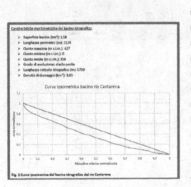 

Fig. 9. Morphometric studies and conditions of instability for slopes

4.2 Urban Planning Comparisons with Diachronic Analysis of Historical Maps

A first interesting analysis was carried out within the Liguria Region Operational Program 2014–2020 - European Social Fund - Axis 3 "Education and Training" by CNR-IRPI Turin and University of Genoa for the superimposition of historical maps with data of the new survey, for the purpose of recognizing artificial morphologies in urban areas [7].

The study was carried out on sample areas and started georeferencing and digitizing the contour lines of Porro's maps "General Defense Map of Genoa (1: 2.000)" produced between 1835 and 1838 for the generation of a 'historical' DTM.

The diachronic analysis with the new digital terrain models was carried out on four very important study areas for the Genoese territory:

a) Sant'Agata Bridge, a critical area for floods of Bisagno river basin;
b) 'Uphill ring' road, the city's hilly road artery;
c) Promontory of San Benigno, a symbolic place for the presence of the Genoa's Lantern and subject to profound alterations in the urban fabric;
d) the area of new San Giorgio Bridge in Val Polcevera, now home to new transformations following the tragedy of the collapse of the Morandi Bridge.

Very significant representations of the changes occurred during two centuries of industrialization and urbanization have been obtained, which can highlight information often hidden or lost, and provide useful elements for territorial planning. Note, as an example, the profound narrowing and modification of the section of the riverbed of Bisagno stream near the Sant'Agata Bridge (Fig. 10) and the significant landscape variation near the promontory of San Benigno (Fig. 11).

Fig. 10. Urban planning comparisons in San'Agata bridge area

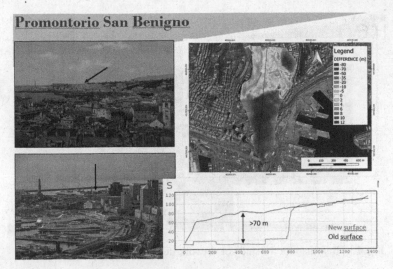

Fig. 11. Urban planning comparisons of San Benigno promontory

4.3 Applications to Water, Gas and Sewage Networks Design

The new detailed surveys have been used in an experimental approach by IRETI Spa, being underway the design of new water supply networks and new extensions of sewage collectors. For the Technical Economic Feasibility Studies, digital models and orthoimages have been used in order to define planimetries and profiles (Figs. 12 and 13).

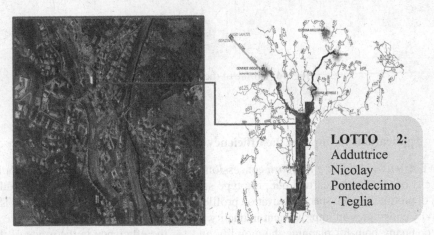

Fig. 12. Cartographic basis of the feasibility study - section in Val Polcevera

Fig. 13. Basemap for the study of network development nearby the coastline

The application of DTM/DSM was also very interesting to estimate excavation volumes with a good margin of precision, to define vents and drains and to draw a detailed aqueduct profile, also on the basis of the survey of detected subservices (Fig. 14).

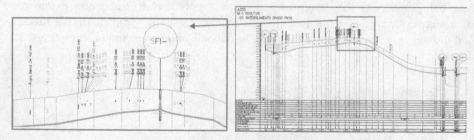

Fig. 14. Profile of the aqueduct level

4.4   Applications to Improve the Efficiency of Public and Sustainable Mobility

AMT, *Azienda Mobilità e Trasporti* concessionaire for public transport in the metropolitan city of Genoa, has carried out prototype studies on many hilly bus routes with the aim of producing each specific elevation profile starting from the planimetric paths. The activity constitutes an improvement in quality and accuracy of information available to the company both for planning the mobility and for the efficiency in the usage of the electric vehicles fleet (Fig. 15).

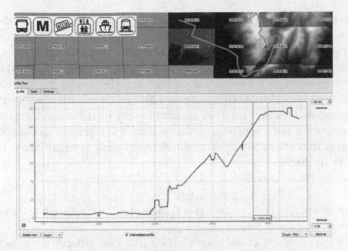

Fig. 15. Elevation profile of one specific bus route

4.5   Applications in the Context of Accessibility Projects

As part of the activities of the LARTU (Laboratory of Territorial and Urban Analysis and Representations - University and Polytechnic of Turin) and of the TAL (Turin Accessibility Lab - Polytechnic of Turin), experiments are underway on the use of metric information extracted from the SmartCity3D platform to walkability projects. A city like Genoa has heavy problems for accesses and public spaces often disputed between various categories of users (motorists, cyclists, pedestrians,…), even more difficult because of significant altimetric differences and steep roads: it is necessary to develop solutions for accessibility improvements, even more if applied to people with motor disabilities. Within studies connected with the implementation of the PEBAs (Plans for the Elimination of Architectural Barriers), the available platform allows generalized measurements throughout the territory, allowing to highlight and classify criticalities, even in the absence of inspections.

5   Conclusions

The Municipality of Genoa fosters medium/long-term strategies to become a 'lighthouse city', that means to be hub of innovation at the crossroads of urban management, environment and business building a multi-level governance in partnership with other Italian and European cities.

For this reason, investing in a new topographic database that improves the vision of the digital twin of the city is a masterpillar for its present and future management [5, 6].

The geospatial information infrastructure that contains the technological, semantic, organizational and legal components (Yang et al. 2010; Granell et al. 2014) is essential to facilitate the information flow envisaged by Gore (1998) and the multidisciplinary research outlined by Goodchild and colleagues (2012). Moreover, improved visualization of massive geospatial features are a key concept for city modelling and advancements in BIM/GIS integration and a way to geosensors, data structures and spatial relations that will be of great importance in emerging applications such as smart cities (Breunig M, Bradley PE et al., 2020).

Genoa's new DBT supports:

- the implementation of grey, green and soft measures for adaptation to climate change (EU Climate Adaptation Strategy);
- the further improvement of adoption of INSPIRE Data Specifications according to Italian national law;
- interoperability latest recommendations of Agency for Digital Italy (AgID), the technical agency of the Italian Presidency of the Council of Ministers for innovation and economic growth.

The data described in this paper are the first and more advanced geospatial output existing at present in Italy (DBT, DEM, DSM, LIDAR, ortophoto) at scale ratio 1:1000 for urbanized areas and 1:2000 for mountain areas, and represent an important technological innovation in the usage of geospatial data for local scale applications, providing better ways to plan, design, and make decisions.

We are also studying the possibility that aerial surveys will no longer have a sporadic character as it has been until now, but will become an annual/biennial commitment, integrating, in addition to LiDAR campaign, the oblique photogrammetric surveys that are spreading in Italy, too.

In this way, as well as having tools to keep the databases up-to-date, it will be possible to implement automatic controls of territorial changes, thus supporting the activities related to Municipality's goals.

References

1. Schade, S., et al.: Geospatial information infrastructures. In: Guo, H., Goodchild, M.F., Annoni, A. (eds.) Manual of Digital Earth, pp. 161–190. Springer, Singapore (2020). https://doi.org/10.1007/978-981-32-9915-3_5
2. Breunig, M., et al.: Geospatial data management research: progress and future directions. ISPRS Int. J. Geo-Inf. **9**(2), 95 (2020). https://doi.org/10.3390/ijgi9020095
3. Junxiang, Z., Jun, W., Xiangyu, W., Yi, T.: Innovative production and construction. In: Chapter 19: An Economical Approach to Geo-Referencing 3D Model for Integration of BIM and GIS, pp. 321–334 (2019). https://doi.org/10.1142/9789813272491_001
4. Jack Dangermond Fall 2013, The Power of GIS is Transforming Our World, Esri International User Conference
5. White, G., Zink, A., Codecà, L., Clarke, S.: A digital twin smart city for citizen feedback. Cities **110**, 103064 (2021). ISSN 0264-2751 https://doi.org/10.1016/j.cities.2020.103064

6. Schrotter, G., Hürzeler, C.: The digital twin of the city of Zurich for urban planning. PFG – J. Photogrammetry Remote Sens. Geoinformation Sci. **88**(1), 99–112 (2020). https://doi.org/10.1007/s41064-020-00092-2
7. Terrone, M., Piana, P., Paliaga, G., D'Orazi, M., Faccini, F.: Coupling historical maps and lidar data to identify man-made landforms in urban areas. ISPRS Int. J. Geo-Inf. **10**(5), 349 (2021). https://doi.org/10.3390/ijgi10050349
8. D.P.C.M. 10 novembre 2011, Regole tecniche per la definizione delle specifiche di contenuto dei database geotopografici (12A01800), GU Serie Generale n.48 del 27-02-2012 - Suppl. Ordinario n. 37

Sensors Performance and Data Processing

A Low-Cost GNSS Prototype for Tracking Runners in RTK Mode: Comparison with Running Watch Performance

Yuri Taddia[1] , Luca Ercolin[2], and Alberto Pellegrinelli[1]([X])

[1] Engineering Department, University of Ferrara, Via Saragat 1, 44122 Ferrara, Italy
{yuri.taddia,alberto.pellegrinelli}@unife.it
[2] Department of Neuroscience and Rehabilitation, Faculty of Medicine,
Pharmacy and Prevention, University of Ferrara, Via Borsari 46, 44121 Ferrara, Italy
luca.ercolin@unife.it

Abstract. GNSS positioning is widely use in every kind of application. Nowadays, low-cost GNSS modules are becoming available to apply the Real-Time Kinematic mode in those applications in which a centimeter-level accuracy would be appreciated for a precise positioning. In this work, we developed a prototype for collecting data in RTK mode with a single-frequency multi-constellation device during some physical tests performed by a professional runner. Prior to do this, we assessed the accuracy in estimating the distance actually covered during a walking on a signalized line. Also, we verified the capability to detect short sprints of about 12–15 s. Finally, we compared the results of our prototype with a Polar M430 running watch during three Cooper tests and a Kosmin test. The comparison highlighted that the running watch overestimated the total distance systematically and did not describe the performance of the athlete accurately in time. The distance overestimation was +4.7% on average using the running watch, whereas our prototype system exhibited an error level of about 0.1%.

Keywords: Low-cost GNSS RTK · Running watch · Cooper test · Kosmin test · u-blox

1 Introduction

Global Positioning System (GPS) has been widely implemented during last decades in almost every field of our life. Car navigation based on the use of standard GPS modules is one of the most common applications since decades. Nowadays, Global Navigation Satellite System (GNSS) positioning, with more constellations than GPS only (GLONASS, Galileo, Beidou) is available on a wide range of devices, such as smartphones for instance. However, the miniaturization of antennas and receivers has spread the use of GNSS positioning also to physical activity and sports. The standard accuracy level of some meters is certainly suitable for car navigation since, essentially, the real position is bound to be on the road. Also, the path followed during hikes or similar non-human activities, such as tracking dogs in the streets [1], is still well described using

E. Borgogno-Mondino and P. Zamperlin (Eds.): ASITA 2021, CCIS 1507, pp. 233–245, 2022.
https://doi.org/10.1007/978-3-030-94426-1_17

standard GNSS positioning. However, a higher level of accuracy is needed whenever the GNSS data collection is further used to evaluate the actual performance of athletes for scheduling training activities.

Nowadays, low-cost GNSS devices are available for mass market. Such instruments are based on small modules able to receive not only C/A codes, but also to perform carrier phase measurements. When this kind of approach is combined to the use of a second module placed on a fixed position, it is possible to operate in Real-Time Kinematic (RTK) mode obtaining a final positioning characterized by a centimeter-level accuracy in optimal conditions [2]. U-blox modules implement this technology and make it available through application boards ready to be integrated in prototypes for almost every kind of positioning-based application [3, 4]. High-precision single-frequency in RTK mode has been successfully developed and validated for vehicle applications [5] and non-human tracking [6]. The development of a small and lightweight system for applying the GNSS RTK positioning to running, both from the point of view of the professionalism and the amateurism, can help to describe in a better manner the performance level of athletes. In fact, test analysis often starts from the total distance covered by the runner to establish which is the actual degree of preparation of the athlete for a certain kind of competition. This is the case of Cooper and Kosmin tests. Cooper test [7], is a way to analyze the performance of an athlete who has a total time of 12 min available and has to cover the longest distance as possible managing its own physical resources. Kosmin test, instead, is predictive for middle-distance competitions and consists of a sequence of running (as fast as possible) and stops (recovery time). The sequence for predicting 1500 m test is: 1-min running, 3-min stop, 1-min running, 2-min stop, 1-min running, 1-min stop and final 1-min running. For instance, Cooper test followed by GPS tracking during football matches has been used to analyze physical performance in adolescents [8] and GPS with accelerometry data to assess benefits of physical activity in seniors [9].

Evaluating the distance with a high level of accuracy can hence make the difference: a wrong classification of the performance with respect to the real one due to too large measurement uncertainties can lead, in the worst scenario, up to muscle strains because of an overexertion. In this research, we therefore developed a simple prototype with the aim of survey the performance of a professional runner during the execution of some technical tests (Cooper and Kosmin). Also, we investigated the level of accuracy obtainable using the prototype, as well as we compared it with some running watches commonly used by the athletes to evaluate their own performance.

2 Materials and Methods

In this work, we used the u-blox RTK application board package C94-M8P, based on u-blox NEO-M8P-2 module, to develop an easily wearable GNSS rover prototype for tracking the path of an athlete. In particular, our system consists of one C94-M8P application board with NEO-M8P-2 module as GNSS receiver, an external GNSS antenna and an external UHF antenna. Both antennas are connected to the main board. The GNSS antenna is fixed to a bike helmet that is worn by the runner during each measurement session. The application board is also connected to a Raspberry Pi 3 Model B+ where the data flow of GNSS solutions epoch per epoch is continuously recorded. The Raspberry

Pi is powered by a compact battery bank and the overall system is contained into a small backpack easily wearable by runners (see Fig. 1).

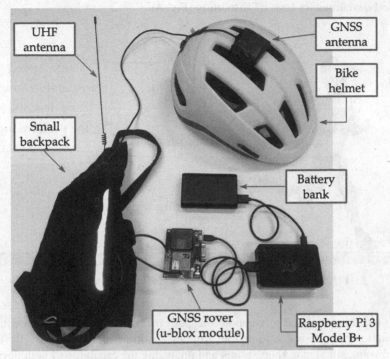

Fig. 1. Description of the wearable GNSS rover prototype system.

At the same time, another application board, acting as a base station for RTK operations, is set up every time. The location of the base station is arbitrary and a survey-in procedure starts every time the base receiver is powered on. After 3 min, the position is assumed as fixed and hence the base starts sending data to the rover through UHF radio for reaching a rover solution in which the carrier phase ambiguities have been fixed. Both the GNSS receivers are single-frequency, multi-constellation and were set up to operate as GPS + GLONASS in RTK mode. The maximum RTK solution rate we tested is 5 Hz, with a solution every 0.2 s. However, in the following we use a rate of 1 Hz with the aim to perform a direct comparison with the data collected using running watches. All the tests were carried out in a running track, placing the base receiver in the lawn inside the track. Hence, the maximum base-rover distance (i.e., the baseline) never exceeded 100 m. No significant obstacles reduced the sky visual, with the only exception of some buildings with a height of 15 m located at about 20 m from one side of the track, that is a common situation for urban running tracks.

Prior to use our prototype on a real athlete, we carried out two preliminary tests. The first consisted in analyzing the lateral uncertainty level when walking along a signalized path around the running track. The prototype (also simply referred to as u-blox in the following) was hence worn as reported in Fig. 2 and the test was conducted with a low speed, following a specific path. The same line, signalized on the ground, was surveyed using a geodetic GNSS receiver (Topcon GR-3) in NRTK mode with the dual purpose to reconstruct the horizontal path and computing its real length. We therefore computed the lateral deviations for each RTK solution (Fig. 4).

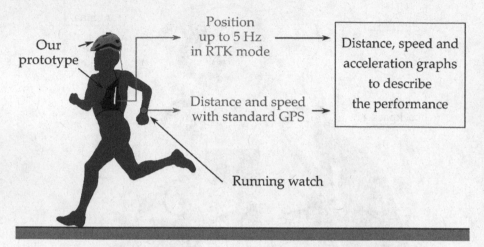

Fig. 2. Data acquisition with both systems worn by the athlete.

The second test aimed to compare the performance of our prototype with those of a common running watch (TomTom Runner 2 Cardio, abbreviated as TomTom in the following), simulating short sprints and analyzing the capability of both devices in detecting them. The position of the runner was hence collected simultaneously. Four sprints were simulated during this test. Sprint durations were ca. 15 s for the first two sprints and ca. 12 s for the last ones. The scheme is also reported in Fig. 3. Distance, speed and acceleration have been computed afterwards. The aim was to evaluate whether the use of our prototype introduced any improvement in describing accelerations and decelerations in short time-frames.

Finally, we collected data during Cooper tests performed by a professional athlete. It is worth noting here that our prototype has been developed with a particular regard to not interact with the performance of the runner. The procedure we applied for acquiring data essentially consisted in powering on both boards every time: in fact, they were set up to operate as a base and a rover respectively. Data recording on the Raspberry Pi automatically starts at power on. The fix of carrier phase ambiguities on the rover is ensured by a led indicator.

A total amount of three Cooper tests and one Kosmin test were surveyed and analyzed in order to assess the difference in using a running watch and our prototype. A high-end Polar M430 device was used instead of the TomTom previously employed during the preliminary comparison. In this work, we aimed to reconstruct the path followed by the runner with a time step of 1 s. Polar M430 directly gave distance and speed as output, whereas our prototype was set to send NMEA GGA strings as output data flow. From such strings, we finally computed East and North coordinates (UTM projection). Linear deformation module was also taken into account when computing the real distance from horizontal UTM coordinates.

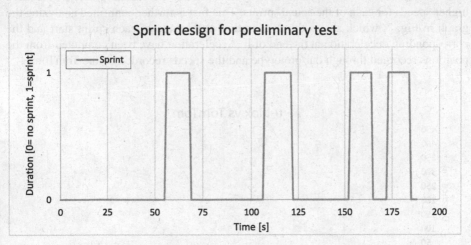

Fig. 3. Duration of sprints during the second preliminary test.

3 Results

The first preliminary test, conducted on a track line, highlighted that the 68% of the lateral deviations were in the range of $0-0.107$ m and the 95% in the range of $0-0.25$ m (Fig. 4). The total number of points that was collected during the test is 478. The total distance covered was twice a lap. The distance computed from the position sampled every second with our prototype showed a mean lap length of 406.06 m. If compared to the real length surveyed using a geodetic receiver (405.69 m), the error is $+0.1\%$.

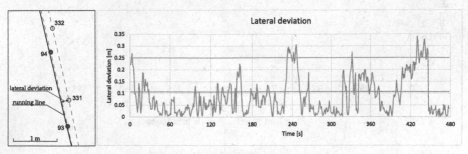

Fig. 4. Lateral deviations from a line during the first preliminary test.

As mentioned in Sect. 2, we also conducted a second preliminary test focusing on the comparison of a TomTom running watch and our prototype. The results, in terms of distance, speed and acceleration graphs are illustrated in Fig. 5, Fig. 6 and Fig. 7 respectively. It is worth noting, especially looking at Fig. 6, how the wristwatch recognized only two of the four sprints made by the athlete, whereas our prototype recorded higher speeds for each of the actual sprints. This fact is further confirmed analyzing the graph in Fig. 7, which shows the acceleration at the time of each sprint start and the corresponding deceleration at the end of it. Acceleration have been computed from the positions recorded through our prototype and the speeds recorded by the TomTom.

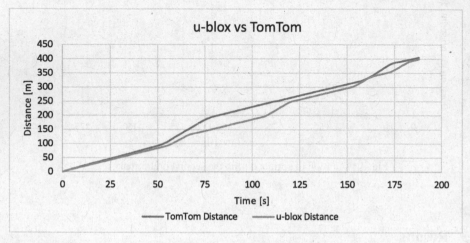

Fig. 5. Distance during preliminary test.

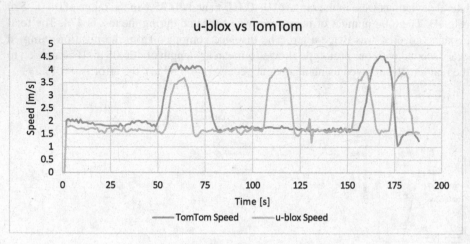

Fig. 6. Speed during preliminary test.

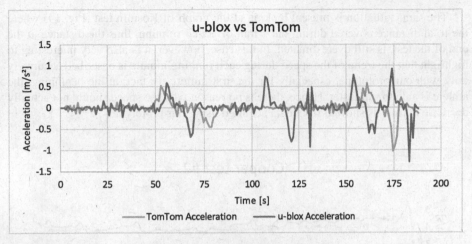

Fig. 7. Acceleration during preliminary test.

Moreover, the duration of the sprints detected by the running watch seems not to be consistent with the actual duration of them. This is clearly noticeable from Fig. 6 and also leads to a deviation of the distance covered from the runner up to ca. 40 m in about 100 s from the start of the test (see Fig. 5). However, at the end of the test, the distance difference decreased to less than 1 m.

The data collection made during the performance of Cooper tests is depicted in Fig. 8, Fig. 9 and Fig. 10 in terms of speed versus time and in Fig. 11, Fig. 12 and Fig. 13 in terms of speed versus total distance covered.

Analyzing the graph of speed versus time, it is possible noting that the running watch (Polar M430 in this case) tends to overestimate the real speed of the runner for almost all the duration of the tests. As a consequence, also the distance covered by the athlete was systematically overestimated using the Polar M430.

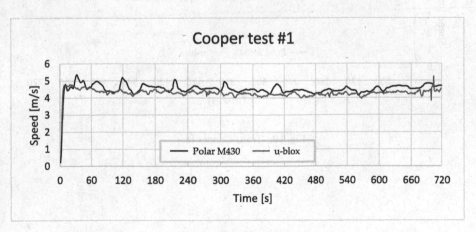

Fig. 8. First Cooper test.

The same situation is present looking at the graph of Kosmin test (Fig. 14) where the total distance covered during the 4 min of actual running, thus the distance at the end of the test, is still overestimated. In this case, however, it is also very interesting to highlight that the trend of the speed during each running minute is described accurately only with our prototype, especially for the first minute. In fact, at the beginning, the athlete is able to run faster. Hence, there is no reason why the speed should not actually decrease in time as showed from data acquired using our prototype.

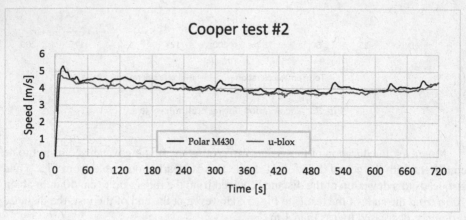

Fig. 9. Second Cooper test.

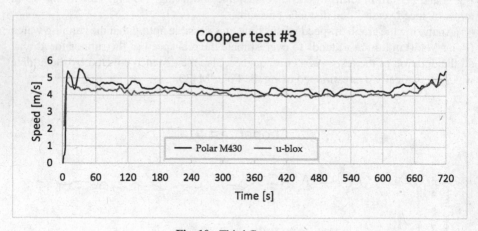

Fig. 10. Third Cooper test.

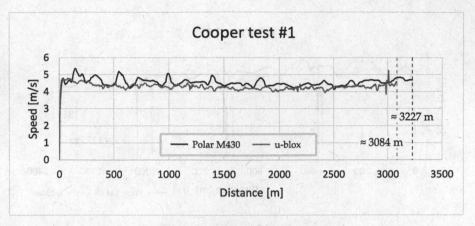

Fig. 11. First Cooper test: total distance.

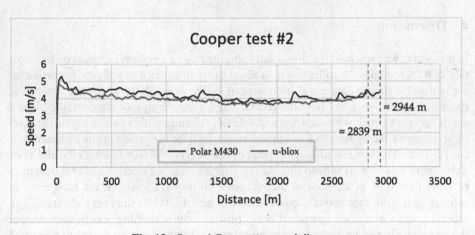

Fig. 12. Second Cooper test: total distance.

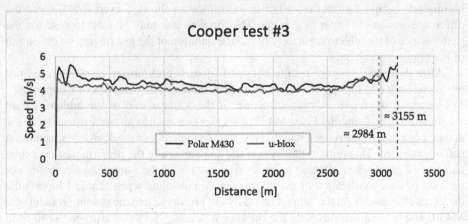

Fig. 13. Third Cooper test: total distance.

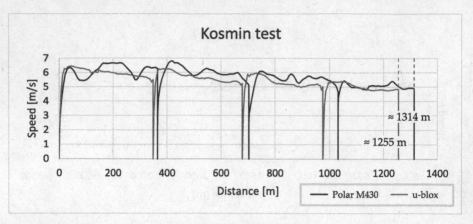

Fig. 14. Kosmin test.

4 Discussion

In this work, we presented the first results obtained using a prototype based on low-cost GNSS RTK modules for collecting data about the performance of athletes. In particular, we realized a simple data acquisition system easily wearable in which the antenna is fixed to a bike helmet and both the receiver and a recording unit are contained into a small backpack. First, we conducted a couple of preliminary tests to investigate the level of accuracy of the system and its capability to describe also short sprints (duration of ca. 12–15 s). The first test highlighted that our prototype, compatibly with the ability of a person to follow a signalized line during walking, did not exceed a lateral deviation of more than 0.25 m for 95% of the recorded positions. Moreover, the total error in estimating the distance actually covered was of about +0.1%, thus very accurate. The second test, in which we compared our prototype with a running watch, showed that the sprints were recognized using our prototype, but they were not correctly identified using the running watch. Also, the distance computed using the two different devices highlighted a gap of more than 40 m in the middle of the test, even if at the end the difference was in the order of a meter. This implies that may be hard to describe the performance of the athlete accurately for all the duration of the test relying on the output of the running watch only.

After these encouraging results obtained in such preliminary tests, we used our prototype on a real runner. We therefore collected data during a series of Cooper tests. In every test, we found an overestimation of the actual speed of the athlete, for all the duration of it, using the Polar M430. This fact causes also an overestimation of the distance covered by the runner, which represents an indicator of the degree of preparation actually reached. This implies that even if the comparison of the performance over time can be still good when affected by an overestimation of the total distance, this is not the case of the classification of the performance in absolute terms. Table 1 reports the distances evaluated from the data recorded by our prototype and the running watch Polar M430. The overestimation using the running watch is +4.7% on average (+140 m in absolute terms). Such error can make the difference in the evaluation of the real result of a Cooper test and about the further considerations regarding the preparation of the runner. It is also worth noting that an actual feedback on the substantial accuracy of the distance estimated using our prototype was given by the fact that the last recorded position was not close to the finish line as pointed out by the data recorded by the Polar M430 (Polar M430 final distance for test #3 is close to 3200 m, thus almost at the end of the 8th lap theoretically). Finally, we also collected data during a Kosmin test. Once again, we found a difference of +4.7% in relative terms between the use of a running watch and our prototype (see Table 1).

Table 1. Comparison of total distance after Cooper tests with our prototype (u-blox) and Polar M430.

Test	u-blox dist. [m]	Polar M430 dist. [m]	Polar M430 overestimation	
Cooper #1	3084	3227	143 m	+4.64%
Cooper #2	2839	2944	105 m	+3.70%
Cooper #3	2984	3155	171 m	+5.73%
Kosmin	1255	1314	59 m	+4.70%

It is worth noting that the Polar M430 is a running watch able to receive only GPS signals and is worn on the wrist, which is not an optimal antenna location. Moreover, positioning algorithms estimating the athlete's path from previous epochs when the signal is partially or temporarily lost are implemented in running watches and excluding them is usually not possible. More recent multi-constellation running watches are available on the market (e.g., GPS + GLONASS), however pseudorange-based standalone positioning has a level of accuracy lower than RTK positioning. The results of this work show that our prototype, based on a GNSS RTK approach, is able to provide a very high level of accuracy in describing the performance of athletes. Positions are recorded every second with a theoretical centimeter-level accuracy. Speed is computed afterwards from the distance between positions at each time.

5 Conclusions

This work presented the first results in using a wearable prototype based on GNSS RTK for the data collection aimed to describe the performance of athletes in a more accurate way than using common running watches. Preliminary tests conducted in a running track show an accuracy of about 0.1% in total distance estimation when using our prototype. Differences in estimating the total distance during both Cooper tests and Kosmin test is instead in the order of +5% using a common model of running watch, if compared with our prototype. This highlights the importance of developing systems to acquire more accurate data when using GNSS-based device. The implementation of RTK mode in a compact device can represent an optimal and very promising solution for this. A local base receiver can be established permanently in a training center or, alternatively, a

Network RTK (NRTK) approach can be adopted. More recent low-cost multi-frequency [10] multi-constellation modules can also be used to increase the potential of the system for reaching fixed solutions. Also, the miniaturization of prototypes is certainly a point to be improved in order to make this technology available for real athletes.

Acknowledgements. The authors are grateful to the students Silvia Sangalli (runner) and Andreas Piva (support during data collection using the prototype) for their contribution during the tests and to Andrea De Vivo (UISP) for having made available to us the running track (test site).

References

1. Paula, P.M.C., Secco, R.A., Molento, C., Filho, P.L.: Construction of a prototype for tracking dogs in the streets using Arduino. Acta Vet. Brno **14**, 61–67 (2020)
2. Garrido-Carretero, M.S., de Lacy-Pérez de los Cobos, M.C., Borque-Arancón, M.J., Ruiz-Armenteros, A.M., Moreno-Guerrero, R., Gil-Cruz, A.J.: Low-cost GNSS receiver in RTK positioning under the standard ISO-17123-8: a feasible option in geomatics. Measur. J. Int. Measur. Confederation **137**, 168–178 (2019)
3. Poluzzi, L., Tavasci, L., Corsini, F., Barbarella, M., Gandolfi, S.: Low-cost GNSS sensors for monitoring applications. Appl. Geomat. **12**(1), 35–44 (2019). https://doi.org/10.1007/s12 518-019-00268-5
4. Cina, A., Piras, M.: Performance of low-cost GNSS receiver for landslides monitoring: test and results. Geomat. Nat. Haz. Risk **6**(5–7), 497–514 (2015)
5. De Bakker, P.F., Tiberius, C.C.J.M.: Single-frequency GNSS positioning for assisted, cooperative and autonomous driving. In: 30th International Technical Meeting of the Satellite Division of the Institute of Navigation, ION GNSS 2017, vol. 6, pp. 4038–4045 (2017)
6. Keshavarzi, H., Lee, C., Johnson, M., Abbott, D., Ni, W., Campbell, D.L.M.: Validation of real-time kinematic (RTK) devices on sheep to detect grazing movement leaders and social networks in merino ewes. Sensors **21**(3), 1–19, art. no. 924 (2021)
7. Alvero-Cruz, J.R., Giráldez García, M.A., Carnero, E.A.: Reliability and accuracy of Cooper's test in male long distance runners. Revista Andaluza de Medicina del Deporte **10**(2), 60–63 (2017)
8. Gawrecki, A., Michalak, A., Gałczyński, S., Dachowska, I., Zozulińska-Ziółkiewicz, D., Szadkowska, A.: Physical workload and glycemia changes during football matches in adolescents with type 1 diabetes can be comparable. Acta Diabetol. **56**(11), 1191–1198 (2019). https://doi.org/10.1007/s00592-019-01371-0
9. Marquet, O., MacIejewska, M., Delclòs-Alió, X., Vich, G., Schipperijn, J., Miralles-Guasch, C.: Physical activity benefits of attending a senior center depend largely on age and gender: a study using GPS and accelerometry data. BMC Geriatr. **20**(1), 1–10, art. no. 134 (2020)
10. Hamza, V., Stopar, B., Ambrožič, T., Turk, G., Sterle, O.: Testing multi-frequency low-cost GNSS receivers for geodetic monitoring purposes. Sensors **20**(16), 1–16, art. no. 4375 (2020)

Performance of Dual-Frequencies Low-Cost GNSS Sensors for Real Time Monitoring

Luca Poluzzi[(⊠)] [iD] and Stefano Gandolfi

University of Bologna, DICAM, Bologna, Italy
`luca.poluzzi5@unibo.it`

Abstract. GNSS technology has now become a viable tool for monitoring applications in geology and civil engineering. Low-cost sensors have been available on the marketplace for more than 10 years in which technology has made great strides forward, and also the performance of these instruments has increased significantly. Until a few years ago only single-frequency receivers were available, which still guaranteed respectable performance, now dual-frequency receivers are also on the market.

In this work, the performance in RTK mode on a very short baseline, in terms of accuracy and convergence time, of two single (M8P) and dual-frequency (F9P) u-blox receivers were compared. Furthermore, three types of GNSS antenna (patch, low-cost, and geodetic class) were tested coupled to the F9P receiver, to evaluate the impact on the performance of the quality of the antenna. The accuracies highlighted by the tests show that this low-cost dual frequency instrumentation is more performing. The convergence times also confirm this aspect. For this reason, these types of sensors can be used not only for real-time monitoring but also for post-processing on long baselines or for Precise Point Positioning [1]. Given the economic convenience of these devices compared to the geodetic class ones, it is possible to think of their increasingly massive use in monitoring.

Keywords: GNSS · Monitoring · Low-cost · Dual-frequency

1 Introduction

Nowadays, GNSS technology constitutes one of the most used tools for monitoring civil structures and territory. Usually, geodetic receivers are used to achieve very high precision measurement. These instruments allow precisions at the centimeter level, or even less, in static mode and very long observation periods. Nevertheless, despite the decreasing cost of such instruments, geodetic class equipment is still quite expensive if compared to other sensors used for structural engineering, such as inclinometers, extensometers, and so on. However, in recent years a new class of low-cost GNSS receivers has become available on the market which can perform centimeter-level positioning. Consequently, many experiments were carried out by the scientific community in order to evaluate their real performance. A considerable amount of literature has been published on this topic, some studies generally describe the potential of this technology in the monitoring field

© Springer Nature Switzerland AG 2022
E. Borgogno-Mondino and P. Zamperlin (Eds.): ASITA 2021, CCIS 1507, pp. 246–258, 2022.
https://doi.org/10.1007/978-3-030-94426-1_18

[2]. Others focus on specific areas such as monitoring of landslides [3, 4] or structure monitoring such as bridges [5, 6] and dams [7, 8]. The technological evolution has led to the great development also of low-cost GNSS sensors, which allow a more massive use and peace of mind in case of breakage or loss. In the last 15 years, many authors have started experimenting with these low-cost sensors. In particular, until a few years ago only single-frequency receivers were commercially available. There are several low-cost receivers on the market, and different papers examine their performance under various conditions [9, 10]. In this paper, we want to evaluate two aspects: the performance of two low-cost receivers and the impact of the antenna type on the quality of the solution in terms of accuracy (standard deviation) and convergence time.

For that reason, two models of u-blox receivers (NEO-M8P and ZED-F9P) and three types of GNSS antennas (ANN-MB patch antenna, low-cost Harxon GPS1000 antenna, and Trimble Zephyr 3 geodetic antenna) were used. The testing took place on the roof of the DICAM Dept. of the University of Bologna, acquiring 1 Hz static RTK solutions on a baseline of about 100 m.

2   Material

U-blox is one of the companies that, for years, has been producing low-cost receivers with different features as shown in Table 1, and which can be used in different contexts.

Table 1. List of u-blox models with main features.

Model (year)	Constellations	Channels	Frequency	RTK module	Price
LEA-4T [11–13]	G	16	Single L1	/	~15 € (chip)
LEA-5T [14–16]	G + (S)	50	Single L1	/	~15 € (chip)
LEA-6T [17–19]	G + (S)	50	Single L1	/	~50 € (chip)
NEO-7P [19–21]	G + R + (S) (2 concurrent constellations)	56	Single L1/L1	/	~65 € (chip)
NEO-M8P [22–24]	G + R + C + (S) (2 concurrent constellations)	72	Single L1/L1/B1	Embedded	~ 75 € (chip) ~175 € (application board)
LEA/NEO-M8T [25–27]	G + R + E + C + (S) (3 concurrent constellations)	72	Single L1/L1/E1/B1	Embedded	~80 € (chip) ~175 € (application board)
ZED-F9P [28–30]	G + R + E + C + (S) (4 concurrent constellations)	184	Dual L1 + L2/L1 + L2/E1 + E5b/B1 + B2	Embedded	~90 € (chip) ~210 € (application board)

The current cost of the chips (to be engineered) ranges from 15 euros for single-frequency GPS only, up to 90 euros for dual-frequency multi-constellation. The number of channels has increased significantly, also a sign of the evident technological evolution of electronics. Since 2015, the RTK module (embedded inside the chips) also allows accurate positioning in real-time. F9P module is the latest chip released by u-blox, which allows you to acquire phase observations on two frequencies and from different constellations.

3 Methods

3.1 Hardware and Software Setting

As mentioned in the introduction, two types of low-cost receivers were used in this work: the first one single frequency (u-blox NEO-M8P) and the second one dual-frequency (u-blox ZED-F9P). Both receivers can work in RTK mode by transmitting RTCM corrections.

In particular, we used the C94-M8P application board (chipset NEO-M8P) that allows two concurrent GNSS (in our case GPS and Glonass) on the L1 frequency and the C099-F9P application board (chipset ZED-F9P) that uses almost all the available constellations and is a dual frequency receiver. Table 2 shows frequencies acquired by the receivers for each constellation.

Table 2. Types of frequencies acquired by M8P and F9P u-blox receivers for each constellation.

Constellation	NEO-M8P Frequencies	ZED-F9P Frequencies
GPS	L1C/A	L1C/A, L2C
Glonass	L1OF	L1OF, L2OF
Galileo	/	E1B/C, E5b
Beidou	/	B1l, B2l

The modules are configured using the u-center software, which also allows acquiring RTK data solutions in proprietary binary format (".UBX") using the USB interface (Fig. 1). Although this software is useful for module configuration, it is certainly not the ideal tool for data acquisition because it binds the use of a PC and does not allow the automation of procedures.

Given the aforementioned problems, a "parser" has been created which could work in any environment (OS) and therefore could be automated within scripts. The code, written in *Python* language, performs the decoding of some of the parameters present in the binary stream. The most important information for a complete explanation of a solution is given in Table 3.

Table 3. u-blox message types decoded by the parser to export useful information.

UBX message type	Information
NAV-TIMEUTC	Reference period (Year, Month, Day, Hour, Minute, Second)
NAV-HPPOSECEF	High Precision Geocentric Coordinates (X, Y, Z) Precision Level: mm
NAV-HPPOSLLH	High Precision Geographical Coordinates (Lat, Lon, h) Precision Level: 10^{-9} deg
NAV-HPPOSLLH	Accuracies (s) associated with coordinates (Horizontal and Vertical)
NAV-PVT	Type of solution (Standalone, Float, Fixed)

As mentioned, we use RTK as survey mode, by setting a master station at known coordinates, which sends corrections to the rover station, positioned on the site to be monitored. The communication between master and rover occurred using a pair of external radios with an RS232 serial interface. This interface was added to the receivers through hardware modifications (TTL converter installation).

The script was put into a Raspberry Pi to have a flexible tool with low energy consumption, also, it was equipped with a 4G dongle to remotely control via VPN (Virtual Private Network). Figure 1 shows the Rover station equipment and the different connections; the Master one only needs radio connections to send RTK corrections.

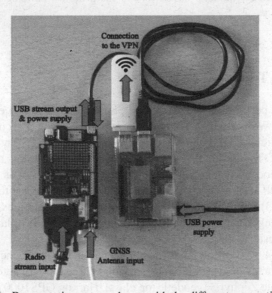

Fig. 1. Rover station setup scheme with the different connections.

The experiments were carried out on the roof of the DICAM Dept. of the University of Bologna (Italy). A baseline of about 96 m was created using two steel pillars bound to the building that allow the insertion of the GNSS antennas (Fig. 2). The results obtained in these tests can be considered valid for short baselines. It is known that for baseline lengths up to 5–10 km, there is no great degradation of accuracy due to poor modeling of atmospheric effects, as a matter of fact, this aspect has a minimal impact on the solution accuracy [18].

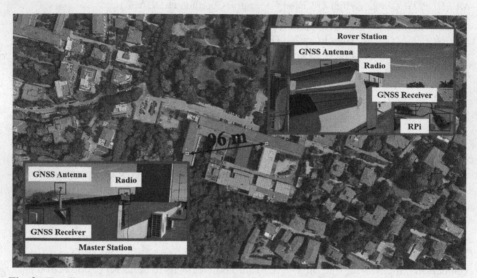

Fig. 2. Baseline used for the tests on the roof of the historical building of DICAM Dept. – University of Bologna.

4 Performed Tests

The first test was performed to evaluate the performance difference between the two chosen receivers. We wanted to evaluate the impact of using a second frequency and 2 more constellations (Galileo and Beidou in addition to GPS and Glonass) on the precision of the RTK solution and the convergence time. With this aim, the ZED-F9P receiver with a geodetic antenna (Trimble Zephyr 3) was chosen as the master station while the ZED-F9P and NEO-M8P were simultaneously connected to the same antenna (Trimble Zephyr 3) using a splitter thus forming the rover stations. RTK corrections were also split using Y-cables on the RS232 interface. Figure 3 explains the connection diagram for this test.

The second test was done to grade the impact of the dual-frequencies GNSS antenna quality on the accuracy of the solution. In particular, three types of antennas were chosen for the test: Trimble Zephyr 3 (geodetic top class), Harxon GPS1000 (low-cost but with high-performance features), and u-blox ANN-MB (very low-cost patch antenna provided together with the Application Board).

Each antenna was connected to the ZED-F9P receiver forming the rover station, while the master station was defined with ZED-F9P receiver and Trimble Zephyr 3 antenna as in the previous test.

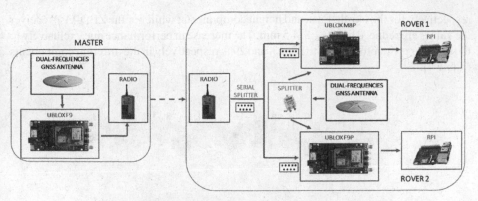

Fig. 3. Operation diagram of the simultaneous survey.

Figure 4 shows the antenna models that were tested with the low-cost dual-frequency receiver, along with their market values.

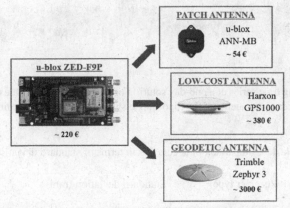

Fig. 4. The three different types of GNSS antenna connected to the u-blox F9P receiver for the test

5   Results

5.1   Test 1

In this test, 7 days of 1 Hz data were acquired simultaneously from each Rover station. Figure 5 shows the comparison between a one-day 1 Hz time series (expressed in a topocentric system ΔN, ΔE, ΔU) produced by the two low-cost receivers. Although both receivers provide an excellent level of repeatability, greater stability of the series in the dual-frequency module ZED-F9P (red dots) compared to that of the NEO-M8P (blue dots) can be noted. This aspect is also confirmed by the standard deviations calculated on an 11-day dataset, which for the NEO-M8P receiver are equal to 3.1, 2.4, 6.3 mm respectively for the North, East, and height components; while for the ZED-F9P receiver the values are reduced to 2.4, 1.8, 4.5 mm. The increase in performance due exclusively to the receiver is therefore equal to 23, 25, and 29% respectively in the different components (Table 4).

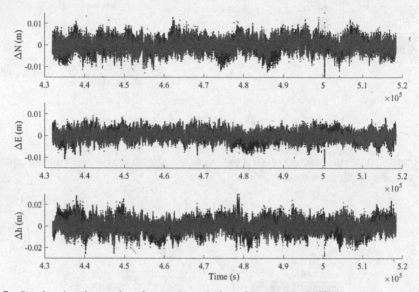

Fig. 5. Overlapping time series of a one-day solution of the receiver M8P (blue dots) and the F9P (red dots) in the three components of the topocentric system. (Color figure online)

Table 4. Comparison of accuracies in terms of standard deviation.

Receiver type	Standard deviation (mm)		
	σ_N	σ_E	σ_U
u-blox NEO-M8P	3.1	2.4	6.3
u-blox ZED-F9P	2.4	1.8	4.5
% Improvement	**23%**	**25%**	**29%**

In the context of monitoring, it is not always required to acquire GNSS data continuously. In the design of a system where energy optimization is necessary, turning on the instrument, acquiring the data, and then turning it off can be done. The number of acquisitions per day will be chosen, based on the dynamic of the phenomenon to be monitored. Therefore, the convergence time of the receiver needs to know, defined as the time elapsed from power on to the highest precision mode (with fixed ambiguity). To do this, 50 tests were carried out, turning on the rover receiver and timing the seconds to resolve the integer carrier phase ambiguities, which is our convergence parameter.

Table 5 shows some statistical values of the timing measurements (mean and maximum values). In particular, we can see how the use of the ZED-F9P receiver leads to an average reduction in times of 19 s (37%), going from 51.1 s with the M8P to 32.3 s. Analyzing also the maximum values, there is confirmation of greater stability of the dual-frequency receiver in which the convergence times have never exceeded the 40 s against the 70 s of the previous receiver.

Note that this parameter is sensitive to some factors such as the power of the radio and any obstacles in the line of sight.

Table 5. Comparison of the convergence parameter.

Receiver type	Convergence time (s)	
	Mean	Max
u-blox NEO-M8P	51.1	70
u-blox ZED-F9P	32.3	41
% Improvement	**37%**	**43%**

5.2   Test 2

As mentioned previously, in this test, three different GNSS antennas were used coupled to the low-cost receiver u-blox F9P. The goal is to evaluate whether the performance of the low-cost quality antenna is closer to a geodetic one or a low-quality one. To do this, 7 days of 1 Hz data were acquired for each above-mentioned antenna.

Figure 6 shows the time series corresponding to the day when the patch antenna was replaced with the geodetic class one. The impact in terms of accuracy is significant and the difference in performance is perceptibly clear.

These results are confirmed by Table 6 which shows the accuracy values, in terms of the standard deviation, of the three components (N, E, U), obtained using the three different antennas together with the ZED-F9P receiver. There is a strong reduction in the standard deviation between the patch antenna results and the geodetic class one, in fact, the values have almost doubled.

Table 7 shows the comparison, in percentage terms, of the accuracies between the low-cost quality antenna (Harxon GPS1000) and the others. It is interesting to note that the STD values obtained with this antenna are very close to the geodetic class ones, with a worsening of the accuracy in percentage terms between 11 and 15%, but very low in absolute terms and always less than a millimeter.

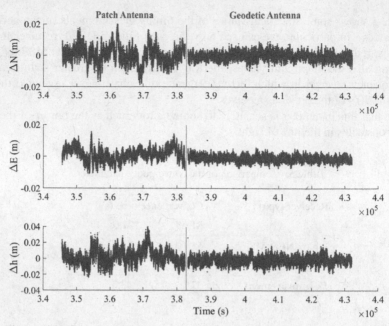

Fig. 6. Time series of the day on which the patch antenna was replaced with the geodetic one in the three components of the topocentric system.

Table 6. Accuracies of the solutions obtained with the three different antennas.

Receiver type	Standard deviation (mm)		
	σ_N	σ_E	σ_U
u-blox ANN-MB	4.4	3.5	8.1
Harxon GPS1000	2.7	2.1	5.3
Trimble Zephyr 3	2.4	1.8	4.5

Table 7. Percentage of improvement in the accuracy of the solutions compared to those obtained with Harxon antenna

Harxon GPS1000 VS	% STD Improvement		
	σ_N	σ_E	σ_U
u-blox ANN-MB	39%	40%	35%
Trimble Zephyr 3	−11%	−14%	−15%

6 Discussion

The tests carried out have shown that technological development can bring great benefits to monitoring activities. In fact, the use of multi-constellation dual-frequency receivers has led to an increase in performance. Nevertheless, the increase in accuracy (in absolute terms) is not particularly lofty but we felt this choice was still preferable even considering that with a dual-frequency receiver it is possible to extend the applications. It is possible to think about its use on long baselines (>10 km). Furthermore, these types of receivers allow post-processing with the Precise Point Positioning approach in non-differentiated mode with centimeter accuracy.

Speaking about second test, it is interesting to show the value for money of the tested antennas (Fig. 7). The result of the low-cost quality antenna (Harxon GPS1000) catches the eye. In fact, it has a price closer to the lower-cost antenna, but the performances are more similar to the geodetic one. For this reason, this antenna can be considered the most suitable for these purposes.

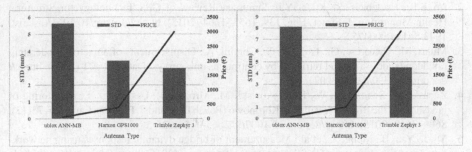

Fig. 7. Histograms of the accuracy in plan (left) and elevation (right) components in relation to the price of the individual antennas (orange line). (Color figure online)

Accuracies obtained in this work can be improved by using algorithms such as moving averages, at the expense of the timeliness with which to identify a movement. In fact, increasing the size of the moving average will improve accuracy but at the same time delay the detection of a potential shift.

7 Conclusion

Different tests were performed to evaluate the performance of low-cost GNSS sensors. In particular, the impact on the accuracy and convergence time of the use of a dual-frequency multi-constellation receiver compared to a single-frequency dual-constellation one was evaluated. The impact of the quality of the GNSS antenna on the accuracy of the solutions was also assessed.

In summary, these results confirm that the ZED-F9P receiver actually offers better performance than the NEO-M8P module both in terms of accuracy (with an improvement of about 25%) and convergence time (with a reduction of about 40%).

As is known, antennas also have a great impact on satellite positioning performance. In particular, it emerged that the low-cost Harxon antenna (coupled with low-cost receivers) offers performances very close to geodetic class ones.

The present findings confirm that the technological evolution of recent years has led to a reduction in the costs of these types of sensors and, at the same time, has driven an improvement in their performance. This means that these tools, once engineered, can be widely used in monitoring contexts.

Acknowledgements. We would like to show our gratitude to "CAE S.P.A." for making GNSS and Radio devices available and for their support in this work.

References

1. Zumberge, J., Heflin, M.: Precise point positioning for the efficient and robust analysis of GPS data from large networks. J. Geophys. Res. Solid Earth **102**, 5005–5017 (1997)
2. Im, S.B., Hurlebaus, S., Kang, Y.J.: Summary Review of GPS Technology for Structural Health Monitoring. J. Struct. Eng. **139**, 1653–1664 (2013). https://doi.org/10.1061/(asce)st.1943-541x.0000475
3. Mulas, M., Ciccarese, G., Truffelli, G., Corsini, A.: Displacements of an active moderately rapid landslide—a dataset retrieved by continuous gnss arrays. Data **5**(3), 71 (2020). https://doi.org/10.3390/data5030071
4. Zabuski, L., Świdziński, W., Kulczykowski, M., Mrozek, T., Laskowicz, I.: Monitoring of landslides in the Brda river valley in Koronowo (Polish Lowlands). Environ. Earth Sci. **73**(12), 8609–8619 (2015). https://doi.org/10.1007/s12665-015-4025-3
5. Yu, J., Yan, B., Meng, X., et al.: Measurement of bridge dynamic responses using network-based real-time kinematic GNSS technique. J. Surv. Eng. (2016). https://doi.org/10.1061/(asce)su.1943-5428.0000167
6. Chen, Q., Jiang, W., Meng, X., et al.: Vertical deformation monitoring of the suspension bridge tower using GNSS: A case study of the Forth Road Bridge in the UK. Remote Sens. **10**(3), 364 (2018). https://doi.org/10.3390/rs10030364
7. Barzaghi, R., Cazzaniga, N.E., De Gaetani, C.I., et al.: Estimating and comparing dam deformation using classical and gnss techniques. Sensors (Switzerland) **18**(3), 756 (2018). https://doi.org/10.3390/s18030756
8. Xiao, R., Shi, H., He, X., et al.: Deformation monitoring of reservoir dams using GNSS: an application to south-to-north water diversion project, China. IEEE Access **99**, 1 (2019). https://doi.org/10.1109/ACCESS.2019.2912143
9. Glabsch, J., Heunecke, O., Schuhbäck, S.: Monitoring the Hornbergl landslide using a recently developed low cost GNSS sensor network. J. Appl. Geod. **3**(3), 179–192 (2009). https://doi.org/10.1515/JAG.2009.019
10. Günther, J., Heunecke, O., Pink, S., Schuhbäck, S.: Developments towards a low-cost GNSS based sensor network for the monitoring of landslides. In: 13th FIG international symposium on deformation measurements and analysis, Lisbon, p. 15 (2008)
11. Schwieger, V.: Accurate High-Sensitivity GPS for Short Baselines (2009)
12. Song, W.Z., Huang, R., Xu, M., et al.: Air-dropped sensor network for real-time high-fidelity volcano monitoring. In: MobiSys 09 - Proceedings of the 7th ACM International Conference on Mobile Systems, Applications, and Services. ACM Press, New York, USA, pp 305–318 (2009)

13. Weston, N.D., Schwieger, V.: Cost effective GNSS positioning techniques (2014)
14. Cina, A., Piras, M.: Performance of low-cost GNSS receiver for landslides monitoring: test and results. Geomatics Nat. Hazards Risk **6**, 497–514 (2015). https://doi.org/10.1080/194 75705.2014.889046
15. Bellone, T., Dabove, P., Manzino, A.M., Taglioretti, C.: Real-time monitoring for fast deformations using GNSS low-cost receivers. Geomatics Nat. Hazards Risk **7**, 458–470 (2016)
16. Jaimes, A., Kota, S., Gomez, J.: An approach to surveillance an area using swarm of fixed wing and quad-rotor unmanned aerial vehicles UAV(s). In: 2008 IEEE *International Conference* on Service-Oriented *System Engineering* SoSE (2008). https://doi.org/10.1109/SYSOSE.2008. 4724195
17. Benoit, L., Briole, P., Martin, O., Thom, C.: Real-time deformation monitoring by a wireless network of low-cost GPS. J. Appl. Geod. **8**, 119–128 (2014). https://doi.org/10.1515/jag-2013-0023
18. Caldera, S., Realini, E., Barzaghi, R., et al.: Experimental study on low-cost satellite-based geodetic monitoring over short baselines. J. Surv. Eng. **142**(3), 04015016 (2016). https://doi. org/10.1061/(asce)su.1943-5428.0000168
19. Tsakiri, M., Sioulis, A., Piniotis, G.: Compliance of low-cost, single-frequency GNSS receivers to standards consistent with ISO for control surveying. Int. J. Metrol. Q. Eng. **8**(2), 11 (2017). https://doi.org/10.1051/ijmqe/2017006
20. Biagi, L., Grec, F., Negretti, M.: Low-cost GNSS receivers for local monitoring: experimental simulation, and analysis of displacementsxs. Sensors (Switzerland) **16**(12), 2140 (2016). https://doi.org/10.3390/s16122140
21. Rademakers, E., De Bakker, P., Tiberius, C., et al.: Obtaining real-time sub-meter accuracy using a low cost GNSS device. In: 2016 European Navigation Conference, ENC 2016. Institute of Electrical and Electronics Engineers Inc. (2016)
22. Kersten, T., Paffenholz, J.A.: Feasibility of consumer grade GNSS receivers for the integration in multi-sensor-systems. Sensors (Switzerland) **20**(9), 2463 (2020). https://doi.org/10.3390/ s20092463
23. Poluzzi, L., Tavasci, L., Corsini, F., Barbarella, M., Gandolfi, S.: Low-cost GNSS sensors for monitoring applications. Appl. Geomatics **12**(1), 35–44 (2019). https://doi.org/10.1007/s12 518-019-00268-5
24. Garrido-Carretero, M.S., de Lacy-Pérez de los Cobos, M.C., Borque-Arancón, M.J., et al.: Low-cost GNSS receiver in RTK positioning under the standard ISO-17123-8: a feasible option in geomatics. Measur. J. Int. Measure. Confed. **137**, 168–178 (2019). https://doi.org/ 10.1016/j.measurement.2019.01.045
25. Krietemeyer, A., ten Veldhuis, M.C., van der Marel, H., et al.: Potential of cost-efficient single frequency GNSS receivers for water vapor monitoring. Remote Sens. **10**(9), 1493 (2018). https://doi.org/10.3390/rs10091493
26. Wilkinson, M.W., McCaffrey, K.J.W., Jones, R.R., et al.: Near-field fault slip of the 2016 Vettore Mw 6.6 earthquake (Central Italy) measured using low-cost GNSS/704/4111/704/2151/134/123 article. Sci Rep. **7**, 4612 (2017). https://doi.org/10.1038/ s41598-017-04917-w
27. Taufik, M., Yuwono, C.M.N., Putra, J.R.: Analysis level of accuracy GNSS observation processing using u-blox as low-cost GPS and geodetic GPS (case study: M8T). In: IOP Conference Series: Earth and Environmental Science, p. 012041. Institute of Physics Publishing (2019)
28. Krietemeyer, A., van der Marel, H., van de Giesen, N., ten Veldhuis, M.C.: High quality zenith tropospheric delay estimation using a low-cost dual-frequency receiver and relative antenna calibration. Remote Sens. **12**, 1393 (2020). https://doi.org/10.3390/RS12091393

29. Semler, Q., Mangin, L., Moussaoui, A., Semin, E.: Development of a low-cost centimet-ric GNSS positioning solution for android applications. In: International Archives of the Photogrammetry, Remote Sensing and Spatial Information Sciences - ISPRS Archives (2019)

30. Hamza, V., Stopar, B., Ambrožič, T., et al.: Testing multi-frequency low-cost GNSS receivers for geodetic monitoring purposes. Sensors **20**, 4375 (2020). https://doi.org/10.3390/s20 164375

Definition of the Local Geoid Undulation Using Non-contemporary GNSS-Levelling Data on Subsidence Area: Application on the Adriatic Coastline

Luca Tavasci [ID], Enrica Vecchi[(✉)] [ID], and Stefano Gandolfi [ID]

University of Bologna, DICAM, Bologna, Italy
{luca.tavasci,enrica.vecchi}@unibo.it

Abstract. The knowledge of the so-called geoid undulation, which represents the height of the geoid above a reference ellipsoid, is a fundamental step to link ellipsoidal heights measured using satellite systems and orthometric heights. Several geoid models are available at the time both at the national or global scale, which can be used for the purpose. Another way to define the geoid undulation is to perform joint measures with GNSS and spirit levelling over common benchmarks. This requires onerous measurements that is seldom possible to perform due to their cost. In this work, we evaluated the possibility to define a local model of the geoid undulation using already available spirit levelling orthometric heights and GNSS ellipsoidal heights measured about 13 years later. The test area is the Emilia-Romagna Adriatic coastline, an area of great interest both from the environmental and economic point of view, which is also undergoing consistent subsidence phenomena.

Test results show that the available measurements allow defining a geoid undulation that is coherent with the shape defined by the gravimetric models and also allows to transform ellipsoidal heights into orthometric ones more consistent with the height reference available on the surveyed area. A 7 cm overall bias with respect to the ITALGEO05 was found, whereas ITG2009 and EGM2008 have higher differences. The use of subsidence models to align over time the coordinates used to define the geoid undulation has proven to be a fundamental step. The analysis on the a-priori uncertainty in the geoid height definition shown that the combined use of much more precise GNSS coordinates and contemporary spirit levelling campaign is necessary to significantly improve the resulting geoid height.

Keywords: Geoid · Subsidence · Geoid height · Geoid undulation · GNSS · Spirit levelling · Emilia-Romagna

1 Introduction

The accurate estimation of the geoid undulation has become fundamental especially in the last decades with the increasing use of GNSS and other spatial techniques for surveying and monitoring. All the techniques that use satellites orbits as constraints for the

© The Author(s) 2022
E. Borgogno-Mondino and P. Zamperlin (Eds.): ASITA 2021, CCIS 1507, pp. 259–270, 2022.
https://doi.org/10.1007/978-3-030-94426-1_19

final coordinates are bound to relate the height component to the geometric surface of the reference ellipsoid. Such a reference does not consider the local gravitational potential, therefore the so-called ellipsoidal height (h) cannot be used in many technical applications, especially the ones involving water management. The geoid, which represents the equipotential surface of the Earth gravity field passing below the topographic masses and approximating the mean sea level, is the more appropriate reference surface to deal with the common concept of "height" and allows to define the orthometric height (H). The geoid undulation (N) represents the separation between the reference ellipsoid and the geoid itself [1]. It allows calculating the orthometric height also for those points surveyed using a space technique directly providing the ellipsoid height only.

Several models of geoid undulation are available both at the global and regional scale. These models have been developed over time starting from satellite gravimetric measurements and modelling the shape of the geoid using of a certain number (up to 2190) of spherical harmonics. Another way to compute the geoid undulation is to compare over a common point the difference between its ellipsoidal height defined using a GNSS receiver and its pseudo-orthometric height measured through spirit levelling [2–4]. This cannot be done at the global scale because of limitations in the application of spirit levelling, but it can be useful at the regional scale.

Coastal areas are environments where the correct use of orthometric heights is fundamental, in particular for those regions characterized by flat terrain such as the Emilia-Romagna Adriatic coastline. On this territory, the regional agency for the environmental protection of Emilia-Romagna (Arpae), together with the Department of Civil, Chemical and Environmental Engineering (DICAM) of the University of Bologna, created in 2016 a geodetic infrastructure called Coastal Geodetic Network (RGC) [5], which is composed of 51 benchmarks both suitable for spirit levelling and GNSS surveying. Its main use is the monitoring of the sand erosion along the coastline, but it can be used as support for any survey about the area since the benchmarks coordinates are defined in the national official reference frame (ETRF2000, epoch 2008.0).

In this paper, we investigated the possibility to calculate a GNSS-levelling derived model for the local geoid undulation on the Emilia-Romagna coastal area. This model could provide a way to correct the ellipsoidal heights more consistently with the orthometric data already available.

One of the key points in this work is the unavailability of contemporary measurements with both GNSS and spirit levelling, combined with the fact that the whole area is affected by significant subsidence phenomena [6–8]. Therefore, an appropriate strategy to overcome this problem is proposed, together with a discussion on the expected accuracy of the geoid undulations estimated on site. To do so, 51 benchmarks belonging to the RGC were used.

The experimental data results have been finally compared with the available data from three gravimetric models, namely the Italian official ITALGEO05 [9] the more recent ITG2009 [10] and the EGM2008 [11] global model. A discussion will be provided whether the opportunity of using already existent geomatic data to estimate local models for the geoid height and the requirements necessary to reach an accuracy sufficient to consider such models a trustable reference and a real improvement with respect to global/national ones.

2 Dataset

The Italian Adriatic coast represents a significant area for the national environmental and economic wealth. For this reason, in the last decades, many different authorities have arranged their own monitoring networks, with points distributed along the coastline. These networks have been managed by IGM, RER, Idroser, Agip and, finally, by Arpa which handled the subsidence monitoring network. In 2016, some of the benchmarks belonging to these monitoring networks have been included in the RGC created from the collaboration between Arpae and the DICAM of the University of Bologna [5]. A requirement for the chosen points was the suitability both for spirit levelling surveys and for GNSS measurements. Moreover, to have a proper distribution of the benchmarks along the coast, the spatial density of about one point every 4 km (Fig. 1) was defined. These benchmarks have been last measured through precise spirit levelling in 1999 and 2005 during campaigns for subsidence monitoring. In the following years Arpa, today Arpae, moved from spirit levelling to the InSAR technique for the monitoring of subsidence phenomena [12], therefore those gathered in 2005 are the most recent data about the orthometric height available for the coastal levelling networks.

In order to reach a more homogeneous spatial distribution of the RGC, during 2019 some new benchmarks were installed and measured. Their orthometric heights have been defined through short levelling stretches linking to the closest existing points belonging to the above-mentioned networks but not suitable for GNSS positioning. Concerning the ellipsoidal heights, GNSS measuring campaigns have been carried out mainly in 2016–2017 for the first set of points and then integrated in 2019. The measuring campaigns involved static observing sessions ranging between 1 and 2 h to compute the short baselines linking contiguous points. Despite the poor redundancy due to the network geometry it was possible to adjust the baselines, thus providing the a-posteriori error matrix for each benchmark.

3 Methods

As already mentioned, both the orthometric and the ellipsoidal heights of the chosen benchmarks were not referred to the same epoch. Although the undulation value is invariant to the subsidence phenomenon, this can impact the calculation in the case of non-contemporary measurements. For this reason, the computation of the local geoid undulation N needed for the updating of both the height values to a common epoch. To take into account the subsidence phenomena we used piecewise linear models of height variations. The chosen epoch to which update the height coordinates has been the 2018.0, being it about the middle of GNSS surveying campaigns and a quite recent time.

Starting from the year 2006, the Emilia-Romagna region provides Subsidence Models for the area based on InSAR data every five years [12–14]: currently there is the availability of models for the periods 2006–2011 and 2011–2016. We extrapolated data of the later periods at epoch 2018.0 since the up-to-date model is still not available.

As for ellipsoidal heights, values for each benchmark were updated at epoch 2018.0 following the formula:

$$h_{2018.0} = h_t + \Delta t * v_s \tag{1}$$

Fig. 1. Location of the 51 RGC benchmarks along the Emilia-Romagna Adriatic coastline.

where h_t is the ellipsoidal height at the measurements epoch, Δt is the time span ranging from such epoch and 2018.0, and v_s is the subsidence rate provided by the most recent model in the position of the considered point.

The orthometric heights were updated at 2018.0 by applying:

$$H_{2018.0} = H_t + \Delta t_1 * v_{s1} + \Delta t_2 * v_{s2} \tag{2}$$

where H_t is the orthometric height at the measurement epoch (mostly 2005, while 1999 in a couple of cases). Δt_1 and v_{s1} are the time span and related subsidence velocities before 2012, whereas Δt_1 and v_{s1} are related to the period 2012–2018.0.

Starting from both the height values at 2018.0, the experimental undulation for each point has been calculated through the simple equation:

$$N = h - H \tag{3}$$

Table 1 reports the values involved in Eq. 3 for each point of the RGC network considered in this work.

With the aim to estimate the a-priori accuracy of the experimental values for the geoid height, we combined the uncertainties of all the involved measures by applying the covariance propagation law. Because of the poor knowledge about the uncertainties to be considered, we focused on defining a single value for all the network instead

Table 1. Ellipsoidal heights (Columns 2, 6) and orthometric heights (Columns 3, 7) at the 2018.0 epoch. Columns 4 and 8 report the experimental undulations in the chosen benchmarks.

RGC id	h (m)	H (m)	N (m)	RGC id	h (m)	H (m)	N (m)
GABI0100	45.33	4.88	40.45	SAPC0400	40.35	1.17	39.18
CARI0100	42.84	2.40	40.44	SAPC0500	40.56	1.38	39.19
CARI0010	42.81	2.38	40.43	SAPC0600	43.34	4.17	39.17
CARI0200	42.32	1.91	40.41	SAPC0650	39.97	0.71	39.25
CARI0210	42.27	1.88	40.38	SAPC0700	41.33	2.05	39.28
CARI0300	43.46	3.15	40.30	PCPG0020	41.96	2.58	39.39
CARI0400	43.69	3.49	40.20	PCPG0010	40.93	1.49	39.44
CARI0500	43.10	3.01	40.08	PCPG0100	41.08	1.64	39.44
CARI0600	42.94	2.96	39.98	PCPG0200	41.68	2.11	39.57
CARI0700	41.72	1.83	39.89	PCPG0300	40.36	0.68	39.68
RICE0100	42.68	2.81	39.87	PCPG0400	41.51	1.68	39.82
RICE0200	42.57	2.77	39.80	PCPG0450	41.57	1.69	39.88
RICE0300	42.33	2.57	39.76	PCPG0500	41.56	1.58	39.98
RICE0400	42.85	3.29	39.56	PCPG0600	41.93	1.78	40.14
RICE0500	41.55	1.97	39.58	PGFV0100	42.08	1.82	40.26
RICE0550	41.01	1.49	39.51	PGFV0200	44.11	3.74	40.37
RICE0600	41.83	2.36	39.47	PGFV0300	43.14	2.53	40.61
RICE0700	42.01	2.54	39.47	PGFV0400	42.73	2.08	40.65
CESA0100	40.99	1.60	39.39	PGFV0500	41.06	0.20	40.86
CESA0200	41.40	2.10	39.30	FVFG0500	42.20	1.43	40.77
CESA0300	41.17	1.96	39.21	PGFV0600	43.58	2.61	40.97
CESA0400	40.74	1.63	39.11	FVFG0400	43.07	2.00	41.07
SAPC0100	43.01	3.90	39.10	FVFG0300	42.44	1.30	41.14
SAPC0150	40.58	1.50	39.08	FVFG0100	41.77	0.55	41.22
SAPC0200	40.49	1.39	39.10	FVFG0200	39.35	−1.92	41.27
SAPC0300	41.41	2.24	39.17				

of a specific one for each benchmark. The accuracy for the subsidence models (σ_{subs}) can be considered about 2 mm/years for both the selected periods as stated in [13, 14]. The accuracy of the orthometric heights (σ_{H_i}) provided by spirit levelling campaigns can be considered about 7 mm, as declared by the involved authorities [15]. For what concerns the levelling measures carried out in 2019 for the newly installed RGC points, we considered an accuracy equal to 1 mm (σ_{lev}) being the involved distances few hundred meters. The last uncertainty to be considered is that of the ellipsoidal height (σ_h) obtained from the GNSS measures. For this evaluation, we considered the a-posteriori standard deviation obtained in the network adjustment, which average value over the 51 benchmarks is about 32 mm.

Due to the error propagation, combining Eqs. 1–2 and 3, we obtained the accuracy associated to our experimental undulation values:

$$\sigma_N = \sqrt{(\sigma_h)^2 + (\sigma_{H_i})^2 + (\sigma_{lev})^2 + (\Delta t_H + \Delta t_h)^2 * (\sigma_{subs})^2} \tag{4}$$

where Δt_H is the time span between the measuring epoch (assumed to be 2005) of the original orthometric heights and the final epoch 2018.0, and Δt_h is the period between the average measuring epoch for the GNSS measures (2017.08) and 2018.0, both expressed in years. It is important to underline that for sake of simplicity the levelling measures have been considered for all the benchmarks, while actually, they involved only 11 points, thus obtaining a slightly overrated final value. Using the mentioned values, the a-priori undulation accuracy is about 4.3 cm.

It was then possible to evaluate the differences between the experimental undulation values and the point-wise ones extracted from different existent geoid models.

The first comparison has been carried out by considering the official national geoid model of Italy, ITALGEO05. This is a gravimetric geoid, integrated with GPS/levelling data, developed by the Politecnico di Milano and adopted by IGM (Istituto Geografico Militare) [9, 16]. This model is delivered to users through gk2 format grids [17] which needed to be converted to allow easier use for our analysis. The gk2 grids have been formatted and densified through a TIN (Triangular Irregular Network) interpolation model with a 100 m spacing (about 0.001° in latitude and longitude). Once obtained the final grid aligned to the ETRS89-ETRF2000 reference system, the geoid undulations over the chosen benchmarks have been extracted using Surfer software (https://www. goldensoftware.com/products/surfer).

The EGM2008 model was also considered, which is a global geopotential geoid released by the U.S. National Geospatial-Intelligence Agency (NGA) EGM Development Team [11]. The global model EGM2008 has proved to give comparable results with those of the ITALGEO05 and to be very effective in fitting data in the Central Mediterranean area [18], therefore we decided to test it. The EGM2008 point-wise undulations have been obtained using the Matlab *geoidheight* function, starting from the benchmarks geographic coordinates.

Finally, the ITG2009, which is the latest geoid model of Italy, has been considered. This regional model is based on the EGM2008, improving its precision and reliability [10] over the Italian area. The computing of the ITG2009 undulations has been carried out using the ISG web service (https://www.isgeoid.polimi.it/Geoid/geoid_rep.html).

Different geoid models usually show biases between them due to the specific choice adopted in terms of datum reference for each one [19]. The comparison between geoid realizations is therefore performed by subtracting to each one a bias that can be modelled through an oriented plane [2, 10, 18]. Because of the particular geometry of the RGC network, which is mostly aligned along a straight direction, we have chosen to solve the biases between the four considered realizations of the geoid undulations using a linear regression.

Differences between the regression lines will provide the generic information about the difference that one would find by applying a model instead of another one to correct ellipsoidal heights measured along the coastline. Differently, the analysis concerning the accuracy of each model in describing the shape of the geoid along the considered area will be discussed by looking at the residual values with respect to the regression lines.

4   Results

First of all, the experimental values of geoid undulation have been superimposed to the ones calculated in the corresponding positions using the three geoid models, as shown in Fig. 2. An overall agreement between the estimations can be noticed, with a better alignment between ITALGEO05 and the experimental values, whereas EGM2008 and ITG2009 are higher and close to each other. This result is not surprising since ITG2009 and EGM2008 are both based on the same computation with a difference in the fitting area [10] and the ITALGEO05 is the official reference for Italy, therefore the one also used to define the orthometric heights considered in the computation of the experimental N.

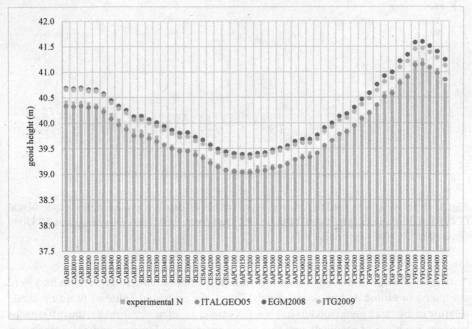

Fig. 2. The chart reports different definitions for the geoid heights over the chosen benchmarks: experimental GNSS-levelling values (grey bars), ITALGEO05 (red dots), EGM2008 (blue dots) and ITG2009 (green dots). (Color figure online)

The regression straight lines for each set of geoid heights were computed and are reported in Fig. 3. A general tilt can be seen moving along the coastline from south to north. The geoid height differences from south to north are 70 cm for the experimental data and 76.5 cm, 74 cm, 82 cm for the ITALGEO05, ITG2009 and EGM2008 respectively. The ITG2009 geoid model, which is the most recent and refined Italian model, shows the tilt closer to the experimental data.

The mean biases between the experimental data and the geoid models are − 7 cm, 23 cm and 30 cm for the ITALGEO05, ITG2009 and EGM2008 respectively. All these values can be considered significant with respect to both the GNSS and spirit levelling precisions in the measurement of the height, therefore such biases have to be taken into account.

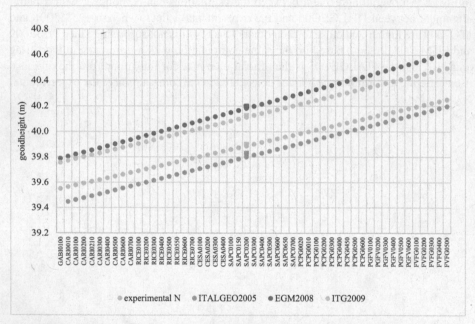

Fig. 3. Regression lines used to define and remove biases between geoid heights: experimental GNSS-levelling values (grey dots), ITALGEO05 (red dots), EGM2008 (blue dots) and ITG2009 (green dots). (Color figure online)

Residual values between each geoid undulation dataset and its regression line were computed to eliminate biases and trends. Then, the averaged value of these residuals relating to the three geoid models has been assumed as reference. Finally, the differences between each set of residuals and this reference were calculated and are reported in Fig. 4. The geoid models show to be scattered around their mean value with an RMS at the 1 cm level, which is within the accuracies declared for their determination [17, 18]. Nevertheless, local differences higher than 4 cm can be found over certain points, in particular between the ITALGEO05 and the EGM2008.

GNSS-levelling geoid heights are more scattered with respect to the reference, meaning 3.4 cm in terms of RMS with a couple of data up to 11 cm far. By considering a normal distribution of the measuring errors and a 3 sigma confidence interval, all these data are compatible with the a-priori uncertainty of 4.3 cm. Differently, taking into account the

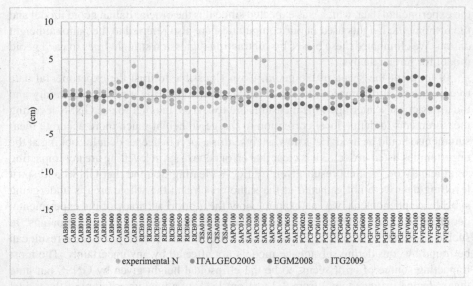

Fig. 4. Local differences between each geoid height determination and the reference defined as the mean value of the three considered gravitational models: experimental GNSS-levelling values (grey dots), ITALGEO05 (red dots), EGM2008 (blue dots) and ITG2009 (green dots). (Color figure online)

a-posteriori dispersion of the measures, the two points FVFG0500 (−11.2 cm) and RICE0400 (−9.9 cm) are not compliant with the measuring errors, which lead to different possible interpretations. On the one hand, these differences between experimental data can be due to gross errors in the measures, but on the other hand, these can be local deviations of the geoid due to particular conditions that cannot be modelled by gravimetric data used to define geoid models at the national/global scale. The latter hypothesis seems not to apply to the RICE0400 point since the area surrounding it is similar at all to the neighbouring coastline. Differently, the FVFG0500 point is located in a very particular area in the North of the regional coast, the Sacca di Goro lagoon, close to the lighthouse at the extremity of a small peninsula. This might induce a gradient in the gravity field close to the area unrecognized by large scale data.

5   Discussion and Conclusion

A definition of the geoid height alternative to the ones provided by three already available geoid models has been calculated over 51 points belonging to the RGC network along the Emilia-Romagna coastline. It was done by combining spirit levelling measures mainly performed in 2005 and GNSS coordinates estimated through static baselines between the years 2016 and 2019. The coherence of the experimental geoid heights has proven to be in line with the expected accuracy of the available data. Widespread biases of several centimetres between the experimental data and the models have been found, because of different references used to identify the geoid. The ITALGEO05 model is the closest to the experimental data, which was expected since it is the official Italian geoid model and the orthometric heights used in our computation are also referred to the national height datum. We eliminated these biases by subtracting regression straight lines to each geoid model for further analysis.

In terms of the shape of the geoid, it isn't possible to trust the experimental data to apply local corrections to the other models, since both the a-priori uncertainty and the a-posteriori scattering of the measures are too large. In order to use GNSS-levelling measurements to define local correction to the geoid height much more accurate measurements should be used. Let's now analyse this aspect in deeper detail. Looking at the uncertainties listed in Sect. 3 it is clear that errors due to spirit levelling are not impacting significantly on the final result given by Eq. 4. Bearing in mind that GNSS and spirit levelling data were not gathered at the same epoch and the whole area is undergoing subsidence phenomena, we can examine how the a-priori accuracy of the experimental geoid undulation would have improved with contemporary measuring campaigns. In such a case, the uncertainty changes from 4.3 to 3.2 cm. Obviously, the same result can be found by considering subsidence models not affected by any uncertainty. The most impacting source of error seems to be the ellipsoidal height given by GNSS but note that reducing its uncertainty from 3.2 to 1 cm leads to a final uncertainty of the model of 3 cm, which is an improvement very similar to what obtainable using simultaneous measurements. Finally, the combined use of contemporary acquired data and ellipsoidal height defined with 1 cm uncertainty lets Eq. 4 give an estimation of the final accuracy of the geoid height about 1.2 cm, which is significantly better than what we dealt with. Such a case would only be possible by performing GNSS observing sessions much longer than 1–2 h in order to significantly improve the accuracy in the height definition.

Nevertheless, we want to highlight that the computed experimental geoid undulation can be used to transform ellipsoidal heights measured using satellite systems into orthometric heights in a way more coherent with the reference already defined in the considered area. Finally, it was fundamental to take into account the subsidence phenomena. In facts, if we estimate the local geoid heights without applying the corrections given by the subsidence models, an overall bias of about 2 cm is introduced, with differences up to 12 cm over the points affected by the higher subsidence ratio. This aspect is fundamental to be considered whenever dealing with surveys performed in different years.

References

1. Rapp, R.H., Wang, Y.M.: Geoid undulation differences between geopotential models. Surv. Geophys. **14**, 373–380 (1993). https://doi.org/10.1007/BF00690565
2. Soycan, M., Soycan, A.: Comparison of several techniques for fitting of the EGM08 to GPS/leveling datum. Arab. J. Sci. Eng. **39**(7), 5637–5651 (2014). https://doi.org/10.1007/s13369-014-1136-1
3. Bjelotomić Oršulić, O., Markovinović, D., Varga, M., Bašić, T.: The impact of terrestrial gravity data density on geoid accuracy: case study Bilogora in Croatia. Surv. Rev. **52**(373), 299–308 (2020)
4. Oluyori, P.D., Ono, M.N., Eteje, S.O.: Computations of Geoid undulation from comparison of GNSS/levelling with EGM 2008 for Geodetic applications. Int. J. Sci. Res. Publ. **8**(10), 235–241 (2018). https://doi.org/10.29322/IJSRP.8.10.2018.p8230

5. Vecchi, E., et al.: Third beach nourishment project with submarine sands along Emilia-Romagna coast: geomatic methods and first monitoring results. Rend. Fis. Acc. Lincei, **31**, 79–88 (2020) https://doi.org/10.1007/s12210-020-00879-w

6. Aguzzi, M., et al.: Stato del litorale emiliano-romagnolo al 2018. Erosione e interventi di difesa, Bologna, Arpae Emilia Romagna, I quaderni di Arpae (2020)

7. Mancini, F., Grassi, F., Cenni, N.: A workflow based on SNAP–StaMPS open-source tools and GNSS data for PSI-based ground deformation using dual-orbit sentinel-1 data: accuracy assessment with error propagation analysis. Remote Sens. **13**, 753 (2021). https://doi.org/10. 3390/rs13040753

8. Teatini, P., Ferronato, M., Gambolati, G., Bertoni, W., Gonella, M.: A century of land subsidence in Ravenna. Italy. In: Environ. Geol. **47**, 831–846 (2005). https://doi.org/10.1007/s00 254-004-1215-9

9. Barzaghi, R., Borghi, A., Carrion, D., Sona, G.: Refining the estimate of the Italian quasi-geoid. In: Bollettino di Geodesia e Scienze affini, vol. 3, pp. 146–157 (2007)

10. Corchete, V.: The high-resolution gravimetric geoid of Italy: ITG2009. J. Afr. Earth Sci. **58**, 580–584 (2010)

11. Pavlis, N.K., Holmes, S.A., Kenyon, S.C., Factor, J.K.: The development and evaluation of the Earth Gravitational Model 2008 (EGM2008). J. Geophys. Res. Solid Earth **117**, B04406 (2012). https://doi.org/10.1029/2011JB008916

12. Bitelli, G., et al.: Updating the subsidence map of Emilia-Romagna region (Italy) by integration of SAR interferometry and GNSS time series: the 2011–2016 period. Proc. IAHS **382**, 39–44 (2020)

13. Emilia-Romagna, A.R.: Rilievo della Subsidenza nella pianura Emiliano-Romagnola. Relazione finale (2012)

14. Emilia-Romagna, A.R.: Rilievo della Subsidenza nella pianura Emiliano-Romagnola. Relazione finale (2018)

15. Emilia-Romagna, A.R.: Misura della rete regionale di controllo della subsidenza, misura di linee della rete costiera non comprese nella rete regionale, rilievi batimetrici. Relazione Finale (2001)

16. International Service for the Geoid (ISG). https://www.isgeoid.polimi.it/Geoid/Europe/Italy/ italgeo05_g.html. Accessed 08 Jan 2021

17. Prezioso, G., Pepe, M., Santamaria, R.: Confronto, su territorio campano, tra modello geoidico EGM2008 e modello di ondulazione da grigliati (2012). https://doi.org/10.13140/RG.2.1. 4354.8003

18. Barzaghi, R., Carrion, D.: Testing EGM2008 in the central mediterranean area, external quality evaluation. Reports of EGM08. Newton's Bull **4**, 133–143 (2009)

19. Barbarella, M., Barzaghi, R., Dominici, D., Fiani, M., Gandolfi, S., Sona, G.: A comparison between the Italgeo'95 and GPS/Leveling data along the coast of Italy. J. Phys. Chem. Earth (ISSN: 1474-7065) **23**(1), 81–86 (1998). [SCOPUS ref. 2-s2.0–0031870497]

Comparative Analysis Among Photogrammetric 3D Models RAW Data vs RGB Images

Alessio Cardaci(✉) [iD], Pietro Azzola, Michele Bianchessi, Ruggero Folli, and Simone Rapelli

Department of Engineering and Applied Sciences, University of Bergamo, Bergamo, Italy
{alessio.cardaci,pietro.azzola}@unibg.it, {m.bianchessi,r.folli, s.rapelli}@studenti.unibg.it

Abstract. The military architecture of the ancient Republic of Venice is a very significant heritage. These are structures with simple volumes in the building and functional in the distribution; they are often little considered because, wrongly, they are considered minor. The cultural capital that must be documented and digitized to preserve, improve and preserve. The case study of the "Torresino da Polvere" in via Beltrami, in the upper town of Bergamo, was used as a pretext for a comparative analysis between the 3D models. Models generated by the direct processing of data from photographic sensors and those obtained from image processing after conventional raw conversion processes. The research, based on rigorous experimentation, proposes a new method of capture and frame management in order to obtain high quality models directly from the raw data. The results allowed some interesting considerations; they highlighted the singular peculiarities of some software in the management of raw data, both for a higher accuracy of the returns, and for an unexpected speed of calculation.

Keywords: 3D integrated survey · Torresini da polvere · Bergamo

1 Introduction

The format commonly referred to as raw contains information related to the light intensity measured by the photometric sensor, a 'digital negative' without modification or alteration. Raw data are sequences of bits stored in proprietary files according to specific codes established by the different constructors and, among them, incompatible with each other. Digital manufacturers, for purely business reasons, were less likely to adopt a universal standard, as demonstrated by the limited success of the DNG format [1, 2]. A format developed by Adobe®, patented, open and without loss and may be boycotted by major brands like Canon®, Nikon® and Sony®.

A photograph, even of the same scene and under the same lighting conditions, will therefore be different if captured with different cameras, both because it is dependent on the different spectral sensitivities of the sensors, and on the different 'preservation' of the information [3]. In addition, the raw data does not represent a structured and visible image thanks to colored pixels but, instead, a list of values recorded by the

E. Borgogno-Mondino and P. Zamperlin (Eds.): ASITA 2021, CCIS 1507, pp. 271–282, 2022.
https://doi.org/10.1007/978-3-030-94426-1_20

photosensitive detectors by means of a filter matrix - reactive to the frequencies of red, green and blue - arranged according to the well-known and usual Bayer Array [4]. The creation of a realistic representation is the result of a conversion performed through raw conversion algorithms which transform the luminosity values of each photoreceptor. Transformation deals sequentially with linear values, white balance, demosaification, color space conversion and gamma correction in an orderly array of RGB data [5].

The main function of raw-converter software is to 'estimate' the amount of light captured by the chamber and make it visible through colorimetric information; a process strongly conditioned both by the electronics of the chamber and by the choices of the operator [6]. The transformation of the raw data into dng, tif or jpg codes is therefore an action that involves both an alteration of the information (caused by the interpretation of the value) and a loss of part of the contents (as a result of compression and/or reduction from bit depth, generally from 14 to 8, as well as noise reduction and increased contrast and sharpness). A process that in the literature is evaluated as an added value as it allows to improve the quality of photographs, both for the correction of errors made during capture (adjustment of colour shades, increase of contrasts, filtering of background noise,…), and for the possibility of adding multiple shots with merging and/or HDR elaborations [7].

The proposed research, taking as a pretext the case study of the 'Torresino da Polvere' in the upper city of Bergamo [8], wanted to conduct a comparative study among the 3D photogrammetric models extracted from the direct processing of the photographic sensor data with those, instead, obtained from the processing of RGB images after the traditional raw-converter treatment.

The work is part of a larger search for the digital documentation of military architectures of the former Republic of Venice (Fig. 1); an extensive patrimony of inestimable value made up of structures with simple volumes in construction and functional in distribution and, perhaps for this reason, little considered because poorly considered as minor.

2   Laser Scanner Survey and Topography Network

The 3D survey of the 'Torresino da Polvere' of via Beltrami, a small architecture with regular geometry and linked to the Venetian Walls of the city, was therefore the necessary study frame for experimentation (Fig. 2).

The strong presence of vegetation on the roof and the partial burial of two of its sides, did not allow the return of the integral model of the building but only part of it; wall sections, however, more than satisfactory for punctual and reliable reflections. Measurements were made using multiple instruments and different acquisition methodologies, a well-established practice in the new integrated investigation procedures [9]. A topographic network has been set up whose vertex coordinates, materialized with prisms placed on fixed tripods, have been determined with total station and operating a forced centring, a method that allows the interchangeability between signal and instrument has allowed an indeterminacy of less than one millimetre. The resolution of the hyperdetermined equations of the network (for the surplus of both angular and distance measurements) was carried out through minimum square compensation software. In this case the well-known commercial product MicroSurvey® Star*Net was used because it was able to combine ease of use and essential functions, with great reliability and high rigor [10]. From the top of the network, through forward intersections and distantly surveys, the coordinates of the centres of paper targets placed on the walls of the building were acquired; they, in large numbers and well-studied in geometry and spatial distribution, have formed the Ground Control Points (GCP) - twelve in total - of the georeferencing system of 3D laser scanner and photogrammetry virtual maquettes. The topographic survey has been integrated with an active sensor survey in order to have a much higher number of cornerstones (twenty-eight in all) at known coordinates; the cloud of points obtained was, in fact, the metric reference for the comparison of the various models [11].

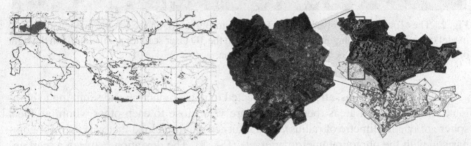

Fig. 1. La The fortress of Bergamo in the context of the ancient Republic of Venice of the 16th century and the 'Torresino da Polvere' in the upper city.

In order to optimize the time, only reflectance information was recorded and not the colorimetric data; the purpose of the experiment was in fact the verification of the accuracy of digital artefacts and not the study and understanding of colour. The creation of a single global project cloud was carried out with an initial alignment of the individual catches on the targets presented earlier and, therefore, an approximation of the various portions by means of 'shape-recognition' algorithms.

The use of external references, such as spheres or chessboards, allowed for the stricter recording of scans as well as verification of inaccuracies based on differences between targets measured with the laser scanner and the position of the top of the topographic network [12, 13]. The recording phase was carried out through the software that owns the instrument, the Faro® Scene, and the verification of the accurateness was carried out through the application of the ATS® Quality Manager, able to perform the calculation of voltages, compensations and return the statistics of ground control points (GCP). The excellent overlap of the individual clouds was thus ascertained with an average approximation contained within the instrumental precision (±1.5 mm).

Fig. 2. The 'Torresino da Polvere' in via Beltrami in Bergamo; on the left the preview of the 3D model (projection of the photogrammetric model on the 3D laser scanner point cloud); on the right of the images of the architecture after the restoration.

The individual scans, after being subjected to noise reduction and sampling to elim-inate the over-posed areas (because they are very close to each other within an ideal sphere of one millimetre of radius), then returned a dense cloud that was used for com-parison with the photogrammetric artefacts (Fig. 3). The deviation between a 'certain' and reliable geometry (that of the 3D laser scanner) and the virtual model recreated on the basis of the different photogrammetric treatments, has therefore made it possible to identify the most accurate archetype.

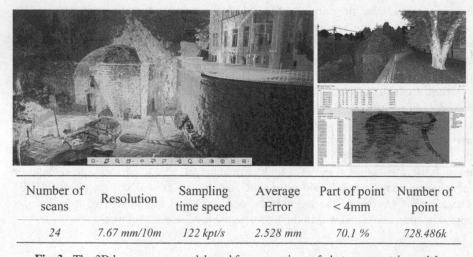

Number of scans	Resolution	Sampling time speed	Average Error	Part of point < 4mm	Number of point
24	7.67 mm/10m	122 kpt/s	2.528 mm	70.1 %	728.486k

Fig. 3. The 3D laser scanner model used for comparison of photogrammetric models.

3 Photogrammetry: Processing Raw Data and RGB Images

Photogrammetric 3D models were created by processing the same photo capture set. The experiment consisted of the creation of five virtual artefacts: two generated by directly processing the sensor data stored on the camera memory card (RAW image sensor and JPG image sensor), three RGB images created after the raw data processing (JPG Raw-Converter, TIF Raw-Converter and DNG Raw-Converter).

Table 1. The image quality index: comparative tables and graphs between the various formats.

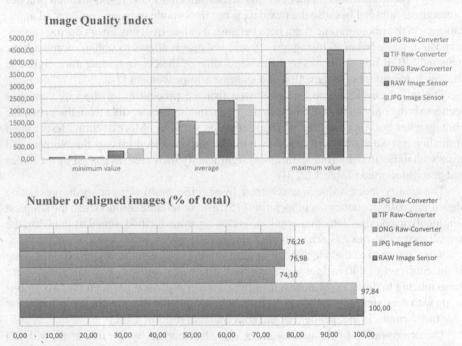

Name	Minimum Quality	Average Quality	Maximum Quality	Image Aligned
JPG Raw-Converter	*60,00*	*2027,50*	*3995,00*	*76,26 %*
TIF Raw-Converter	*98,00*	*1550,00*	*3002,00*	*76,98 %*
DNG Raw-Converter	*48,00*	*1103,00*	*2158,00*	*74,10 %*
JPG Image Sensor	*402,00*	*2221,00*	*4040,00*	*97,84 %*
RAW Image Sensor	*309,00*	*2393,50*	*4478,00*	*100,00 %*

The conversion was carried out through the Adobe@ Camera Raw software by applying to all photographs of the group the same transformation parameters and, therefore, saving them in different formats: DNG, TIF and JPG. Graphical information from the RAW Image Sensor and transformed RGB images - JPG Raw-Converter, TIF Raw-Converter and DNG Raw-Converter - was captured/stored at the same resolution as about 21 Mega-Pixels (5616 × 3744), while JPG Image Sensor was slightly lower at 5.2 Mega-Pixel (2784 × 1856). It is because of the settings of the device used, a mark II EOS 5D Canon@ reflex with fixed lens Canon@ 24 mm/1.4, put to get small files. In all, a hundred shots were taken with an overlap between the images between 60% and 75%. The digital development of raw sensor information is recommended practice - sometimes hobbled because the raw data is not importable in many commercial applications - in the photographic field, both because it can correct any errors during capture (exposure, white balance, histogram…), and because it allows to obtain more realistic 'personal' RGB images thanks to the manipulation of the colour temperature, light and shadow regulation, noise reduction and sharpness improvement [14].

The initial checks immediately showed that the processing of the raw converter seems to bring only an improvement in the visual quality, perceptible from the eye of the photographer but not from the 3D reconstruction software. More accurate tests aimed at quality assessment have in fact shown that in the processed images the blurring and areas with uniform colouring textures has significantly increased, as shown by the tables and graphs reported (Table 1 [2, 3]).

The quality index value was returned by specific multi-slate analysis processing algorithms with frequency decomposition [15], a more reliable solution than the simplest commonly used edge detection applications. A rigorous method aimed at knowing the overall characteristics of each individual image [16].

When returned to the table, the minimum value, average value, and maximum value of the entire set of 140 images were reported. The best results, as you can guess, were those relating to direct raw catches; it surprised the comparison between the two groups in jpg with very similar parameters, as if to demonstrate that the raw-converter treatment - for this format - is independent of the conversion algorithm used.

The deterioration of the quality index was also marked by the first steps with 3D Image Based Reconstruction software, in which a reduction of about 30% of the images used for the external positioning of the cameras was evident. The greater number of non-aligned photographs, from careful observation of the models, was caused both by the smaller number of keypoints recognized by the software, and by the greater inaccuracy in the positioning of target centres; this feature, as will be emphasized below, will result in less accuracy of the model. In fact, the deviation between the coordinates of the references attributed by the software (for the lower sharpness and greater blurring of the edges) and those forced by the direct assignment of the values measured with the topographic network, is the cause of a greater error of RMS reprojection.

The experiment was based on the use of the latest version of the 3DFlow® Zephyr; in fact, it is one of the few commercial applications for photogrammetry that can import raw data. The tests were able to take advantage of the possibilities offered by the new Windows Imaging Component (WIC) Raw Format engine that can support most of the raw formats of large photographic equipment manufacturers.

Specifically, the software utilizes the potential of the codec pack developed by Microsoft® as part of the LibRaw project. It is a free and open source software library [17] that can process the raw files of many manufacturers while maintaining metadata, bit-data depth (up to 32 bits per channel) and the high dynamic range of the sensor.

The choice of a single application penalises the generalization of the problem as the results can be conditioned by the structure of the programme; aware of this limitation, the authors are conducting the same tests with multiple software (in order to be able to make general hypotheses not dependent on the applications used) but this, at the moment, is not related to the treatment of the essay because the findings are still unripe and deserve further study.

In principle, however, they appear to confirm the hypotheses advanced so far. The creation of the photogrammetric models followed the usual workflow distinguished, first of all, by a single choice of parameters for the various processing steps for all reconstructions. Standard values have been set of the variables that regulated the creation of the artefacts, avoiding extremes and particular situations that could have altered the generality of the results favouring one specific format over another.

The first phase saw the recognition by the software of particular points in the photographs and therefore the subsequent combination of them between the homologous frames; based on these 3DF® Zephyr indications continued by operating the spatial positioning of the chambers and the consequent generation of the scattered clouds.

The next steps were to build the dense cloud, convert the discontinuous point model to the continuous mesh model, and finally, reprojection on the faces of individual RGB image triangles (after accurate blending to ensure uniformity of exposure and colour). The georeferencing of the model and its 'scale' was carried out on the basis of the spatial coordinates of the Ground Control Points (GCP) which also fulfilled the role of Quality Control Points (QCP); as in the procedures concerning the data acquired by passive sensors, in fact, some cornerstones were used for the comparison of differences and differences between the coordinates of the models and those of the topographic network (Table 2, Fig. 5).

In order to achieve a better result instead of proceeding with the processing of the entire set of images within a single environment - more burdensome in terms of time and hardware resources - partial processing of the images was chosen and then the models were brought together. In particular, the two façades were rebuilt separately, keeping the areas close to the edge and roof as common joining elements.

This artifice has also made it possible to obtain more points (both scattered and dense cloud) as well as smaller and more 'interpretative' meshes of the real geometry of the building, thanks to the double processing of common frames (Fig. 5).

The comparison between the models highlights, with absolute clarity, how the best reconstructions are those obtained from the raw data, both in terms of accuracy and in the percentage of parts returned. The reconstruction of the cover, from shots captured in poor conditions with the inclined and more distant chamber, is guaranteed by the sensor information (raw and jpg) and not possible with RGB images after raw-converter treatments. It is important to highlight the results obtained by the jpg image sensor format because it is the result of pictures with much lower resolution and high compression ratio.

Table 2. Quantitative comparison tables between the various photogrammetric models.

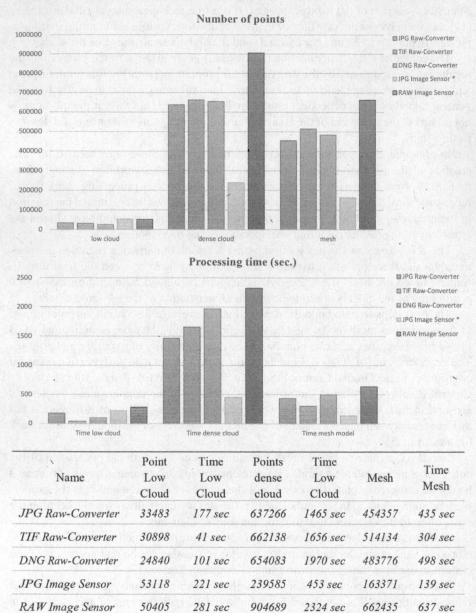

Name	Point Low Cloud	Time Low Cloud	Points dense cloud	Time Low Cloud	Mesh	Time Mesh
JPG Raw-Converter	33483	177 sec	637266	1465 sec	454357	435 sec
TIF Raw-Converter	30898	41 sec	662138	1656 sec	514134	304 sec
DNG Raw-Converter	24840	101 sec	654083	1970 sec	483776	498 sec
JPG Image Sensor	53118	221 sec	239585	453 sec	163371	139 sec
RAW Image Sensor	50405	281 sec	904689	2324 sec	662435	637 sec

Fig. 4. Model comparison: scattered point cloud, dense point cloud and mesh model (from left to right); retashing from the JPG Raw-Converter, JPG Raw-Converter, DNG Raw-Converter, JPG Image Sensor, and RAW Image Sensor image set (up to down).

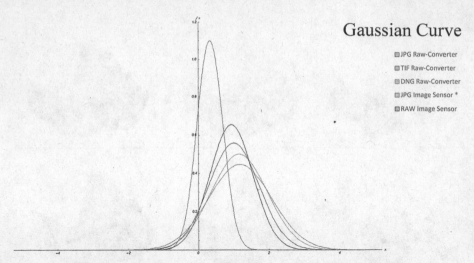

Fig. 5. Comparing the accuracy between models of the RMS index.

This is actually the basis of shorter processing times and less points and triangles making up clouds and meshes. A model that, although less accurate (it must not mislead the graph because it is compared with groups of photographs of different resolutions) has nevertheless reconstructed the model in its entirety, including the roof (Fig. 6).

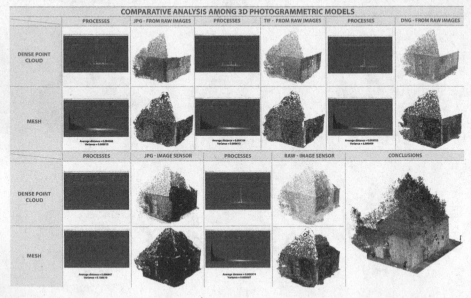

Fig. 6. Comparative analysis between photogrammetric models and the 3D laser scanner cloud.

4   Conclusions

Image Based Reconstruction 3D photogrammetry is based on the use of digital photos but many software does not allow the direct processing of raw files but only that of RGB images.

The first consideration is the convenience of using raw data for the creation of virtual artefacts based on photographic captures, because they can combine high metric accuracy with processing times that are still contained. The lack of digital development of the shots, while allowing to reduce 'time and work', is a constraint for greater attention during the capture of the scene; in fact, it is not possible to correct any 'grip' errors because, to date, it is not allowed to make changes to raw files within the software.

The external transformation of the raw data (not carried out by the chamber processor and/or with proprietary software) has instead shown a general 'loss' of information quality; the same raw jpg data saved directly from the camera allows the creation of models much more accurate than those obtained as a result of raw-converter transformations and saved in dng, tif and jpg formats.

This manifested itself with particular evidence in the very 'glimpsed' photographic sockets (such as the roof to the left of the roof photographed from below and up close by the presence of a wall) where the number of recognized keypoints was even insufficient to reconstruct the geometry.

Important reflection should be done for jpg images provided directly from the camera and produced with proprietary algorithms from different manufacturers. They are of far better quality than those generated by external software (ex: Abobe @CameraRaw); however, they have the disadvantage of preventing the photographer from intervening on the conversion parameters and, therefore, adjusting white balance, brightness,…, because everything is decided by the machine.

Acknowledgements. The study was conducted within a collaboration between the University of Bergamo and the Municipality of Bergamo, aimed at the knowledge, conservation and enhancement of the complexes of the Venetian Walls of Bergamo. The authors thank the 3DFlow team for valuable information and advice regarding the structure and optimal use of Zephyr software.

References

1. Triantaphillidou, S., Allen, E.: Digital image file formats. In: Allen, E., Triantaphillidou, S. (eds): The Manual of Photography and Digital Imaging, pp. 315–328. Routledge, New York (2010)
2. Schewe, J.: Il negativo digitale: file RAW con Photoshop, Lightroom e Camera RAW. Apogeo, Milano (2014)
3. Nguyen, R., Prasad, D.K., Brown M.S.: Raw-to-raw: mapping between image sensor color responses. In: Proceedings on IEEE Conference on Computer Vision and Pattern Recognition, pp. 3398–3405 (2014). https://doi.org/10.1109/CVPR.2014.434
4. Fraser, B.: Understanding Digital Raw Capture. Adobe Systems Incorporated, San Jose (2004) http://www.adobe.com/digitalimag/pdfs/understanding_digitalrawcapture.pdf
5. Rojtberg, P.: Processing RAW images in Python (2017). LNCS. http://www.researchgate.net/publication/314239357_Processing_RAW_images_in_Python

6. McHugh, S.T.: Understanding Photography: Master Your Digital Camera and Capture that Perfect Photo. No Starch Press, San Francisco (2018)

7. Verhoeven, G.J.J.: It's all about the format–unleashing the power of RAW aerial photography. Int. J. Remote Sens. **31**(8), 2009–2042 (2010)

8. Cappellini P.: Le polveriere venete. Tipografia Cesare Ferrari, Bergamo (1987)

9. Cardaci, A., Versaci, A.: Rilievo e restauro: un binomio imprescindibile: approcci metodologici e applicazioni operative finalizzate alla conoscenza e alla conservazione del patrimonio culturale. Aracne, Roma (2018)

10. Bonfanti C.: Topographic and photogrammetric approaches for the multiscale documentation. Parthica: incontri di culture nel mondo antico (17), 57–62 (2015)

11. Shan, J., Toth, C.K.: Topographic Laser Ranging and Scanning: Principles and Processing. Routledge, New York (2018)

12. Liscio, E., Hayden, A., Moody, J.: A comparison of the terrestrial laser scanner & total station for scene documentation. J. Assoc. Crime Scene Reconstr. **20**, 1–8 (2016)

13. Cox, R.: Real-world comparisons between target-based and targetless point-cloud registration in Faro Scene, Trimble RealWorks and Autodesk Recap. (2015). LNCS. https://eprints.usq.edu.au/29195/

14. Carpiceci, M.: Fotografia digitale e architettura, elaborazioni con le odierne attrezzature fotografiche e informatiche. Aracne, Roma (2012)

15. Pirotti, F., Vettore, A., Guarnieri, A.: Algoritmi di classificazione contextual con GRASS. Geomatics Workbooks **6**, 1–12 (2016)

16. Alfio, V.S., Costantino, D., Pepe, M.: Influence of image TIFF format and JPEG compression level in the accuracy of the 3D model and quality of the orthophoto in UAV photogrammetry. J. Imaging **6**(5), 30 (2020)

17. http://www.libraw.org *Sample Heading (Forth Level).* The contribution should contain no more than four levels of headings. The following gives a summary of all heading levels

Photogrammetric Techniques and Image Segmentation via Machine Learning as Supporting Tools in Paving Asphalt Mixtures Studies

Andrea Piemonte$^{(\boxtimes)}$ ⓘ and Gabriella Caroti ⓘ

Civil and Industrial Engineering Department, University of Pisa,
Largo Lucio Lazzarino 2, 56122 Pisa, Italy
andrea.piemonte@unipi.it

Abstract. Research activities in the field of bituminous aggregates composition for roadway paving (asphalt) often require 2- and 3-D geometric measurements. In some cases, these can provide support in studying aggregate arrangement within bituminous matrices subjected to stress and evaluating 3D trends in the tyre/road contact interface. The current job investigates the potentialities of photogrammetry in handling these issues, presenting and checking two methodologies, i.e. the tested and well-established homographic transformation for 2D investigations, and the more innovative, 3D approach of Structure from Motion (SfM) + Multi-View Stereo (MVS). Both theoretical provisions and test findings confirm that photogrammetry can offer effective solutions to surveying issues in this specific field. Accuracy of geometric measures and photographic quality are appropriate for investigating aggregate dimension and dislocations ranging at 10^{-4} m. Finally, some possible applications of Machine Learning (ML) algorithms for segmentation and classification of photogrammetry imagery are discussed. Automatic image segmentation leads to less than 2% mismatch in the interest classes.

Keywords: Structure from Motion · Homography · Paving asphalt mixture · Machine Learning

1 Introduction

The ability of photogrammetry to simultaneously yield both visual and metric information of objects has led to its wide exploitation in several fields. A specific application lies in the investigations of asphalt mixtures for roadway paving [1]. These materials are the object of several measurements, both directly, on the roads on which they are implemented, and on core samples extracted from the same roads [2]. Laboratory tests carried out on asphalt samples provide, among other, both the measurement of any aggregate deformation or displacement in the granular matrix when cores are subjected to stress and the analysis of macro- and micro-texture of the tyre/road contact interface (ISO 13473–1:1997 and EN ISO 13473–1:2019 standards). Based on needs, measures can

© Springer Nature Switzerland AG 2022
E. Borgogno-Mondino and P. Zamperlin (Eds.): ASITA 2021, CCIS 1507, pp. 283–297, 2022.
https://doi.org/10.1007/978-3-030-94426-1_21

be restricted to analysis of planar shifts or involve the creation of a 3D model. In order to meet the diverse requirements, it is possible to employ different surveying and post processing photogrammetry methodologies.

Photogrammetry is a versatile methodology, providing several procedures to extract 2- and 3-D information from images. In particular, the present paper focuses on two methodologies: the rectification of a single image, in the case of surveys of flat elements, and stereo-photogrammetry in its current versions linked to Structure from Motion (SfM) techniques for generation of 3D models. The ongoing developments in digital technologies and Computer Vision (CV)-derived tools, crucial for photogrammetry automation [3], have greatly reduced calculation procedures and extended possible scenarios for photogrammetry applications, foremost in the field of close-range photogrammetry.

Notably, in this context of transformation and evolution, photogrammetry still retains stringent requirements as regards accuracy, reliability, performance and process robustness.

Images still provide the core raw data for both single- and multi-image photogrammetry, with their optical, radiometric and geometric qualities, along with shot settings, directly affecting quality of the end product. Although several investigations have covered both photogrammetric surveying and factors affecting image quality, to date the interactions between these have not, to the Authors' knowledge, been properly researched, possibly due to the high number of variables involved.

Currently, photogrammetry is mainly used to generate 3D point cloud models through SfM and MVS [4]. The combination of these multi-image techniques features high automation and seemingly low skill requirements and is able to process images collected at different scales, with different camera positions and from different sensors, since it does not necessarily entail exact image control as a starting point in the processing workflow. Thanks to their special algorithms, SfM and MVS almost never fail to produce a point cloud, which is the semi-finished product to be fed into subsequent processing to achieve orthophotographs, surface models, planar sections etc., for use in different scientific fields as metrically correct knowledge bases of the survey object. On the other hand, achieving metrically correct results actually requires in-depth knowledge of the multiple issues brought about by the methodology, which also affect the end product quality of the survey. In close-range applications on small (10^{-2} m range) objects, with surface equally developed along all dimensions, and a 10^{-4} m precision range target, image collecting requires special care to achieve high-quality datasets. Particular attention must be paid to radiometric and geometric sampling resolution, distance between object and camera central point, properties of camera sensor and lens, field depth, mutual overlapping and shooting position of input images, cast shadows, etc. [5].

The lack of a prevailing dimension requires careful analysis of the involved factors and highlights the remarkable complexity of finding the right balance.

With objects developed along principal planes, photogrammetric surveys take advantage of a methodology exploiting homographic transformation [6]. In this case, the object surface must be assumed as planar, which allows to streamline the search for the best procedures of image acquisition, also easing the issues linked with focusing the object, so that the quest for the right balance between lens, sensor and shooting range (to ensure that the entire object lies within the field depth) is usually carried out without resorting to special supports or dedicated devices.

The theoretical end accuracy of the different photogrammetric products is defined per the fundamental photogrammetry laws [7].

Photogrammetric methodologies are rarely used in standard laboratory tests on bituminous conglomerates although there is no lack of literature references on the topic [8, 9]. Consistently, no ISO standard yet considers such methodologies despite their potential effectiveness in this type of measures [10, 11]. This paper proposes some photogrammetric techniques as support means for survey issues in two different cases: the analysis of stress-induced aggregate arrangement within bituminous conglomerate matrices via 2D measurements on a single rectified image, and the analysis of surface macrotexture in bituminous conglomerates via 3D photogrammetry model measurements.

In both cases, the achievable accuracies and the advantages that a high quality photographic metric product can lead to are highlighted.

2 Materials and Methods

2.1 Analysis of Stress-Induced Aggregate Arrangement Within Bituminous Conglomerate Matrices

Road surface stress causes its deformation, with ensuing dislocation of both bituminous matrix and any included aggregate. As regards the analysis of bituminous conglomerate composition, it is interesting to note that changes in aggregate arrangement are linked to variations in their distance from the contact surface of the stress-inducing object [12]. Lab tests investigate these dislocations by subjecting a cylindrical core sample to a vertical load simulating the pressure exerted by a wheel rolling on the road. Figure 1 shows the same core sample before and after performing the test.

Fig. 1. Asphalt core samples

In order to ease result analysis, the core sample is sliced along a plane parallel to the cylinder axis prior to the test, exposing a core section where granulometric composition and arrangement of the conglomerate is easily detectable.

Since the analysis at issue refers to a planar surface, a simplified photogrammetry procedure has been followed, i.e. the rectification of a single image relative to the section plane.

A rectangular frame, covered in graph paper, is laid coplanar with the section plane, in order to enclose the conglomerate section to be evaluated. Two images are collected, one of the intact core sample prior to the test (at time T0) and the other of the deformed core sample after the test (at time T1); both are then rectified according to well-known homography relations. In order to evaluate the homography parameters, 20 control points, homogeneously arranged along the edge of the frame, are used. There is no need to place the frame in the same position relative to the core sample, as it only provides planar (for rectifying) and metric (for scaling) references. Since parts of the sample furthest away from the stress surface suffer no deformation throughout the test, the well-defined edges of the aggregates in these parts can be used to rototranslate both rectified images by overlaying undeformed regions.

Images have been shot with a Nikon D700 digital SLR camera (full frame sensor, 36.0×23.9 mm @ 4256×2832 pixel), fitted with a f $= 85$ mm lens in order to minimize lens-induced radial distortion. The ensuing mean Ground Sampling Distance (GSD) is $= 0.1$ mm at a mean shooting distance of 90 cm.

2.2   Analysis of Surface Macrotexture in Bituminous Conglomerates

Road pavement texture is defined, according to ISO regulation 13743, as the deviation of the pavement surface from a perfectly flat reference. The macrotexture represents the part of texture referring to the wavelength range included between 0.5 mm and 50 mm.

Usually, lab tests for macrotexture definition provide use of laser profilometers and trend assessment of a set of single sections from a cylindrical core sample of the road surface [13]. By implementing a photogrammetry approach, it is possible to achieve the so-called "digital twin" of the core sample, i.e. its digital replica, and extend the investigation to the entire 3D surface rather than restricting it to the single sections. The choice photogrammetric methodology relies, for its processing phase, on SfM and MVS algorithms, which opens new possibilities, previously unattainable due to time requirements and complexity, for this otherwise traditional surveying methodology. Generally speaking, a possible restriction to this approach lies in the surface texture of the survey object, in detail if homogeneous or with little detail variations and, even more so, with reflecting elements. In these conditions, the resulting point clouds are very noisy and therefore unsuitable for accurate and strict surface definition.

However, this is not the case for asphalt core samples, whose surface is both rough and heterogeneously textured. In this case, SfM + MVS perform quite well, achieving 3D accuracy matching theoretical results of an ideal predictive model [7].

The test object is a cylindrical ($\emptyset = 150$ mm, h $= 70$ mm) asphalt core sample (Fig. 2).

The geometric resolution of photogrammetry models depends mostly on shooting distance. On the other hand, accuracy depends upon many factors, including proper

Fig. 2. Cylindrical asphalt core sample for macrotexture analysis

overlap between adjacent photograms and overall shooting geometry; as already seen for homography, however, the most important one is photographic quality of the image, i.e. the actual survey raw data. Image sharpness, which in turn is affected by several issues such as unintentional movements during exposure, poor lighting or uneven focus, must therefore be carefully checked.

In order to achieve both resolution and precision in the 10^{-4} m range, all these aspects must be taken care of.

Since the shortest wavelength to analyse is $= 0.5$ mm, the photographic shooting design aims for a GSD $= 0.1$ mm.

Images are shot with a Nikon D700 digital SLR camera (full frame sensor, 36.0×23.9 mm @ 4256×2832 pixel), fitted with a f $= 50$ mm lens. In this configuration, the required GSD is achieved at a shooting distance of 60 cm.

In order to ensure even lighting of the sample surface and avoid cast shadows, use of a lightbox photo studio allows shooting with aperture f/11, which in turn ensures the required field depth to have the entire object surface properly focussed.

In classic photogrammetry, small objects are usually surveyed by moving the camera around the object. On the other hand, the same approach results in noisier point clouds, as the most part of the scene is out of focus, and poorer performance and accuracy of the matching algorithms.

In this case, both data collection and model generations are improved by using an electrically rotatable dish, conveniently synchronized with the camera shutter, so to have a rotating object and a stationary camera. Even though the lightbox walls and surfaces remain unchanged throughout every image, they can be easily masked out by means of automated procedures in bitmap graphics software.

In order to provide the model with a scale, two reference L-shaped ($250 \times 160 \times 25$ mm and $200 \times 130 \times 25$ mm, respectively) graph paper-covered rulers are used (Fig. 2).

Three Ground Control Points (GCPs), identified on the graph paper, provide the model with a scale and a local reference system. At the same time, 18 Check Points (CPs) are collimated on the graph paper to provide known scale bars against which model accuracy can be checked.

2.3   Image Segmentation via Machine Learning (ML) Algorithms

ML algorithms [14], a part of Artificial Intelligence (AI), allow to make predictions and classify new observations based on known sample datasets, and are therefore widely used in semantic segmentation processes as well as in the analysis of 3D architectural data [15, 16]. Their use in the latter field exploits features derived from both 3D models (e.g. depth map, roughness, aspect etc.) and model-linked photographic information (e.g. texture, colour, extracted boundaries etc.).

Even in case the survey data and the processing results include 2D images, the semantic segmentation can be performed relying on pixel classification via ML algorithms. The latter allow, based on chosen features suitably extracted from the input data (e.g. hue, saturation brightness, Gaussian blur, Sobel filter, Hessian values of the original image), to create stacks of images and, based on class definitions, to perform boundary detection, semantic segmentation, or object detection and localization.

In this case, processing relies on semantic segmentation processes in order to suitably distinguish asphalt and aggregates: an appropriate portion of the set is originally chosen as training set, a set of examples used for the learning process. Then, thanks to the selection of an appropriate set of features, a classifier is constructed allowing to automatically segment the whole image.

This process, allowing to highlight aggregate displacement and deformation within bituminous matrices, is performed thanks to the Trainable Weka Segmentation (TWS) plugin, implemented in the open-source image processing program ImageJ [17]. The ML model is constructed via an ensemble classifier, the Fast Random Forest (FRF) algorithm [18]: this algorithm combines the output of multiple individual learning models and thus results more robust to errors and noise than a single classification tree. The four classes identified over the considered asphalt sample and the related annotations used for training are shown in Fig. 3.

In terms of pixels count, the training set consisted of almost 6% of the entire image: the percentages, broken down by each class, are displayed in Table 1.

Table 1. Training set single class pixel percentage (image pixels number: 246706)

Class	Training set [pixel n.]	Training set [pixel %]
Asphalt	3252	1.32%
Aggregate	1659	0.67%
Graph paper	7949	3.22%
Background	1728	0.70%

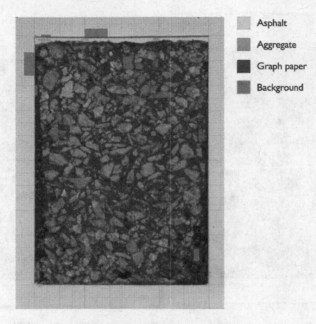

Asphalt

Aggregate

Graph paper

Background

Fig. 3. Training classes on asphalt section

3 Results and Discussion

3.1 Analysis of Stress-Induced Aggregate Arrangement Within Bituminous Conglomerate Matrices

The results of the homographic transformation of the images before and after deformation are used in the analysis of aggregate arrangement within the bituminous matrix (Fig. 4).

Since far more double points than those strictly needed have been used to define homographic parameters, it is possible to analyse the deviations between coordinates calculated via the graph paper reference system and those resulting from the transformation.

Table 2 displays all the residuals, also highlighting that, considering the 2D composition (resXY) of the residuals as X (resX) and Y (resY), mean deviation is 0.11 mm and 0.09 mm, and maximum deviation is 0.23 mm and 0.19 mm, for T0 and T1 respectively. Mean values match the designated GSD @ $\pm 10^{-4}$ m and also conform to the precision estimate for defining point coordinates on graph paper.

Accuracy of geometric measures and photographic quality are appropriate for investigating aggregate dislocations ranging at 10^{-4} m, also allowing to trace possible aggregate disruption by comparing both rectified images.

Fig. 4. Rectified images of the sample section at time T0 (left) and T1 (right)

Table 2. Check points coordinates residual

	T0			T1		
	resX [mm]	resY [mm]	resXY [mm]	resX [mm]	resY [mm]	resXY [mm]
dx_A	−0.01	0.20	0.20	−0.08	0.07	0.11
dx_B	0.13	0.15	0.20	−0.05	0.05	0.07
dx_M	−0.04	−0.10	0.11	0.07	−0.07	0.09
dx_MAA	−0.06	0.07	0.09	−0.01	0.04	0.04
dx_MBB	0.01	0.08	0.08	0.06	0.03	0.06
dx_MMA	−0.09	−0.13	0.15	−0.03	0.03	0.04
dx_MMB	−0.02	−0.03	0.03	−0.01	−0.04	0.04
M_A	0.04	−0.01	0.05	0.09	−0.11	0.14
M_B	0.03	−0.11	0.11	0.02	−0.06	0.06
MMdx_A	−0.04	−0.09	0.10	−0.04	0.03	0.05
MMdx_B	0.07	−0.12	0.14	0.04	−0.05	0.06
MMsx_A	0.07	−0.11	0.13	0.03	−0.08	0.08
MMsx_B	−0.02	0.01	0.02	−0.01	0.02	0.02
sx_A	0.02	0.19	0.19	−0.13	0.14	0.19

(continued)

Table 2. (*continued*)

	T0			T1		
	resX [mm]	resY [mm]	resXY [mm]	resX [mm]	resY [mm]	resXY [mm]
sx_B	−0.10	0.21	0.23	−0.15	0.09	0.18
sx_M	−0.03	−0.11	0.11	0.08	−0.08	0.11
sx_MAA	0.10	−0.04	0.11	−0.01	0.02	0.02
sx_MBB	−0.02	−0.01	0.02	−0.01	0.00	0.01
sx_MMA	−0.01	−0.02	0.02	0.12	−0.08	0.14
sx_MMB	−0.05	−0.05	0.07	0.04	0.03	0.05

3.2 Analysis of Stress-Induced Aggregate Arrangement Within Bituminous Conglomerate Matrices

The end result of SfM/MVS processing is a so-called dense point cloud, to set it apart from the intermediate processing result, I.e. the point cloud including only the tie points detected by the matching algorithms (E.G. SIFT- scale-invariant Feature Transform) and used to calculate orientation parameters in the bundle adjustment phase. Dense point clouds are very high-resolution 3D representations of the object surface (Fig. 5), and can be used to extract sections, or to define fitting planes for volume calculations or actual deviations measurements.

Fig. 5. 3D model of core sample surface macrotexture

Table 3 displays model deviations at the provided scale bars. The resulting standard deviation = 0.3 mm conforms to the theoretical precision of a standard stereophotogrammetry restitution [7], which, in the given conditions, is = 0.2 mm.

3.3 Image Segmentation via Machine Learning Algorithms

Figure 6 shows, on the left, the rectified image of the asphalt core section, and, on the right, its segmentation in the four classes fed into the FRF classifier, based on training

Table 3. Deviations at scale bars

Scale bar	Deviation [mm]
L_10_L_50	−0.1
L_10_L_190	−0.7
L_100_L_150	−0.2
L_150_L_190	−0.2
M_10_M_50	−0.1
M_10_M_150	−0.6
M_100_M_150	−0.2
P_10_P_50	0.0
P_10_P_100	0.0
P_50_P_100	0.0
S_10_S_50	0.0
S_10_S_240	0.3
S_100_S_150	0.1
S_200_S_240	0.0
MEAN [mm]	−0.1
STDV [mm]	0.3
RMSE [mm]	0.3

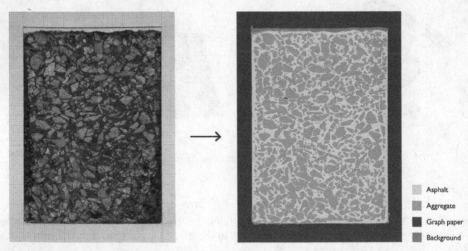

Asphalt
Aggregate
Graph paper
Background

Fig. 6. 3D model of core sample surface macrotexture

features processed by means of the TWS algorithm. class "Aggregate" is well defined and separate from the bituminous matrix.

By isolating class "Aggregate" in a separate image and comparing the segmented images before and after applying stress, it is possible to describe the aggregate dislocation and deformation.

To validate the resulting segmentation, a held-out sample of the image is considered, corresponding to the 25% (Fig. 7). The predictions for this part of the dataset are compared with a manual segmentation performed by the authors by hand by filling similarly coloured areas with a class colour. This process takes place via Adobe Photoshop, a widely used software for image processing.

The comparison between manual and automated segmentation for the sample at time T_0 is shown in Fig. 8-left and 8-right respectively.

Fig. 7. Validation set: the upper left of the image of the sample at time T_0

The validation set gives an unbiased estimate of the ML model performance, by comparison between true and predicted values. The graphical difference between the two images, obtained via MATLAB Image Processing Toolbox, is displayed in Fig. 9 (false negatives in pink and false positives in green exiting the automatic segmentation via ML), while the difference computed in terms of pixels and split for each class is illustrated in Table 4. The mismatch in the asphalt and aggregate classes is less than 2%.

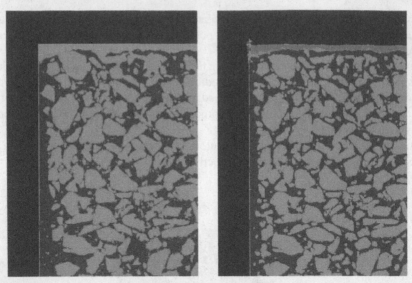

Fig. 8. Comparison between manual (left) and automated (right) segmentation for the validation set at time T_0

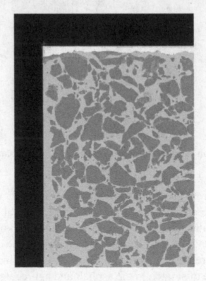

Fig. 9. Graphical comparison between manual and automatic segmentation

Table 4. Comparison in terms of pixel number between manual and automatic segmentation

Class	Manual seg. [pixel n.]	Automatic seg. [pixel n.]
Asphalt	91963	93791
Aggregate	117945	115622
Graph paper	80409	82564
Background	6992	5332

4 Conclusion

Both photogrammetry methodologies discussed, i.e. rectifying and SfM + MVS, allow to achieve suitable results, in terms of both metric accuracy and photographic quality, to support analysis of bituminous conglomerates.

In particular, while SfM + MVS is the only approach providing a 3D survey of the asphalt sample, when investigations only involve a planar section of the sample, single-image rectification attains the best results as regards accuracy. Besides, since homography aims at rectifying single images, it also achieves better results for image quality. In fact, any orthophotograph relative to the same section plane as the rectification of the model achieved via SfM + MVS would be a paste-up of many tiles coming from different images. No matter how strict the operations of collage and blending, to achieve even brightness and hue across the different images, the resulting orthophotograph will not achieve better quality than a single image, shot and optimized for the specific plane of interest.

This means that even a20 + years-old, well-established and simplified photogrammetry processing technique as homographic rectification can still provide an effective support for several surveying requirements, with particular reference as the analysis of aggregate arrangement within the bituminous matrix in specific control sections of asphalt samples.

Anyway, should investigations extend in 3D space, modern photogrammetry methodologies of the SfM + MVS type allow to achieve excellent results in terms of both metric accuracy of 3D models and quality of derived images such as perspective views, orthoimages etc.

Both these approaches of photogrammetry surveying and processing require very high-quality images as regards lighting, focus, and blur absence, which entail the use of *ad hoc* photo box and professional lighting kits, as well as careful drafting of a photogrammetry shooting design, defining GSD according to the values of expected displacements or frequencies and, as a consequence, focus and camera-object distance based on sensor size. Field depth can then be calculated based on the higher aperture setting possible without affecting image quality. Survey objects extending beyond the field depth require either applying masks in the processing step, or exploiting techniques such as focus stacking, to collect and merge different images, shot from the same camera position with different focal planes. All these attentions to image quality allow to achieve results with very high resolution and very low noise levels, therefore also suitable for automated interpreting exploiting the potentialities of Machine Learning segmentation applied to imagery.

Acknowledgments. The research presented in this article is partially funded by the Pisa University project PRA_2020_28 - Smart and Sustainable Use Phase of Existing Roads (S-SUPER) and by the project PRIN2017 - Extended resilience analysis of transport networks (EXTRA TN): Towards a simultaneously space, aerial and ground sensed infrastructure for risks prevention.

References

1. Tan, Y., Li, Y.: UAV photogrammetry-based 3D road distress detection. IJGI **8**, 409 (2019). https://doi.org/10.3390/ijgi8090409
2. Sefidmazgi, N.R., Tashman, L., Bahia, H.: Internal structure characterization of asphalt mixtures for rutting performance using imaging analysis. Road Mater. Pavement Design **13**, 21–37 (2012). https://doi.org/10.1080/14680629.2012.657045
3. Granshaw, S.I., Fraser, C.S.: Editorial: computer vision and photogrammetry: interaction or introspection? Photogram Rec. **30**, 3–7 (2015). https://doi.org/10.1111/phor.12092
4. Remondino, F., Spera, M.G., Nocerino, E., Menna, F., Nex, F.: State of the art in high density image matching. Photogramm. Rec. **29**, 144–166 (2014). https://doi.org/10.1111/phor.12063
5. Remondino, F., Spera, M.G., Nocerino, E., Menna, F., Nex, F., Gonizzi-Barsanti, S.: Dense image matching: comparisons and analyses. In: 2013 Digital Heritage International Congress (DigitalHeritage), pp. 47–54. IEEE, Marseille, France (2013). https://doi.org/10.1109/Digita lHeritage.2013.6743712
6. Hemmleb, M.: Digital Rectification and Generation of Orthoimages In Architectural Photogrammetry, 8 October 1997
7. Kraus, K.: Photogrammetry. V.1.: Fundamentals and standard processes., Bonn: Dummler (1994)
8. Jiang, J., Ni, F., Dong, Q., Yao, L., Ma, X.: Investigation of the internal structure change of two-layer asphalt mixtures during the wheel tracking test based on 2D image analysis. Constr. Build. Mater. **209**, 66–76 (2019). https://doi.org/10.1016/j.conbuildmat.2019.02.156
9. Cannelle, B., Beltzung, F., Thiémard-Spada, M.: Application of Photogrammetry and Image Processing for the Study of Porous Surface Courses. 5 (2020)
10. Chun, C., Ryu, S.-K.: Road surface damage detection using fully convolutional neural networks and semi-supervised learning. Sensors **19**, 5501 (2019). https://doi.org/10.3390/s19 245501
11. Mazzini, D., Napoletano, P., Piccoli, F., Schettini, R.: A novel approach to data augmentation for pavement distress segmentation. Comput. Ind. **121** (2020). https://doi.org/10.1016/j.com pind.2020.103225
12. Wei, F., Guan, B., Li, S., Shan, J.: Determination of optimal pretreatment method for existing pavement surface in high-friction surface treatment construction. J. Transp. Eng. Part B: Pavements **147**, 04021003 (2021). https://doi.org/10.1061/JPEODX.0000257
13. Losa, M., Leandri, P.: The reliability of tests and data processing procedures for pavement macrotexture evaluation. Int. J. Pavement Eng. **12**, 59–73 (2011). https://doi.org/10.1080/102 98436.2010.501866
14. Breiman, L.: Machine Learning. Mach. Learn. **45**, 5–32 (2001). https://doi.org/10.1023/A: 1010933404324
15. Croce, V., Caroti, G., De Luca, L., Jacquot, K., Piemonte, A., Véron, P.: From the semantic point cloud to heritage-building information modeling: a semiautomatic approach exploiting machine learning. Remote Sens. **13**, 461 (2021). https://doi.org/10.3390/rs13030461

16. Teruggi, S., Grilli, E., Russo, M., Fassi, F., Remondino, F.: A Hierarchical machine learning approach for multi-level and multi-resolution 3D point cloud classification. Remote Sens. **12**, 2598 (2020). https://doi.org/10.3390/rs12162598

17. Arganda-Carreras, I., et al.: Trainable Weka Segmentation: a machine learning tool for microscopy pixel classification. Bioinformatics **33**, 2424–2426 (2017). https://doi.org/10.1093/bioinformatics/btx180

18. Lindner, C.: Automated image interpretation using statistical shape models. In: Statistical Shape and Deformation Analysis, pp. 3–32. Elsevier (2017). https://doi.org/10.1016/B978-0-12-810493-4.00002-X

Towards a FOSS Automatic Classification of Defects for Bridges Structural Health Monitoring

Elena Belcore[1]([✉]) [iD], Vincenzo Di Pietra[1] [iD], Nives Grasso[1] [iD], Marco Piras[1] [iD],
Francesco Tondolo[2] [iD], Pierclaudio Savino[2] [iD], Daniel Rodriguez Polania[2],
and Anna Osello[2] [iD]

[1] Department of Environmental, Land and Infrastructure Engineering (DIATI),
Politecnico di Torino, C.so Duca degli Abruzzi 24, 10129 Turin, Italy
{elena.belcore,vincenzo.dipietra,nives.grasso,
marco.piras}@polito.it
[2] Department of Structural, Geotechnical and Building Engineering (DISEG),
Politecnico di Torino, C.so Duca degli Abruzzi 24, 10129 Turin, Italy
{francesco.tondolo,pierclaudio.savino,
s258085}@studenti.polito.it, anna.osello@polito.it

Abstract. Bridges are among the most important structures of any road network. During their service life, they are subject to deterioration which may reduce their safety and functionality. The detection of bridge damage is necessary for proper maintenance activities. To date, assessing the health status of the bridge and all its elements is carried out by identifying a series of data obtained from visual inspections, which allows the mapping of the deterioration situation of the work and its conservation status. There are, however, situations where visual inspection may be difficult or impossible, especially in critical areas of bridges, such as the ceiling and corners. In this contribution, the authors acquire images using a prototype drone with a low-cost camera mounted upward over the body of the drone. The proposed solution was tested on a bridge in the city of Turin (Italy). The captured data was processed via photogrammetric process using the open-source Micmac solution. Subsequently, a procedure was developed with FOSS tools for the segmentation of the orthophoto of the intrados of the bridge and the automatic classification of some defects found on the analyzed structure. The paper describes the adopted approach showing the effectiveness of the proposed methodology.

Keywords: Bridge defect detection · Unmanned aerial vehicles (UAV) · FOSS · Machine learning · Random forest · OBIA · Photogrammetry · MicMac

1 Introduction

The management of existing bridges is a widespread problem throughout the world. In Italy and many other countries, bridges are nearing the end of their useful life and show

© The Author(s) 2022
E. Borgogno-Mondino and P. Zamperlin (Eds.): ASITA 2021, CCIS 1507, pp. 298–312, 2022.
https://doi.org/10.1007/978-3-030-94426-1_22

significant deterioration conditions. During its life cycle, each infrastructure will face deterioration depending on several factors such as the natural aging, the execution of works, the material quality, the planned maintenance, and the environmental condition. In recent years, many Italian bridges have been affected by severe failures or collapses that have caused significant economic and human lives losses. The main defects are related to phenomena of cracking, spalling and delamination, which significantly shorten the useful life of the bridge and make it more fragile against the traffic on wheels with a consequent increase of safety-related risks.

The current situation would require in-depth analyses to be carried out on all infrastructures in order to assess the actual level of safety, according to current regulations, and to take appropriate measures. It is a costly procedure in terms of time and money and the number of infrastructures on which it should be applied is very high, about one million bridges and viaducts just in Italy. Many of these are of mixed competence, about 30 thousand are managed by local authorities with reduced financial capacity, and as many as 1,425 viaducts are without an identified owner and manager [1]. The strategic approach suggested by the decision-making bodies is defining and developing simple and efficient methods for assessing the structural risk associated with infrastructures throughout the national territory. These assessments must be carried out following the classification and identification of deterioration and damage.

To this end, Superior Council of Public Works of the Ministry of Infrastructure and Transport has issued the "Guidelines for the Classification and Risk Management, Safety Assessment and Monitoring of Existing Bridges" [2]. They are intended to provide a procedure for managing the safety of existing bridges in order to prevent inadequate levels of damage by making the risk acceptable. One of the various aspects described by the guidelines is the classification of risk by identifying defects following a visual inspection. The guidelines explain how to identify these issues through photographic identification, measurement and geometric survey. This lends itself to automation as it is a well-structured methodology.

This automation has started with the advent of computer vision and machine-learning techniques, which provides effective tools for automatic analysis and detection of defects in bridge pictures. Image enhancement, morphological operators, object segmentation algorithms have been used on images for several years [3–5]. With the technological development of imaging sensors and the increased amount of data acquired, machine-learning techniques [6–8] and artificial neural networks [9, 10] have become of great interest in this field.

A further step forward has been the spread of remotely piloted aircraft, which allowed georeferenced images of large parts of the infrastructure to be acquired. In the specific case of bridges, these are generally complicated structures to detect due to limited access to the structure itself. This often means increased risk for the operators involved in the inspection procedures, as well as the need to stop traffic, which increases costs. The use of drones could be a solution to these problems and could also provide an effective tool for cost saving with respect to traditional techniques [11]. Unmanned Aerial Vehicles (UAV) have already been used in bridge inspection and also developed in order to acquire those non-conventional data [12, 13] for documentation. In this scenario, photogrammetric techniques are effective tools to perform more in-depth analyses: i.e. georeferencing, measuring and quantifying defects in bridges. In fact, digital photogrammetry provides three-dimensional models and metrically accurate solid orthophotos, which could be used as a rich dataset for machine learning classification techniques [14].

This work aims to automate the procedure by means of geomatic and machine-learning techniques for the identification and automatic classification of structural defects in bridges. A UAV was modified for carrying a low-cost camera facing upward in order to acquire images of the intrados of a bridge. The automatic identification of the defects was made thorough a semiautomatic object-oriented (OBIA) supervised machine learning classification. The input data used as training sets were an orthoimage and a digital surface model results of the photogrammetric processing. All the steps of the work were made by means of free and open-source software (FOSS).

2   Case Study

The procedure proposed in this contribution was tested on the Stura bridge. The Stura river is crossed by this 150 m length double bridge, located on the motorway connection RA10, which allows the communication between Turin and the international airport Sandro Pertini (Fig. 1). The Stura Bridge is realized with two separated structures, one next to the other, each one of them corresponding to a direction of travel and 11 m wide. Each structure has five spans of variable lengths formed by a three main pre-stressed concrete girder beams system and complemented with squared sections transversal beams.

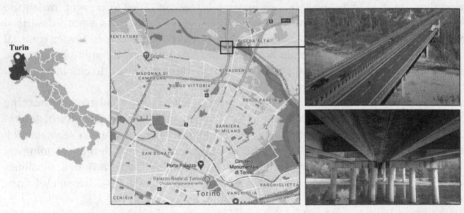

Fig. 1. Location of the Stura bridge on the RA10, its top and bottom view.

Given its strategic importance, the Stura bridge has been subject to various monitoring activities in recent years. Regardless of the nature of the inspection technique, monitoring the bridge's intrados is arduous because most of its length crosses the Stura river, and therefore it is hard to reach. This is especially true for geomatics approaches, which rely on different instruments. To this purpose, a novelty procedure for realising a photogrammetric survey with an upward camera installed on a UAV and the automatic classification of the defects was realized and applied on the second span of the bridge, 35 m long and 22 m wide.

3   The Methodology

The methodology consists of three macro-steps: data acquisition, data processing and the visual restitution of the results. It was entirely realized using FOSS (Fig. 2).

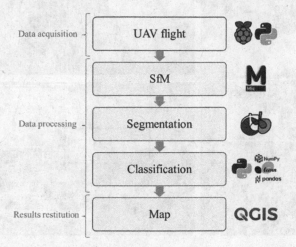

Fig. 2. FOSS workflow for the detection of structural damages.

3.1   Data Acquisition

The input data used in this work for the automatic classification of the structural defects of the bridge was the orthophoto of its intrados. The realization of this product required a novelty approach, which involved the use of an upward camera installed on a UAV platform. Typically, the commercial UAV solution integrates a camera gimbal that can be oriented at an angle of 90°, from zenith to nadiral view. In some cases, where it is necessary to inspect particular structures that cannot be observed and analysed effectively with other instruments, such as the intrados of a bridge, the possibility of exploiting an upward tilt can be decisive.

For the survey, a common Dji Phantom 4 aircraft was used. The quadrotor has a flight autonomy of about 20 min and a maximum upward orientation of the camera of 30°, which is insufficient for the complete photogrammetric reconstruction of the intrados. For this purpose, the UAV was equipped with a Raspberry Pi Camera Module 2 connected and managed by a Raspberry Pi (RPi) 3 system (Fig. 3). The advantage of this solution is the limited cost (<60 euro), their light weight and their simplicity to be used and embedded. Moreover, the RPi system can be exploited to control and process data collected from other sensors, such as inertial platforms and GNSS receivers, in order to perform the direct photogrammetry, where environmental conditions allow it [15].

Fig. 3. The photogrammetric system integration composed of the Raspberry Pi Camera Module V2 (in green), the Raspberry Pi 3 (in blue) and the power-bank (in red). (Color figure online)

A power-bank with 5000 mAh capacity was connected to the RPi, guaranteeing the autonomy of about 7 h. The devices were fixed with some cable ties to the camera gimble clamp of the drone and a support for a particular optical sensor (not used in this study) so as not to unbalance the platform. The total weight of the devices and the mounting components amounted to about 220 g. The RPi RGB camera module was installed upwards on the UAV to capture images with an orientation of 45° with respect to the zenith view. This camera sensor has an 8 MP resolution, but, for this study, a video recording at a lower resolution was set (1029 × 702 pixel) in order to automatically acquire images with a higher frame rate (2 fps) and ensure sufficient overlap between consecutive frames. To this purpose, a specific application in Python was developed to set the images acquisition with RPi camera and to store them automatically on an SD card inside the RPi. The application can be launched before the start of the flight. Due to the lack of GNSS signal, the flight was manually performed. In order to cover the entire study area, a flight path, at a distance of about five meters from the intrados, was followed, consisting of five survey lines corresponding to the spans of the bridge, each travelled in both directions. Table 1 summarizes the flight plan parameters and the characteristics of the acquired data.

Table 1. Flight plan parameters

Number of images	498
Flying altitude	5.29 m
Ground resolution	6.6 mm/pix
Image resolution	1024 × 720

As the external orientation of the images was unknown, external markers and photogrammetric points, easily identifiable on the images, were used as Ground Control Points (GCPs) to reference the model and to predict its accuracy. Therefore, the first step of the survey involved the construction of a topographic network composed of six vertices. Two vertices, identifying the primary network, were surveyed through a GNSS Leica GS-18 double frequency and multi-constellation receiver in static modality, standing on each point for about 1 h. The coordinates have been estimated considering a single-base solution (through the Leica Geo Office® software v.8.4) with the Torino permanent station of CORSs (Continuous Operating Reference Stations) network by Piedmont district, with an accuracy of about 3 mm.

Starting from this reference network, it was possible to acquire the position of four other points materialized on the ground under the bridge using a Leica MS-50 total station and a prism. The position of three artificial markers and of ten photogrammetric points spread on the intrados was measured from the station points of the topographic network and adjusted with the MicroSurvey StarNet v.7.0 software in order to obtain the final coordinates: the root mean square (RMS) of the estimated coordinates was lower than 1 cm.

4 Data Processing

The data processing regards the reconstruction of the orthophoto of the bridge's intrados and the supervised machine learning classification of the damages of the structure.

4.1 Photogrammetric Data Processing

Photogrammetric processing allows reconstructing of different scenarios from a set of images acquired from different points of view in the form of 3D digital model and ortho-imagery of the surveyed area. In order to maintain the FOSS approach, the free open-source photogrammetric suite MicMac (Multi-Images Correspondances, Methodes Automatiques de Correlation) from the French National Geographic Institute (IGN) [16, 17] has been used. The first step of the point cloud reconstruction is the identification of relevant features visible in multiple images, which is performed with the well-known SIFT algorithm [18]. Thanks to these common features, the position of the camera centre and the calibration parameters are computed. The MicMac libraries use the Structure from Motion procedure in order to accurately reconstruct the scene, generating the dense point cloud from which the digital elevation model (DEM) and the orthomosaic map are extracted. All these steps are applied by running sequentially five libraries: Tapioca, Tapas, Malt, Nuage2Ply and Tawny. During the process, some known reference points measured with a Total Station has been used to scale and georeference the model (GPSBascule tool). An optimization procedure which minimizes the coordinate errors is performed by Campari tool and the overall discrepancies between the reference coordinates and the estimated ones are reported in Table 2. From this procedure a DEM with resolution of 2.5 cm and an orthophoto with resolution of 0.6 cm have been extracted.

Table 2. Overall RMSE of the photogrammetric points on the intrados measured with the total station.

RMSE East	RMSE North	RMSE Up
7.27 mm	3.38 mm	5.68 mm

4.2 Damage Classification

The damages were identified thorough a semiautomatic object-oriented (OBIA) supervised machine learning classification.

In the Very High Resolution (VHR) image classification realm, the OBIA approach dominancy is undiscussed. Ontologically, OBIA allows the identification and extraction of real-world features more accurately than pixel-based solutions and reliably from remotely sensed data only on more appropriate scales [19].

The OBIA classification is generally organized in six steps [20]:

a. Segmentation;
b. Features extraction and data preparation;
c. Training and validation datasets generation;
d. Classification algorithm;
e. Feature selection;
f. Validation of the classification.

The segmentation is the core process of OBIA, and several steps generally characterize it. Starting with individual pixels, OBIA algorithms merge contiguous pixels into groups (i.e., objects) based on three parameters: scale, shape, and compactness [20–22]. The objects should represent the classification features of interest (i.e. structural damages and non-damaged areas) [19]. The scale represents the degree of spectral heterogeneity allowed in each object. Generally, the higher the scale value (that is unitless), and larger the object will be because it is more heterogeneous [19, 22]. The compactness can be defined as the degree of similarity of a polygon to a circumference. The compactness parameter optimizes the resulting objects regarding the compactness.

The segmentation was realised on three-dimensional information of visible spectral information imagery using ORFEO toolbox [23], an open-source library for remote sensing application. The ORFEO project was funded in 2006 by the French space agency and it has rapidly evolved into a reliable toolbox for remote sensing practitioners. The OTB Large-Scale Mean-Shift segmentation workflow (LSMS) was applied [24]. First, the Red-Green-Blue image was smoothed with a range radius of 10 and a spatial radius of 2. Then the smoothed dataset was segmented using LSMS segmentation algorithm, with 2 as spatial radius and 5 as range radius. The LSMS Small region merging algorithm allowed the merging the smallest segments by setting the minimum segment size (i.e. 100). Finally, the segmentation was vectorised using the LSMS vectorization algorithm.

Effective use of features as input data for a classification procedure can improve classification accuracy [20, 25, 26]. Thus, the classification dataset was enriched with derivative features, namely, spectral-, textural-, and statistical-based features. The extraction of features was based on the literature classification research [27–32] and the authors' personal experience. Since the OBIA approach allows the analyst to introduce into the classification model features regarding the segmented objects' geometric characteristics and their relationship with the neighbourhood's objects, the shape, the extent and the compactness of the segments were computed too. 156 features were computed for each object. Table 3 reports the used measures for segmentation and classification. For each segment were computed the mean, the standard deviation, the median, the variance, the skewness and the kurtosis of spectral, histogram and textural features of Table 3.

Five classes describe the existing damages over the study area: Drainage; uncovered metal bar (UMB); Oxidized rebar (OR); Non-damaged intrados; and Non-damaged beam (Table 4). For each class were visually identified 100 segments to be used as training and test (70% training – 30% test). Reaching 100 samples was not always possible since some classes are more frequent (in terms of area coverage) than others, and some other classes, although covering large areas, are spectrally homogeneous and thus described by large segments. This lead to small and unbalanced training datasets that can negatively affect the classification results. Thus, the training dataset was oversampled in Python environment. The oversampling [34] creates synthetic samples by interpolation of the feature values of the nearest neighbours. The Synthetic Minority Oversampling Technique (SMOTE) was applied considering the 6 nearest neighbour samples (n) to reach the largest available class (100 samples of *Drainage*). The final training dataset was composed of 500 samples. Then, data were scaled according to each feature minimum-maximum values.

The classification was performed in Python environment using Pandas, NumPy and Sklearn libraries. Random Forest classification [35] model was trained using the smoted dataset. One-thousand trees with Gini criterion for the node splitting were used. The Random Forest algorithm can compute the Gini gain of each feature [36]. A simplified description of the GINI gain defines it as the sum of impurity decreases from two nodes and the parent node. The GINI is calculated for each variable of the classifier. This parameter is a proxy of the importance of each feature within the model: the variables that have high GINI gain (so they have less impurity) are more important. Features that have GINI importance less than the median values of the feature importance values were excluded from the classification.

Table 3. Features selected for the classification input dataset. They were computed using ORFEO toolbox.

Category	Features
Spectral-based	Color Index
Statistical-based Over the GREEN band In 5 × 5 neighbourhood	Variance
	Mean
	Skewness
	Kurtosis
Grey level co-occurrence matrix measures Over the GREEN band In 5 × 5 neighbourhood [33]	Mean
	Variance
	Dissimilarity
	Sum Average
	Sum Variance
	Sum Entropy
	Difference of Entropies
	Difference of Variances
	Image Correlation 1
	Image Correlation 2
	Energy
	Entropy
	Correlation
	Inverse Difference Moment
	Inertia
	Cluster Shade
	Cluster Prominence
	Haralick Correlation
Elevation	Digital Elevation Model
Geometric	Extension (Number of Pixels)
	Flat
	Roundness
	Longness
	Perimeter

Table 4. Classes of the model.

Class	Description	
Drainage	Area of the bridge that have evidence of present, or past, drainage	
Uncovered metal bar (UMB)	Metal bars of the beam that are not covered by concrete rebar	
Oxidized rebar (OR)	The concrete covering the bars with a evident oxidation process going on, thus, potentially evolving in Uncovered metal bars	
Non-damaged intrados	No evidence of damages	
Non-damaged beams	No evidence of damages	

The classification model was assessed using cross-validation approach. The cross-validation splits the test dataset in k folds of equal size and test the k-model on each fold. Since the test dataset is small (i.e. only 30 samples per class), the Leave-One-Out cross-validation (LOOCV) algorithm was applied [37, 38]. The LOOCV is a k-fold method where the number of folds is equal to the number of test samples. Thus, each fold's has only one test sample. In the case of correct classification, the fold validation is 1, and it is 0 in the case of wrong classified test samples. The assessment of the results is the mean of the assessment measures calculated on each fold. The precision, the Recall, and the F1-score were computed. It is important mentioning that the SMOTE was applied inside the LOOCV cycle.

5   Results and Discussion

The segmentation resulted in 8068 segments characterised by 156 feature each. Figure 4 provides the visual restitution of the classification. The feature selection reduces the input classification variables from 156 to 74 without losing in accuracy. Indeed the overall accuracy of the model moved from 0.816 (without feature selection) to 0.819 (with feature selection). Table 5 reports the F1-score, Precision and Recall values of each class.

Table 5. Accuracy metrics calculated with LOOCV.

Metric	Uncovered metal bar (UMB)	Drainage	Oxidized rebar (OR)	Non-damaged intrados	Non-damaged beam
F1-score	0.846	0.938	0.602	0.770	0.792
Precision	0.860	0.929	0.676	0.731	0.776
Recall	0.831	0.948	0.543	0.814	0.809

The classification is well-performant in almost all the classes. Indeed, the F1-score is never below 0.750, except for the Oxidized rebar class. The latter provides the lowest accuracy; the F1-score is only 0.602. This aspect is quite interesting since there should be a clear difference over the Red band of the orthophoto. Nevertheless, within the damages classification, OR class less affects the infrastructure's stability. Precision and recall measures mirror the F1-score and are quite well balanced. The Recall value of class OR relates to a high false-negative rate. The non-damaged areas class shows opposite behaviour with respect to OR. The Recall is high, indicating a low number of false positive, but the precision is relatively low relating to high false positive.

It should be noted that in the specific case of the bridge intrados, the final result of the classification could be influenced by environmental lighting conditions. The limited illumination that characterizes this area of the infrastructure, influences both the reconstruction of the photogrammetric block and therefore the accuracy of the final model, as well as the radiometric values of the orthophoto, causing a loss of accuracy in the result of the classification procedure.

Fig. 4. Result of the classification.

6 Conclusion

This study has proposed an automatic approach for the detection of bridge defects as support for managing the safety of existing bridges in order to prevent inadequate levels of damage. The approach is intended to follow the directives of the Italian Ministry of Infrastructure and Transport, expressed in the "Guidelines for the Classification and Risk Management, Safety Assessment and Monitoring of Existing Bridges". Nevertheless, the procedure can be extended for defect classification of bridges worldwide. In particular, the intent of this work is to check the potential of FOSS-focused unconventional photogrammetry for the classification of infrastructures' damages. A commercial UAV has been modified with a low-cost imaging sensor managed by an opensource environment to acquire images of the intrados of a bridge. Those images have been processed in an open-source photogrammetric suite to extract an orthomosaic map and a digital surface model. Again, open source libraries for remote sensing image processing has been used to perform supervised classification. Uncovered metal bar, Drainage, oxidized rebar, non-damaged intrados and non-damaged beam has been classified with good results and metrics.

Although the application resulted in accurate results, they can be further improved by enlarging the input dataset by using sensors sensitive to infrared light. Additional studies should explore the possibility of spectral calibration to ensure the model's replicability.

References

1. Viadotti: 1.425 sono senza un proprietario e nessuno fa la manutenzione | Milena Gabanelli. https://www.corriere.it/dataroom-milena-gabanelli/viadotti-1425-sono-senza-proprietario-nessuno-fa-la-manutenzione-ponti-crolli-ecco-mappa/ae3102d2-263f-11e9-9b5e-1a58eb 1d569a-va.shtml. Accessed 5 Mar 2021

2. Mit. Approvate Le Linee Guida per La Sicurezza Dei Ponti|Mit. https://www.mit.gov. it/comunicazione/news/mit-approvate-le-linee-guida-per-la-sicurezza-dei-ponti. Accessed 5 Mar 2021

3. Marchewka, A., Ziółkowski, P., Aguilar-Vidal, V.: Framework for structural health monitoring of steel bridges by computer vision. Sensors **20**, 700 (2020). https://doi.org/10.3390/s20 030700

4. Prasanna, P., Dana, K., Gucunski, N., Basily, B.: Computer-vision based crack detection and analysis. In: Proceedings of the Sensors and Smart Structures Technologies for Civil, Mechanical, and Aerospace Systems 2012; International Society for Optics and Photonics, April 6 2012, vol. 8345, p. 834542 (2012)

5. Dinh, T.H., Ha, Q.P., La, H.M.: Computer vision-based method for concrete crack detection. In: Proceedings of the 2016 14th International Conference on Control, Automation, Robotics and Vision (ICARCV), November 2016; pp. 1–6 (2016)

6. Hoang, N.-D.: Image Processing-Based Recognition of Wall Defects Using Machine Learning Approaches and Steerable Filters. https://www.hindawi.com/journals/cin/2018/7913952/. Accessed 5 Mar 2021

7. Park, J.-K., Kwon, B.-K., Park, J.-H., Kang, D.-J.: Machine learning-based imaging system for surface defect inspection. Int. J. Precision Eng. Manuf. Green Technol. **3**(3), 303–310 (2016). https://doi.org/10.1007/s40684-016-0039-x

8. Flah, M., Nunez, I., Ben Chaabene, W., Nehdi, M.L.: Machine Learning algorithms in civil structural health monitoring: a systematic review. Arch. Comput. Methods Eng. **28**(4), 2621–2643 (2020). https://doi.org/10.1007/s11831-020-09471-9

9. Xue, Y., Li, Y.: A fast detection method via region-based fully convolutional neural networks for shield tunnel lining defects: a fast detection method via region-based fully convolutional neural networks for shield tunnel lining defects. Comput.-Aided Civ. Infrastruct. Eng. **33**, 638–654 (2018). https://doi.org/10.1111/mice.12367

10. Hassan, S.I., et al.: Underground sewer pipe condition assessment based on convolutional neural networks. Autom. Constr. **106**, 102849 (2019). https://doi.org/10.1016/j.autcon.2019. 102849.

11. Wells, J., Lovelace, B.: Unmanned Aircraft System Bridge Inspection Demonstration Project Phase II Final Report; Minnesota Department of Transportation: St. Paul, MN (2017)

12. Hernandez, I., Fields, T., Kevern, J.: Overcoming the challenges of using unmanned aircraft for bridge inspections. In: AIAA Atmospheric Flight Mechanics Conference; American Institute of Aeronautics and Astronautics

13. Gillins, D.T., Parrish, C., Gillins, M.N., Simpson, C.: Eyes in the Sky: Bridge Inspections with Unmanned Aerial Vehicles (2018)

14. Gopalakrishnan, K., Gholami, H., Vidyadharan, A., Choudhary, A., Agrawal, A.: Crack damage detection in unmanned aerial vehicle images of civil infrastructure using pre-trained deep learning model. Int. J. Traffic Transp. Eng. **8**, 1–14 (2018). https://doi.org/10.7708/ijtte.2018. 8(1).01

15. Piras, M., Grasso, N., Abdul Jabbar, A.: UAV photogrammetric solution using a raspberry pi camera module and smart devices: test and results. In: Proceedings of the ISPRS - International Archives of the Photogrammetry, Remote Sensing and Spatial Information Sciences; Copernicus GmbH, August 24 2017; Vol. XLII-2-W6, pp. 289–296 (2017)

16. MicMac. https://micmac.ensg.eu/index.php/Accueil. Accessed 5 Mar 2021
17. Deseilligny, M.P., Clery, I.: Apero, an open source bundle adjustment software for automatic calibration and orientation of set of images, 8 (2011)
18. Lowe, D.G.: Object recognition from local scale-invariant features. In: Proceedings of the Proceedings of the Seventh IEEE International Conference on Computer Vision, September 1999, vol. 2, pp. 1150–1157 (1999)
19. Hussain, M., Chen, D., Cheng, A., Wei, H., Stanley, D.: Change detection from remotely sensed images: from pixel-based to object-based approaches. ISPRS J. Photogramm. Remote Sens. **80**, 91–106 (2013). https://doi.org/10.1016/j.isprsjprs.2013.03.006
20. Lu, D., Weng, Q.: A survey of image classification methods and techniques for improving classification performance. Int. J. Remote Sens. **28**, 823–870 (2007). https://doi.org/10.1080/01431160600746456
21. Meneguzzo, D.M., Liknes, G.C., Nelson, M.D.: Mapping trees outside forests using high-resolution aerial imagery: a comparison of pixel- and object-based classification approaches. Environ. Monit. Assess. **185**, 6261–6275 (2013). https://doi.org/10.1007/s10661-012-3022-1
22. Rastner, P., Bolch, T., Notarnicola, C., Paul, F.: A comparison of pixel- and object-based glacier classification with optical satellite images. IEEE J. Sel. Top. Appl. Earth Obs. Remote Sens. **7**, 853–862 (2014). https://doi.org/10.1109/JSTARS.2013.2274668
23. Orfeo ToolBox – Orfeo ToolBox Is Not a Black Box
24. Michel, J., Youssefi, D., Grizonnet, M.: Stable mean-shift algorithm and its application to the segmentation of arbitrarily large remote sensing images. IEEE Trans. Geosci. Remote Sens. **53**, 952–964 (2015). https://doi.org/10.1109/TGRS.2014.2330857
25. Maxwell, A.E., Warner, T.A., Fang, F.: Implementation of machine-learning classification in remote sensing: an applied review. Int. J. Remote Sens. **39**, 2784–2817 (2018). https://doi.org/10.1080/01431161.2018.1433343
26. Salah, M.: A Survey of Modern Classification Techniques in Remote Sensing for Improved Image Classification. **11**, 21 (2017)
27. Jin, Y., Liu, X., Chen, Y., Liang, X.: Land-cover mapping using random forest classification and incorporating NDVI time-series and texture: a case study of central shandong. Int. J. Remote Sens. **39**, 8703–8723 (2018). https://doi.org/10.1080/01431161.2018.1490976
28. Lewiński, S., Aleksandrowicz, S., Banaszkiewicz, M.: Testing texture of VHR panchromatic data as a feature of land cover classification. Acta Geophys. **63**(2), 547–567 (2015). https://doi.org/10.2478/s11600-014-0250-5
29. Zhang, X., et al.: Monitoring vegetation phenology using MODIS. Remote Sens. Environ. **84**, 471–475 (2003). https://doi.org/10.1016/S0034-4257(02)00135-9
30. Drzewiecki, W., Wawrzaszek, A., Krupiński, M., Aleksandrowicz, S., Jenerowicz, M.: Multi-fractal parameters in prediction of land-use components on satellite images. In: Proceedings of the 2019 Signal Processing: Algorithms, Architectures, Arrangements, and Applications (SPA), September 2019, pp. 296–301 (2019)
31. Merciol, F., Balem, T., Lefèvre, S.: Efficient and Large-Scale Land Cover Classification Using Multiscale Image Analysis, 5 (2019)
32. Pelletier, C., Valero, S., Inglada, J., Dedieu, G., Champion, N.: An assessment of image features and random forest for land cover mapping over large areas using high resolution satellite image time series. In: Proceedings of the 2016 IEEE International Geoscience and Remote Sensing Symposium (IGARSS), July 2016, pp. 3338–3341 (2016)
33. Haralick, R.M., Shanmugam, K., Dinstein, I.: Textural features for image classification. IEEE Trans. Syst. Man Cybern. **SMC-3**, 610–621 (1973). https://doi.org/10.1109/TSMC.1973.4309314
34. Chawla, N.V., Bowyer, K.W., Hall, L.O., Kegelmeyer, W.P.: SMOTE: synthetic minority over-sampling technique. J. Artif. Intell. Res. **16**, 321–357 (2002). https://doi.org/10.1613/jair.953

35. Breiman, L.: Random forests. Mach. Learn. **45**, 5–32 (2001). https://doi.org/10.1023/A:101 0933404324
36. Hastie, T., Tibshirani, R., Friedman, J.: Random forests. In: Hastie, T., Tibshirani, R., Friedman, J. (eds.) The Elements of Statistical Learning: Data Mining, Inference, and Prediction; Springer Series in Statistics, pp. 587–604. Springer, New York (2009). ISBN 978-0-387-84858-7
37. Breiman, L., Spector, P.: Submodel selection and evaluation in regression. The X-Random Case. Int. Stat. Rev. Rev. Int. Stat. **60**, 291 (1992). https://doi.org/10.2307/1403680
38. Kohavi, R.: A Study of Cross-Validation and Bootstrap for Accuracy Estimation and Model Selection, 8

Geomatics and Soft Computing Techniques
for Road Infrastructure Monitoring

Antonino Fotia$^{(\boxtimes)}$ ⓘ and Vincenzo Barrile$^{(\boxtimes)}$ ⓘ

Department of Civil, Energy, Environment and Materials Engineering (DICEAM), University
Mediterranea of Reggio Calabria, Via Graziella, Feo di Vito, 89128 Reggio Calabria, Italy
{Antonino.fotia,vincenzo.barrile}@unirc.it

Abstract. In the context of the monitoring and control of the Italian transport
infrastructure heritage, both with regards to existing network and infrastructure
works, an experiment has been developed: it combines geomatic and soft computing techniques in order to produce a system which aimed at both solving
Early Warning problems and it is able to generate a forecasting system on the
infrastructure's behavior over time, mainly exploiting geomatics parameters.

The proposed integrated/early warning predictive system is based on the initial realization and integration of multiple models (geometric/structural) which
represents the object of study (infrastructure) and the necessity for training and
subsequently in the implementation of a neural network, that requires in input
only the data, which can be acquired from the sensors, positioned on the infrastructure to produce different risk levels. Particular attention has been paid to the
displacement measurement phase by GPS (Global Position System) signal.

The proposed integrated predictive system's experiment was carried out in the
viaduct "Annunziata" in Reggio Calabria (Southern Italy), already used as a case
study in the context of other research activities conducted by the Geomatics laboratory of DICEAM (Civil, Energetic, Environmental and Material Engineering
Department - University Mediterranea of Reggio Calabria).

Keywords: Monitoring · Sensors · GPS · Neural network

1 Introduction

Bridges are certainly among the most important structures of any road network. During their life service, they are subject to deterioration that can reduce their safety and
functionality.

In Italy, the bridges' problems mainly concerns the old construction, so it is necessary
to create tools that allow to understand the infrastructure behavior in a predictable way
and to ensure that it is possible to make a correct distribution of the available maintenance
budget.

There are several considerations in relation to the possibility of using innovative
monitoring systems even at the design stage, considering the benefits in both economic
and risk prevention terms.

E. Borgogno-Mondino and P. Zamperlin (Eds.): ASITA 2021, CCIS 1507, pp. 313–324, 2022.
https://doi.org/10.1007/978-3-030-94426-1_23

In this context, the activities carried out in this note, attempt to overcome the limits deriving from the use of traditional monitoring systems, presenting, implementing, and experimenting a methodology that integrates Geomatic and Soft Computing techniques, in order to produce a prototype system that aims both to solve early warning problems and to generate a forecasting system mainly using geomatic parameters.

2 Materials and Methods

2.1 The Proposed System

The proposed methodology aims both to use and integrate geomatics technologies to the resolution of Early Warning problems and, through soft computing techniques, to produce a prototype useful for the infrastructures monitoring using a predictive system.

Therefore, the goal is to create a risk predictive system in real time that simulating different scenarios and, clearly, various infrastructures behaviors, is able to alert the subjects in charge, in case of imminent alert.

The proposed system uses different data (also in the preventive phase to define the various scenarios of infrastructure behaviors on the structural model), then reworking them through machine learning techniques, in order to obtain predictive values to be compared with limit thresholds representing different levels of risk.

The architectural system (regardless of the initial data: agent loads on the infrastructure are both artificial - average daily traffic - and natural - wind, any water flow, capacity of the soil) consists of:

- a Data Acquisition System (UAV Systems - GNSS Systems - accelerometers);
- a System for Structural Modeling;
- a Soft Computing system to produce the level of risk that uses a suitable neural network both in training (using the different scenarios of infrastructure behavior) and in the predictive phase (requiring as input, once that the neural network has been trained, only displacements data- static and dynamic), to produce the risk level;
- a System for processing and displaying results.

The results of the system and therefore any criticality reports are obtained through the analysis and simulation of any future scenarios on a "final" structural model built by the integration of the following representative models of the object of study (infrastructure):

- a 3D model detected by a drone (useful to deploy it in the initial state because it can monitories geometric information of the structure);
- a structural model that simulate as many scenarios (scenario n) at instant "0", where multiple boundaries conditions are varied to.

The final model obtained is integrated with the data, acquired in real-time by the sensor system (displacements).

The data are then processed through a system of neural networks properly built on Google Colab (Platform to run code in Python language), used to implement the neural network that allows to return the predictive behavior over time of the infrastructure in the face of the movements detected.

Then these data are transmitted via internet to a suitable monitoring platform properly realized. Figure 1 shows an explanatory flow chart of the entire proposed procedure.

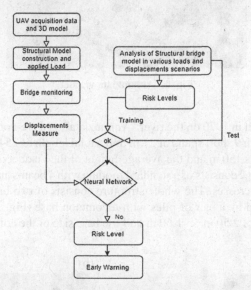

Fig. 1. Flow chart implemented system

The value of the proposed system lies in the possibility of evaluating and determining a specific "risk class" for each structural element (beams, spans, piles, bases), characterizing the infrastructure under investigation. These classes predicts the behavior of the structure, using soft computing techniques and only displacement data and not a whole series of parameters that are instead used only initially for the training phase of the neural network.

The prototype is therefore based on a control unit, installed near the viaduct that collects the data of the various sensors and sends them to a data processing platform (central server located inside the premises of the Geomatics laboratory of DICEAM of the University Mediterranea of Reggio Calabria), where the system is implemented. An operator, able to view the output data both in relation to the Early Warning phase and in relation to the predictive phase on the behavior of the infrastructure over time, can control the prototype.

3   Case Study

A first analysis was carried out on the motorway viaduct located on the A2 Mediterranean Motorway in the city of Reggio Calabria with the proposed methodology (Fig. 2).

Fig. 2. Annunziata viaduct

The viaduct, built in 1970 on the river "Annunziata", is a pre-compressed reinforced concrete viaduct with 9 short spans of 27 m and a total length of 254 m (cornering). The radius of curvature is 150 m and the average height of the viaduct is 25 m above sea.

The viaduct bridge consists of a standard module with 4 beams and 3 pre-compressed reinforced concrete crosses. The whole structure consists of two bridges (one for each direction), supported by a pair of piles with a common base (Fig. 3). The piles have a rectangular section of 2.50 m × 1.60 m and the base size of the columns is 8 m × 3 m.

(a)   **(b)**

Fig. 3. (a) Structure of the viaduct, (b) Base of columns

3.1   UAV Survey (3d Modeling and Automatic Extraction of Infrastructure Geometry)

The main objective of the important activity was the complete acquisition of the Annunziata viaduct with subcentimetric precision through a suitable UAV survey and the consequent extraction of the infrastructure's geometric characteristics.

The aerial survey was carried out using a commercial four-rotor DJI UAV, Mavic 2 Pro. On the Fig. 4 we report the cloud of the points obtained.

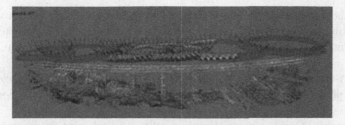

Fig. 4. Sparse cloud of circular mission points processed with SFM algorithm

To reconstruct the 3D scale model and to geo-reference it, an area survey was conducted using a Leica GS1250 plus GPS and total station flex line series model TS02–7", where there were several ground control points (GCP), evenly distributed over the area.

The extraction of relevant geometric information from the model under investigation was carried out through a semi-automatic methodology. This procedure extracts the shape from the segmented structural parts and automatically inserts the data into a predefined spreadsheet. The structural parts, already classified, are transformed from a point cloud into a 3d mesh object using Screened Poisson Surface Reconstruction (Fig. 5) and consequently from the three-dimensional models obtained, the geometric information (Plinth, Beams, Scaffold), related to the viaduct, is automatically extrapolated.

Fig. 5. Viaduct 3d model and geometric features extraction system

3.2 The Sensor Detection System

The viaduct main parameters were acquired through a network of sensors with a dual purpose:

- Provide information only in the initial and preliminary phase of the work in order to know the different load conditions of the structure to be used in the preliminary phase (only once) to analytically and structurally model the infrastructure (bridge and viaduct);
- Subsequently provide time displacement values over various parts of the structure in order to determine on one hand a real-time early warning system and on the other a predictive system.

Below there is a list of the instruments and methodologies used. The sensors used to determine time displacement values on various parts of the structure in order to determine Early Warning and predictive study of infrastructure behavior over time are:

– A LEICA-GMX30 receiver (VADASE firmaware) with antenna (24-channel L1/L2 code and phase, 20 Hz data rate, Smart Track technology for high precession, accuracy of 1 mm + 0.5 ppm (orizz.), 2 mm + 1 ppm (ver.));
– A network of 9 GNSS sensors (mainly used to monitor joint failures and displacements) consisting of low-cost GNSS sensors (consisting of pairs of single-frequency receivers, u-blox C94-M8P, associated with a Trimble bullet 360 antenna) and a dual-frequency geodesic class receiver the Leica GM30 GNSS (single frequency static mode data processing with synthetic frequency construction L2);
– Two Leica-1250 GPS receivers (16-channel L1/L2 code and phase, 20 Hz data speed, Smart Track technology, 1 mm + 0.5 ppm accuracy (orizz.), 2 mm + 1 ppm (ver.)) used in predominantly relative static mode (double frequency static mode data processing);
– Low cost experimental system composed of the combination of smartphones and antennas (smartphone methodology data processing).

The effectiveness of the system and the goodness of the measurements, obtained both from low-cost sensors and experimental systems based on the use of smartphones, was therefore evaluated in terms of repeatability and accuracy of the measurements (σ and δ) (Fig. 6).

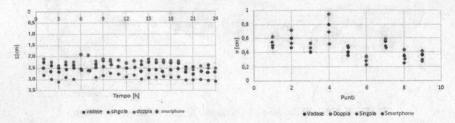

Fig. 6. Beam monitoring results

Figure 6 shows a good adaptability of the results obtained with the various methodologies.

3.3   Implementation of Final Model

In order to have an initial model to use for training the neural network and then proceed with the predictive phase of the infrastructure behavior over time, these steps were followed:

• Geometry and construction details' acquisition from Drone survey and 3D modeling;
• Information's acquisition related to the mechanical properties of materials and soils through project documentation;

- Loads' acquisition through on-site sensor system;
- Final structural model creation using FEM methodology.

By using the RFEM software, the geometric features, extracted from the 3d model, were inserted into the structural model.

In the Fig. 7, it is shown the obtained final model (integrated with the geometry) that allows to analyze the behavior of the infrastructure by changing the applied loads and, consequently, the training of an experimental predictive neural network, suitably implemented, in order to know the predictive behavior over time related to the infrastructure examined.

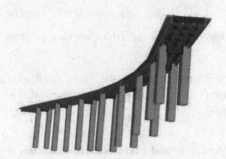

Fig. 7. Final model (integrated with geometry) of the finite element viaduct

On the basis of the final model we obtained a thousand simulations using RFEM software (varying the combinations of the parameters relating to the loads operating on the infrastructure), in order to obtain a value of reliance and corresponding risk classes. We could obtain both the parameters necessary for the training of the neural network and those necessary for the identification of the span of many subject to stress on.

Calculation of Threshold Values

Four risk classes have therefore been identified according to the different software calculations:

Class A: Negligible. Infrastructures that do not show significant signs or defects, (all elements with green coloring are displayed on the Spreadsheet).

Class B: Low. Infrastructure that manifests some elements with slight defects. (Some yellow elements are displayed on the platform.)

Class C: Moderate. The infrastructure belonging to this class manifests elements with significant defects (in the platform some elements with orange coloring are displayed).

Class D: High. The infrastructure belonging to this class manifests elements with significant defects (on the platform some elements with red coloring are displayed).

In order to use the system tested and proposed with early warning finalization, once the risk classes (and therefore the threshold values have been obtained and defined), the system has been programmed in such a way that the threshold value is "trivially" compared with the value measured by the sensor, associating with each comparison the class to which it belongs and possibly producing, displaying and signaling the alarm signal.

Figure 8 shows an analysis and consequent allocation of the various risk classes individually, for each monitored element.

Fig. 8. Example of a risk class view per item.

The example in Fig. 8 shows us with the green color obtained, the elements that are a in a "negligible level" of risk (since the data transmitted by the sensor have never exceeded the set threshold).

3.4 Soft Computing Analysis and Platform Visualization

Once the "final" structural model had been built (having both the acting loads on the infrastructure and the displacement data provided by the sensors installed), a neural network is implemented in order to obtain predictive values of the infrastructure behavior as the measured displacements varied.

In particular, a 3-layer neural network (based on the back propagation algorithm) with two input levels (displacements, loads), two hidden layers and an output level have been implemented in Google Colab. The number of nodes in the input layer is determined by the dimensionality of the data, while the number of risk classes (previously defined) determines the number of nodes in the output level. Figure 9 shows the code string for network activation.

```
model = keras.Sequential([
                        keras.layers.Dense(50, activation=tf.nn.relu,
                                           input_shape=(train_x.shape[1],)),
                        keras.layers.Dropout(0.2)
                        keras.layers.Dense(30, activation=tf.nn.tanh),
                        keras.layers.Dropout(0.2)
                        keras.layers.Dense(9)
                        ])
model.compile(loss='mse',
              optimizer='Adam',
              metrics=['mae']
```

Fig. 9. Python code string on Google Colab for neural network training

From an operational point of view, the neural network has been trained as follows:

- On the structural software have been implemented several loading actions (wind, earthquake…) and different displacements (associated with failures chosen for network training) in different scenarios in order to highlight the different responses of the structure.
- Out of 1000 scenarios implemented, 200 have been used as tests to verify the correct training of the neural network by entering as input only the previously chosen displacement data set and used, thus comparing the correspondence of the risk levels obtained between software and neural network in the various scenarios.

The results obtained, as expected, vary very little as the complexity of the network changes, except for the eras necessary to train the model.

In relation to the "displacement" output parameters provided by the neural network, Fig. 10 shows the result of the conformance between the expected results and those obtained on the span that was most requested through RFEM analysis.

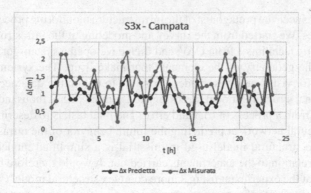

Fig. 10. Comparison between the results obtained and those expected on the long span x

Once the neural network has been trained, the displacement values obtained by the sensors (and not from the model) are applied as inputs directly through the recall of the.csv file generated by the sensors. After that, we will obtain, in the output phase for each of the elements of the infrastructure, an expected displacement and rotation value and a consequent coloring according to the attributed risk class. The values will not change regardless of the positioning of the sensors that provided the sensor input data.

For the final display phase of the results (both for the Early Warning phase and for the structural behavior prediction phase, the same principle of platform display applies) a display platform was used, implemented in the WordPress environment, integrating SSL security protocols, which provide a fundamental level of online security, essential when transmitting sensitive information. In the specific case, in Fig. 11, it can be observed that both the early warning phase and the predictive phase, the structure is not prompted by actions such as to identify a risk class to be attentive: in fact, as previously mentioned, the green coloring base indicates the belonging of all the structural elements investigated (pillars, beams, spans) to a very low risk class.

Fig. 11. Screen shot of monitoring horizontal elements

4   Conclusion

The research has seen the protagonist of the infrastructure monitoring process by addressing all its phases. We started from the survey and modeling of the infrastructure, through photogrammetric techniques from UAV, and then developed a system for the automatic extraction of the geometry of the elements that make it up. The system, clearly also used as a tool for visual analysis, made it possible to obtain the data necessary for the creation of a final structural model, necessary to examine over a thousand possible scenarios coming from a process of trial and error. The final task is to describe in detail the training of a neural network at predicting the future behavior of the infrastructure.

Clearly, the structural model used in this trial is a simplified model, even if it is performing in relation to the experiments carried out. It would therefore be desirable to be able to repeat the experiment using a more complex structural model (variable loads) and to verify it on a test infrastructure on which to monitor more important movements.

The trained neural network has been "calibrated" so that it can predict the displacements (scenario n + 1), that will occur on the infrastructure in the next 24 h, in a four-week cycle.

However, it's desirable to refer to further results checks (because of all the simplifications made), since both the training and the test phase took place on the virtual model and it was not possible to make a comparison with the actual behavior of the infrastructure. In fact, although no "real" displacements were measured that could somehow test the viability of the predictive system we used for viaduct test the parameters measured on the final structural model.

The research work has therefore tried to provide a proactive contribution for the resolution of problems related to the monitoring and management of infrastructures all meant at proposing an alternative solution to the systems used to date.

In fact, it is researched that having the possibility to monitor fewer parameters, in particular those of displacement, to know the behavior of the entire infrastructure, could be an excellent tool at the service of the managing bodies for the supervision of quotas resources to be dedicated to maintenance as well as an excellent solution to identify the safety of end users.

References

1. Huang, Y., Ludwig, S.A., Deng, F.: Sensor optimization using a genetic algorithm for structural health monitoring in harsh environments. J. Civil Struct. Health Monit. 6(3), 509–519 (2016). https://doi.org/10.1007/s13349-016-0170-y
2. Li, J., Zhang, X., Xing, J., Wang, P., Yang, Q., He, C.: Optimal sensor placement for long-span cable-stayed bridge using a novel particle swarm optimization algorithm. J. Civ. Struct. Health Monit. 5(5), 677–685 (2015)
3. Yi, T.-H., Li, H.-N., Wang, C.-W.: Multiaxial sensor placement optimization in structural health monitoring using distributed wolf algorithm. Struct. Control Health Monit. 23(4), 719–734 (2016)
4. Jin, C., Jang, S., Sun, X., Li, J., Christenson, R.: Damage detection of a highway bridge under severe temperature changes using extended Kalman filter trained neural network. J. Civil Struct. Health Monit. 6(3), 545–560 (2016). https://doi.org/10.1007/s13349-016-0173-8
5. Farrar, C.R., Worden, K.: Structural Health Monitoring. A Machine Learning Perspective. Wiley, Hoboken (2013)
6. Rao, A.R.M., Lakshmi, K.: Damage diagnostic technique combining POD with time-frequency analysis and dynamic quantum PSO. Meccanica 50(6), 1551–1578 (2015)
7. Diez, A., Khoa, N.L.D., Makki Alamdari, M., Wang, Y., Chen, F., Runcie, P.: A clustering approach for structural health monitoring on bridges. J. Civil Struct. Health Monit. 6(3), 429–445 (2016). https://doi.org/10.1007/s13349-016-0160-0
8. Zhou, Q., Zhou, H., Zhou, Q., Yang, F., Luo, L., Li, T.: Structural damage detection based on posteriori probability support vector machine and Dempster-Shafer evidence theory. Appl. Soft Comput. 36, 368–374 (2015)
9. Gonzalez, I., Karoumi, R.: BWIM aided damage detection in bridges using machine learning. J. Civil Struct. Health Monit. 5(5), 715–725 (2015). https://doi.org/10.1007/s13349-015-0137-4
10. Das, S., Saha, P., Patro, S.K.: Vibration-based damage detection techniques used for health monitoring of structures: a review. J. Civil Struct. Health Monit. 6(3), 477–507 (2016). https://doi.org/10.1007/s13349-016-0168-5
11. Neves, A., Simões, F., Pinto da Costa, A.: Vibrations of cracked beams: discrete mass and stiffness models. Comput. Struct. 168, 68–77 (2016)
12. Abaqus FEA (2017) ABAQUS Inc. http://www.3ds.com/products-services/sim-ulia/products/abaqus/. Accessed May 2017
13. Chen, S., Truong-Hong, L., Laefer, D., Mangina, E.: Automated Bridge Deck Evaluation through UAV Derived Point Cloud, September 2018
14. Cryderman, C., Mah, S.B., Shufletoski, A.: Evaluation of UAV photogrammetric accuracy for mapping and earthworks computations. Geomatica 68(4), 309–317 (2014)
15. Eschmann, C., Wundsam, T.: Web-based georeferenced 3D inspection and monitoring of bridges with unmanned aircraft systems. J. Surv. Eng. 143(3), 04017003 (2017)
16. Escobar-Wolf, R., Oommen, T., Brooks, C.N., Dobson, R.J., Ahlborn, T.M.: Unmanned Aerial Vehicle (UAV)-based assessment of concrete bridge deck delamination using thermal and visible camera sensors: a preliminary analysis. Res. Nondestruct. Eval. 29(4), 183–198 (2018)
17. Gerke, M., Przybilla, H.-J.: Accuracy analysis of photogrammetric UAV image blocks: in- fluence of onboard RTK-GNSS and cross flight patterns. Photogramm. Fernerkund. Geoinformation 2016(1), 17–30 (2016)

18. Gienko, G.A., Terry, J.P.: Three-dimensional modeling of coastal boulders using multi-view image measurements. Earth Surf. Process. Landf. **39**, 853–864 (2014)

19. Hackl, J., Adey, B.T., Woźniak, M., Schümperlin, O.: Use of Unmanned Aerial Vehicle photogrammetry to obtain topographical information to improve bridge risk assessment. J. Infrastruct. Syst. **24**(1), 04017041 (2018)

20. Ham, Y., Han, K.K., Lin, J.J., Golparvar-Fard, M.: Visual monitoring of civil infrastructure systems via camera-equipped Unmanned Aerial Vehicles (UAVs): a review of related works. Vis. Eng. **4**(1), 1–8 (2016). https://doi.org/10.1186/s40327-015-0029-z

21. Holst, J.M.F.G., et al.: Eurocode 8 Part 3: assessment and retrofitting of buildings. J. Constr. Steel Res. **54**(2), 18–20 (2011)

22. Hug, C., Krzystek, P., Fuchs, W.: Advanced Lidar data processing with Lastools. In: International Society for Photogrammtry and Remote Sensing (ISPRS), pp. 12–23, July 2012

23. Kazhdan, M., Hoppe, H.: Screened poisson surface reconstruction. ACM Trans. Graph. **32**(3), 1–13 (2013)

24. Khaloo, A., Lattanzi, D., Cunningham, K., Dell'Andrea, R., Riley, M.: Unmanned Aerial Vehicle inspection of the Placer River Trail Bridge through image-based 3D modelling. Struct. Infrastruct. Eng. **14**(1), 124–136 (2018)

25. Lovelace, B.: Unmanned Aerial Vehicle Bridge Inspection Demonstration Project, p. 214, July 2015

26. Mader, D., Blaskow, R., Westfeld, P., Maas, H.G.: UAV-based acquisition of 3D point cloud a comparison of a low-cost laser scanner and SFM-tools. Int. Arch. Photogramm. Remote. Sens. Spat. Inf. Sci.-ISPRS Arch. **40**(3W3), 335–341 (2015)

27. Marcus, W., Fonstad, M.: Earth Surf. Process. Landf. **33**, 1491–1501 (2008)

28. Fotia A – Tecniche di Geomatica e soft computing per il monitoraggio del territorio e del costruito. Tesi di dottorato (2021)

Automatic Co-registration of Copernicus Time Series via Synchronization

Luigi Barazzetti[1] (ID), Andrea Fusiello[2] (ID), Marco Gianinetto[1,3] (ID),
Eleonora Maset[2] (ID), Francesco Niccolò Polinelli[1], and Marco Scaioni[1(✉)] (ID)

[1] ABC Department, Politecnico di Milano, Via Ponzio 31, Milan, Italy
{luigi.barazzetti,marco.gianinetto,francesconiccolo.polinelli,
marco.scaioni}@polimi.it
[2] DPIA, Università di Udine, Via Delle Scienze 206, Udine, Italy
{andrea.fusiello,eleonora.maset}@uniud.it
[3] Institute for Electromagnetic Sensing of the Environment, National Research
Council of Italy, Via Bassini 15, Milan, Italy

Abstract. This paper presents a satellite image co-registration procedure aiming at simultaneously estimating multiple affine transformations between a set of multi-temporal or multi-source satellite images, reducing error accumulation and improving metric precision. The approach is based on *synchronization*, a method that seeks to infer the unknown states of a network of nodes, where only the ratio (or difference) between node pairs can be measured. In our case states represent affine transformations. The proposed method globally combines via synchronization pairwise transformations computed for all the image combinations of the multi-temporal sequence, beyond the traditional image-to-base approach available in remote sensing and GIS packages. Results obtained with Landsat and Sentinel-2 images reveal that the algorithm can be used not only to perform the actual co-registration, but also as a diagnostic tool to evaluate the quality of transformation parameters through a comparison with basic co-registration methods, as well as with global least squares adjustment.

Keywords: Registration · Satellite images · Synchronization · Diagnostic · Copernicus · Sentinel

1 Introduction

Since the first Sentinel launch in 2014, the availability of free and open access satellite images has increased exponentially [11]. Nevertheless, before the release of Level-2 products (i.e., surface reflectance and surface temperature), the enormous amount of information recorded by optical satellites could not be used effectively for geophysical/biophysical analyses. This situation drastically changed in 2018 when the European Space Agency started producing atmospherically-corrected Sentinel-2 images, following the U.S. Geological Survey's best practice for their Landsat missions. Consequently, today the end-users can fully exploit

E. Borgogno-Mondino and P. Zamperlin (Eds.): ASITA 2021, CCIS 1507, pp. 325–336, 2022.
https://doi.org/10.1007/978-3-030-94426-1_24

the increasing potentialities of cloud-based computing platforms for the automatic processing of long time series of images (e.g., Google's Earth Engine). Furthermore, the EU is developing its cloud ecosystem, made of the Copernicus Data and Information Access Services (or DIASes) for commercial applications [10], as well as the free Sentinel Hub for non-commercial use [8].

In this fast-changing scenario, cloud-based tools usually focus on the core methods for data analysis, requiring the user to take care of all the necessary radiometric and geometric pre-processing. Regarding the geometric uncertainties, archived Sentinel-2 images have a 2σ geolocation accuracy of 12.5 m when processed with Ground Control Points (GCPs) [9]. Similarly, Landsat images archived in the Tier 1 collection have a geolocation RMSE of 12 m [25]. Consequently, the time-series analysis or multi-source analysis (e.g., Landsat and Sentinel) might need geocoding refinement to avoid errors due to an insufficient co-registration accuracy. For this reason, many studies were published in the last years about this specific topic [18,23].

The current available strategies for precise *co-registration* (or simply *registration*, or *alignment*) of time-series are illustrated and discussed in [20]. In the case of medium-resolution images, the application of standard pre-processing steps reduces the co-registration process to the computation of a 2D geometric transformation mapping the space of each image into a reference *datum* [16] (a.k.a. *image-to-map* approach). When working with a single image, this task can be accomplished by measuring some GCPs, whose coordinates are retrieved from higher-accuracy digital data or from direct measurement (e.g., by using GNSS positioning). GCPs are then used, together with their corresponding observations in the image, to estimate the parameters of the 2D transformation able to obtain the georeferencing in the given *datum*. An alternative approach for co-registration is based on the *image-to-image* techniques, where images are directly co-registered without external data. While manual measurements of tie-points has been the standard practice since the beginning of Remote Sensing (RS), the development of image matching techniques has allowed to transform this task into an automatic operation (see, e.g., [15]).

When working with time series including several overlapping images, the basic image-to-image co-registration approach – called *image-to-base*[1] – is to select a reference (*base*) image and register all the remaining images to it using basic co-registration processes that works on pairs of images (see, e.g., [13,23]).

On the other hand, some authors have proposed an alternative approach based on the Bundle Block Adjustment (BBA), where the co-registration of a time series is computed by considering tie-points between all overlapping images, and not only w.r.t. the base image [6]. An obvious key feature of BBA is that also images that do not directly share any tie-point with the base image, for example because of some changes in land cover, can be registered together. But, as described in [20], this approach has another feature that becomes very important when tie-points are automatically extracted using image matching algorithms.

---

[1] The traditional "master-to-slave" terminology has been replaced here with this one, which, albeit not standard, fulfill politically correctness requirements.

Since also robust matching techniques may leave behind wrong observations, the redundancy of tie-points that are used within a BBA can be exploited for a more efficient detection and rejection of errors, according to the theory of *reliability* that has been widely investigated in Geodesy [12]. Such an operational workflow is recommended where many images must be aligned in an automatic way. In this case, the redundancy of tie-points is used to control the quality of the final results.

In this work, an alternative procedure for solving the global co-registration problem called *synchronization* (see Sect. 3) is presented and compared against Multi-Image Robust Alignment (MIRA), a global least squares adjustment approach that was presented in [20]. The effort of developing an alternative technique to solve for the BBA has multiple aims. First of all, to see whether some cases of failures in the co-registration (e.g., due to the low number or poor distribution of tie-points) can be overcome. Second, the look for a more efficient approach under computational point-of-view. Indeed, when working with massive data sets (hundreds of images in the time series) and with thousands of tie-points, the computational burden of the traditional least squares adjustment may be too much time-consuming also for modern workstations and cloud computing. Third, the availability of two independent approaches for the co-registration of images can be used for mutual validation of the results. This aspect, together with the application of the reliability analysis, is expected to enforce the controllability of the final co-registration.

2   Multi-image Robust Alignment

Multi-Image Robust Alignment (MIRA) is a global least squares adjustment approach that was presented in [20] with the aim to provide a fully automatic pipeline for the geometric co-registration of satellite time series with sub-pixel accuracy, based on the least squares solution of a system of parametric equations. The method does not depend on external information or user interaction and addresses the following requirements:

- Generic applicability to multi-sensor time series of satellite images;
- Robustness against illumination geometry, atmospheric conditions, land cover changes, image quality, and spatial resolution; and
- Possibility to be easily integrated into existing (RS) processing pipelines.

MIRA is composed of several sequential steps, the first one being keypoint extraction via a SIFT-like approach (found also in [24]). More in detail, the keypoint detector is the one proposed by [17], where blobs with associated scale levels are detected from scale-space extrema of the scale-normalized Laplacian. As for the descriptor, MIRA implements a 128-dimensional radial descriptor, based on the accumulated response of steerable derivative filters.

To detect pairwise matches, a nearest neighbor approach is applied, followed by a robust method based on M-estimator SAmple Consensus (MSAC) to estimate 2D transformations between pairs of images. Finally, a base image is chosen and an affine transformation able to map each image to the base one is computed with a global least squares adjustment strategy, as described in [6]. In short, each tie-point provides two linear equations where the unknowns are the parameters of the affine transformation of the images. The resulting over-constrained linear system is solved with least squares fitting.

3   Image Registration via Synchronization

In this section, we introduce the global approach known as *synchronization*, that can be applied to image co-registration.

Given a network of nodes (or a graph), where each node is characterized by an unknown state and pairs of nodes connected by an edge can measure the ratio (or difference) between their states, the goal of synchronization [22] is to recover the unknown states from the pairwise measures.

As an example, one can think of topographic levelling as a synchronization problem, where absolute height is the state, differences in elevation between pairs of points are measured, and one wants to retrieve the height of each point.

Mathematically, states are represented by elements of a group Σ. Different instantiations of Σ lead to different variants of the synchronization problem. Among them, it is worth citing the special linear group $SL(d)$ for *homograpy synchronization* [21] and the General Affine group $GA(d)$ for *affine matrix synchronization* [7], where d denotes the dimension, two in our case.

Thanks to the formalism of synchronization, several photogrammetric and computer vision problems [4] can be addressed without relying on features or points, since the problem is formulated in frame space, or, more abstractly, in a group [2]. In [19], e.g., the image mosaicking problem is solved exploiting homography synchronization to align and stitch multiple images and affine synchronization to compute global color corrections. In this paper, the attention is focused on synchronization over $GA(2)$, for multi-temporal or multi-source satellite images are registered applying affine transformations.

In order to formally define the problem and its solution, let $*$ denote the operation in the group Σ. Suppose that the relations between the index pairs $(i, j) \subseteq \{1, ..., n\} \times \{1, ..., n\}$ are known, and refer to them as z_{ij}. *Synchronization* can be formulated as the problem of recovering $x_i \in \Sigma$ for $i = 1, ..., n$ such that the following *consistency constraint* is satisfied

$$z_{ij} = x_i * x_j^{-1}. \tag{1}$$

The solution is defined up to a global (right) product with any group element, i.e., if $x_i \in \Sigma$ satisfies (1) then also $x_i * y$ satisfies (1) for any (fixed) $y \in \Sigma$.

Pairwise measures are usually noisy, so the consistency constraint cannot be satisfied exactly. Thus, we search the solution that minimizes the *consistency error*:

$$\epsilon(x_1, x_2, ..., x_n) = \sum_{(i,j)} \delta(z_{ij}, x_i * x_j^{-1}) \tag{2}$$

where $\delta : \Sigma \times \Sigma \to \mathbb{R}^+$ is a metric function for Σ [3].

3.1 Synchronization over $(GL(d), \cdot)$

Let us first consider the synchronization problem over the General Linear group $GL(d)$, which is the set of all $d \times d$ invertible matrices, where the group operation $*$ is matrix multiplication and the identity element is I_d. Let $X_i \in \mathbb{R}^{d \times d}$ and $Z_{ij} \in \mathbb{R}^{d \times d}$ denote the matrix representations of $x_i \in \Sigma$ and $z_{ij} \in \Sigma$, respectively. Using this notation, Eq. (1) can be rewritten as $Z_{ij} = X_i X_j^{-1}$.

Let us collect the unknown group elements and all the measures in two matrices $X \in \mathbb{R}^{dn \times d}$ and $Z \in \mathbb{R}^{dn \times dn}$ respectively, which are composed of $d \times d$ blocks:

$$X = \begin{bmatrix} X_1 \\ X_2 \\ \cdots \\ X_n \end{bmatrix}, \quad Z = \begin{bmatrix} I_d & Z_{12} & \cdots & Z_{1n} \\ Z_{21} & I_d & \cdots & Z_{2n} \\ \cdots & & & \cdots \\ Z_{n1} & Z_{n2} & \cdots & I_d \end{bmatrix}. \tag{3}$$

If not all the pairwise measures Z_{ij} are available, the input matrix becomes $Z_A := Z \odot (A \otimes \mathbf{1}_{d \times d})$, where $\odot$ denotes the Hadamard product, A is the adjacency matrix, $\mathbf{1}_{d \times d}$ represents a $d \times d$ matrix filled by ones and the Kronecker product with $\mathbf{1}_{d \times d}$ is required to match the block structure of the measures. The $n \times n$ adjacency matrix is constructed as follows: $A_{ij} = 1$ if the pairwise measure Z_{ij} exists, $A_{ij} = 0$ otherwise. Accordingly, the consistency constraint writes

$$Z_A = (XX^{-b}) \odot (A \otimes \mathbf{1}_{d \times d}) \tag{4}$$

where $X^{-b} \in \mathbb{R}^{d \times dn}$ denotes the block-matrix containing the inverse of each $d \times d$ block of X.

It can be shown [1] that the following relation holds

$$Z_A X = (D \otimes I_d) X \tag{5}$$

where D is the degree matrix defined as $D = \text{diag}(A\mathbf{1}_{n \times 1})$. Thus, the eigenvectors of $(D \otimes I_d)^{-1} Z_A$ corresponding to the d largest eigenvalues represent an estimate of X. This is also known as the *spectral solution*.

3.2 Synchronization over $GA(d)$

The previously described formulation allows us to easily retrieve the solution also for the synchronization over the General Affine group $GA(d)$. This is the set of invertible affine transformations in d-space, which admits a matrix representation through $(d+1) \times (d+1)$ matrices

$$GA(d) = \left\{ \begin{bmatrix} M & \mathbf{v} \\ \mathbf{0}' & 1 \end{bmatrix}, \; s.t. \; M \in \mathbb{R}^{d \times d}, \mathbf{v} \in \mathbb{R}^d \right\}. \tag{6}$$

$GA(d)$ is a subgroup of $GL(d+1)$, therefore, following Eq. 5, the synchronization problem can be solved by computing the top $d+1$ eigenvectors of $(D \otimes I_{d+1})^{-1} Z_A$. Since this approach leads to an algebraic solution, it does not enforce constraints that matrices in $GA(d)$ should satisfy. Going into detail, the output matrix U will not have vector $[\mathbf{0}_{1 \times d} \ 1]$ in rows multiple of $d + 1$, in general. In order to obtain X from U, one must choose a different basis for the resulting eigenvectors that satisfies such constraint. This can be obtained by solving a linear system of equations, as explained in [5].

To solve the problem of satellite images co-registration, in this work we apply synchronization over $GA(2)$ to convert pairwise affine transformations into global ones. In this way, all transformations between overlapping images are considered simultaneously, minimizing the errors among the whole set of images.

The method is also attractive for its simplicity, as it enjoys an easy and compact Matlab implementation[2]. Moreover, it requires only to store pairwise transformation parameters, with benefits in terms of memory footprint and computing time when compared to other global methods such as MIRA, that relies on the tie-points extracted during the matching phase.

4   Experiments and Results

The novel approach based on affine synchronization (henceforth dubbed AS) is compared with traditional image-to-base approach using the MIRA solution [20] as the baseline.

These approaches were tested with sets of data imaged on different locations, in different seasons and/or years, with different illumination, land cover and cloud coverage as well as different sensors. The common stages of keypoints extraction and matching were performed using the Satellite Automatic Multi-Image Registration (SAMIR) software [14].

4.1   Dataset Sevilla

The Sevilla dataset captures a typical Mediterranean landscape, with flat and hilly topography. All the image tiles were downloaded from Sentinel Hub (https://www.sentinel-hub.com) as already geocoded to the UTM zone 29N - WGS84 (EPSG:32629) reference system and have a footprint of 110 km × 110 km. More specifically, the dataset Sevilla is made up of 5 images: 4 Sentinel-2/MSI cloud-free images collected over Sevilla (Spain) on 27-APR-2019 (image S2-0), 26-JUN-2019 (image S2-1), 09-SEP-2019 (image S2-2), and 18-NOV-2019 (image S2-3); and 1 additional cloudy Sentinel-2/MSI image collected over Sevilla on 20-AUG-2019 (S2-4). Image co-registration was carried out by using the image acquired on 27-APR-2019 (i.e., S2-0) as base image.

As a first test to validate the co-registration algorithms, only the cloud-free images were taken into account. Figure 1 shows the location of the extracted tie-points: one can notice that the spatial distribution is not homogeneous over the images and most of them are detected in urban areas, which have a better texture.

---

[2] Code available at http://www.dpia.uniud.it/fusiello/demo/acs/.

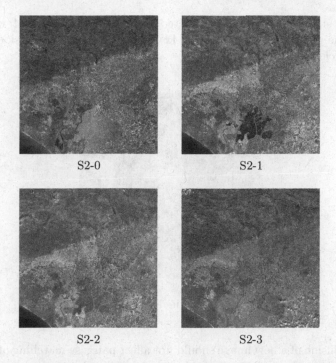

Fig. 1. Tie-points for the cloud-free images acquired over Sevilla.

The number of tie-points and their distribution was very good for all image combinations, therefore similar parameters were found for the affine transformations computed using different strategies. The number of matched tie-points is always larger than 6,000 for all image combinations (see Table 1). Adding more points would make no sense for they tend to fall in already populated areas.

Taking MIRA as the gold standard method, we performed a comparison with the other two co-registration approaches, namely image-to-base and AS, taking the translation error:

$$\Delta T = \sqrt{\left(T_x^{\text{MIRA}} - T_x^{\text{AS}}\right)^2 + \left(T_y^{\text{MIRA}} - T_y^{\text{AS}}\right)^2} \tag{7}$$

as a figure of merit. We use translation because scale and rotation errors have been found to be negligible, and translations in pixels can be easily related to the error in metric units knowing the ground sampling distance (GSD).

For this first dataset, differences between tested methods are very small: the mean value of ΔT, averaged on the three images, is 0.027 pixel ($\sigma = 0.014$ pixel) for image-to-base vs MIRA and 0.017 pixel ($\sigma = 0.016$ pixel) for AS vs MIRA. This test confirms that the different co-registration algorithms provide the same transformation parameters when a good point distribution can be achieved on all the images of the dataset. It also proves the correctness of the algorithms, and it demonstrates that in the case of few images with a very good overlap with the base, a simple image-to-base approach is sufficient.

Figure 2 shows the keypoints extracted on the cloudy image S2-4, when introduced in the process. As expected, no keypoints were matched inside the areas covered by clouds.

Fig. 2. Cloudy Sentinel-2/MSI image S2-4.

The inclusion of a new image should not affect pairwise matching of the previous images, nevertheless, the process is not repeatable due to random component inside MSAC. To overcome this issue, we did not perform again the matching step but just updated the tie-points with the new combinations including S2-4. Table 1 clearly shows that image matching involving S2-4 have a significant smaller number of keypoints.

Table 1. Matched points, including the additional cloudy image.

	S2-0	S2-1	S2-2	S2-3	**S2-4**
S2-0	0	8,072	7,864	6,142	**2,898**
S2-1	8,072	0	22,430	9,316	**5,028**
S2-2	7,864	22,430	0	11,126	**4,476**
S2-3	6,142	9,316	11,126	0	**2,590**
S2-4	**2,898**	**5,028**	**4,476**	**2,590**	0

All the co-registration methods performed slightly worse when including the cloudy image. In this case, the mean value of ΔT is 0.058 pixel ($\sigma = 0.038$ pixel) for image-to-base vs MIRA and 0.047 pixel ($\sigma = 0.028$ pixel) for AS vs MIRA.

4.2   Dataset Venice

The Venice dataset features both Sentinel-2/MSI and Landsat-8/OLI images (Fig. 3) and includes flat, hilly and mountain regions, and several urbanized areas. Landsat images were downloaded from Earth Explorer (https://earthexplorer.usgs.gov) as geocoded images in UTM zone 33N - WGS84 reference system and have a footprint of 185 km × 185 km. Sentinel-2 images were downloaded as described in the Sevilla dataset.

Overall, the dataset is made up of 5 Sentinel-2/MSI images and 5 Landsat-8/OLI images collected over Venice (North-East Italy). Landsat images were collected on 11-JUN-2017 (LS-0), 03-OCT-2019 (LS-1), 10-OCT-2018 (LS-2), 22-NOV-2017 (LS-3), and 20-DEC-2017 (LS-4). Sentinel images were collected on 20-NOV-2017 (S2-5), 15-DEC-2018 (S2-6), 01-NOV-2019 (S2-7), 17-AUG-2018 (S2-8), and 03-JUL-2019 (S2-9).

The co-registration process was carried out using spectral band B03 for both Sentinel-2/MSI (542–578 nm) and Landsat-8/OLI (530–590 nm). We made that choice to make our co-registration pipeline suitable to the processing of any satellite image. Specifically:

- These sectors of the visible spectrum are covered by all the adopted sensors;
- The use of images with similar wavelengths makes easier the detection of corresponding tie-points;
- In the visible spectrum, green has more image contrast because it has a smaller Rayleigh scattering (about 1/4 of total path radiance) compared to blue (about 2/3 of total path radiance).
- In vegetated areas, green has higher contrast (reflectance about 10%–12%) compared to red (reflectance about 4%–5%).

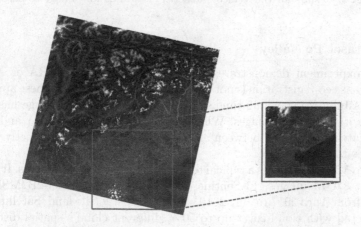

Fig. 3. The different overlap between Sentinel-2/MSI and Landsat-8/OLI.

In this case the use of different cameras, orbits, spatial resolution, and product geocoding accuracy generate larger errors in the registration between mixed sensors. The correspondence between the Landsat 8 images is relatively good (less than 2 pixel). The results for Sentinel-2 images show larger discrepancies superior to 3 pixels between the different co-registration methods (Fig. 4). Overall, the mean difference between image-to-base and MIRA methods is 1.755 ± 1.506 pixel, while the comparison between AS and MIRA shows slightly lower error values (1.553 ± 1.108 pixel). Such result is worse than previous figures, and unveils that point distribution in the images is not sufficiently good for a reliable co-registration procedure. In this sense, applying 3 different co-registration algorithms (which however are based on the same set of corresponding points) can reveal if the tie-points are sufficiently good to ensure reliable co-registration, which is a fundamental preliminary procedure in remote sensing.

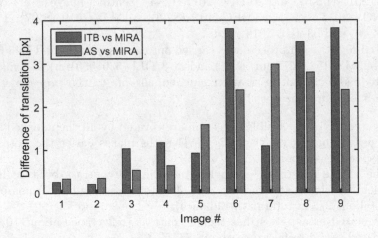

Fig. 4. Results for the Venice dataset. ITB stands for "image-to-base".

4.3 Dataset Po Valley

The last experiment demonstrates the advantage of using MIRA or AS when image-to-base co-registration is not feasible. As a matter of fact, these approaches can successfully register long time series only when the base image has enough matches with the other images. When this is not the case, MIRA and AS can exploit matches extracted between all image pairs, therefore indirectly tying all the images to the base one.

The Po Valley dataset is a typical test for agricultural applications. It includes 9 Landsat-8/OLI images, 13 Sentinel-2A/MSI and 6 Sentinel-2B/MSI images collected from April 2017 to July 2019 in Italy's most fertile land. Satellite images were selected with cloud cover up to 50%, different cloud's spatial distribution and size, to test the robustness against cloud coverage. Besides, the satellite data were not corrected/compensated for the atmospheric effect. That makes the image matching even more challenging.

Unlike the Venice dataset, the image matching was done with the near-infrared spectral bands: band #8a for Sentinel-2 (854–875 nm), and band #5

(850–880 nm) for Landsat-8/OLI. The near-infrared is widely used to monitor farmlands and also partially reduces the impact of the different atmospheric conditions, contrasting crops with different growth stages.

Comparing the parameters estimated via the MIRA method and AS shows that differences are rather small (on average, 0.045 pixel with $\sigma = 0.032$ pixel) and confirms that the two methods provided equivalent results. As mentioned, the comparison does not include the image-to-base strategy which cannot be applied in this scenario for the impossibility to match the base image with all the others images.

5   Conclusion

Synchronization has a wide range of interesting applications [2]. In this paper we applied it to the co-registration of remote sensing images as an alternative to the more traditional image-to-base approach. Both MIRA and AS can overcome the lack of co-registration results when the base image does not share matches with all the remaining images in the dataset. In fact, image-to-base co-registration strategies usually available in remote sensing/GIS software packages cannot automatically complete the co-registration workflow for those images. The use of methods able to handle also matches extracted between other (all, in principle) image pairs can overcome this limitation. Experiments in the paper have shown that a discrepancy between the computed parameters with both AS and MIRA could indicate an unreliable set of matches extracted automatically in the image dataset. Comparing the parameters estimated with both methods can be therefore intended as an additional diagnostic tool able to verify the reliability of the extracted set of tie-points.

References

1. Arie-Nachimson, M., Kovalsky, S.Z., Kemelmacher-Shlizerman, I., Singer, A., Basri, R.: Global motion estimation from point matches. In: Proceedings of the Joint 3DIM/3DPVT Conference: 3D Imaging, Modeling, Processing, Visualization and Transmission (2012)
2. Arrigoni, F., Fusiello, A.: Synchronization problems in computer vision with closed-form solutions. Int. J. Comput. Vis. **128**(1), 26–52 (2020)
3. Arrigoni, F., Fusiello, A., Rossi, B.: Camera motion from group synchronization. In: Proceedings of the International Conference on 3D Vision (3DV), pp. 546–555 (2016)
4. Arrigoni, F., Maset, E., Fusiello, A.: Synchronization in the symmetric inverse semigroup. In: Battiato, S., Gallo, G., Schettini, R., Stanco, F. (eds.) ICIAP 2017. LNCS, vol. 10485, pp. 70–81. Springer, Cham (2017). https://doi.org/10.1007/978-3-319-68548-9_7
5. Arrigoni, F., Rossi, B., Fusiello, A.: Spectral synchronization of multiple views in SE(3). SIAM J. Imag. Sci. **9**(4), 1963–1990 (2016)
6. Barazzetti, L., Scaioni, M., Gianinetto, M.: Automatic co-registration of satellite time series via least squares adjustment. Eur. J. Remote Sens. **47**(1), 55–74 (2014)

7. Bernard, F., Thunberg, J., Gemmar, P., Hertel, F., Husch, A., Goncalves, J.: A solution for multi-alignment by transformation synchronisation. In: Proceedings of the IEEE Conference on Computer Vision and Pattern Recognition, pp. 2161–2169 (2015)
8. ESA: Sentinel Hub. https://www.sentinel-hub.com. Accessed 19 Feb 2020
9. ESA: Sentinel online. https://earth.esa.int/web/sentinel/technical-guides/sentinel-2-msi/performance. Accessed 19 Feb 2020
10. European Commission (EC): DIAS. https://www.copernicus.eu/en/access-data/dias. Accessed 19 Feb 2020
11. European Commission (EC): Copernicus sentinel data access 2018 annual report (2018). https://scihub.copernicus.eu/twiki/pub/SciHubWebPortal/AnnualReport2018/COPE-SERCO-RP-19-0389_-_Sentinel_Data_Access_Annual_Report_Y2018_v1.0.pdf. Accessed 19 Feb 2020
12. Förstner, W.: Generic estimation procedures for orientation with minimum and redundant information. In: Gruen, A., Huang, T.S. (eds.) Calibration and Orientation of Cameras in Computer Vision. Springer Series in Information Sciences, vol. 34. Springer, Heidelberg (2001). https://doi.org/10.1007/978-3-662-04567-1_3
13. Gianinetto, M.: Automatic co-registration of satellite time series. Photogram. Rec. 27(140), 462–470 (2012)
14. Gianinetto, M., Barazzetti, L., Dini, L., Fusiello, A., Toldo, R.: Geometric registration of remotely sensed data with SAMIR. In: 3rd International Conference on Remote Sensing and Geoinformation of the Environment, vol. 9535, p. 95350Q (2015)
15. Gianinetto, M., Scaioni, M.: Automated geometric correction of high-resolution pushbroom satellite data. Photogram. Eng. Remote Sens. 74(1), 107–116 (2008)
16. Goshtasby, A.A.: 2-D and 3-D Image Registration: For Medical, Remote Sensing, and Industrial Applications. Wiley, Hoboken (2005)
17. Lindeberg, T.: Feature detection with automatic scale selection. Int. J. Comput. Vis. 30, 79–116 (1998)
18. Roy, D.P., et al.: Landsat-8 and Sentinel-2 burned area mapping - a combined sensor multi-temporal change detection approach. Remote Sens. Environ. 231, 111254 (2019)
19. Santellani, E., Maset, E., Fusiello, A.: Seamless image mosaicking via synchronization. ISPRS Ann. IV-2, 247–254 (2018)
20. Scaioni, M., Barazzetti, L., Gianinetto, M.: Multi-image robust alignment of medium-resolution satellite imagery. Remote Sens. 10(12), 1969 (2018)
21. Schroeder, P., Bartoli, A., Georgel, P., Navab, N.: Closed-form solutions to multiple-view homography estimation. In: 2011 IEEE Workshop on Applications of Computer Vision (WACV), pp. 650–657 (2011)
22. Singer, A.: Angular synchronization by eigenvectors and semidefinite programming. Appl. Comput. Harmon. Anal. 30(1), 20–36 (2011)
23. Stumpf, A., Michéa, D., Malet, J.P.: Improved co-registration of Sentinel-2 and Landsat-8 imagery for earth surface motion measurements. Remote Sens. 10(2), 160 (2018)
24. Toldo, R., Gherardi, R., Farenzena, M., Fusiello, A.: Hierarchical structure-and-motion recovery from uncalibrated images. Comput. Vis. Image Underst. 140, 127–143 (2015). https://doi.org/10.1016/j.cviu.2015.05.011
25. USGS: Landsat Collection 1. https://www.usgs.gov/land-resources/nli/landsat/landsat-collection-1?qt-science_support_page_related_con=1#qt-science_support_page_related_con. Accessed 19 Feb 2020

Geomatics and Land Management

Living Labs and Open Innovation
to Support Local Development Policies

Pietro Battistoni[✉] ⓘ, Michele Grimaldi ⓘ, Monica Sebillo ⓘ,
and Giuliana Vitiello ⓘ

University of Salerno, 84084 Fisciano, SA, Italy
{pbattistoni,migrimaldi,msebillo,gvitiello}@unisa.it

Abstract. The term Living Lab was first used at MIT and originates
from purpose-built labs where volunteer research participants were provided with facilities of a regular home and were observed with all sorts of
devices while testing new technologies. The concept has evolved over the
years and now it represents a systematic user co-creation approach that
integrates research and innovation processes in real life communities and
settings. The research described in this paper focuses on the role that
Living Labs can play in strengthening the skills of territory by increasing
knowledge deriving from it also by improving users' engagement in the
process itself of creation and instantiating relationships among actors. In
particular, an innovative approach to the design and use of Living Labs
is studied, aimed at integrating territorial intelligence and ICT to better
understand territorial phenomena and interpret local dynamics involving
citizens, institutions and organizations. To support the achievement of
this goal, in this paper a technological solution conceived to increase the
automation process for knowledge creation and sharing is also described.
It allows users to query thematic datasets and visualize (geolocated)
information. Each new information produced by aggregating and mining processes can be in turn integrated as a resource belonging to the
heritage of the spatially enabled territory.

Keywords: Living labs · Supply data chain · Open government ·
Citizens' engagement

1 Introduction

The information technology (IT) available today enables citizens to contribute
in a new form of participatory democracy where private actors, associations and
individuals, participate in making decisions and bring together their experiences
to enrich local resources. This form of citizen engagement is currently known
as collective intelligence and represents an indispensable step towards the actu-
alization of the three pillars of the Open Government (OG) paradigm, namely
transparency, participation and collaboration [2,13,14,20]

Supported by MIUR, PRIN 2017 grant number 2017JMHK4F_004.

E. Borgogno-Mondino and P. Zamperlin (Eds.): ASITA 2021, CCIS 1507, pp. 339–350, 2022.
https://doi.org/10.1007/978-3-030-94426-1_25

Examples of how people are involved in these community-based activities are now becoming common enough and they mainly refer to the civic consultations in defense of cultural and environmental heritages. However, the scope where the collective intelligence may result fruitful is quite wider and ranges from natural environment to healthcare, from safety to mobility, thanks to the pervasive impact of the unifying element of those domains, namely the territory underlying a community and the information deriving from it. In fact, the geographic information itself plays a relevant role within the collective intelligence building process since it synthesizes and aggregates homogeneous collections of data, thus preparing a base to enable people to cooperate for a problem solution. When such shared collections of data heritage generated by territory are then regularly organized through a system of models, methods, processes, people and tools, the collective intelligence assumes a specific territorial connotation and becomes Territorial Intelligence (TI) [9,17,18].

The term TI relates the development of a territory and communities acting on it, to pursue its valorization through a continuous improvement of its economic, social, environmental and cultural (sustainability) dimensions. This claim explains the important role that TI is gaining for organizations and companies belonging to the same geographic area: it works as a collector of information deriving from multiple sources and, by processing it, TI produces knowledge relevant to the underlying territory and supports the exchange of know-how among local actors of different cultures [1]. Moreover, activating the citizens' participation in civil life of a territory modifies their role from only information consumers to information consumers and producers, namely information prosumers. It is known in fact that citizen's contribution to collect meaningful data about an event has turned out to be significant in many situations, such as the volunteered geographic information provided by the Haitians people after the devastating earthquake in 2010 that notably contributed to the (digital) humanitarian community [19].

Handling the multidisciplinary complexity of data coming from a spatially enabled territory and supporting a fruitful exchange of it represent the goals of the research we are conducting at the Laboratory of Geographic Information Systems (University of Salerno). In this field, we are investigating a digital ecosystem, as an open and shared environment with properties of scalability and sustainability, capable to realize services through the integration of four basic territory-oriented elements, namely content, communities, practices and policy, and technology.

The research described in this paper focuses on a specific theme within the wide context previously described, that is the role that Living Labs (LL)s can play in strengthening the skills of the territory by increasing knowledge deriving from it also by improving users' engagement in the process itself of creation and instantiating relationships among actors [5].

To deepen this topic of interest, an innovative approach to the design and use of LLs is studied, aimed at integrating TI and Information Technologies (IT) to better understand territorial phenomena and interpret local dynamics involving citizens, institutions and organizations. In particular, when properly collected, shared and crossed with data on users and services through IT tools, TI can provide decision makers with appropriate territorial indicators useful to conceive new development models aligned with the sustainable development models.

To support the achievement of this goal, in this paper we present a technological solution conceived to increase the automation process for knowledge creation and sharing. On the basis of a digital infrastructure, we discuss how users are allowed to query thematic datasets and visualize (geolocated) information. Each new information produced by aggregating and mining processes can be in turn integrated as a resource belonging to the heritage of the spatially enabled territory.

The paper is organized as follows. Section 2 recalls the concept of LL and its diverse implementations. In Sect. 3, the rationale that stimulated the rethinking of the design and implementation processes of LLs, is discussed, and the approach used to outline the information flow pattern is presented. Section 4 presents the architectural principles adopted to design a LL with special focus on both the metadata collection framework and the module addressed to the citizens' engagement. The prototype is depicted in Sect. 5 where the basic functionality is presented through the fruition of territorial services. Conclusions are drawn in Sect. 6.

2   Living Labs

When faced with complex challenges in an evolving real-life context with multiple factors to consider, it becomes very difficult, if not impossible, for a single actor, to find the right solution. For this reason, the LL strategy becomes the best choice to adopt as it offers the possibility to design solutions with end users and stakeholders through collaboration and co-creation. In this way, complexity and uncertainty are reduced and the possibility of finding a sustainable and advantageous solution increases.

In the following, the concept of LL is recalled and a brief overview on its evolution is given. The ENoLL network is also described.

2.1   Living Labs as User-Centred, Open Innovation Ecosystems

The term LL was first used by MIT's Prof William (Bill) Mitchell and originates from purpose-built labs where volunteer research participants were provided with all facilities of a regular home and were observed with all sorts of devices while testing new technologies [5]. The concept has evolved over the years and the current rationale underlying LLs is based on a systematic user co-creation approach that integrates research and innovation processes in real life communities and settings. Instead of recreating a natural context in a laboratory setting, users are in fact observed in their everyday habitats. This "living" approach, namely placing the citizen at the centre of innovation, improves the ability to benefit from the opportunities offered by new IT solutions to satisfy requirements coming from local contexts.

According to the European Network of LLs [5] 5 key elements are paramount for a LL, namely

1. active user involvement,
2. real-life setting,
3. multi-stakeholder participation,
4. a multi-method approach, and
5. co-creation.

In particular, elements 3 and 4 emphasize the involvement of technology and service providers, and institutional and private actors to create cross-fertilization through the combination of methods and tools originating from several and diverse disciplines.

2.2 European Network of Living Lab (ENoLL)

ENoLL is the international federation of benchmarked Living Labs in Europe and worldwide. It was founded in November 2006 under the auspices of the Finnish European Presidency. The European approach to LLs was created in the Unit "Collaborative working environments" of the DG CONNECT and the original LL concept was updated to open innovation environments to attract investments, both intellectual and financial [11] Today, ENoLL counts over 150 active LLs members worldwide and it is present in five continents. It provides co-creation, user engagement, test and experimentation facilities addressed to innovation in many different domains, such as energy, media, mobility, healthcare, agrifood. Figure 1 shows the distribution of LL members dated at 2015. The most common topics are Health and Wellness, Social inclusiveness, Smart Cities and Social Innovation. Other themes of interest are Education, Mobility, Energy, Public administration, Culture and creativeness.

Fig. 1. The 2015 world distribution of LL members [6]

3   The LL Architecture, Resources, Actors and Roles

A LL is a distributed, adaptive, open socio-technical system with self-organization and sustainability properties. It is embedded within a set of satellite applications, Web portals, externals systems, legacy systems, and corporate DBs, representing the Technology and Infrastructure component that integrates the LL and the IT Infrastructure and Hardware meta-elements.

As for the users, clustering according to their role allows for simpler management of services allocated to them. Single users, thematic communities, organizations/institutions, regulatory bodies are generic examples of clusters of users who access and produce information through the LL component that coordinates the aspects related to fruition, competition, and collaboration for resources among diverse entities. This facility is based on the underlying spatial interactions that set the involved locations on a continuous space at multiple scales with spatio-temporal constraints. The heterogeneous spatial connectivity derived from this approach affects the search strategies and determines a differently distributed topology of the landscape.

It is worth to noting that, although these characteristics obstruct the adoption of a uniform approach for problem-solving, they allow for speeding critical issues solutions by focusing on specific problems.

Figure 2 depicts the general schema of an "ideal" LL showing the interactions between the various hardware, software, and "human" resources.

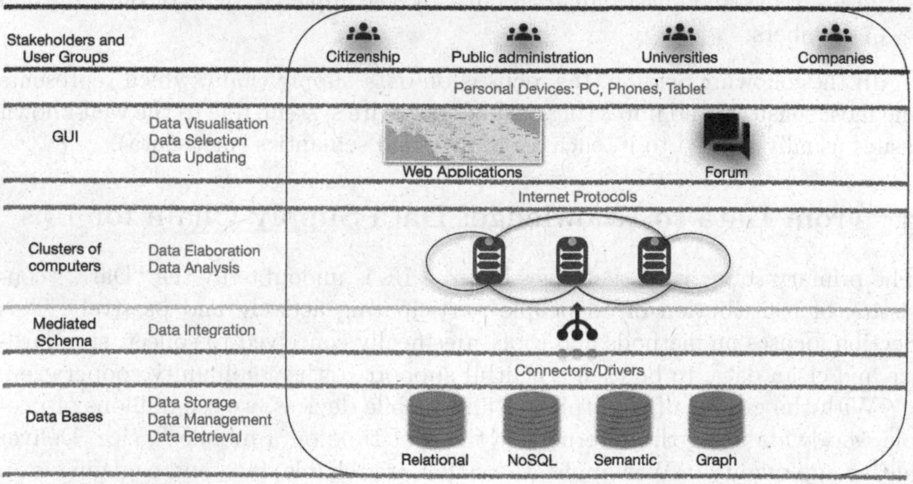

Fig. 2. A general schema showing a LL architecture and its interactions

The lowest level is associated with data, which has already been extracted, standardized, cleaned, loaded in a database, and is ready to be saved, managed, and queried through drivers made available by various programming languages.

At the second level, a mediated schema between the various databases and servers is necessary, which is created through a data integration process, and offers the illusion of having a single endpoint for accessing information. The task of this layer is receiving the queries from the servers, sending them to the individual databases involved, collecting the results in a single response and sending it back to the servers. The layer plays a fundamental role in collecting requests sent by the user, which may concern the simple retrieval of already available data or new knowledge production through data analysis processes. The transmission of the requests and their answers occurs through the classic transmission protocols adopted for the web.

The Graphic User Interface (GUI) level consists of two components: a Web-GIS application that supports the research and development team's activities and a forum connecting all community members through easily accessible devices, such as PCs and smartphones. The application visualizes both traditional data in tables and spreadsheets, and geo-referenced data on maps, also allowing the basic operations of insertion, modification, and deletion. Moreover, it offers the user the possibility of applying clustering algorithms, statistics functions, graphs creation, and other data operations. Other necessary features are:

- a "Registration" section to enroll each person;
- a "Sharing" section where share news, files, objectives and results;
- a "Learning" section allowing users to attend courses;
- a "Talking" section where it is possible to discuss on a particular topic or problem, expose ideas, opinion, and knowledge, answer direct questions, propose surveys and questionnaires that can be completed by all or only a group of members.

In the following Section, the focus is on data supply chain, which represents the most sensitive and impacting part of the entire system, due to the well-known issues usually related to it, such as quality and semantics (metadata).

4 From Data to Knowledge: Data Supply Chain for LLs

The primary component that gives life to a LL is undoubtedly the "Data," consisting of contribution of all people participating actively and passively. This Section focuses on methods and tools specifically conceived to collect, standardize and clean data, to be then a fruitful support to the community cooperation.

With the growth of smartphones and mobile devices, we see millions of people worldwide using the Internet for the first time on a mobile device. Deliver native-app quality in Web applications that are reliable, fast, and engaging is an essential tool for a LL.

A general framework valid for any application domain is proposed in the Fig. 3, describing all the steps required to build a queryable knowledge base capable of supporting research and development activities.

The first and more challenging step is data collection. Each person in a LL community can contribute to putting data and transferring her/his personal experience.

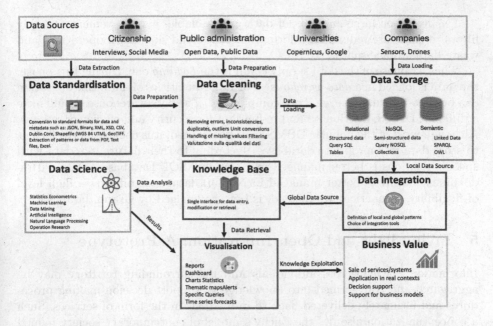

Fig. 3. Integration and analysis of data from multiple sources

The acquired data could be already clean and communicated in a standard way, such as data coming from Open Data sources by governments, or need Extract, Transform, Load (ETL) phases [4]. Data can be extracted from structured formats, such as other databases and Web Application Programming Interface (API). Alternatively, it can be extracted from unstructured sources, such as text documents, Web pages [15] and messages, and more. This process is done during the data *Extraction* phase. Data extracted from the source is raw and need to be cleansed, mapped, and transformed in a defined standard structure. The *Data Cleaning* process is invoked during the *Transformation* phase. It is addressed to clean data from redundancy and inconsistencies and represents a sophisticated process, which can be both automatically performed as proposed in [16], and supervised.

During the *Cleaning* process, the management of missing or partial values is addressed by defining an action strategy. There are various alternatives that can be adopted, such as removing the partial information, replacing the missing parts with non-indicative values, inserting an estimation based on the existing data or logical reasoning.

Another quality to check is data consistency, that is values expressed by same units of measurement. Analogously, outliers, duplicate values and measurement errors, should be removed, as they only generate noise and are not valid for statistical purposes.

Finally, when large amounts of data are available, it is convenient to apply filters to eliminate redundant information that could slow down operations and waste data storage space.

The last phase of the data supply chain is the *Loading* one. During this phase, the data is loaded in a *data warehouse*. For large quantities of data, this operation can be time-consuming, even if not complicated. The data warehouse should have a different DBMS, distributed and redundant for security and efficiency reasons. Although most of the popular DBMSs can be adapted, it is usually more efficient to store data in appropriate databases, according to their nature. So, data with specific relations is better managed in Relational SQL Databases. Data with a document nature is better managed in NoSQL databases, offering a high level of flexibility. Semantic data, instead, is better managed by Graph databases.

5   Living Labs and Open Innovation: A Prototype

Information flowing across individuals and the surrounding territory may be aggregated and transformed into knowledge to support decision-making procedures and ultimately delivered back to individuals in the form of services. Such a conceptualization also fits the Flichy's model of contemporary society named "connected individualism," which emphasizes the role of communities and networks for individual growth and empowerment [7]. Within this transformation, the goal of information sharing and cooperative exploitation can be achieved by a profitable combination of territorial knowledge with personal data and events organized through a software infrastructure conceived for the development of special-purpose applications meant to improve users' experience while creating public value for services.

In order to design and develop such a platform, the factors of primary importance that should be taken into account are the need for a shared communication protocol among all the involved entities, extensibility (i.e., the ability to add new features without affecting the existing components), and the opportunity to hide the format differences of data coming from heterogeneous data sources. In particular, to this aim, it is necessary to identify people who produce information, to aggregate/disaggregate it, and to include slices of them as part of the system, thus satisfying the need of accessing and providing both prior knowledge (static) and information generated in real-time (dynamic).

As a proof-of-concept, this Section presents a prototype of the LL, built on a Web platform. It supports citizens' activities and allow service providers to create, monitor and share different services. The whole community may leverage such services and the derived (possibly aggregated) information, with a potential growth in territorial knowledge.

Starting from the data extraction to the visualization of the analysis results, the proposed application creates a single platform where it is possible to apply most of the phases previously described. In particular, based on the data available it is possible to generate maps of the local territory to identify any trends and phenomena occurring in one or more municipalities. It is also possible to quickly and intuitively group geographically distant municipalities sharing the same characteristics.

The goal of the scenario used to run the prototype was to develop and implement policies to promote economic regeneration of local areas. In particular, the knowledge derived from the platform and visualized through the maps has become fundamental support for expert users, such as urban planners and engineers, to understand which Smart Specialization Strategy is best suitable to stimulate local economic development.

In terms of data, the first source in terms of municipalities, census sections, provinces, and regions is the National Institute of Statistics (ISTAT). However, despite providing certified, verified, and reliable data, the ISTAT portal is quite complex to build the desired queries, even for experienced users. From this concern, the development of a simplified application arises, which allows direct requests through a faster and more natural interface, thanks to a technologically advanced system that handled the ISTAT data warehouse in machine-to-machine mode via web service. This service, free of charge and freely available, allows bodies and organizations to formulate specific requests, download data of interest, and quickly receive them in their databases, web portals, and applications [8]. The queries can be sent through programming languages, such as PHP, C#, JAVA, and VB.NET, while the query formulation follows the Statistical Data and Metadata eXchange (SDMX), adopted for the transmission of statistical data by the most important international organizations.

It is possible to query web service by selecting and inserting information, such as the category and the territory of interest at the regional, provincial or municipal level. The expected results are displayed on the map and in tabular form. In order to apply the geo-referencing algorithm, the data transformation requires a supervised action where the user manually indicates which fields contain the municipality or census section code to which data refers.

In addition to data loading and map visualization, the proposed application performs statistical functions, data analysis functions, interactive diagrams and composite index to identify specific phenomena or deficiencies in a given territory.

An example of a composite index building is the application of the Mazziotta-Pareto Index (MPI) [12]. It summarizes a set of individual indicators assumed to be non-substitutable, i.e., all components must be balanced [3]. MPI + is usually chosen for "positive" multidimensional phenomena (the higher the value, the better the performance), such as well-being, quality of life, development, and infrastructure provision. In contrast, MPI − is chosen for "negative" multidimensional phenomena (the higher the value, the worse the performance), such as poverty, mortality, and pollution. Figure 4 displays the trend of the composite index representing the combination of socio-economic variables on a municipal basis.

It is also possible to execute the Principal Component Analysis, whose purpose is to reduce the greater or lesser number of variables describing a data set to a smaller number of latent variables, limiting the loss of information as much as possible [21]. When combined with the K-means algorithm, this technique allows to build clusters, which minimize the total intra-group variance

[10]. Figure 5 shows an application of these two combined analyses, where the resulting clusters represent groups of municipalities that are homogeneous with respect to the given socio-economic variables.

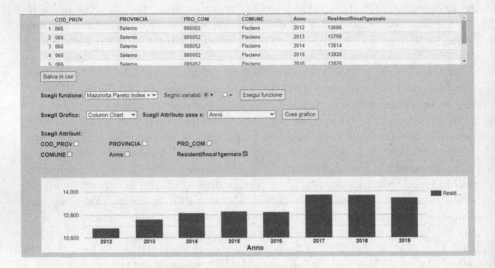

Fig. 4. Mazziotta-Pareto Index application

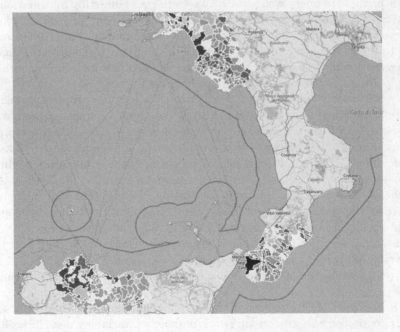

Fig. 5. Clusters of municipalities for socio-economic parameters

6 Conclusions

The prototype described in the paper represents the initial results of the SOUND Project (Smart Open Urban-rural iNnovation Data - PRIN - National Interest Research Project), which experiments a multidisciplinary, place-sensitive approach for the implementation of the Smart Specialisation Strategies (S3) - by taking into account the evolving and multi-scalar territorial characteristics. The ultimate goal of SOUND is to build a Smart Platform based on the LL approach aimed to empower the connection between innovation dynamics and territorial capital through the ICT support.

This paper proposes an architecture and a software application to re-think LL activities to improve the citizens' engagement and produce knowledge dynamics as is envisaged by the S3. Kept a territorial regeneration as an exemplary case for using a LL, a web application has been developed as a spatial decision support system for domain experts and decision makers to facilitate contextualised open innovation processes.

Future work is addressed to the integration of the existing data heritage produced by multiple sources, such as the Copernicus EO program and traditional cartographic maps. Such an integrated platform will be then experimented on a real case study as proposed in the SOUND project, which aims to create connections among S3 and Emerging Industries clusters. The resulting platform is then meant to explore hidden relationships featuring new territorial clusters of open innovation.

References

1. Bertacchini, Y., Rodriguez-Salvador, M., Souari, W.: From territorial intelligence to compositive & sustainable system. Case studies in Mexico & in Gafsa university. In: International Conference of Territorial Intelligence, Huelva 2007, Huelva, Spain, pp. 106–124 (October 2007). https://halshs.archives-ouvertes.fr/halshs-00516033
2. Canares, M.P., Marcial, D., Narca, M.: Enhancing citizen engagement with open government data. J. Commun. Inf. **12**(2) (2016). https://doi.org/10.15353/joci. v12i2.3240. https://doi.org/10.15353%2Fjoci.v12i2.3240
3. De Muro, P., Mazziotta, M., Pareto, A.: Composite indices of development and poverty: an application to MDGs. Soc. Indic. Res. **104**(1), 1–18 (2011). https:// doi.org/10.1007/s11205-010-9727-z
4. Deufemia, V., Giordano, M., Polese, G., Tortora, G.: A visual language-based system for extraction-transformation-loading development. Softw. Pract. Exp. **44**(12), 1417–1440 (2014). https://doi.org/10.1002/spe.2201
5. European Network of Living Labs. https://enoll.org/
6. European Network of Living Labs (2015). https://openlivinglabdays16.wordpress. com/2015/12/10/the-10th-wave-for-enoll-membership-is-now-open/
7. Flichy, P.: Connected individualism between digital technology and society. Réseaux **124**, 17–51 (2004)
8. ISTAT: Web service sdmx per l'accesso ai dati di istat (October 2020). https:// www.istat.it/it/metodi-e-strumenti/web-service-sdmx

9. Laurini, R.: Geographic Knowledge Infrastructure. Applications to Territorial Intelligence and Smart Cities. Elsevier (2017)

10. Likas, A., Vlassis, N., Verbeek, J.: The global k-means clustering algorithm. Pattern Recogn. **36**(2), 451–461 (2003)

11. Living Labs and Open Innovation (February 2016). https://ec.europa.eu/digital-single-market/en/news/living-labs-and-open-innovation

12. Mazziotta, M., Pareto, A.: On a generalized non-compensatory composite index for measuring socio-economic phenomena. Soc. Indic. Res. **127**(3), 983–1003 (2016)

13. Obama, B.: Transparency and open government (January 2009). Online

14. Partnership, O.G.: Open government declaration (September 2011). Online

15. Patel, J.: Introduction to Web Scraping, pp. 1–30. Apress, Berkeley (2020). https://doi.org/10.1007/978-1-4842-6576-5_1

16. Pellegrino, M.A., Postiglione, L., Scarano, V.: Detecting data accuracy issues in textual geographical data by a clustering-based approach. In: 8th ACM IKDD CODS and 26th COMAD, CODS COMAD 2021, pp. 208–212. Association for Computing Machinery, New York (2021). https://doi.org/10.1145/3430984.3431031

17. Sebillo, M., Tortora, G., Tucci, M., Vitiello, G., Ginige, A., Giovanni, P.D.: Combining personal diaries with territorial intelligence to empower diabetic patients. J. Vis. Lang. Comput. **29**, 1–14 (2015)

18. Sebillo, M.M.L., Vitiello, G., Grimaldi, M., De Chiara, D.: A territorial intelligence-based approach for smart emergency planning. In: Chinnici, M., et al. (eds.) Data Science and Big Data Analytics in Smart Environments, pp. 135–156. Routledge Taylor & Francis Group (2021)

19. USHAIDI: Ushaidi. https://www.ushahidi.com/

20. Wirtz, B.W., Birkmeyer, S.: Open government: origin, development, and conceptual perspectives. Int. J. Pub. Adm. **38**(5), 381–396 (2015)

21. Wold, S., Esbensen, K., Geladi, P.: Principal component analysis. Chemometr. Intell. Lab. Syst. **2**(1), 37–52 (1987). Proceedings of the Multivariate Statistical Workshop for Geologists and Geochemists. https://doi.org/10.1016/0169-7439(87)80084-9. https://www.sciencedirect.com/science/article/pii/0169743987800849

Analysis of Geospatial Behaviour of Visitors of Urban Gardens: Is Positioning via Smartphones a Valid Solution?

Francesco Pirotti[1,2](✉) , Marco Piragnolo[1,2] , Alberto Guarnieri[1,2] ,
Marco Boscaro[1], and Raffaele Cavalli[1]

[1] TESAF Department, University of Padova, Viale dell'Università, 16, 35020 Legnaro, PD, Italy
`francesco.pirotti@unipd.it`
[2] CIRGEO Interdepartmental Research Center in Geomatics, University of Padova,
Viale dell'Università, 16, 35020 Legnaro, PD, Italy

Abstract. Tracking locations is practical and speditive with smartphones, as they are omnipresent devices, relatively cheap, and have the necessary sensors for positioning and networking integrated in the same box. Nowadays recent models have GNSS antennas capable of receiving multiple constellations. In the proposed work we test the hypothesis that GNSS positions directly recorded by smartphones can be a valid solution for spatial analysis of people's behaviour in an urban garden. Particular behaviours can be linked to therapeutic spots that promote health and well-being of visitors. Three parts are reported: (i) assessment of the accuracy of the positions relative to a reference track, (ii) implementation of a framework for automating transmission and processing of the location information, (iii) analysis of preferred spots via spatial analytics. Different devices were used to survey at different times and with different methods, i.e. in the pocket of the owner or on a rigid frame. Accuracy was estimated using distance of each located point to the reference track, and precision was estimated with static multiple measures. A chat-bot through the Telegram application was implemented to allow users to send their data to a centralized computing environment thus automating the spatial analysis. Results report a horizontal accuracy below ~2.3 m at 95% confidence level, without significant difference between surveys, and very little differences between devices. GNSS-only and assisted navigation with telephone cells also did not show significant difference. Autocorrelation of the residuals over time and space showed strong consistency of the residuals, thus proving a valid solution for spatial analysis of walking behaviour.

Keywords: Navigation · Global navigation satellite systems · Smartphone · Low-cost positioning · Health and well-being (H&WB)

1 Introduction

Higher accuracy geolocation solutions are increasingly making their way in mass-market sectors as devices increase their ability to perform low-end mapping and surveying activities [1]. Global navigation satellite systems (GNSS) are now served by multiple constellations. Multiple constellations mean that there are more satellites thus a higher probability

E. Borgogno-Mondino and P. Zamperlin (Eds.): ASITA 2021, CCIS 1507, pp. 351–365, 2022.
https://doi.org/10.1007/978-3-030-94426-1_26

of having an unobstructed line of sight (LOS) between the receiver and the space vehicle (SV). They also provide a higher probability of an improved satellite configuration, thus lower values of position dilution of precision (PDOP). GNSS receivers in smartphones are now capable of collecting information from multiple constellations. This capability is becoming more common also in lower cost smartphones, that can now receive United States' Global Positioning System - GPS (GPS), Global'naya Navigatsionnaya Sputnikovaya Sistema - GLONASS (GLO), Europe's Galileo (GAL), Japan's Quasi-Zenith - QZSS (QZS), China's BeiDou (CMP), and India's Indian Regional Navigational Satellite System - IRNSS (IRN).

Satellite navigation system data are shared through several standard formats. The GNSS chipset in the smartphone can provide coordinates in the NMEA (National Marine Electronics Association) protocol, which comes in different versions. NMEA 0183 is the most common format to this day, providing communication of position and information on the quality of satellite geometry. NMEA files provide position calculated through the Standard Positioning Service (SPS) or, if the chipset allows, real time differential corrections. In general, an SPS receiver can provide position information with an error of less than 10 m. In this particular case the NMEA data was used.

Investigations using low-cost and smartphone-based receivers have already been extensively carried out. There is a high interest in understanding the possibility of using such devices for surveying and monitoring [2], both in real time kinematic and also with post-processing of observation data, even online as was tested in [3]. Pirazzi et al. [4] tested GPS+GAL single frequency antenna in a smartphone in different scenarios, finding metric accuracy in dynamic surveying and decimetric accuracy in static surveying. Dabove and Di Pietra [5] tested two smartphones and an external receiver, finding decimetric accuracies with centimetric precision in real time if a reference station is available. Dabove in [6] also tested GNSS NMEA acquisitions from two smartphones in two scenarios, one scenario providing mostly fixed solutions, and one with only floating solutions and reasonably multipath error sources. Results of comparing with reference positions from a total station showed horizontal deviations respectively ~3 m–5 m. Lately also dual-frequency GNSS receivers (L1/E1/ and L5/E5 signals) have become available in few models of smartphones, which have been analysed for performance in [7] showing an improvement from ~5 m to ~1 m. Positions recorded in time also allow to record velocities, and Android smartphone (Xiaomi Mi 8) was tested also in this sense, finding root mean square errors (RMSE) of a few millimeters per second in east and north directions [8].

2   Materials and Methods

Different devices are tested under controlled conditions in different scenarios. In particular locations under different types of canopy cover were tested, as the accuracy reduction due to canopy cover is the main object of investigation.

2.1   Study Area

The tests were carried out in the premises of the University of Padova, Villa Revedin Bolasco (VRB), located in the city of Castelfranco Veneto (province of Treviso).

Historical Background. The area, where today the villa and the garden stand, was historically owned by noble families, Tempesta, Morosini and since 1509, to the Venetian patrician family Corner which built their residence. Italian garden decorated with statues, the work of Orazio Marinali (1643–1720) was called "The Paradise". The garden was designed as a Romantic English garden designed by Meduna and other famous landscape designers such as Francesco Bagnara and Marc Guignon from France. Today, the historical garden extends over an area of 7.63 ha (Fig. 1), and it counts over 1,000 trees. Owning to the many elements that are involved, a specific database was also implemented for management of maps, profiles and other topographical information [9].

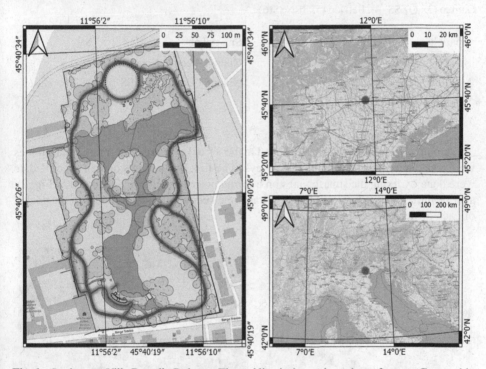

Fig. 1. Study area, Villa Revedin Bolasco. The red line is the track used as reference. Geographic coordinates refer to the WGS84 datum (Color figure online).

2.2 Surveys

In this note the term "survey" is used to indicate the collection of coordinates over a defined time-lapse. In the reported tests the "Rinex ON" application was used [10, 11]. Rinex ON was also used in other investigations [12–15], and allows to collect data from the NMEA protocol. Rinex ON also stores GNSS observations and navigation messages in Receiver Independent Exchange (RINEX) format that can be used for further post-processing, but this will be done in a future investigation on this topic and is not in the scope of this paper.

Five smartphones were used for repeated surveys. Surveys were carried out, individually and, in one specific day, 3 February 2021, with all smartphones tested simultaneously. On that day three surveys were done with all smartphones in the same frame (see Fig. 2). The frame keeps a consistent relative position of all four smartphones during movement and allows more rigorous comparisons. The frame was positioned at a height of 1.8 m to make sure that it is above the heads of surveyors, thus avoiding signal obstruction by body parts (e.g. head) (Table 1).

Table 1. Date and type of test survey. Constellation references (**Sat**): GPS (1), GLONASS (2), Galileo (3), QZSS (4), BeiDou (5), IRNSS(6)

Smartphone	Sat	Smartphone	Sat
Blackview - BV4900	1, 2, 3, 5	Xiaomi - Redmi Note 8T	1, 2, 5
Motorola - Moto E (4) Plus	1	Xiaomi - Redmi Note 9S	1, 2, 3, 5, 6
Samsung - SM-A515F	1, 2, 3, 5		

A total of 19 surveys were carried out. On the 3rd of February 2021, more smartphones were tested simultaneously in three surveys. The first two surveys on that specific date were done by fixing the smartphones on a frame positioned above the head (see Fig. 2), and the third and last survey of that day was done keeping the smartphones in the pocket of each owner.

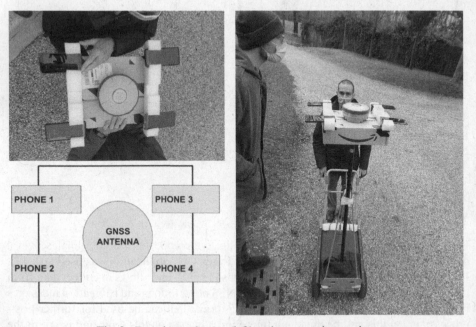

Fig. 2. Experimental setup (left) and survey using carriage.

Each survey lasted about 26 min:20 min of mobile measures, and three minutes of static measurements at the beginning and three minutes at the end. Starting times of the campaign were respectively at 11:31 AM, 12:08 AM and 12:32 AM (see Table 2). Each round-trip along the track collected around 1500 coordinates.

The following sample design was applied for this day: (i) smartphones were positioned in a specific spot and Rinex ON application was started; (ii) smartphones were left to collect measures statically for three minutes; (iii) the smartphones were carried through navigation at constant walking speed on a closed-ring trip on the middle of the track in Fig. 1; (iv) the navigation stopped along the track in two predetermined spots for about 10 s; (v) the smartphones were positioned back to the initial spot and were left there for three minutes again to statically collect data; (v) Rinex ON was stopped and the NMEA file sent to the server via Telegram through the T-BOT (see next section).

Table 2. Survey at single date (2021-02-03) with multiple smartphones.

ID	Survey smartphone model	ID	Survey smartphone model
1	11:31:00 Xiaomi - Redmi Note 8T	7	12:08:00 Xiaomi - Redmi Note 8T
2	11:31:00 Xiaomi - Redmi Note 9S	8	12:32:00 Xiaomi - Redmi Note 8T
3	11:31:00 Samsung - SM-A515F	9	12:32:00 Xiaomi - Redmi Note 9S
4	12:08:00 Blackview - BV4900	10	12:32:00 Blackview - BV4900
5	12:08:00 Samsung - SM-A515F	11	12:32:00 Motorola - Moto E (4) Plus
6	12:08:00 Xiaomi - Redmi Note 9S		

2.3 NMEA File - Transmission and Analysis via T-BOT

To automate the process of collecting the data from the surveys and streamlining them on a workflow for processing, a specific system was deployed. Transmission over the internet was implemented by creating a Telegram chat-bot (T-BOT) and collecting the files to a database through server-side. Analysis was successively carried out in the R CRAN (R) environment. Figure 3 depicts the data flow and the points below summarize it.

1. The user downloads to the smartphone an app that supports recording GNSS data and provides results in the NMEA format (Rinex ON in our tests).
2. The user starts the app and collects positions, just like in our tests.
3. The user ends the survey and shares the results through the T-BOT.
4. R functions processes data to detect preferred spots and analyse behaviour of visitors.

In our case the last point included processing accuracy metrics because the users walked on the reference track. The NMEA files provided through Rinex ON also contain the date and time of the start of the survey and also the model of the smartphone in the header. This allows to automatically keep track of the individual survey, because the

T-BOT receiving the NMEA file provides information about the user sending the file. Therefore it is possible to record information on the user, the smartphone model and the date/time of the survey.

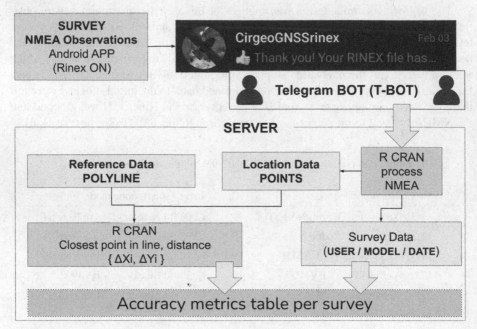

Fig. 3. Semi automatic workflow for ingesting and processing NMEA data from the survey via a ChatBOT developed in Telegram application.

2.4 Analysis of Geolocation Quality

The points were recorded every second always along a reference track (Fig. 1), so in each survey campaign they can be considered a time series, i.e. a sequence of measurements of the same variables made over time. Points are recorded as geographic coordinates in latitude and longitude in the WGS84 coordinate reference system (CRS) frame. For further processing geospatial coordinates were transformed to the projected UTM CRS in zone 32 ETRS89 (EPSG code 25832).

The reference track in Fig. 1 was surveyed using a total station instrument, with monumentation of points for each station for a closed polygonization. The polyline consisted of points surveyed on the track every ~1 m from the stations. The closure of the polyline allowed it to minimize the errors by a least-squares approach and assess the measurement error, that was <0.19 m. The assessment was done by moving along this track. It is therefore reasonable to say that the distance between measured points and this track is a proxy of accuracy. Being the track circular, we can also assess, to a certain degree, any directional bias regarding the residuals.

Accuracy. Estimated accuracy was calculated for each survey by measuring the residuals for each recorded coordinate, x_0 and y_0. Residuals were calculated by considering as real coordinate the point on the polyline of the reference track (see Fig. 1) that was closest to x_0 and y_0 with the following formula:

$$x = \frac{b(bx_0 - ay_0) - ac}{\sqrt{a^2 + b^2}} \quad y = \frac{b(-bx_0 + ay_0) - bc}{\sqrt{a^2 + b^2}} \tag{1}$$

where x and y are the coordinate values of the point on the line which is closest to x_0 and y_0, and a, b and c are constants where a and b cannot both be zero.

It must be noted that this is an empirical way to assess accuracy, as the closest point on the reference line is not necessarily the real coordinate. Another way to look at this shortcoming is that the directional component of the residuals that corresponds to the orientation of the segment will not be detected. This is an empirical method that is sensitive to the components of the residuals that are perpendicular to the direction of the segment considered of the polyline, i.e. the nearest one to the considered point, and is not sensible to errors in the same direction. This is a necessary drawback to assess a mobile survey, but it is acceptable because the goal is not to assess accuracy of the single point, but provide an idea of the average accuracy for a full survey. Being the track a circular path, sensibility to errors in all directions will also be assessed. This will be further discussed in the next sections.

Precision. The replicability of the measure was estimated by leaving the smartphones positioned statically for three minutes at the beginning and at the end of each survey, as described in Sect. 2.2. The standard deviation from the mean was calculated in the east and north directions to provide an estimation of precision.

Temporal and Spatial Error Correlation. Something is temporally correlated when its values are similar over different moments in time. Temporal and spatial autocorrelation of GNSS residuals have been investigated and found to be significant [16–19]. Previous work has shown that accuracy changes at a defined rate, e.g. in the work of Olynik [21] 5 cm in 50 s was observed. This is an advantage in the application that is proposed in this work, because the target is to detect when visitors move and when they stop or slow down; in other words the determination of velocity of the movement of the visitor. Velocity is calculated by distance between position in two successive intervals t0 and t1 (one second at the sampling rate of the surveys). If the error between t0 and t1 is very similar, then the difference of the two positions will partly remove the error. As noted in Ranacher et al. [20] "if there is a strong autocorrelation between any two consecutive position estimates, they have very similar errors. These errors cancel out when average speed, distance or direction is calculated along the trajectory."

3 Results and Discussion

The objective of this work is to verify the feasibility of using personal devices (smartphones) for determining the behaviour of visitors in an urban garden context. In particular to understand if the coordinates recorded at a rate of 1 Hz through smartphones are precise enough to understand which are the favored spots where visitors linger longer periods. The point to consider is the following: are GNSS NMEA data suitable for implementing a system where smartphones can transmit positions to a central analysis system that will be able to process data to find hot-spots and thus analyse behaviour? In this context factors that can decrease the quality of the geolocation data are vegetation canopy cover, sensitivity loss of GNSS antenna due to the position (smartphone will realistically be carried by the user in the hand or in the pocket or purse) and, to a lesser extent, multi-path from buildings. First accuracy and precision are reported in the following section, then discussion on the feasibility of spatial analysis focused on user behaviour is reported.

3.1 Quality of Geolocation

Accuracy. The accuracy is reported in two plots Fig. 4 and Fig. 5 below.

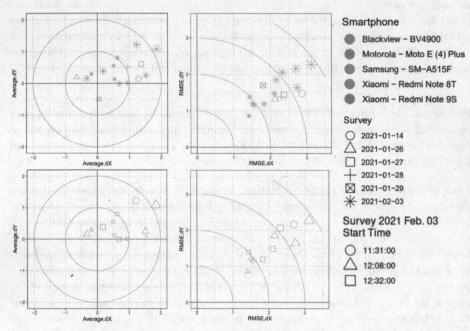

Fig. 4. Distribution of average of residuals (left column), and RMSE of residuals (middle column) and legends (right column).

Again it is important to note that the estimation of accuracy here was done using a reference track, thus a linear geometry which underestimates the residual component with a cosine law of the direction of the closest segment to each considered point. Nevertheless, the number of measurements and the circular shape of the track allows to sample all directions. Results do show a slight anisotropy in the east-west direction, as many ellipses shown in Fig. 4 show directionality. This is likely due to the fact that the track is oriented in the north-south direction, thus most readings will be compared with

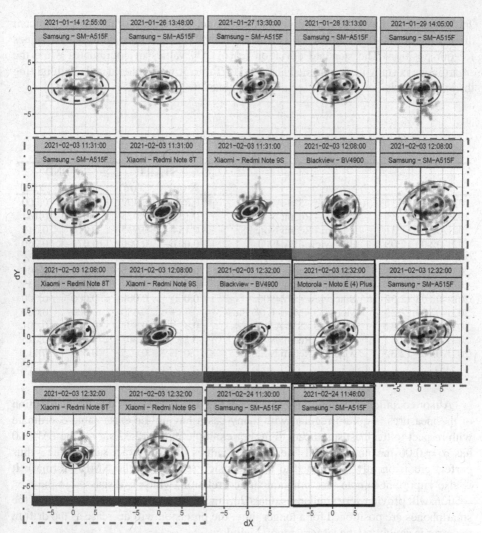

Fig. 5. Distribution of residuals. Green blue and red ellipses respectively indicate 68% 95% and 99% confidence intervals and denote estimated accuracies. Boxes with black borders indicate surveys without phone cell signal (aero mode). Red dashed line indicates the concurrent survey campaign on 3rd of February 2021 with multiple smartphones. Thick bottom ribbon color indicates the date of simultaneous surveys. (Color figure online)

segments that have a north-south direction, thus diminishing that component of the error and weighting more the east-west component.

Precision. The three minutes of static measures with the smartphones at the beginning and the end of the survey allowed us to calculate the replicability of the measure, also known as the precision. It must be noted first the intrinsic precision of the NMEA format. The NMEA format provides coordinates as *ddmm.mmmmm* where "d" is degrees and "m" is minute - thus 4 factional digits of the minute. The weight of the least significant digit is therefore ~0.186 m and ~0.131 m respectively for latitude and longitude values for our position. The standard deviation (σ) of 100 values of coordinates while the smartphone is statically positioned is shown in Table 3, with colored cells highlighting the lowest precisions. It can be seen that all values are below 1 m.

Table 3. Precisions (1σ) from static positioning during 2021-02-03

Survey	Sensor	START		END	
		X (m)	Y(m)	X(m)	Y(m)
2021-02-03 11:31	Samsung - SM-A515F	0.824	0.499	0.000	0.000
2021-02-03 11:31	Xiaomi - Redmi Note 8T	0.133	0.025	0.028	0.104
2021-02-03 11:31	Xiaomi - Redmi Note 9S	0.154	0.935	0.014	0.043
2021-02-03 12:08	Blackview - BV4900	0.001	0.000	0.074	0.260
2021-02-03 12:08	Samsung - SM-A515F	0.145	0.422	0.127	0.861
2021-02-03 12:08	Xiaomi - Redmi Note 8T	0.094	0.125	0.166	0.601
2021-02-03 12:08	Xiaomi - Redmi Note 9S	0.076	0.058	0.275	0.943
2021-02-03 12:32	Blackview - BV4900	0.000	0.000	0.000	0.000
2021-02-03 12:32	Motorola - Moto E (4) Plus	0.783	0.630	0.000	0.000
2021-02-03 12:32	Samsung - SM-A515F	0.335	0.393	0.026	0.001
2021-02-03 12:32	Xiaomi - Redmi Note 8T	0.275	0.305	0.033	0.015
2021-02-03 12:32	Xiaomi - Redmi Note 9S	0.016	0.025	0.056	0.113

A more detailed description is provided in Fig. 6 which shows that the distribution of the measures is quite irregular, with many cases having the exact same coordinate with respect to the least significant digit. For example in the 12:32 survey the BV4900 has $\sigma = 0.00$ meaning that all one hundred values had the exact same values, thus perfect precision (always limited to the intrinsic precision of the NMEA format). It is also important to note that temporal autocorrelation, which is discussed in the next section, will provide very similar residuals during the three minutes, and therefore if the smartphones are positioned for a longer time, the precision will decrease as the drift in the error is caught by the larger temporal window.

3.2 Autocorrelation

As mentioned it is proven in previous investigations that the residuals are not random over time, but change gradually, thus change at a certain rate. It is important for the goal of this investigation, because the application of using positions is to detect movement and speed, and not absolute location information. The coefficient of correlation between two values in a time series is defined by the autocorrelation function (ACF). Figure 7 shows the results of this metric over most surveys done in March 03 2021. The plots report a lag time of 2 min and show that on average all surveys are still significantly correlated on a 30 s lag, consistently over the X and Y components. It means that the residual can be modelled using the previous residuals in time. These results are coherent with the ones from [16–19] where GNSS residuals have been investigated and found to

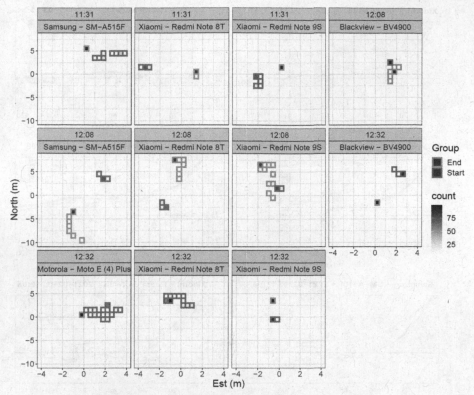

Fig. 6. Distribution of coordinates during the static measures at the start and the end of the surveys. Dark dots mean that all measures are inside that bin, light color inside the bins means very few measures. (Color figure online)

be significant, as well as from the work of Olynik [21] where a change of 5 cm in 50 s was observed.

3.3 Clustering "Hotspots"

The final result is the detection of the three spots where the simultaneous surveys stopped for around 10 s. The spots correspond to benches along the track. These are depicted in Fig. 8. Four spots are detected because the bottom left one corresponds to the start/end position, where the smartphones measured statically for three minutes and thus were identified as a stopping spot. As mentioned in the previous section, autocorrelation allows to abate the effect of the error when calculating the speed of the movement by simply the first derivative of distance over time. For best results it was observed that a low-pass median filter over a 5 s time window helps to remove noise, thus false positive stops. For false positives it is meant that two or three successive points might be very close in space due to the effect of the error, even if in reality there was movement that caused the points to be apart. Considering only two-three points would provide a false

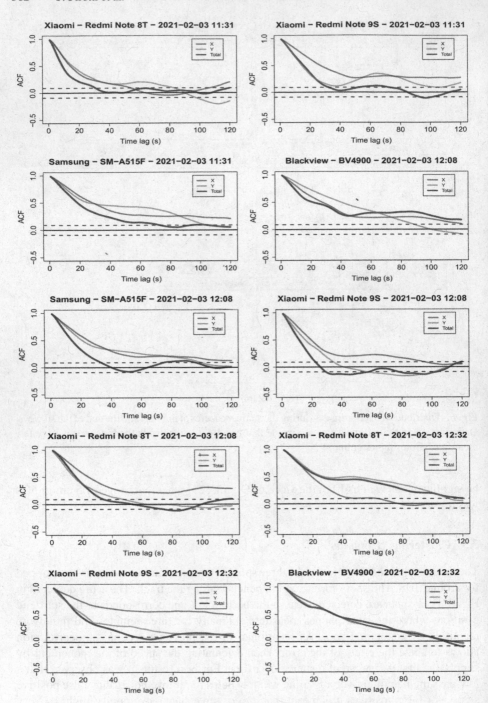

Fig. 7. Autocorrelations values on a lag time up to 2 min.

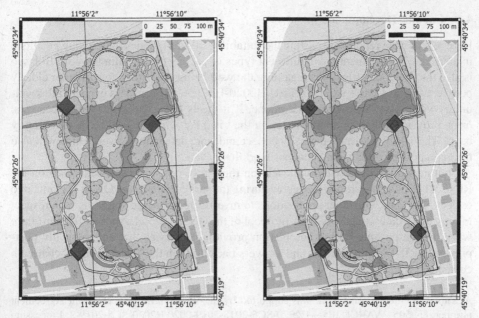

Fig. 8. Detection of "preferred" spots from filtering geolocations which did not change significantly for 10 s or more. Left is the first survey (rigid-frame) and right is the last survey (hand-held) in date 03 March 2021.

signal of the smartphone stopping. To avoid this a low-pass filter removes these false signals.

4   Conclusions

It is well known that the rigorous estimation of accuracy requires to compare a measured value with another value that was measured with an instrument with several orders of magnitude higher accuracy. In this work a rougher estimation of accuracy is enough for the intended focus, which is to test how well a smartphone allows us to understand the behaviour of a visitor in terms of relative position in time. In other words we want to know if it is possible, carrying a smartphone in a garden with varying cover conditions, to understand if a person slows down in certain points or speeds up on other areas which maybe are not as pleasant. Results show that positions have overall errors that range a couple of meters from the reference, but also that this error remains constant enough to be able to define speed accurately enough to detect changes in movement. It is also reported that data can be streamed via a chat-bot to automate processing and remove time-consuming file transfers via other means. Another part worth noting is that all smartphones tested provided similar results, without significant differences, even if they had different capabilities in terms of how many constellations they received and model of GNSS antenna.

4.1 Further Development

Here results were reported regarding the suitability of smartphones for tracking positions in a specific environment, i.e. a different types of canopy cover. Villa Revedin Bolasco is also the site of investigations regarding the well-being of visitors, in particular elderly people, as part of the VARCITIES EU H2020-EU.3.5.2 project. It is expected that voluntary visitors use their own smartphone, if it meets the criteria for GNSS receivers, or be provided with a smartphone during the visit. Participation will be on a voluntary basis. The T-BOT will automatically collect and store data in the server, which will also trigger a post-processing and analysis workflow.

Future work will look more closely on the use of post-processing methods on the RINEX files which were also collected during the survey with Rinex ON. It is planned to collect more data with other applications to investigate improved solutions with respect to only using data from the NMEA protocol of the GNSS chipset. Another further future work will be pushing further automation providing a service that automatically post-processes RINEX observations and answers back through the Telegram BOT chat with corrected positions.

Acknowledgements. This work was supported by the VARCITIES project, Grant Agreement number: 869505—VARCITIES—H2020-SC5-2018-2019-2020/H2020-SC5-2019-2. Processing was carried out by support from the Hyperearths project - ISREDI7542.

References

1. European GNSS Supervisory Authority: GNSS user technology report. Issue 3, 2020 . Publications Office, LU (2020)
2. Poluzzi, L., Tavasci, L., Corsini, F., Barbarella, M., Gandolfi, S.: L'uso di strumenti GNSS a basso costo per applicazioni di monitoraggio. Boll. SIFET **4**, 10–15 (2018)
3. Belcore, E.: Potenzialità e limiti dei servizi PPP online per il posizionamento di stazioni master: caso studio sul fiume Sirba (Africa sub-Sahariana). Boll. SIFET **2**, 76–83 (2018)
4. Pirazzi, G., Mazzoni, A., Biagi, L., Crespi, M.: Preliminary performance analysis with a GPS+Galileo enabled chipset embedded in a smartphone. In: 30th International Technical Meeting of the Satellite Division of the Institute of Navigation, ION GNSS 2017 (2017). https://doi.org/10.33012/2017.15260
5. Dabove, P., Di Pietra, V.: Towards high accuracy GNSS real-time positioning with smartphones. Adv. Space Res. (2019). https://doi.org/10.1016/j.asr.2018.08.025
6. Dabove, P.: What are the actual performances of GNSS positioning using smartphone. InsideGNSS (2014)
7. Robustelli, U., Baiocchi, V., Pugliano, G.: Assessment of dual frequency GNSS observations from a Xiaomi Mi 8 android smartphone and positioning performance analysis. Electron. Switz. **8**, 91 (2019). https://doi.org/10.3390/electronics8010091
8. Fortunato, M.: Ricostruzione di movimenti rapidi in tempo reale con osservazioni GNSS da smartphone android. Boll. SIFET **4**, 24–30 (2018)
9. Guarnieri, A., Masiero, A., Piragnolo, M., Pirotti, F., Vettore, A.: A geodatabase for multi-source data applied to cultural heritage: the case study of villa revedin bolasco. Int. Arch. Photogramm. Remote Sens. Spat. Inf. Sci. **XLI-B5**, 267–271 (2016). https://doi.org/10.5194/isprs-archives-XLI-B5-267-2016

10. FLAMINGO. https://www.flamingognss.com. Accessed 02 Mar 2021
11. Data Quality from the Dual Frequency Xiaomi MI 8. http://gmvnsl.com/about-nsl/nsl-blog/15-products-and-services/56-xiaomi-mi8-2
12. Aggrey, J., Bisnath, S., Naciri, N., Shinghal, G., Yang, S.: Use of PPP processing for next-generation smartphone GNSS chips: key benefits and challenges. In: Proceedings of the 32nd International Technical Meeting of the Satellite Division of the Institute of Navigation, ION GNSS+ 2019, pp. 3862–3878 (2019)
13. Baiocchi, V., et al.: Use of the sensors of a latest generation mobile phone for the three-dimensional reconstruction of an archaeological monument: the survey of the Intihuatana stone in Machu Picchu (Peru'). In: IOP Conference Series: Materials Science and Engineering, p. 012106. IOP Publishing (2020)
14. Fortunato, M., Ravanelli, M., Mazzoni, A.: Real-time geophysical applications with Android GNSS raw measurements. Remote Sens. **11**, 2113 (2019)
15. Uradziński, M., Bakuła, M.: Assessment of static positioning accuracy using low-cost smartphone GPS devices for geodetic survey points' determination and monitoring. Appl. Sci. **10**, 5308 (2020)
16. Miller, C., O'Keefe, K., Gao, Y.: Time correlation in GNSS positioning over short baselines. J. Surv. Eng. **138**, 17–24 (2012). https://doi.org/10.1061/(ASCE)SU.1943-5428.0000057
17. El-Rabbany, A., Kleusberg, A.: Effect of temporal physical correlation on accuracy estimation in GPS relative positioning. J. Surv. Eng. **129**, 28–32 (2003). https://doi.org/10.1061/(ASCE)0733-9453(2003)129:1(28)
18. Wang, J., Satirapod, C., Rizos, C.: Stochastic assessment of GPS carrier phase measurements for precise static relative positioning. J. Geod. **76**, 95–104 (2002). https://doi.org/10.1007/s00190-001-0225-6
19. Howind, J., Kutterer, H., Heck, B.: Impact of temporal correlations on GPS-derived relative point positions. J. Geod. **73**, 246–258 (1999). https://doi.org/10.1007/s001900050241
20. Ranacher, P., Brunauer, R., Trutschnig, W., Van der Spek, S., Reich, S.: Why GPS makes distances bigger than they are. Int. J. Geogr. Inf. Sci. **30**, 316–333 (2016). https://doi.org/10.1080/13658816.2015.1086924
21. Olynik, M.C.: Temporal characteristics of GPS error sources and their impact on relative positioning (2002). https://www.ucalgary.ca/engo_webdocs/MEC/02.20162.MOlynik.pdf

Land Abandonment and Its Impact on the Landscape Character of Val Borbera (Northern Apennines)

Rebekka Dossche[1](✉) and Veerle Van Eetvelde[2]

[1] Università di Genova, 16126 Genova, Italy
Rebekka.dossche@unige.it
[2] Ghent University, 9000 Gent, Belgium

Abstract. The Northern Apennines are characterized by a long history of local land management, adapted to limited environmental conditions without causing ecological degradation. These agro-silvo-pastoral land use systems resulted in land covers such as meadows, chestnuts, vineyards and woodland interspersed with mercantile trails. Since 1950s, its local actors started emigrating the Apennine valleys causing an abandonment and marginalization of the land and an extensification of the landscape.

The research is focusing on two cases in the valley 'Val Borbera' (NE of Italy). For both cases, an historical analytical approach was executed based on the combination of interdisciplinary sources like historical maps, land register maps, aerial photographs, topographic maps and field survey. Through the regressive cartographic analysis, the landscape changes and dynamics since the 19th century and the relationships between the land cover and land use are being mapped. These insights can benefit to a better understanding of the spatial character of the cultural rural mountain landscape.

Keywords: Spatial landscape character · Regressive cartographic analysis · Land use & land cover

1 Dynamics and Processes of Rural Mountain Landscapes

During the last decennia, historical cultural landscapes of the European countryside are vanishing due to large-scale land abandonment. Spontaneous nature development takes over and dominates landscapes used intensively for centuries within a couple of decades (Vos and Meekes 1999). One of the landscape types that changed most drastically through time, are rural mountain areas.

In the Mediterranean region, these cultural landscapes comprised intensive land management regimes and an economic context where inhabitants combined self-sufficiency with a limited export of their local products. Local practitioners who were managing the land using a multiple system (Vos and Meekes 1999; Moreno 1990; Cevasco et al. 2007), integrating forests and tree pastures (e.g. for forest grazing, charcoal burning, fire-wood,

© Springer Nature Switzerland AG 2022
E. Borgogno-Mondino and P. Zamperlin (Eds.): ASITA 2021, CCIS 1507, pp. 366–384, 2022.
https://doi.org/10.1007/978-3-030-94426-1_27

timber, manuring, and all kinds of utensils), rough grazing lands (e.g. heathlands, phry-gana, garrigues), water systems (e.g. for irrigation, fertilization), etc. (Vos and Stortelder 1992). Every site and every tree was used being part of a trinity of trees, arable cultures and grazing (Le Coz 1990; Joffre 1992; Joffre et al. 1991; Vos and Meekes 1999). The resulting agro-silvo-pastoral systems were regionally differentiated by their adaptation to climate, physiography and local cultures through a continuous change of practices and production.

In general, the historically integrated agro-silvo-pastoral land use systems reached their optimum in the second half of the 19th century. At that moment, the high popula-tion pressure and the need for subsistence caused a diversified use of nearly the entire landscape. Livestock became the central component, because of their meat, milk, wool and hides, but also for their manure, animal power, and transport capacities. Despite this transition, the agro-silvo-pastoral systems kept a balance between the increasing population and farm production, being sustainable for a long time. But the equilibrium was fragile and very much alive to catastrophes, periodic overpopulations and effects of wars and epidemics (Vos and Meekes 1999). After the Second World War and until the 1970s–1980s, the rural mountain areas became largely abandoned by its population, with severe consequences for the land. Since the end of the 20th century, pastures and fields (mainly on terraces) have been abandoned, coppice is changing into high forest, chestnut plantations have become neglected, and monocultures have been introduced in forestry (Pinto-Correia 1993). Nevertheless, the spatial character of the present-day landscape still reflects the agricultural structure of the first decades of this century, which gradually developed from probably the 12th century onwards.

Hence, the landscapes of the agro-silvo-pastoral systems represent a continuous and endless interaction between the land, how it is used, and by whom it is used. The results of this interaction are structured in specific land use patterns. Land use is considered as the result of local practices of the environmental sources. It represents the use and management of the land and its resources to produce goods and services, and, therefore, includes the relation of the land, its environment and the related actors. Land cover relates to the occupation (vegetation, infrastructure, water, etc.) that covers the land or the soil (Antrop 2007b; Lambin et al. 2006; Geist et al. 2006). The current vegetation cover is an evident indicator for the former land use and is therefore one of the primary palimpsest sources. Both land use and land cover are essential aspects in landscape research (Antrop 2007a). The first is the underlying significance of the interrelation between environment and actor, noticeable through the actor's local management practices, and the second because of its valuable environmental information on the former land use. The one cannot be seen without the other.

Land use and cover analyses are a useful way to discover the strengths and weak-nesses of a landscape, and to give information about the future possibilities and threats (Carvalho-Ribeiro et al. 2013; García-Frapolli et al. 2007). Therefore, land use and cover change studies (LUCC) are interesting for landscape research, intending to construct a sustainable future development, because understanding the landscapes of the past is an important asset for the landscape of the future (Antrop 2005).

The base of a historical approach in landscape research lies in the United Kingdom and Ireland, where both archaeology and history were the focus for landscape research (Crawford 1953: 1951; Hoskins 1955). The approach, and especially the method of multiple sources in a local context, was referred to by other European historical geographers in the mid-twentieth century (e.g. Flatrès 1957; Turner 2013; Braudel 1972). But it was Oliver Rackham who introduced historical ecology into historical geography (Rackham 1986; Grove and Rackham 2003). In Italy, this approach was adapted and transformed by Moreno et al. (1990), who underlined the importance of historical research within the landscape research discourse.

Still today, landscape research in Italy is largely controlled by geomorphology or landscape ecological patterns in explaining landscape structure and planning (Pignatti 1994; Romani 1994; Farina 1998), with a relatively reduced interest in human influence, often resulting in an artificial division between natural features and anthropogenic features of the territory (Agnoletti 2006). Consequently, there is a need to develop specific methodologies to assess human influence, including a historical approach into landscape analysis, a history no more limited to the use of written or printed sources but able to combine different tools and techniques (Agnoletti 2000).

This paper aims to grasp the spatial character of the landscape and how the land abandonment process changed this character through time. It wants to underline the importance of the trinity of trees, arable cultures and grazing land and how and where they were the base of those cultural landscapes that currently are considered as natural landscapes due to the overwhelming impact of the land abandonment. The method draws on several interdisciplinary sources to visualize the evolution of the cultural landscape. The research was illustrated by the story of one particular valley in the North Italian Apennines, Val Borbera. The valley covers a surface of 213,63 km^2 and is situated in the region of Piedmont, province of Alessandria (see Fig. 1).

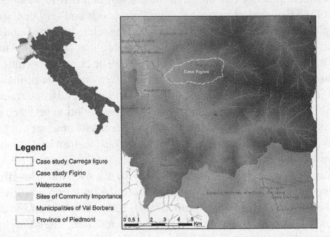

Fig. 1. Localization of the two case studies (Carrega Ligure and Figino) in Val Borbera (Alessandria – Piedmont)

The area is mainly hilly and mountainous (max. 1700 m a.s.l.). With a predominant marly clay/marly calcareous substrate. The mountain belt (1100–1700 m a.s.l.) of the area is covered by herbaceous and shrubby vegetation, covering the geological formation of Monte Antola limestone (Castelli 2001).

The landscape is an example of the rural mountain landscapes and is therefore relevant to explore empirically. Two case studies from Val Borbera were studied and compared. Both cases, Carrega Ligure and Figino (hamlet of municipality Albera Ligure), were chosen based on their geographic situation (respectively higher and lower part of the valley), their accessibility by road, the state of abandonment and the (non)present economic activities. They are representative in terms of both environmental features and socio-economic driving forces within Val Borbera.

2   A Transdisciplinary Methodology: Regressive Spatial Analysis

The method applied in this paper combines the Historic Landscape Characterisation (HLC - Herring 1998; Crow 2009; Turner and Crow 2010) and a Historical-analytical Approach (Cevasco 2002; Moreno 1995). Both ways originate from a historical (archaeological) perspective, study the landscape in a regressive or retrospective way and base themselves on a wide range of sources.

The transdisciplinarity of historical cartography in a GIS environment has been largely studied in international literature (Svenningsen and Linnet Perner 2019; Levin and Svenningsen 2019; Konkoly-Gyurò et al. 2019). It consists on the one hand on the combination of different types of sources (analogue or digital) to get a more holistic understanding of landscape dynamics. On the other hand, the transdisciplinarity lies in the combination of quantitative and qualitative data, in this case study collected through archival documents and field survey. A part from the advantages of HGIS, the approach still has a series of challenges to tackle (Gregory and Ell 2007; Knowles 2005; Grava et al. 2020), such as georeferencing old maps, applying the right projection, dealing with differences in scale and symbolization (Monmonier 2014; Vuorela 2002; Moreno 1999; Cevasco 2002; Gabrielli 2002; Keates 1996). As Eriksson (2010) states, the challenge lies in handling inconsistencies between historical maps without violating the inherent semantic potential. At the end, it is worthwhile to emphasise the need to integrate information extracted from old maps into modern data processing environments and at the same time stress the importance of systematic and well-documented work methods in any such effort (Vuorela 2002).

An important element is the sensitivity of each of the sources (Knowles 2005). The interpretation of maps and aerial images is challenging because of several aspects, even when using modern technological tools. Understanding the origin and a critical assessment of each data source (period, producer, mapping methods, users, goals) is therefore essential (Vuorela 2002; Petit and Lambin 2002; Cevasco 2002; Gabrielli 2002; Gambi 1970; Svenningsen 2015). A critical analysis of the metadata and selection of the sources is thus necessary.

This study focuses on a local scale with the aim to enlarge the temporal scale which is necessary to come to a better and holistic view of the individual and collective landscape dynamics. The cases were deliberately located in the higher and lower part of the valley to be able to extrapolate the results to the scale of the valley and its landscape dynamics.

The regressive spatial approach in this paper is based on two baselines:

Firstly, the combination of different types of sources (historical/archival documents and texts, historical cartography, land cover and land use analysis, oral history) is relevant for the understanding of the local dynamics, analysed in a very detailed way and within a large time scale. Moreover, every individual time layer was the result of a combination of different data of that specific historic moment. The term 'cartographic filtering' was introduced by Moreno (1995), which contains the collection of a sequence of cartographic and photographic material of different eras, mostly of a specific place or site, that is analysed and compared to each other.

Secondly, fieldwork and the production of field sources, combined with cartographic filtering and other techniques, are used for a realistic decryption of the sources themselves. The regressive history of landscapes requires a specific historical-analytical approach to documentary and archival sources in tandem with evidence derived from in situ field studies (Beltrametti 2013).

The regressive approach enables the observation of discontinuities thereby facilitating a greater understanding of the historical asynchronies and anomalies that can appear in sedimentary evidence, therefore avoiding simplistic generalisations concerning system disturbances (Cevasco et al. 2015).

2.1 Data Sampling

Used Sources and Their Characteristics

Different types of spatial data sources were used for the regressive analysis, covering a time period of over 200 years, based on historical maps (1828, 1852), land register maps (1811, 1950) and aerial photographs (1936, 1954, 1981, 2000, 2009–2010, 2014), in combination with the available topographic maps (1877, 1902, 1935, 1937, 1959) (Table 1).

As stated by Cevasco (2002) and Moreno (1990), the 'Minute di Campagna' form an important and exceptional cartographic source to reconstruct the context of the historic agro-silvo-pastoral system of the Apennines. This collection of maps, called tavolette (tables), covers the whole territory of the former Ligurian Republic, and was executed by military topographers on a large scale (from 1/9.450 until 1/20.000). By confronting the symbology with the legend of the second historical collection (the 'Gran Carta degli Stati Sardi di Terraferma', maps Bobbio and Torriglia), it became possible to understand the first map better. Also, the information of the topographical maps of the same time era was of additional importance for the interpretation. All historical maps of 1828 and 1853 were found in the local archive of the Laboratorio di Archeologia e Storia Ambientale (LASA - University of Genova, Department of Antiquity, Philosophy and History) and were integrated in a GIS-environment through georectification.

Both the Napoleonic (1811) and the modern land registers (1950) of Carrega Ligure and Figino were obtained in the corresponding municipalities. Land register maps, other than the information of land cover, also represent the socio-political dynamics of the era. The Napoleonic land registers were the first made in the area and were an artificial 'privatisation' of the land. The current land register was used in a vector format. The information of the land registers was collected for some small areas or pilots. Based on this information and in combination with other data, specific land uses could be confirmed or specified, considering a margin of error.

Table 1. Overview of used cartographic and photographic material

Name	Date	Scale	Made by	Carrega Ligure	Figino
Historical maps					
Minute di Campagna, Corpo di Stato Maggiore	1828	1:20.000	Sig. Cap.no Cav.Mariani	X	
- 88 'Porzione di Carrega – Prov. di Novi'		1:20.000	Drawn by Sig. Ing.		X
- 93 'Porzione di Cantalupo – Prov. di Novi'		1:50.000	Brambilla	X	X
- O.14 'Rocchetta' 20					
Gran Carta degli Stati Sardi di Terraferma	1853	1:50.000		X	X
- F62.Bobbio				X	
- F68. Torriglia					
Topographic maps					
F.71 Forotondo III SE F.71 Rocchetta Ligure III SO	1877	1:25.000	IGM		X
F.83 Carrega IV NE	1902	1:25.000	IGM	X	
F.71 Cabella Ligure III SE F.71 Rocchetta Ligure III SO	1935	1:25.000	IGM		X
F.83 Carrega IV NE - della Carta d'Italia – serie M891, edizione 3	1937	1:25.000	IGM	X	
F.71 Cabella Ligure III SE F.71 Rocchetta Ligure III SO	1959	1:25.000	IGM		X
Carta Tecnica Regionale (196050-196060-196090-196100-196110-196140-196150-214020-214030)		1:10.000	Region of Piedmont	X	X
Land registers					
Napoleonic Land Register	1811		Local municipalities	X	X
Recent Land Register	1950 and beyond		Local municipalities	X	X
Physiographic maps					
DEM		5m	Region of Piedmont (ARPA)	X	X
Photographs					
Aerial photographs	1936		IGM	X	
Aerial photographs	1954	1:55.000	IGM	X	X
Aerial photographs	1981	1:30.000	Region of Piedmont	X	X
Aerial photographs	2000		Region of Piedmont	X	X
Orthographic photographs	2009-2011		Region of Piedmont	X	X
Google Earth	2014		Google	X	X

A series of aerial photographs were used from different time eras (1936, 1954, 1981, 2000, 2009–2010, 2014). The black and white aerial photographs of 1954 are considered the oldest images that are visualising the historic rural landscape. The use of colour digital aerial orthophotos of the year 2000 and later allowed us to analyse the present landscape, but their interpretation was accompanied by fieldwork as data validation. The aerial photographs were analysed in combination with the topographical maps of the same period. The reason for using this material was their rich temporal availability and the detailed spatial resolution required on a local scale. The aerial photographs of 1981 and 2000, the orthographic photograph of 2009–2010, and the Digital Elevation Model with a resolution of 5 m. The other aerial photographs and the topographic maps were acquired at the Military Geographical Institute (IGM. All the material was digitalized, georectified when necessary, and integrated in a GIS-environment.

Understanding, Mapping, Landscape Elements Through Field Survey

By including field survey to the data collection, the preliminary results based on the cartographic analysis can be validated, the information of the topographical maps can be checked with the field knowledge of the vegetation cover, and the final hypothesis of the historical land cover can be improved. This method does not only give the possibility to assess the spatial land cover/use dynamics, but can be used to valorise the current vegetation mosaic and the landscape formation.

The field survey was executed through field observation and documentation. In total 21 field visits were done, of which 17 by the author, and 4 in company of one or more external experts and/or local actors. They were organised in different moments of the year to have a better knowledge of and insights into the seasonal changes of the landscape.

The field notes were collected through standardized forms in combination with panoramic or punctual photographs. The first type of photographs was collected to grasp different horizontal views and directed vistas of the landscape, while the latter were taken as illustrations of certain landscape types, for which an individual form was completed. The forms were largely focussing on the description of the individual landscape, the accessibility of the area, the level of abandonment, and contained a more detailed part on geomorphology, openness of the landscape, presence of roads, water, landscape elements, etc.

2.2 Construction of the Database

The GIS-database integrating the spatial and non-spatial data was constructed in three steps:

1. Organising the data sources into time slices
2. Mapping land cover, land use and function, hillslope and field structure
3. Linking additional attributes with information on the presence of terraces, small landscape elements and the state of abandonment, with the individual polygons.

Step 1: Organising the Data Sources into Time Slices

To picture the dynamics of the landscape over 200 years, a longitudinal analysis about five points in time was executed: 2014, 1980, 1936–1954, 1852 and 1828. This regressive analysis gives insights into the trajectory of the different land use categories, i.e., the land use situation between 1828 and 2014. Those time slices are based on the available cartographic, photographic material, and other non-spatial sources.

Step 2: Mapping Land Cover, Land Use and Function, Hillslope and Field Structure

Information about land cover was obtained through visual interpretation of aerial photographs and topographic maps and validated by the field survey. Twelve main land cover categories were defined; seven as vegetation, three as infrastructural and two as hydrographic coverage. For each land cover category, several subcategories were defined (Table 2). The largest mapping units varied between 0,85 m^2 (Carrega) and 1,72 m^2 (Figino).

Table 2. Definition of categories and subcategories during the spatial analysis (source: Castelli et al. 2001)

(SUB)CATEGORIES	Definition
VEGETATION COVERAGE	
WOODLAND	Area dominated by trees
1: Woodland dominated by secondary vegetation	Mixture post-cultural vegetation, shrub and forests of neo-formation (*Geranio nodosi-Laburnetum alpine ass. Nova*)
2: Coppice woodland	Small trees – used in the traditional way for coppice (*Quercus cerris, Fagus sylvatica, ...*)
3: Middle woodland	Middle high trees – dominant tree *Quercus cerris*
4: High woodland	High trees – dominant tree *Fagus sylvatica* (*Trochiscantho-Fagetum, sorbetosum aucupariae Gentile 1974*)
5: Pine woodland	High trees – dominant tree *Pinus nigra*
PLANTATIONS	Area dominated by active fruit plantation
1: Chestnut	For chestnut production
2: Hazelnut	For hazelnut production
3: Fruit trees	For fruit production
GRASSLAND	Polygon dominated by grassland (rich & poor)
1: Grassland on higher altitude	Positioned on higher altitudes (> 1300 masl) (*Festuco gracilioris-Brometum erecti ass. Nova, arnicetosum montanae subass. Nova, aggruppamento a Nardusstricta L., Vaccinio-Hypericetum richeri, Pirola e Corbetta 1971*)
2: Grassland on lower altitude	Positioned on lower altitudes (< 1300 masl)
SHRUBLAND	Polygon dominated by a non-fertile land and covered by mixture of grasses and shrubs with stones.
1: Rough land	Land dominated by rocks, stones, and some shrubs (*Festuco gracilioris-Brometum erecti ass. Nova variante a Sesleria cylindrical (Babis) DC; Poo badensis – Sedetum monregalensis ass. Nova*)
2: Bushland	Land dominated by remnant vegetation or is disturbed but still retains a predominance of the original floristics and structure (Draper & Richards, 2009) (*Arabido brassicae-Genistetum radiatae ass.nova*)
NON-COVERED	Polygon dominated by sand, clay, rocks
1: Non-covered substrate	Area dominated by clay, sand, rock
CULTIVATED LAND	Polygon dominated by land that is being cultivated and elaborated
1: Horticulture land	For private production e.s. vegetable garden
2: Arable land	For agricultural production (wheat, corn, ...)
3: Vineyard	For wine production
4: Beans	For bean production (fagioli)
OTHER COVERAGES	Areas dominated with other coverage
1: Recreation area	Areas with predominant function for recreation (soccer, tennis, playground ...)
2: Cemetery	For cemeteries that are separate to churchyards and including associated buildings and car parks.
3: Agritourism	For agritourisms and attached car parks
INFRASTRUCTURAL COVERAGE	
HOUSING	Polygon dominated by buildings for residential use
1: Medieval housing	Housing that has medieval roots
2: Modern housing	Modern housing
3: Ruins	Ancient housing that was destroyed
HISTORIC BUILDING	Polygon dominated by buildings with historic roots
1: Castle	Castles and associated yards
2: Church	Churches and associated churchyards, car parks and grounds
INDUSTRIAL INFRASTRUCTURE	Area dominated by productive infrastructure
1: Mill	Water mills and associated yards
2: Stable	Stand-alone stables with associated yards
3: Hydro-electric installation	Energy supplying installation with associated yards
HYDROGRAPHIC COVERAGE	
WATER SURFACE	Polygon dominated by stable water, either natural or artificial
1: Pool	Still standing water with a diameter larger than 10m wide
2: Source	
WATER COURSE	Polygon dominated by a flow water, either natural or artificial
1: River	Waterways larger than 3m wide

One shape file was set up, with the information of all 5 time slices. Every time slice (2014, 1980, 1954/1936, 1852, 1828), every polygon was interpreted and given a code for a corresponding category and subcategory. Furthermore, every (sub)category was described through a series of additional attributes (Table 3) (Vink 1980; Van Eetvelde 2007).

According to Vink (1980) and Van Eetvelde (2007), different types of attributes can be outlined. The first type of attributes determines the delineation of the polygons and are therefore called differentiating attributes (Table 3). They have a major contribution on the composition of the landscape and consist of relevant information to answer the research questions in this largely abandoned area. Land use/function, hillslope and field structure were elected as relevant differentiating attributes.

Step 3: Linking Additional Attributes to the Land Cover Polygons

Next to the differentiating attributes, the descriptive attributes and diagnostic attributes are ascribed to each of the delineated polygon. Those attributes give an extra characterisation of the main (sub)categories and consist out of peculiarities describing every polygon. The choice of those attributes is depending on the research question of the evolution of this largely abandoned landscape. In this case, the presence of terraces, small landscape elements and clearly visible passages are considered descriptive attributes. The state of abandonment represents the events and processes that are relevant for the landscape change and is therefore seen as a diagnostic attribute since it is indicating a specific process of change.

Table 3. Definition of the different types of attributes

ATTRIBUTES	CODES
DIFFERENTIATING	
FUNCTION/USE	0: no function; 1: only grazing; 2: only hay production; 3: only cultivations; 4: only fruit production; 5: only wood production; 6: hay and grazing; 7: wood production and grazing; 8: fruit, grazing and wood production
HILLSLOPE	0: flat (<6%); 1: slightly flat (6-16%); 2: hilly (16-24%); 3: steep (24-33%); 4: very steep (33-63%)
FIELD STRUCTURE	0: no; 1: Strip fields perpendicular to the slope; 2: Strip fields parallel with the slope; 3: Blocky fields
DESCRIPTIVE	
PRESENCE OF TERRACES	0: no terraces; 1: earth terraces with small pendance; 2: terraces made by stone walls (stairs) 3: mixed terraces
SMALL LANDSCAPE ELEMENTS	0: no; 1: hedgerows; 2: treelines
CLEARLY VISIBLE PASSAGES	0: no passages; 1: less visible passages; 2: clearly visible passages
DIAGNOSTIC	
STATE OF ABANDONMENT	0: not abandoned, intensive use of the land; 1: medium abandoned, extensive use of the land; 2: completely abandoned, no activity is going on

3   Results

3.1   Five Main Landscape Trends

The landscape character of the two individual case studies is analysed for the last 200 years in a very detailed way. All the (sub)categories are explored in relation to their attributes and their surface in every time period. The results of the analysis on the evolution of the landscape of each case study is exposed based on 5 main landscape trends: the exponential growth of woodland, the decrease of plantations, the decrease and later increase of grasslands, the increase and later decrease of shrubland, and the disappearance of cultivation. Table 4 and Figs. 2 and 3 illustrate the results.

Table 4. Evolution of land cover (%) of Carrega Ligure and Figino (1828–2014)

(Sub)categories of Land Cover	1828		1852		1936		1980		2014	
	Carrega Ligure	Figino	Carrega Ligure	Figino	Carrega Ligure	Figino	Carrega Ligure	Figino	Carrega Ligure	Figino
WOODLAND	27,16	12,06	30,90	11,85	30,67	14,35	50,58	55,00	61,64	66,80
Secondary vegetation	2,06	0,22	5,22	0,68	6,61	2,84	12,03	4,48	20,14	12,21
Coppice woodland	12,04	11,27	4,86	10,74	9,77	11,06	3,05	0,00	5,71	0,00
Middle woodland	6,17	0,56	4,68	0,43	6,16	0,43	21,44	48,26	23,09	46,23
High woodland (fagus)	6,90	0,00	16,13	0,00	8,13	0,02	11,65	0,00	13,10	0,00
Pine woodland	0,00	0,00	0,00	0,00	0,00	0,00	2,41	2,26	2,57	8,36
PLANTATION	3,97	22,70	5,40	18,00	5,58	26,36	2,87	0,14	0,00	0,12
Chestnut plantations	3,97	22,70	5,40	18,00	5,58	26,36	2,87	0,00	0,00	0,00
Fruit plantations	0,00	0,00	0,00	0,00	0,00	0,00	0,00	0,14	0,00	0,12
GRASSLAND	15,10	10,61	11,46	0,00	12,57	9,17	10,31	22,62	17,48	19,11
Grasslands on high altitudes	15,10	10,61	11,46	0,00	12,51	0,01	10,16	0,00	8,94	0,00
Grasslands on low altitudes	0,00	0,00	0,00	0,00	0,05	9,16	0,15	22,62	8,53	19,11
SHRUBLAND	19,22	11,21	20,16	26,81	25,25	19,20	17,06	9,02	14,00	5,57
Rough land	8,45	11,21	14,96	26,81	21,59	18,05	6,19	7,36	6,00	5,57
Bushland	10,77	0,00	5,20	0,00	3,66	1,15	10,87	1,65	8,00	0,00
NON COVERED	0,28	0,00	0,43	0,00	1,13	0,00	0,68	0,00	0,93	0,02
Non covered substrate	0,28	0,00	0,43	0,00	1,13	0,00	0,68	0,00	0,93	0,02
CULTIVATED LAND	31,61	38,42	28,98	38,32	22,08	25,98	15,71	8,22	0,05	2,96
Horticulture	0,00	0,00	0,05	0,00	0,05	0,29	0,05	0,41	0,05	0,62
Arable land	31,61	12,07	28,93	8,36	22,03	22,14	15,66	6,47	0,00	1,39
Vineyard	0,00	26,32	0,00	29,96	0,00	1,33	0,00	0,69	0,00	0,80
Beans	0,00	0,02	0,00	0,00	0,00	2,22	0,00	0,66	0,00	0,14

An Exponential Growth of Woodland

Figure 2 and Table 4 show that different types of woodland, considering secondary vegetation (Carrega 20,14%; Figino 12,21%), coppice woodland (Carrega 5,71%), middle woodland (Carrega 23,09%; Figino 46,23%), high woodland (Carrega 13,10%) and pine woodland (Carrega 2,57%; Figino 8,36%), take a large part of the current landscape, while the same land covers take only 27,16% of the surface in 1828 in Carrega, and 12,06% in Figino. This large increase of woodland during the last 200 years, but mostly from the second half of the 20th century onwards, is mostly due to the increase of secondary vegetation (Carrega 2,06%; Figino 0,22% in 1828) and middle woodland (Carrega 6,17%; Figino 0,56% in 1828) and the introduction of the pine woodlands in the area. Over time, the amount of middle woodland increased, mainly because of the abandoned coppice woodland that transformed more and more into middle woodlands, even if there are still traces of the coppice management. The middle woodland is the only type of woodland that primarily declined, and even disappeared. Even though the woodland itself did not disappear, the rural technique of coppice management was not practised anymore. The general increase of woodland is in relation with the decrease of other land covers as grasslands, shrubland and cultivated land.

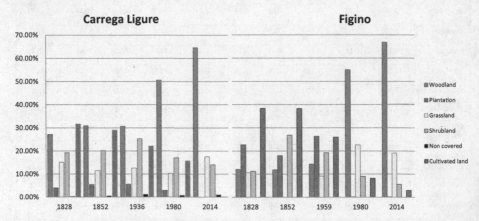

Fig. 2. Evolution of land cover of Carrega Ligure and Figino

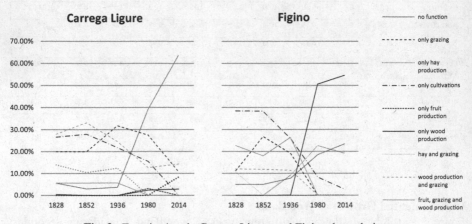

Fig. 3. Function/use in Carrega Ligure and Figino through time

The different types of woodland cover were clearly recognized for the first time on the aerial photographs of 1936 for Carrega and 1959 for Figino. The coppice woodland

(Carrega 12,04%; Figino 11,27%) and the high (coppice) woodland in Carrega (13,10%) took the largest amount of the wooded cover. Even considering the smaller details of the historical maps, we can see a higher coverage of high woodland in the 19th century than at the beginning of the 20th century. Especially in Carrega, a decrease of both coppice and high woodland is noticeable during and after the first World War (1915–1918 in Italy). This evaluation corresponds with the beginning of the industrialisation and modernisation, the First World War and the large amount of organic fuel (wood) needed for the machinery (Leardi 1997). 1936 was probably the most nude period for the forest coverage. After the cutting phase, the proportion of coppices continued decreasing, while the secondary vegetation and middle woodland started invading the area. These transformations are interrelated. The coppiced woodland is a type of woodland that needs a continuous maintenance and was historically included in the rural practices of the area. When the large abandonment started and the area depopulated, the maintenance of the coppiced woodland got into decline. This caused an easy and fast invasion of secondary and invading species, which transformed the areas into middle-high woodland. The expansion of the high woodland in the second half of the 20th century is also related to the decrease of livestock during the same time period (Leardi 1997).

Decrease of Plantations

Also, the plantations were covered by secondary vegetation and transformed into middle woodland. The chestnut plants were historically maintained intensively, like any other part of the rural landscape, but got abandoned mainly between 1936 and 1980 in Carrega and from 1959 in Figino. Similar to the coppices, the plantations became invaded by other species. They were abandoned in a later phase than the coppices since the chestnut plants were producing fruit, which was a rural practice that survived slightly longer. In Carrega, the former chestnut plantations remained categorised as coppice, since the difference with the other coppice woodland that transformed into middle woodland is large. The number of chestnut plantations was much larger in Figino and they all changed relatively homogeneously into middle woodland through time.

Decrease and Increase of Grasslands

In Carrega the number of grasslands remained stable through time (around 15%), but when focussing on the types of grasslands, a landscape transformation is clearly visible. Until 1980, only grasslands located above 1200 m.a.s.l., like the historic permanent grasslands around Monte Carmo, were present. From the second half of the 20th century onwards, a shift in types of grasslands can be noticed. In 2014, the total amount of grasslands is equally divided by grasslands on lower and higher altitudes. This means that the permanent upper hill grasslands decreased through time to 8%. The highest amount of these grasslands was detected in 1936, corresponding with the deforestation phase of the high woodland, and in 1828, but this interpretation is maybe due to a smaller precision of the historic maps. Similar to the land abandonment, and notably present notable 1980 onwards, the historical permanent meadows changed slowly into simple grazing fields. The intensive land use became more extensive.

The small number of grasslands on higher altitudes in Figino completely disappeared in 1852. Grasslands were mapped on the 1828 historical map, but probably it contained a poorly type of shrubland were cattle was brought for grazing. The 'new' grasslands, like in the case for Figino, have increased largely. They are positioned on the former cultivated land, but are slightly in decrease (Fig. 4).

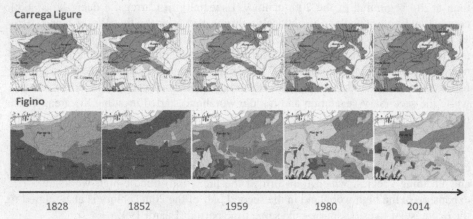

Fig. 4. Exponential growth of woodland in Carrega and disappearance of cultivations in Figino

Increase and Decrease of Shrubland

The shrublands were also largely invaded by secondary vegetation. In both cases the rough land was historically positioned on the less fertile grounds on the southern and steepest slopes, containing stones and rocks, and little shrubs. This less suitable land was historically used for grazing but were the first to be abandoned. From 1980 onwards, the large-scale land abandonment caused a decline in cattle and therefore affected also the rough land, which made them shift to bushland (where rough land was still recognisable) or secondary vegetation woodland. Another large part of the shrubland disappeared with the plantation of the pine woodlands (see before) or the invasion of secondary vegetation. The peak of rough land in 1936 (Carrega) and 1852 (Figino) results from of the wood-cutting policy as explained before, and before the invasion of secondary vegetation.

Disappearance of Cultivations

The secondary vegetation started invading mostly the cultivated land. They probably initiated from hedgerows, treelines, solitary trees or small bushes that were historically installed in the area to delimit the parcels. Especially in Carrega, the massive (large quantities) and fast (short time) abandonment of the cultivated land made it easy for the invasive species to cover over 14% more of the territory than in 1936. The cultivations were located on the strip fields parallel to the slope around the village (infield).

The decline of the arable land is visible in both cases, from 20 to 30% until non-existing in 200 years. As explained before, the arable land changed mostly to grasslands and shifted from an intensive use, e.g. cultivations, to an extensive one, e.g. hay production. Those fields are not completely abandoned, but changed dominantly from an intensive to an extensive use.

In both Figino and Carrega, some private vegetable gardens are still present. The inhabitants garden in the surroundings of their houses and need to fence their land because of the large presence of wild boars and deer who destroy their production.

Figino historically was covered less by arable land but had a large number of vineyards. This decline in land cover was a consequence of the price decline and an increase of diseases for the vineyards. People had difficulties to live from viticulture and most of them kept some vineyards for private use, but dropped the large production. A small increase (0,69% to 0,80%) is noticeable in Figino, related with the recovery of old and plantation of new vineyards by a new local farming family.

3.2 Leading to Three Main Landscape Transformations

From Heterogeneous to Homogeneous

The decline in land management had a substantial impact on the landscape. The abandoned cultivated areas were susceptible to the expansion of secondary vegetation starting from existing treelines and hedgerow. The reduction of goat and bovine population and the increasingly extensive pastoral resource management allowed the spread of shrubs and recolonisation on grasslands and rough lands. The lack of maintenance of the historical coppices changed them easily into mixed, impenetrable middle woodlands. Apart from the invasion of the woodland, grasslands are noticeable in the valley, including both grasslands on higher and lower altitudes. While the first is still used for extensive grazing, the latter is used for hay production. The vegetation dynamics are thus producing a more homogeneous environment in which the forest is closing up, except for the remaining or transformed grasslands.

The disappearance of various land covers through time and the dominance of just one, namely woodland, leading to a first conclusion, namely the homogenisation of the rural mountain areas. However, this homogenisation is not only a process that is present in relation to abandonment. It also is a result of industrialisation of areas, of modernisation processes and of mono-cultures. Therefore, this process is an outcome of the world we currently live in, a world in which one activity and purpose of landscapes is concentrated mainly in one location, in contrast with the past when several activities were executed in the same landscape and when the landscape was considered multifunctional. The cultural landscapes of the Mediterranean were characterised by landscapes with a large variety in land cover. Today, those diverse landscapes are largely transformed into homogeneous landscapes, but the landscape of the past still has its remains.

From Multiple so Single-Use

The agro-silvo-pastoral landscape of the Val Borbera had historically a lot of different functions and uses on the same land cover. The high population pressure and the need for subsistence caused a diversified use of nearly the entire landscape. The multifunctionality of the landscape is characterized by farming activities on the one hand and forestry on the other hand, both being executed on the same place. The historical rural system was based on five different functions: grazing of the cattle; production of hay; cultivations of wheat, potatoes, vegetables and corn; fruit production like chestnuts, hazelnuts, peaches, etc. and wood production. The land cover provided all of these functions, as single or multiple uses.

Until 1936–1959, 40 to 50% of the landscape was occupied by a multiple (grazing in combination with hay production, wood production and/or fruit production) use. The grazing activities were mostly present over the whole territory, using woodland, shrubland, grassland and even plantations, and always combined with another function. The arable land was only reserved for cultivations. The wood production in combination with grazing, together with the cultivations (both almost 30%) were historically the most important functions of Carrega, and this situation remained until the beginning of the 20th century. Figino was characterised mainly by cultivations as wine and beans as well as fruit and wood production in the chestnut plantations. The grazing activities took place on the shrubland and everywhere else in the landscape, but no specific pastures were present. Until the beginning of the 1900s, the single grazing activity increased in both cases, together with the combination of hay production in Figino, while the other multiple functions start to decline. This assures the concentration of the rural system on animal husbandry, more than combining different activities for survival, as was the case in the 19th century.

The multifunctionality of the territory starts to fall apart from the second half of the 20th century onwards. Certain, mostly multiple functions completely disappeared (hay and grazing, fruit-grazing-wood production, cultivation, fruit production) and especially single functions as hay production, grazing and wood production remain. With this change, the multiple uses of hay production on the higher pastureland changed into a monofunctional use. This simplification process of the land use is firstly noted in the outfield and moves later on to the higher positioned meadows, which are still in use. They are used for grazing on the uphill pastureland in combination with wood production in the high beech woodland. An important aspect is the decline of all functions and the transformation of more than 60% in 2014 without any productive function. This trend started from the second half of the 20th century and continues exponentially until now.

From Intensification to Extensification

Historically, the multiple land use system of the Apennine valley required an intensive maintenance of the land, with functions as cultivations, fruit, hay and wood production. The multiple activities of the land created an intensively elaborated rural area, concentrated the variation of animal husbandry, cultivations, etc., which obtained 70 to 80% of the case study of Carrega. At the same time, about 20% of the area was used in extensively, referring to the single grazing areas.

The extensification process is primarily geographically related. In Carrega, the trend started first in 'lower' areas, close to the river, and after it shifted uphill towards the east. There was first an extensification of the middle and coppice woodland and later of the meadows uphill. In Figino, the shrublands used for grazing on the southern slope became used extensively and remained as such through time. The former chestnut plantations followed and finally the cultivations became also largely completely abandoned.

Apart from the link with the land use, this extensification shift is also related to the hillslope of the area. The very steep areas are the first to be extensified and later abandoned. Also, the field structure is a representation of the extensification. The landscape of today is not a representation of the land register. While the latter contains a large variety of very small parcels, the landscape of today seems quite homogeneous and field boundaries are difficult to recognize since a lot of them disappeared. Several fields have been merged and are collectively in common property. Especially the formerly cultivated land, which is now largely used as grassland for hay production, is used by a small number of farmers who use several parcels together. This is easy for the machinery and thus small landscape elements like hedgerows disappeared. The other land use where field boundaries are not necessary are the higher positioned pasture lands since the grazing function is managed in common. The pasture land of Carrega is although separated by a fence from the one of Connio. When parcels are not merged, they have a larger probability to be abandoned, or they are used for cultivation purposes like a private vegetable garden, a fruit plantation or a vineyard.

The conclusion is that there is a large ambiguity of the field structure in the land registers in comparison with the visual landscape and how the fields are actually used. This large division of parcels can create problems for the future development of the rural area. The low economic value of the agricultural land, the private ownership, the large number of owners for just one parcel, the difficulty to trace them back and the lack of interest in land management by those owners are all aspects that create difficulties in the current and future sustainable management of the landscape. Newcomers, new initiatives, future projects encounter problems when looking for land or even housing in the largely abandoned areas.

4 Conclusion

The historical agro-silvo-pastoral system had a large impact on the construction of the cultural landscape for centuries, with the coppice woodlands and chestnut plantations, the large meadows alternated by coppice beech woodland on mountain tops and higher slopes, cultivations on less steep and fertile slopes and shrublands on steep and southern oriented ones. The results of the analysis of the spatial character showed that the landscape of Val Borbera remained relatively stable from the end of the 19th century until the first half of the 20th century. But with from the second half of the 20th century, the spatio-temporal changes undertook a large turning point; modernisation, industrialisation and consequential rural depopulation led to a progressive abandonment of this mountain landscape with a more complex and intense land cover. The typically rural area underwent a spatial transformation of increasing woodland and secondary vegetation and decreasing coppices, plantations and cultivated land. Fallow land or shrubland and the spread of forests are a direct consequence of the end of the traditional agro-silvo-pastoral system. The speed of landscape transformations is clearly shown by diachronic analysis of photographic archives.

The spatial transformations detected in the two case studies of the Val Borbera, can be led to three main trends: From a heterogeneous to a homogeneous landscape; From multiple to a single-use; From intensification to extensification.

The spatial analysis and the detection of the spatial landscape character can help us value the historic landscape on a broader scale. Appreciating the landscape's temporal aspect can assist local authorities and others to set priorities for management and planning for the future (Fairclough and Grau Moller 2008; Crow and Turner 2009). Thus, proposed changes which reinforce the coherence of the historic gain might be encouraged; those that would disrupt or destroy it might be altered or prevented. The results reveal that this landscape is not uniform but has a complex history that demands to be understood and appreciated. It shows clearly that field systems of diverse types are largely correlated with the land use, the positioning of the village, and the infield-outfield system.

References

Agnoletti, M.: Introduction: factors and process in the history of forest research. In: Forest History: International Studies on Socioeconomic and Forest Ecosystem Change, pp. 1–19. CAB International, Wallingford and New York (2000)

Agnoletti, M.: The development of a historical and cultural evaluation. Approach in landscape assessment: the dynamic of Tuscan landscape between 1832 and 2004. In: Agnoletti, M. (ed.) 2006 The Conservation of Cultural Landscapes, CABI, p. 3 (2006)

Antrop, M.: Why landscapes of the past are important for the future. Landsc. Urban Plan. **70**(1–2), 21–34 (2005)

Antrop, M.: Perspectieven op het landschap: achtergronden om landschappen te lezen en te begrijpen. Academia Press (2007a)

Antrop, M.: The preoccupation of landscape research with land use and land cover. In: Key Topics in Landscape Ecology, pp. 173–191. Cambridge University Press. Cambridge (2007b)

Beltrametti, G.: Un esercizio di storia territoriale: fonti e temi in una controversia sui diritti collettivi in Alta Valle Trebbia (XIX sec). In: Cevasco, R. (ed.) La natura della montagna, vol. 1, pp. 172–188 (2013)

Braudel, F.: The Mediterranean and the Mediterranean World in the Age of Philip II. Collins (1972)

Carvalho Ribeiro, S., Loupa Ramos, I., Madeira, L., Barroso, F., Menezes, H., Pinto Correia, T.: Is land cover an important asset for addressing the subjective landscape dimensions? Land Use Policy **35**, 50–60 (2013)

Castelli, M., Biondi, E., Ballelli, S.: La vegetazione erbacea, arbustiva e preforestale del piano montano dell'Appennino piemontese (Valli Borbera e Curone – Italia). Fitosociologia **38**(1), 125–151 (2001)

Cevasco, R.: La copertura vegetale dell'Alta Val Trebbia nelle ricognizioni topografiche del Corpo di Stato Maggiore Sardo (1816–1852): Approccio storico all'ecologia dei siti. Archeologia Postmedievale **6**(6), 195–214 (2002)

Cevasco, R., Moreno, D.: Microanalisi geo-storica o geografia culturale della copertura vegetale?: sull'eredità ambientale dei paesaggi culturali. In: Trame nello spazio, pp. 83–112 (2007)

Cevasco, R., Moreno, D., Hearn, R.: Biodiversification as an historical process: an appeal for the application of historical ecology to bio-cultural diversity research. Biodivers. Conserv. **24**(13), 3167–3183 (2015)

Crawford, O.G.S.: Archaeology in the Field. Praeger (1953)

Crow, J., Turner, S.: Silivri and the Thracian hinterland of Istanbul: an historic landscape. Anatol. Stud. **59**, 167–181 (2009)

Fairclough, G., Grau Moller, P.: The management and protection of landscape in Europe, a summary by the action COST A27 LANDMARKS. In: Landscape as Heritage, p. 79. Geographica Bernensia, Berne (2008)

Farina, A.: Introduction to landscape ecology. In: Farina, A. (ed.) Principles and Methods in Landscape Ecology, pp. 1–21. Springer, Dordrecht (1998). https://doi.org/10.1007/978-94-015-8984-0_1

Flatrès, P.: Géographie rurale de quatre contrées celtiques. Irlande, Galles, Cornwall & Man. Librairie Universitaire J. Plihon (1957)

Gabrielli, E.: Saggio di confronto cartografico per l'esame delle variazioni storiche della copertura vegetale in Alta Val Trebbia (1973–1995). Archeologia Postmedievale 6(6), 133–143 (2002)

Gambi, L.: Cartografia storica, in AAVV., La storiografia italiana negli ultimi vent'anni, Marzorati, Milano, pp. 1361–1378 (1970)

García-Frapolli, E., Ayala-Orozco, B., Bonilla-Moheno, M., Espadas-Manrique, C., Ramos-Fernández, G.: Biodiversity conservation, traditional agriculture and ecotourism: land cover/land use change projections for a natural protected area in the northeastern Yucatan Peninsula, Mexico. Landscape Urban Plann. 83(2), 137–153 (2007)

Geist, H., McConnell, W., Lambin, E.F., Moran, E., Alves, D., Rudel, T.: Causes and trajectories of land-use/cover change. In: Lambin, E.F., Geist, H. (eds.) Land-Use and Land-Cover Change, pp. 41–70. Springer, Heidelberg (2006). https://doi.org/10.1007/3-540-32202-7_3

Grava, M., Berti, C., Gabellieri, N., Gallia, A.: Historical GIS. Strumenti digitali per la geografia storica in Italia (2020)

Gregory, I.N., Ell, P.S.: Historical GIS: Technologies, Methodologies, and Scholarship, vol. 39. Cambridge University Press (2007)

Grove, A.T., Rackham, O.: The Nature of Mediterranean Europe: An Ecological History. Yale University Press, Ehrhardt (2003)

Herring, P.C.: Cornwall's Historic Landscape: presenting a method of historic landscape character assessment. Cornwall Archaeological Unit, Cornwall County Council (1998)

Hoskins, W.G.: The Making of the English Landscape. Hodder and Stoughton, London (1955)

Joffre, R., Hubert, B., Meuret, M.: Les systemes agro-sylvo-pastoraux mediterraneens: enjeux et reflexions pour une gestion raisonnee. Dossier MAB (UNESCO), no. 10 (1991)

Joffre, R.: The Dehesa: does this complex ecological system have a future? In: Teller, A., Mathy, P., Jeffers, J.N.R. (eds.) Responses of Forest Ecosystems to Environmental Changes, pp. 381–388. Springer Netherlands, Dordrecht (1992). https://doi.org/10.1007/978-94-011-2866-7_35

Knowles, A.K.: Emerging trends in historical GIS. Hist. Geogr. 33, 7–13 (2005)

Konkoly-Gyuró, É., Balázs, P., Tirászi, A.: Transdisciplinary approach of transboundary landscape studies: a case study of an Austro-Hungarian transboundary landscape. Geografisk Tidsskrift-Dan. J. Geogr. 119(1), 52–68 (2019)

Lambin, E.F., Geist, H., Rindfuss, R.R.: Introduction: local processes with global impacts. In: Lambin, E.F., Geist, H. (eds.) Land-Use and Land-Cover Change, pp. 1–8. Springer, Heidelberg (2006). https://doi.org/10.1007/3-540-32202-7_1

Leardi, E.: Il Novese. Segni e radici di un'identità Stamperia Editrice Brigati Glauco, 310 p. (1997)

Levin, G., Svenningsen, S.R.: Digital transdisciplinarity in land change science – integrating multiple types of digital data. Geografisk Tidsskrift-Dan. J. Geogr. 119(1), 1–5 (2019)

Le Coz, J.: Espaces mediterraneens et dynamiques agraires: etat territorial et communautes Rurales (1990)

Moreno, D.: Dal documento al terreno. Storia e archeologia dei sistemi agro-silvo-pastorali. Il Mulino-Ricerche, Bologna (1990)

Moreno, D.: Une source pour l'histoire et l'archeologie des ressources végétales. Les cartes topographiques de la montagne ligure (Italie). In: BOUSQUET-BRESSOLIER, C. L'oeil du cartographe et la répresentation géographique du moyen âge à nos jours. Actes du colloque européen sur la cartographie topographique tenu a Paris les, vol. 29 (1995)

Petit, C.C., Lambin, E.F.: Impact of data integration technique on historical land-use/land-cover change: comparing historical maps with remote sensing data in the Belgian Ardennes. Landscape Ecol. 17(2), 117–132 (2002)

Pignatti, S.: Ecologia del Paesaggio. Unione Tipografica Editrice Torinese (UTET) (1994)

Pinto-Correia, T.: Land abandonment: changes in the land use patterns around the Mediterranean basin. Cahiers Options Méditerranéennes 1(2), 97–112 (1993)

Rackham, O.: The History of the Countryside. M. Dent and Sons, London (1986)

Romani, V.: Il paesaggio: teoria e pianificazione. Milano, Franco Angeli (1994)

Svenningsen, S.: Historical cartography and aerial photographs in geography and landscape research. Ph.D. thesis, Roskilde University, Denmark (2015)

Svenningsen, S., Perner, M.P.: The potential of a digital, transdisciplinary approach to landscape change and urbanization around Copenhagen in the 20th century. Geografisk Tidsskrift-Dan. J. Geogr. 119(1), 30–37 (2019)

Turner, S., Crow, J.: Unlocking historic landscapes in the Eastern Mediterranean: two pilot studies using Historic Landscape Characterisation. Antiquity 84(323), 216–229 (2010)

Turner, S.: Landscape archaeology. In: Howard, P., Thompson, I., Waterton, E. (eds.) The Routledge Companion to Landscape Studies, pp. 131–142. Routledge, London (2013)

Van Eetvelde, V.: Van geografische strekenkaart tot landschapsdatabank. Gebruik van GIS, informatietheorie en landschapsmetrieken voor het karakteriseren van landschappen, toegepast op België. Ph.D. thesis Geography, UGent, Belgium (2007)

Vink, A.P.A.: Landschapsecologie en landgebruik. Bohn, Scheltema & Holkema (1980)

Vos, W., Meekes, H.: Trends in European cultural landscape development: perspectives for a sustainable future. Landsc. Urban Plan. 46(1), 3–14 (1999)

Vos, W., Stortelder, A.: Vanishing Tuscon landscapes: landscape ecology of a submediterranean-montane area (Solano'Basin, Tuscany, Italy). Pudoc (1992)

Vuorela, N., Alho, P., Kalliola, R.: Systematic assessment of maps as source information in landscape-change research. Landsc. Res. 27(2), 141–166 (2002)

From Remote Sensing to Decision Support System for Industrial Quarry Basins

Cinzia Licciardello[✉], Antonio Di Marco[✉], Stefania Biagini[✉], Khalil Tayeh[✉], and Diego Palazzuoli[✉]

ARPAT, via Nicola Porpora 22, 50144 Firenze, Italy
{c.licciardello,a.dimarco,s.biagini,k.tayeh,
d.palazzuoli}@arpat.toscana.it

Abstract. Remote Sensing data and techniques play a great role in quarry and mining activity monitoring: UAVs, aerials and terrestrials LiDAR and optical sensors are widely used in quarry management in evaluating extraction phases and compliancy to working stages. Environmental management of large quarry areas requires not only precise 3D data to assess yearly volume changes, but also availability of datasets useful in monitoring compliancy to natural soil consumption previsions and water/extraction waste management rules issued by public authorities.

Integration of both remotely sensed and environmental information systems' data is required to define waste production indicators related to extraction activities. A novel set of indicators over Carrara extractive basin has been proposed by integrating surface and volume changes over the years with production and waste management data: the proposed indicators have been evaluated over all active quarry located in Carrara extraction basin.

The indicators, integrated in a Decision Support System (DSS), can be used to classify all quarries by environmental management performances' scores, thus allowing planning of in-situ controls related to water and marble quarry/cutting waste (MQW/MCW) management according to risk management quantitative criteria.

Prototyping time-varying data on dynamic maps and 3D navigation interfaces have been proposed to support environmental controls' planners in yearly extraction waste production and land cover changes monitoring.

1 Introduction

Quarry and mining industrial activities have been identified as a major source of environment and natural resources loss and degradation caused by extraction wastes [1, 2, 12]: Marble Cutting Wastes slurry (MCW, in Italian '*marmettola*') is involved in Apuan Alps' karst water dynamics leading to both groundwaters and surface waters' environmental impacts [12, 14]. Regarding to Marble Quarry Waste (MQW), centuries of intense extraction activity in the Carrara industrial basin led to massive landscape changes and permanent in-situ debris disposals' growth over extensive areas (see Fig. 1). Nowadays only few of them are allowed to receive, for a limited time, additional debris volumes,

© Springer Nature Switzerland AG 2022
E. Borgogno-Mondino and P. Zamperlin (Eds.): ASITA 2021, CCIS 1507, pp. 385–404, 2022.
https://doi.org/10.1007/978-3-030-94426-1_28

while their permanent in-situ disposal is regarded as unauthorized waste deposit and therefore forbidden by both regional and national regulations. Indeed, surface and volume changes' tracking play a relevant role in assessing current activity state of MCW in-situ disposals.

Sustainable use of marble resources requires both (a) limitation of MCW and MQW production by properly identifying promising extractive areas and proper planning of marble cuts [10], and (b) proper management of MCW and MQW in producing new building material, included the exploitation of historical in-situ MCW/MQW disposals [10, 13].

Regional laws require that quarry owners must issue yearly report of ornamental stones, other sub-products and MCW/MQW production rates to both local and public bodies involved in activities authorization processes. In addition, according to national laws MCW and MQW yearly reports (Environmental Reporting Model, i.e., 'MUD' report) must to be issued by owners to regional and national authorities charged by general waste managements' controls: these data stored in the ARPAT Regional Environmental Information System (SIRA).

Environmental controls in quarry areas issued by ARPAT are primarily focused on both assessing proper water cycle and waste management according to both national and regional regulations; such controls require both careful planning and rapid response capabilities in some limited cases. Tracking MCW/MQW volumes' *in-situ* disposals for Carrara basin's quarries over the years would be a valuable additional resource, allowing – if combined with existing data sources available in the Regional Environmental system – to both prioritize environmental controls basing on waste management performances and to monitor sustainable waste management's goals achievement.

A regional project issued in 2016 involved the Regional Environmental Agency of Tuscany (ARPAT) in developing new waste monitoring methodologies basing on recent remote sensing advances: a number of remote sensing methods have been used for deriving areal and volume datasets, which have been then used to calculate a set of experimental indicators related to potential MQW/MCW impact over the whole industrial Carrara basin. These indicators have been integrated in a prototyping Decision Support System (DSS) to allow *in-situ* controls' planners to decide appropriate time intervals between each control.

Many environmental impact and state/response indicators have been studied for high-level plans monitoring; while impact indicators are primarily based on Life-Cycle Assessment (LCA) method applied to buildings materials [15, 20], the influence of best industrial practices adoption [20] or other hybrid approaches [16], state/response indicators are primarily targeted to assess natural habitat restoration [11]. While these indicators are more suitable to regional plan monitoring, indicators proposed in this work are targeted to local monitoring of single quarries.

The multidimensionality nature of the proposed indicators, varying in time and space, requires additional work to ease indicators usage by decision makers. Therefore, development of proper user interfaces based on dynamic web maps with time-dependent data and 3D representations highlighting critical areas play an important role in environmental controls' planning.

2   Study Area

Carrara industrial basin, located about 1.5km from Carrara city center, is centered on the geographic coordinates (WGS84) 44°05′53.412″and 10°07′44.922″ (Fig. 1); the basin covers an approximate surface of 1076 ha and hosts dozens of inactive quarries, while 104 are still active. The whole area is historically divided in the four main basins of Miseglia (south area), Torano (west area), Fantiscritti (central area) and Colonnata (east area).

Starting from pre-roman times marble extraction have played a key role in local economy. Quarry dimensions and extraction capabilities have increased over the years, due to the introduction of new extraction technologies like explosives' usage (XVI century), cutting wire (first decade of XX century), cutter machines (last decades of XX century) leading to massive waste production usually disposed in nearby areas (*ravaneti*) or used to build both provincial and service roads (Fig. 1).

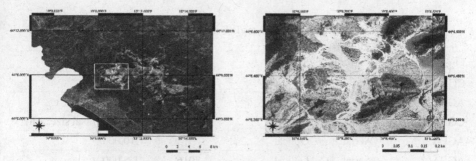

Fig. 1. Carrara industrial basin: 1:100.000 general view (left) and 1:2.000 detail (right) with quarries and old in-situ MCW/MQW disposals. Background: 2019 orthoimage.

As stated before, nowadays only temporary MCW/MQW in-situ disposals are allowed, subjected to a prior approval of MCW/MQW management cycle by public authorities in presence of removal plans at the end of extraction activities. Old-dated *in-situ* MCW/MQW disposals coming from past extraction activities are a source of geomorphological changes, due to the removal of marble debris for subsequent exploitation in industrial processes where calcium carbonate plays an important role. On the other hand, historical *ravaneti* (pre-XXX century MCW/MQW disposals) are the witness of past industrial extractions' techniques and are now under protection as part of Carrara's industrial heritage.

3   Materials and Methods

3.1   Datasets

Remote Sensing techniques play a great role in yearly monitoring extraction activities in Carrara industrial basin: while UAV and/or terrestrial LiDAR are often used for single quarry surveys, the basin's extension and morphology make very challenging their usage at basin scale.

Aerial/satellite high resolution images and aerial LiDAR surveys allow a cost-effective basin coverage; aerial high resolution orthoimages acquired on a tri-annual basis by National Agency for Agriculture Founding (AGEA) are publicly distributed by Tuscany Regional Information System by mean of Geoscopio Web Map Service (WMS).

Archived 2018 tasking tri-stereo 2020 high resolution Pléiades satellite images covering Carrara industrial basin have been granted to the Tuscan Regional Environmental Agency (ARPAT) by the European Spatial Agency (ESA) following Project Proposal id61779.

The large availability of high resolution orthoimage between 2009 and 2020 allow near yearly land cover changes identification, while 2012 and 2017 aerial LiDAR data allow elevation's change detection between 2012 and 2017. Stereo processing of 2020 Pléiades tri-stereo acquisition allows additional elevation's change detection between 2017 LiDAR terrain models and 2020 stereo extracted model.

Table 1. High resolution images/LiDAR surveys publicly available

Flight/Satellite	Platform	Sensor	Year	Reference scale
CGR S.p.a	Aerial	Optical	2009	1:2.000
AGEA	Aerial	Optical	2012	1:10.000
CGR S.p.a	Aerial	LiDAR	2012	~1:10.000 (pixel size: 1m)
AGEA	Aerial	Optical	2013	1:10.000
AGEA	Aerial	Optical	2016	1:5.000
CGR S.p.a	Aerial	Optical + LiDAR	2017	1:5.000
Pléiades	Satellite	Optical	2018	~1:10.000 (pixel size: 1m)
AGEA	Aerial	Optical	2019	1:5.000
Pléiades	Satellite	Optical	2020	~1:10.000 (pixel size: 1m)

As stated before, yearly production data must be sent by quarry owners to Local and Regional bodies involved in authorization management: these data include production volumes of (a) ornamental stone (primary product), (b) other secondary products to be used in stone products, (c) debris. Top 15 quarries with the highest ornamental stone production rates have been selected for further comparison of reported production volumes and detected volume changes between 2017 and 2020.

National Waste Reporting actually in charge to quarry owners includes all waste products coming from extraction activities: only yearly reports between 2009 and 2019 of MCW in various physical states – gravelly, sandy, silty and slurry – have been extracted for each quarry located in Carrara extractive basin and joined to the vector point layers representing quarries' locations.

The Regional Ornamental and Building Stones dataset (BDPIOR)[1] made by LAMMA Consortium for the Tuscany Regional Administration has been used in assess volume changes in Carrara *in-situ* MQW disposals, being the official reference in delineating old *in-situ* MQW disposals until the approval of Carrara extractive basins' plans.

3.2 Land Cover Changes

Extraction activities lead to various land cover changes: natural soil loss occurs when portions of rock or vegetated soil are removed to access marble strata. Natural soil loss

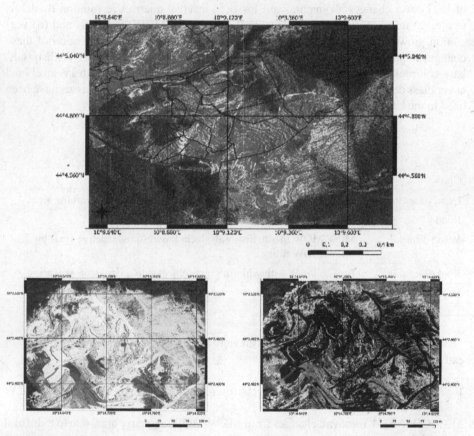

Fig. 2. 3D and 2D processing techniques for high resolution quarry areas classification. Upper image: 1:10.000 map with 2017 DEM slope analysis NW of Colonnata. In red: areas with slope < 15° identifying quarry extraction areas. Black outlines represent quarries' own properties extents. Lower left image: 2019 aerial 1:5.000 orthoimage. Lower right images: Structural Feature Set Texture Analysis (523 False Color Composite 8-set Haralick base set extracted with CNES Orfeo Toolbox) in a sample quarry (1:1.000).

---

[1] http://159.213.57.103/geoweb/CONTINUUM/BD_PIOR/BD_PIOR.zip.

can be mapped with (a) high resolution photo visual interpretation or (b) automatic and semi-automatic spectral classification techniques.

Due to artificial processes' complexity involving quarry areas, visual inspection and interpretations can be regarded as the preferred method to track land cover changes, while spectral classification can be used only for rough identification of both vegetated and artificial areas. Only advanced computer vision and texture analysis techniques [3, 4] combined with 3D information can be used to detect extraction areas characterized by regular block cuts, service areas and quarry MQW disposals: processed images can be used as ancillary bands to gain better spectral separability in spectral distance-based image classifiers (Fig. 2).

Image interpretation classes have been organized to obtain four relevant categories of land cover changes: (a) natural soil loss, (b) inactive quarries restoration by debris usage, (c) in-situ Marble Cutting/Quarry Waste (MCW/MQW) removals and (d) vegetation growth over inactive quarries and old MCW disposals. Identification of these changes requires mapping of four classes: active areas, in-situ MCW/MQW disposals, bare soil/rock and vegetation changes. These classes are consistent with IV level land cover class defined in Regional Official Land Cover dataset; the same classes have been used in the Extractive Basins' plan of the Carrara municipality.

Table 2. Classes used in land cover changes' digitizing

Class	Content
Quarry area	Service roads and infrastructures, block storage areas, working areas
Road	Service roads not included in active areas
Waste disposal	MCW/MQW in-situ disposals, including restored inactive areas by MCW/MQW filling
Rock/Bare soil	Bare soil/rock with/without grass subjected to quarry area expansion
Vegetation	Trees, bushes

Only three kinds of changes are relevant in assessing environmental impact of extractive activities over land use:

1. **Natural soil loss**: changes from vegetation/rock/bare soil to quarry area/road/MCW and/or MQW disposal
2. **MCW/MQW removal**: changes from MCW/MQW to quarry area, due to industrial exploitation of old in-situ disposals
3. **MCW/MQW fills**: changes from quarry areas to MCW/MQW, due to filling of unused quarries (final restoration activities)

Land cover changes data are presented in paragraph 4.

3.3   Volume Changes

As stated before, 3D changes from different acquisitions are a valuable tool to boost both automatic image classification and identification of extraction sites: both LiDAR aerial data and high-resolution satellite stereo acquisitions can be used to obtain precise localization, taking into account elevation precision influence on elevation changes assessment. In the latter case, a digital surface model (DSM) has been extracted from Pléiades tri-stereo acquisition by using s2p stereo pipeline [6] within a Docker container: the surface model has been compared with 2017 LiDAR DSM to assess both surface and volume changes between 2018[2] and 2020 over authorized areas and in-situ MCW/MQW disposals (Fig. 3).

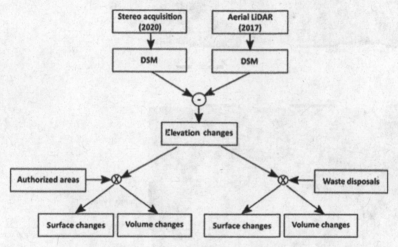

Fig. 3. Processing chain of LiDAR and stereo satellite acquisition for automatic surface and elevation change detection

Manual digitizing of both extracted and in-situ volumes has been done over 11 sample quarries showing values higher than 5 m: this threshold has been selected in accordance with the 2–3 m Root Mean Square Error (RMSE) assessed for tri-stereo extracted terrain models in urban environment [7] to highlight relevant elevation changes.

4   Results

4.1   Land Cover Changes

Both high resolution aerial and 2018/2020 satellite photos in Table 1 have been used in digitizing changes from 2009 to 2020: digitization of all land cover classes in Table 2 has been done over all available images inside each authorized quarry areas.

---

[2] Late 2017 LiDAR acquisition (end of October) has been intended as initial 2018 reference, due to the small number of working days remaining until the end of 2017 (November/first days of December). Their contribution to both blocks and waste production is then negligible compared to February/October working days.

Land cover dataset derived from high resolution photo interpretation has been processed over each sensing period (Fig. 4).

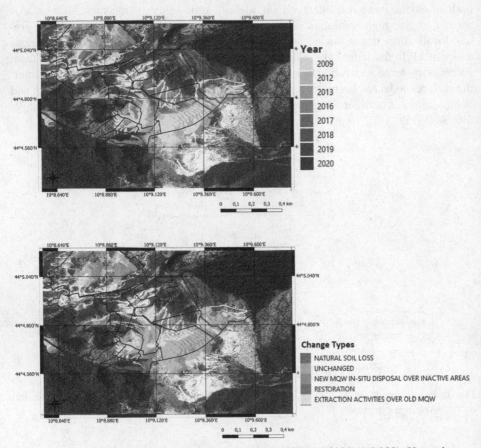

Fig. 4. Sample site with land cover changes between 2009 and 2020 (1:5.000). Upper image: yearly detected changes. Lower image: relevant change types between 2009 and 2020: (a) Natural Soil Loss (red), Extraction Activities Over Old MCW/MQW (yellow), New MCW/MQW in-situ Disposals Over Inactive Areas (cyan). Black outlines represent quarries' own properties extents. Background: 2019 orthoimage. (Color figure online)

As stated in Table 3, land cover changes occurred mainly between 2013 and 2016. Areas subjected to natural soil loss and MCW/MQW removals between 2009 and 2020 are higher than the ones interested by MCW/MQW fills, being respectively the 29% and 35% of total land cover changes' surface; however, between 2017 and 2020 natural soil loss has been significatively lowered with respect to years 2009–2016.

4.2 Volume Changes and Waste Management Indicators

3D volume changes precision has been assessed by comparison with reported production and MCW/MQW data only in 11 of the first 15 sample quarries showing the highest

Table 3. Land cover changes by category: (a) old MCW/MQW removal (b) inactive quarry areas restoration by filling with MCW/MQW (c) natural soil loss near expanding quarry areas

2009–2020 land cover changes

Time interval	MCW/MQW removal		MCW/MQW fills		Natural soil loss		Total	
	Area (m^2)	% (year)	Area (m^2)	% (year)	Area (m^2)	% (year)	Area (m^2)	% tot
2009–2012	6.87	71.4	1.99	7.9	0.76	7.9	9.62	11.4
2012–2013	11.26	46.7	4.33	35.3	8.52	35.3	24.11	28.5
2013–2016	9.29	31.7	3.68	55.6	16.31	55.6	29.34	34.7
2016–2017	4.76	48.8	2.78	22.8	2.23	22.8	9.77	11.6
2017–2018	5.20	85.0	0.10	13.4	0.82	13.4	6.12	7.2
2018–2019	3.66	72,5	0.50	17.5	0.88	17.5	5.04	6.0
2019–2020	0.49	90	–	10.0	0.06	10.0	0.55	0.6
2009–2020	**41.53**	**49.1%**	**13.38**	**15.8%**	**29.57**	**35%**	**84.54**	**–**

production rates, since in four of them extracted 2020 terrain models cannot be used due to matching errors in complex morphology areas.

Figure 5 highlight the good agreement between the whole volume reported (production + waste, in blue) and extracted volume/in-situ MCW/MQW (in orange/gray) detected by both semi-automatic and manual methods. On the top chart, reported global volumes (production + waste) of samples 7, 10 and 11 appears to be from 30% to 75% lower than the ones calculated with semiautomatic methods. While in the case of samples 10 and 11 this can be related to in-situ displacement of extracted volumes (grey bars), sample 7 shows a lack of agreement between reported and calculated volumes. Further investigations for this quarry highlighted unsatisfactory 2020 DSM accuracy.

Extracted and in-situ MCW/MQW volumes on the second chart are evaluated using manually digitized contours: while extracted volumes show minimal differences with the ones obtained by semiautomatic methods, in-situ MCW/MQW volume is far lower except for sample 8. In addition to require better DSM precision, these results highlight that in-situ MCW/MQW is mainly composed of low-height disposals that might have been discarded in manual digitizing.

Thus negligible in volumes with regard to MQW, MCW (*marmettola*) represents the main driver of environmental impact affecting water resources [12, 14]: marble powder, mixed with cooling water and/or other fluids, can be found in nearby rivers thus resulting in a major source of additional costs in water depuration processes.

The amount of MCW can be estimated in three different ways: (a) as a percentage (5–3%) of block production, due to cutting and refining operations, (b) from yearly national waste Reporting contents, or (c) as predicted values during activity authorization. Marble blocks production is reported from quarry owners and verified during transportation at weigh stations, while waste reports only include the amount of MCW sent to waste

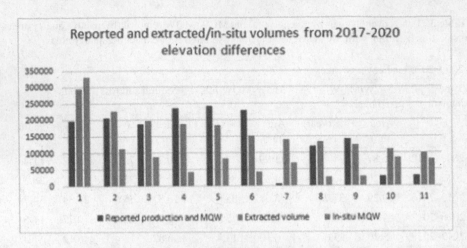

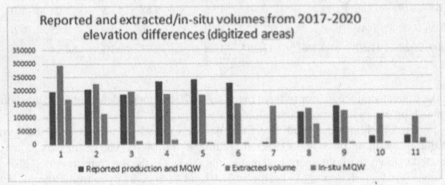

Fig. 5. Reported (blue, including production and MCW/MQW) and extracted volumes from DSMs differences in sample quarries, including extracted (orange) and in-situ (grey). Top: automatic volume extraction, bottom: extraction from manually-digitized areas. (Color figure online)

treatment plants, thus excluding untreated MCW used on site for service infrastructure management.

Other extraction wastes, mainly debris (MQW), have to be removed from extraction site or used for building infrastructures and service roads: 3D elevation differences from DSMs can be used to highlight disposals areas and roughly quantify waste volumes. Indicators used to assess both fine-grained debris are explained in the next two sections.

4.3 Marble Cutting Waste ('marmettola')

Gravel, sandy, silty and slurry MCW are committed to external plants or used in quarry areas for service roads and wall management; in the latter case they can migrate through underwater basins to surface waters.

Committed MCW reports must be sent to national authorities: each waste category being treated outside production sites requires prior classification based on waste codes are established at European level (EWC codes).

MCW are classified with code 010413, i.e., 'wastes from stone cutting and sawing other than those mentioned in 010407': national reports from 2012 to 2019 issued by quarry owners have been normalized, geocoded and assigned to each quarry in order to extract MCW volume and weight values, taking into account special cases of both quarry and sawing plants' owners[3].

In order to check consistency of reported MCW quantities with estimated values from reported blocks production, silty MCW require weighting by the average estimated

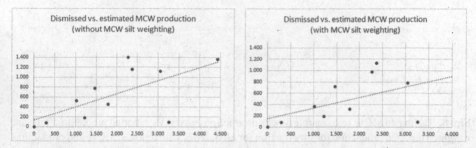

Fig. 6. Estimated MCW from blocks production (x axis) vs, reported production (left) and weighted reported production for silty fraction for sample quarries.

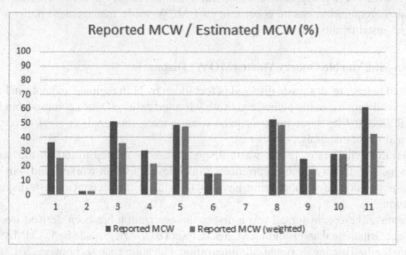

Fig. 7. Reported (sum and weighted sum) 2018–2020 MCW by sample quarries as a fraction of estimated MCW (5% of block production).

---

[3] Sawing plants are a major source of fine-grained wastes, but must not be taken into account in evaluating extraction activities impact of waste production over water resources located in extractive basins.

concentration of the solution, typically between 70% and 80%: avoiding this weighting factor leads to overestimation of reported MCW [21–23].

Figures 6 and 7 shows that the average ratio between reported and estimated MCW is around 25%, while a little amount of the sample shows very little agreement between estimated and reported production due to in-situ disposals. On the converse, Fig. 8 shows a different path for quarries with low production rates (<1.000 T of marble blocks): such results were somehow expected due to minor capabilities in MCW dismission for industrial purposes.

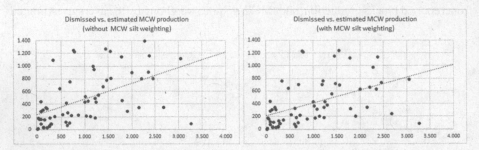

Fig. 8. Estimated MCW from marble blocks production (x axis) vs. reported production (left) and weighted reported production for silty fraction for all quarries with reported MCW and production. The trend is consistent with the one highlighted in Fig. 5 for sample data.

When ratio between reported and estimated MCW is largely below 50%, some further analysis is required to ensure consistency of MCW waste management policies with regional sustainability goals.

4.4   In-Situ Marble Quarry Waste (MQW) Disposals

As stated before, in-situ waste disposal is forbidden by both regional and national regulations while not explicitly authorized in very limited cases: 3D data coming from UAV, LiDAR and satellite stereo images can be used to track changes over areas covered by historical waste disposals.

Elevation changes of in-situ waste disposals can be related to terrain movements due to local instability: such occurrences, thus relevant to both workers and – in some cases – population safety monitoring, have not been taken into account in waste disposals' monitoring.

As stated before, historical waste disposals localization has been derived from the Regional Ornamental and Building Stones dataset (BDPIOR)[4] made by LAMMA Consortium for the Tuscany Regional Administration: elevation changes between 2017 aerial LiDAR survey and 2020 DSM extracted from Pléiades stereo images have been checked over these areas, while precise 6-month difference have been checked over a major waste disposal by two UAV survey-derived DSMs. This latter test, being limited for research purposes, has not been used in whole industrial area monitoring: other available UAV surveys, being limited to quarry active areas, have not been taken into account.

---

[4] http://159.213.57.103/geoweb/CONTINUUM/BD_PIOR/BD_PIOR.zip.

Each waste disposal has been related to a quarry basing on its inclusion on quarry authorized area (overlay) (Fig. 9).

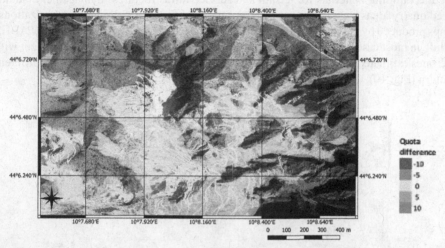

Fig. 9. 1:5.000 north-east area of Carrara industrial basin: elevation changes between 2017 and 2020 over digitized waste disposals' areas (dataset BDPIOR from LAMMA Consortium: in yellow). Excavated areas (red) and new disposals (blue) area highlighted. Background: 2019 orthoimage. (Color figure online)

Both extracted and disposed volumes over old MQW disposals areas have been evaluated by zonal statistics GIS techniques over 500 ha MQW area at global and sub-basin details: 4% of global old MQW surface has been subjected to extraction activities[5], while roughly 10% has been subjected to WQM disposals.

Table 4. In-situ MQW Surface and Volume Changes (2018–2020) for each sub-basin.

Sub-basin	Area (ha)		Volume (m^3)	
	Extracted	Disposed	Extracted	Disposed
Torano	7,0175	13,2	675.706	7.556.162
Fantiscritti	8,0032	12,5	623.237	7.847.711
Colonnata	8,9262	27,7	939.528	11.479.306
Tot	**23,9469**	**53,4**	**2.238.471**	**26.883.179**

---

[5] Elevation changes greater than 5 m due to MCW/MQW landslides are negligible compared with the ones related to extraction activities.

4.5 MQW Disposals in Active Quarries

As stated before, temporary MQW disposals are allowed in active quarries' areas to be used as building materials for terrain and service infrastructures' management: authorized quarry areas have been digitized from national cadaster, following authorizations' maps produced by the Carrara Municipality for the Extraction Management Plan (PABE). While in most cases, especially for big quarries, reported MQW data are consistent with the ones estimated from 3D changes, small quarries seem to follow a slightly different pattern (Fig. 10).

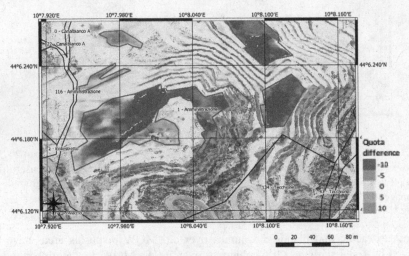

Fig. 10. Detail of 1:1.000 digitized areas for 2017–2020 volume changes evaluation (red: extraction areas, blue: disposals' areas), Black borders define authorized extraction areas. (Color figure online)

Two different approaches have been used in analyzing trends in MQW management: the first is based on accurate analysis of a subset[6] of quarries showing the highest production rates, while the latter relies on automatic extraction and data cleaning over all quarries with high production rates.

In the first case disposals areas have been digitized manually where elevation changes were over 4/5 m, taking into account elevation tolerances of the two 1 m × 1 m 2017 and 2020 DSMs[7]: volumes have been calculated in QGIS by applying digitized boundaries to the raster difference of the two DSMs. Figure 11, where x axis represents extracted volumes and x axis new MCW in-situ disposed volumes, highlights a good agreement

---

[6] Quarries included in the study are the top 10 showing relevant volume changes between 2017 and 2020 (over/near 100.000 m^3).

[7] While 2017 aerial LiDAR DSM dataset show very high precision (<1 m), elevation tolerance of 2020 stereo-derived DSM lies in the range 1–2 m. Elevation difference tolerances can be evaluated as the sum of the two tolerances (3 m), and 4 m has been chosen as reference level for excavation and MCW/MQW disposals' changes assessment.

for both methods, thus assessing a rough correlation between extracted volumes and new MCW disposals for the majority of the quarries under investigation.

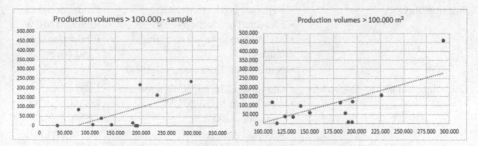

Fig. 11. Extracted volumes (x axis) vs. new MQW disposals in quarry areas: manually-refined areas over a quarry sample (left) and automatic area extraction (right)

Therefore, in both cases it can be stated that extracted volume equals new MCW disposals: taking into account fine debris, silt and sand volume expansion by using an average weight of 40–60%, average production rates and dismissed wastes can be evaluated as 60–40% of extracted volume.

4.6 Data Integration and Proposed Indicators

All derived datasets have been processed to extract both potential impact indicators and spatial data at global and local scale: trends of land coverage changes, MCW and production data have also been evaluated from 2012 to 2019.

Derived key indicators can be roughly classified as sustainable and environmental policies ones: sustainable policy indicators, relying mostly on reported production data, are more suitable in monitoring regional level plans subjected to Strategic Environmental Assessment (SEA), while the so-called environmental impact indicators are more suitable at municipal level, including environmental controls planning. Sustainability indicators at local scale can also be used in local policies' monitoring (i.e., quarry restorations and reusing od old *in-situ* MQW disposals) and assessment.

Table 4 highlights the indicators that could be included in a Decision Support System (DSS): each indicator, while not natively including a spatial component, can be 'spatially-enabled' with join operations based on quarry identifier (Table 5).

Chart representations of key indicators for sustainability policies have been established to highlight their trends over the years: production rate, i.e., the ratio between marble blocks and debris coming from quarry managers yearly reports, is a key indicator in measuring sustainability policies and can be examined over a temporal extent compared to planning targets at regional planning level. This dataset can be used, combined with volume changes, to obtain potential impact indicators to be used in environmental controls' planning (Fig. 12).

Table 5. Indicators to be included in the Decision Support System (DSS)

Class	Indicators	Involved datasets
Sustainability	• Reported production rates • Measured production rates • MCW transferred to recycling industry • Natural Soil Loss (area/volumes)	Production data Reported MCW Production data Land cover
Environmental impact assessment	• Old in-situ MCW/MQW removals • New in-situ MCW/MQW (area/volumes) • Restored quarries	Land cover DSMs DSMs

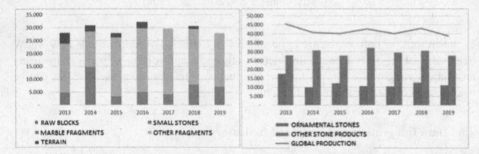

Fig. 12. Example of 2013–2019 production indicators for a sample sub-basin derived from owners' reports. Left image: sub-products' details in cubic meters per year (raw non-ornamental blocks, fragments, debris, small stones). Right image: production rates and trends for both ornamental stones and other derived stone products in cubic meters per year.

2018–2020 production data have been used, in association with 3D volume changes between 2017 and 2020 over a sample of 9 quarries[8], for assessing 2018–2020 consistency of MCW/MQW management and reusing. In the following charts (Fig. 13 and 14) reported 2018–2020 production rate, i.e., ratio between reported production and extraction debris, is compared to the ratio between reported 2018–2020 production and extracted volumes evaluated from elevation changes between 2017 and 2020 (estimated production rates referring to the whole extracted volume).

---

[8] Quarries included in the study are the top 9 showing relevant volume changes between 2017 and 2020 (over/near 100.000 m^3) with 2018 production data.

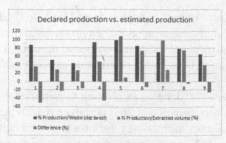

Fig. 13. Reported production rates compared with volume changes in sample sites. Blue: reported production rate, orange: production rate as ratio of production and extracted volume. Differences should be related to in-situ MCW/MQW temporary disposals and/or quarry area infrastructures' management. (Color figure online)

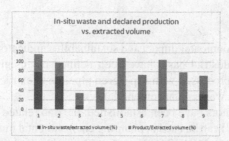

Fig. 14. Extracted volume comparison (%) with in-situ MCW/MQW changes during 2017–2020 (in blue) and production data (in orange) in sample sites. Sites 1, 2 and (partially) 9 show relevant in-situ MCW/MQW disposal, therefore requiring additional data check and/or in-situ control, while other sites are characterized by a quasi-absence of in-situ MCW/MQW disposals, therefore suggesting proper MCW/MQW management. (Color figure online)

5   Discussion

Waste management and land cover changes' indicators highlighted in paragraph 4, compared with production data and waste yearly reports, allow to assess waste management performances achieved by each quarry. Since long-dated MCW/MQW disposal (*ravaneti*) and quarry areas is forbidden, except for building new service infrastructures or repairing existing ones, these indicators allow to track in-situ waste management over the years.

While general criteria for environmental controls in quarries and mines have been established [25] and risk assessment methods have been proposed for controls prioritization in industrial plants with high potential environmental impact [24] by the European Union Network for the Implementation and Enforcement of Environmental Law (IMPEL), this work aims to fill the gap between the above frameworks and quarries' controls' planning. These indicators, established at quarry level, are intended to be integrated in a Decision Support System to give a 'risk score' mainly related to waste management performances.

Existing environmental impact indicators based on Life Cycle Assessment (LCA) methods, although useful in measuring global environmental performance of extractive activities, do not take into account local environmental impacts like MCW/MQW in-situ disposals, that are proven to be a source of groundwater and surface water quality loss in the Apuan karst.

Additional work has to be done on improving terrain models' availability over the years by integration of aerial/satellite stereo acquisition with periodic local UAS surveys in quarries with complex morphology unfit for stereo extraction of terrain models. Proposed indicators should be properly weighted to obtain a single environmental risk assessment score: when integrated with other indicators related to biodiversity preservation and land cover changes, they might be useful in high level environmental monitoring and controls planning.

6 Conclusions

A set of potential environmental impact and sustainability indicators for extractive activities in the Carrara industrial basin have been defined by integrating high resolution remotely sensed data, processed with s2p stereo pipeline to extract terrain models, with marble production and waste management datasets.

Two class of indicators have been established: the one related to quarry waste management (MCW/MQW) can be used in planning environmental monitoring and controls, while the other, related to MQW/MCW exploitation in the building materials' industry and land cover changes, is mostly intended for high level plans monitoring.

Integration in a web-based DSS of data and indicators useful in both production sustainability and environmental protection goals' monitoring over quarry areas in Carrara sub-basins is in progress: once the web-based DSS would be accessible to controls planners and decision makers, it could play a great role in increasing global sustainability of extraction activities.

Acknowledgements. The authors wish to thank the General Manager of ARPAT Quarries Spercial Project, dott. Gaetano Licitra, their colleague dott. Giovanni Menga for his precious contributions on MCW estimation from production data, and the local ARPAT services located in Pietrasanta and Massa for supporting the authors in planning and managing UAV sample surveys performed by the Department of Earth Sciences survey team of Florence University.

References

1. Darwish, T., Khater, C., Jomaa, I., Stehouwer, R., Shaban, A., Hamzé, M.: Environmental impact of quarries on natural resources in Lebanon. Land Degrad. Dev. **22**, 345–358 (2011). https://doi.org/10.1002/ldr.1011
2. Sarraf, M., Larsen, B., Owaygen, M.: Cost of environmental degradation – the case of Lebanon and Tunisia. World Bank Environmental Economics Series, paper no. 97 (2004)
3. Haralick, R., Shanmugam, K., Dinstein, I.: Textural features for image classification. IEEE Trans. Syst. Man Cybern. **SMC-3**(6), 610–621 (1973). https://doi.org/10.1109/TSMC.1973.4309314

4. Xin, H., Zhang, L., Li, P.: Classification and extraction of spatial features in urban areas using high-resolution multispectral imagery. IEEE Geosci. Remote Sens. Lett. **4**(2), 260–264 (2007)
5. Bradley, F.: Marble quarrying – L'escavazione del marmo. Promorama (1999). ISBN 9788888761077
6. de Franchis, C., Meinhardt-Llopis, E., Michel, J., Morel, J.-M., Facciolo, G.: An automatic and modular stereo pipeline for pushbroom images. ISPRS Ann. Photogramm. Remote Sens. Spatial Inf. Sci. **II–3**, 49–56 (2014). https://doi.org/10.5194/isprsannals-II-3-49-2014
7. Poli, D., Remondino, F., Angiuli, E., Agugiaro, G.: Evaluation of pleiades-1A triplet on trento testfield. Int. Arch. Photogramm. Remote Sens. Spatial Inf. Sci. **XL-1/W1**, 287–292 (2013). https://doi.org/10.5194/isprsarchives-XL-1-W1-287-2013
8. Coeurdevey, L., Fernandez, K.: Pléiades Imagery. User Guide. Report No. USRPHR-DT-125-SPOT-2.0 (2012)
9. Liguori, V., Rizzo, G., Traverso, M.: Marble quarrying: an energy and waste intensive activity in the production of building materials. WIT Trans. Ecol. Environ. **108**, 197–207 (2008). https://doi.org/10.2495/EEIA080201
10. Vagnon, F., Dino, G., Umili, G., Cardu, M., Ferrero, A.: New developments for the sustainable exploitation of ornamental stone in carrara basin. Sustainability **12**(22), 9374 (2020). https://doi.org/10.3390/su12229374
11. Zhang, Q., Zhang, T., Liu, X.: Index system to evaluate the quarries ecological restoration. Sustainability **10**, 619 (2018). https://doi.org/10.3390/su10030619
12. Piccini, L., Lorenzo, T., Costagliola, P., Galassi, D.: Marble slurry's impact on groundwater: the case study of the apuan alps karst aquifers. Water **11**, 2462 (2019). https://doi.org/10.3390/w11122462
13. Dino, G., Chiappino, C., Rossetti, P., Franchi, A., Baccioli, G.: Extractive waste management: a new territorial and industrial approach in Carrara quarry basin. Italian J. Eng. Geol. Environ. **2017**, 47–55 (2017). https://doi.org/10.4408/IJEGE.2017-02.S-05
14. Nannoni, A., et al.: Innovative approaches for the sedimentological characterization of fine natural and anthropogenic sediments in karst system: the case of the Apuan Alps (Central Italy). Front. Earth Sci. **9**(2021), 1–16 (2021). https://doi.org/10.3389/feart.2021.672962
15. Bianco, I., Blengini, G.: An analytical and flexible approach for the Life Cycle Assessment of stone products. In: Proceedings SUM2016, Third Symposium on Urban Mining, 23–25 May 2016 (2016)
16. Capitano, C., Peri, G., Raimondi, C., Rizzo, G., Traverso, M.: Energy and environmental analysis of marble productive sites: "by phases" and "by single process" combined approach. Energy Procedia **148**, 1183–1190 (2018). https://doi.org/10.1016/j.egypro.2018.08.023
17. Capitano, C., Traverso, M., Rizzo, G., Finkbeiner, M.: Life cycle sustainability assessment: an implementation to marble products (2011)
18. Traverso, M., Rizzo, G., Finkbeiner, M.: Environmental performance of building materials: life cycle assessment of a typical Sicilian marble. Int. J. Life Cycle Assess. **15**, 104–114 (2010). https://doi.org/10.1007/s11367-009-0135-z
19. Capitano, C., Peri, G., Rizzo, G., Ferrante, P.: Toward a holistic environmental impact assessment of marble quarrying and processing: proposal of a novel easy-to-use IPAT-based method. Environ. Monit. Assess. **189**(3), 1–16 (2017). https://doi.org/10.1007/s10661-017-5825-6
20. Zabalza, B.I., Capilla, A.V., Aranda, U.A.: Life cycle assessment of building materials: Comparative analysis of energy and environmental impacts and evaluation of the eco-efficiency improvement potential. Build. Environ. **46**(5), 1133–1140 (2011). https://doi.org/10.1016/j.buildenv.2010.12.002
21. Mancini, R., Fornaro, M., Dino, G.A.: Impatto ambientale dei limi di segagione. Rapporto finale del Progetto Interreg-III (2005). http://www.naturalstoneinfo.com/download/interregIII.03.pdf

22. Torini, S., Bruno, P.: Piano Provinciale di gestione dei rifiuti speciali anche pericolosi. Volume terzo (2005). https://docplayer.it/20340276-Piano-provinciale-di-gestione-ii-stralcio-volume-terzo-dei-rifiuti-speciali-anche-pericolosi-legge-regionale-n-25-1998.html

23. Allegato, C.:Piano Regionale delle Attività Estrattive di recupero delle aree escavate e di riutilizzo dei residui recuperabili (P.R.A.E.R.) (2007). http://www.roccastradagovernodelter ritorio.it/ambiente/caveminiere/praer%20cave/Allegato%20C.pdf

24. Kramers, R., Büther, H.: easyTools – risk assessment guidance book, report 2011/05. In: IMPEL, European Union Network for the Implementation and Enforcement of Environmental Law. Report adopted at IMPEL General Assembly in Copenhagen, 07–08 June 2012 (2012). http://impel.eu/wp-content/uploads/2014/08/easyTools_-Guidance-Book_-2012-06-21.pdf

25. Holzgraefe, G., et al.: Guidance for environmental and nature protection inspections of quarries and open cast mining in Natura 2000. In: IMPEL, European Union Network for the Implementation and Enforcement of Environmental Law. Report adopted at IMPEL General Assembly Meeting May 2018 (2018). https://www.impel.eu/wp-content/uploads/2018/06/FR-2017-19-1-Guidance-inspection-of-quarries-1.pdf

Airborne and Spaceborne Remote Sensing Data Integration for 3D Monitoring of Complex Quarry Environments

Ing. Cinzia Licciardello[✉]

ARPAT, via Nicola Porpora 22, 50144 Florence, Italy
c.licciardello@arpat.toscana.it

Abstract. Environmental and landscape planning of large quarry areas require precise 3D data to assess yearly volume changes. While unmanned aerial vehicles (UAV) are widely used in single quarry 3D monitoring, large extractive areas like Carrara industrial basin require a different approach to detect yearly volume and surface changes, based on both airborne and spaceborne data.

LiDAR airborne sensors allow precise terrain models' acquisition, thus requiring fairly complex planning and testing processes for each flight: high resolution satellite data are less expensive and can be acquired quickly (<1 month), allowing digital surface models (DSMs) extraction with stereo processing pipelines.

A relatively recent acquisition mode offered by Airbus for the Pléiades constellation, the tri-stereo acquisition one, has been successfully used in DSM generation in dense urban areas, thus suggesting similar results even in quarry areas characterized by complex morphology.

A pair of Pléiades archive images and a new tri-stereo acquisition have been granted by European Space Agency (ESA) under acceptance of a project proposal: CNES s2p Stereo Pipeline and NASA Ames Stereo Pipeline have been used in processing each image set over four sample sites (three quarries and a long-dated waste disposal site).

While tri-stereo-derived digital surface models shows good agreement with LiDAR-based ones, usage of archived satellite images not natively acquired as stereo pair but with suitable B/H ratio cannot allow precise image matching due to terrain modification between the two acquisitions, thus limiting DSM reconstruction to unchanged areas.

1 Introduction

Since many decades Carrara extractive basin has been a major source of environmental conflicts spreading around marble quarry activity. Current public planning actions involve both achievement of environmentally sustainable and waste management best practices' goals, in order to reduce the environmental impacts of fine-grain cutting waste (the so-called *marmettola*) and long-dated *in-situ* waste disposals (*Ravaneti*).

E. Borgogno-Mondino and P. Zamperlin (Eds.): ASITA 2021, CCIS 1507, pp. 405–422, 2022.
https://doi.org/10.1007/978-3-030-94426-1_29

Surface and volume change detection by terrain model's comparison are the building block to derive indicators of both marble cutting and quarry waste production (MCW/MQW), allowing in addition a more precise soil consumption assessment compared to visual interpretation-based methods: precise terrain models with Ground Sample Distance (GSD) less than 1m can be obtained as direct measure of sensor-to-target distances by LiDAR airborne sensors or by mean of satellite/aerial optical stereo image processing.

While LiDAR flight campaigns are quite expensive in planning, execution, processing and product testing, satellite images' acquisition is nowadays an agile method to obtain a digital surface/terrain model (DSM/DTM) using stereo processing techniques. Delivery times for satellite images standard tasking orders, typically less than 30 days, grant final availability of extracted terrain model in about 1 month/1 month and a half over extended regions (minimum extent required per task: 100 km² for Pléiades images). Compared to Unmanned Aerial Vehicles (UAV), widely used in precision surveys of single quarries and mines that allows terrain models generation until 5 cm of GSD over a typical area of 500 × 500 m per half a day, satellite image acquisitions are undoubtedly a more cost-effective solution per square kilometer of extracted terrain models.

Satellite stereo images have been widely used to extract digital terrain models by both manual and automatic methods (see reviews in [24] and [25]): quality assessment of digital extracted models from WorldView-2 and WorldView-3 stereo pairs with commercial software over different land covers showed a good agreement between extracted models and LiDAR surveys [24], while limitations on urban canyons have been well documented [23]. Since quarry active areas morphology is characterized by the presence of both horizontal and vertical marble cuts, it is expected that extracted stereo models could suffer of the same limitations seen in urban areas in both area coverage and elevation precision.

Existing works [1–3] targeted on tri-stereo Pléiades satellite acquisitions in urban areas report vertical Root Mean Square Error (RMSE) values of tri-stereo extracted terrain models on reference points far less than 10 m (see Table 1) and a low percentage of rejected pixels expected for stereo pairs in mountain areas [16]. In natural areas (best case scenario) greater precision can be obtained [3], even lesser than 1m [29].

Table 1. Vertical RMSE of Pléiades triplets derived DSMs in urban areas (review)

Reference	Site	Vertical RMSE
Nasir et al. [1]	Melbourne (urban/mainland)	5.2
Panagiotakis et al. [2]	Athens, urban [DSM]	1.17
Poli et al. [3]	Trento, center	6.1
	Trento, Railway Station	6.5
	Trento, Fersina	8.5
Palaseanu-Lovejoy et al. [29]	Mount Etna	0.78

These values, being the minimum marble cut height and width is around 10 m, suggest that tri-stereo extracted terrain models at year *i* could be effectively use to assess annual extraction activities progress by elevations comparison between terrain models at years *i-h* (being *h* an integer arbitrary value), provided that terrain models with 1m of GSD and RMSE ~2–3 m are available at that time. Natural areas vertical RMSE values highlighted in [3] and [29] indicates that stereo extracted DEMs could be used in addition to assess both stability of historical waste disposals and unauthorized waste discharging nearby active areas.

In this work the potential of both stereo and tri-stereo Pléiades high-resolution images in deriving digital terrain models of active quarry areas with RMSE <5 m has been investigated over 4 test sites located in the Apuan Alps, in order to (a) locate areas of intensive quarry activities and/or waste discharging, and (b) evaluate volume changes. A reference terrain model, acquired at the end of 2017 during a LiDAR aerial survey founded by Soil Defense and Civil Protection Regional Directorate of Tuscany Regional Administration and managed by LAMMA consortium, has been used in both quality assessment of extracted models and 2017–2020 surface and volume change detection. The potential of archived 2018 images, with similar B/H ratio but not natively acquired in a stereo configuration has also been investigated in evaluation of pre-2020 surface and volume changes.

2 Available Data

LiDAR data acquisition in the Apuan Alps has been required by the Regional Directorate for Soil Protection during the Regional Quarry Project started in 2016: the flight, planned by LAMMA Consortium, was taken by CGR S.p.a. in the last days of October, 2017. Derived high resolution terrain models covers a great amount of the Apuan Alps, including Carrara extractive basin centered on the geographic coordinates (WGS84) 44°05'53.412" and 10°07'44.922" (area: 1076 ha), and two minor subareas characterized by intense extraction activities near the towns of Seravezza and Cardoso (Fig. 1). A pair of Pléiades images for mid-2018 (archived) and a new tri-stereo acquisition taken in October 2020 have been granted to the Tuscan Regional Environmental Agency (ARPAT) by the European Spatial Agency (ESA) following Project Proposal id61779: Pléiades images footprints for 2020 acquisition are restricted to small portions of the three areas above, while archived images acquired are restricted to the Carrara extractive basin.

Since Pléiades archive does not include any native stereo acquisition covering Carrara industrial basin, a pair of images has been selected aiming to ensure the best B/H ratio for stereo processing [4], while tri-stereo acquisition parameters have been selected by Airbus tasking managers. Appropriate B/H ratio has a great influence on terrain models' elevation accuracy, thus affecting visibility in urban areas and steep mountains: a large B/H ratio grants more precise elevation values, but increases masked out extents in complex morphology environments like dense urban areas and quarries [5]. While B/H ratios between 0.5 and 0.9 have been found to be the best values for terrain model generation by aerial photos [6], even smaller ratios (0.25) are recommended for tri-stereo automatic DSM extraction [20, 21]. Details of LiDAR data and Pléiades images' characteristics are discussed in the next two paragraphs (Fig. 2).

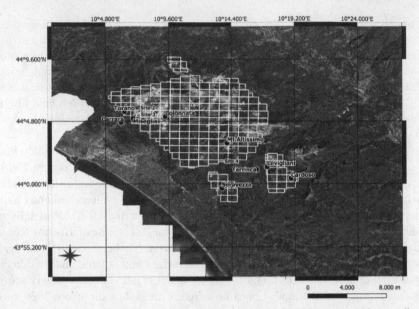

Fig. 1. 1:00.000 2017 LiDAR survey coverage areas (grid in WGS84 geographic coordinates). North: Apuan Alps (including Carrara extractive basin), Seravezza (south), Cardoso (south east).

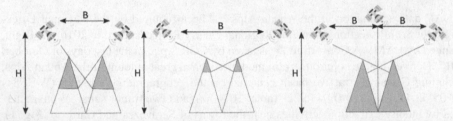

Fig. 2. Influence of B/H over stereo visibility in mountain areas. Left: low B/H ratio in standard stereo configuration (left and right views), center: high B/H ratio, right: tri-stereo configuration with high B/H ratio between left and right views.

2.1 LiDAR DSM and Control Point Dataset

LiDAR products of 2017 flight consist in four datasets: (a) orthoimages (b) digital surface and (c) elevation models (DSM+DEM) with a GSD of 0.5×0.5 m, and (d) original point clouds in ply binary format. DSMs and DTMs can be used as a reference to assess average elevations of both CNES s2p and NASA AMES Stereo Pipeline extracted' DSMs. Exterior orientation metadata of 2017 aerial survey include both orthometric and ellipsoidal height for each aerial photo.

Since quarry areas are characterized by both the absence of man-made manufacts and relevant terrain changes over the years, control points (CP) in unchanged areas must be carefully selected in quality assessment of terrain models by 2017 and 2020 terrain models' comparison. While marble cuts' areas are subjected to active work, service roads' location and extension exhibit a more constant path over the years and can then be safely used in digitizing control points for vertical accuracy quality assessment (QA); old marble cuts not subjected to extraction activities between 2017 and 2020 can also be used. A set of control points has been manually digitized over unchanged areas in each test site assessed by visual comparison of (a) 2017 orthoimage and (b) orthorectified 2020 tri-stereo Pléiades center image: as stated before, CP are mainly located over service roads or old marble cuts and cover the whole test site area. 15 CP have been digitized over test sites 1, 2 and 4, while only 7 CP have been digitized for site 3 due to both quarry limited extent and visual interpretation problems of 2020 orthoimage due to large wall shadows in Pléiades satellite images. CP locations are highlighted in Sect. 4.2.

2.2 Pléiades Archived Images

Since investigation of past volume and surface changes could play a key role in *a-posteriori* assessment of terrain changes in quarry areas, a pair of Pléiades archived images have been required to investigate the feasibility of using standard acquisition to derive 3D terrain models. Images acquired in 30/06/2018 and 12/10/2018 have been selected, being (a) along-track angles wide enough to have a good elevation estimation quality, and (b) the acquisition interval long enough to show a worst-case scenario of strong terrain changes between the two acquisitions, potentially avoiding good pair point matching. However, lost coverage could play an interesting role in delineating areas subjected to extraction activities between the two acquisitions (Table 2).

Table 2. Acquisition angles and B/H ratio of archived Pléiades images (2018)

Img set	Incidence angles		Overall	Sun angle		B/H
	Across track	Along track		Azimuth	Elevation	
001	−2.40	7.92	8.27	166.50	37.69	0.44
002	−0.07	−14.60	19.90	143.91	65.72	0.44

2.3 Pléiades Tri-stereo New Acquisition

A new tri-stereo acquisition has been taken in October 2020, 09th, being the central image P002 acquired with a quasi-nadiral geometry ($-1.25°$): according to [9], along-track and across-track incidence angles of the triplet can be used to obtain B/H ratio. If incidence angle is available, for instance in Airbus GeoStore, B/H ratio can be evaluated by using image-pairs-stereo-capacity IPGP FOSS source code[1] (Table 3).

While B/H ratio for 1-2 and 2-3 pairs is quite small, B/H ratio for 1-3 pair is almost identical to Pléiades recommended value of 0.25 [20, 21]: thus, great capability in getting terrain details masked by high walls for 1-2 and 2-3 pair is expected, with less precision achievable with respect to 1-3 pair due to parallax effects.

---

[1] https://github.com/IPGP/image-pairs-stereo-capacity (Institut de Physique du Globe de Paris).

Table 3. Acquisition angle and B/H Ratio of new tri-stereo on demand Pléiades images (2020)

Img set	Incidence angles		Overall	Sun angle		B/H
	Across track	Along track		Azimuth	Elevation	
001	−9.27	4.67	10.34	169.61	32.13	0.21 0.11
002	−7.70	−1.25	7.80	169.30	32.10	0.11 0.11
003	−6.14	−7.17	9.40	169.30	32.10	0.21 0.11

2.4 Test Sites

Marble quarries are characterized by quite varying terrain morphology: while most of them show a typical open pit configuration slowly degrading according to local slope, some of them – the so-called 'pit' quarries – are delimited by high vertical walls. Furthermore, nearby terrain is often covered by old-dated waste disposals characterized by local landslides.

Four sites (Table 4) have been selected in representation of various terrain morphology characterizing marble quarries and nearby waste disposals, three of them located in the industrial Carrara marble basin and one in the mount Altissimo area.

Site 1, a quarry in the famous Fantiscritti industrial basin with regular marble cuts, has been chosen as a best-case scenario (slowly degrading walls), while Site 2 is a long-dated waste disposal area (so-called 'ravaneto') with constant slope and minimal height changes over the years. Site 3 is a more morphologically-complex quarry with steep walls' slope ('pit' quarry, worst case scenario), while Site 4 is a quarry located on the top of a mountain characterized, like Site 4, by a complex structure of high walls making it pretty similar to an urban canyon (Fig. 3).

Table 4. Test sites

Test site	Center	Scenario
001	44°06'11.7612" 10°08'01.9248"	Best case (slowly-degrading walls)
002	44°06'30.024" 10°08'21.0192"	Slow changes over the years (local landslides)
003	44°05'58.4448" 10°08'22.704"	Worst case (steep walls)
004	44°02'22.74" 10°14'42.8064"	Worst case (many high walls, urban canyon-like)

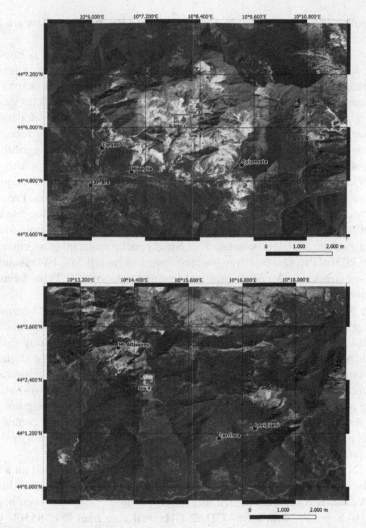

Fig. 3. 1:25.000 map of Carrara industrial basin (upper image) and mount Altissimo (lower image) test sites. Site 1: quarry with regular slope (best case scenario), Site 2: inactive waste disposal area (unchanged area), Site 3: quarry with high walls (worst case scenario), Site 4: quarry with urban canyon-like terrain morphology (worst case scenario). Background image: 1:5.000 Orthoimage (2019).

3   Methods and Tools

While epipolar geometry reconstruction by manual homologous point specification has been the standard stereo processing method for many years, recent acquisitions in photogrammetry processing and 3D object reconstruction by using Computer Vision tools have been used for building fully-automated stereo pipelines working on several images (Multi-View approach). The first approach is used in several photogrammetry suites for satellite image processing, while the latter is used in IGN MicMac [12], NASA AMES

Stereo Pipeline [11] and CNES s2p Stereo Pipeline [10]: both products are available under FOSS licenses and can run under Linux Operating Systems.

In CNES s2p Stereo Pipeline [10] an approximated sensor model is implemented limiting to single image tiles to reduce discrepancy between epipolar curves in horizontal disparity map estimation: both RPC functions and Shuttle Radar Topography Mission (SRTM) terrain model are used for per-tile altitude estimation. The Multi-View Stereo approach allows simultaneous processing of multiple stereo images with default More Global Matching (MGM) method [26], merging all results basing on reconstruction quality: however, the user can choose between a wide range of matching algorithms (tvl1, msmw, hirschmuller08, hirschmuller08_laplacian, sgbm, mgm, mgm_multi) by mean of a JSON configuration file. This approach is targeted for precise 3D reconstruction of urban areas using hundreds of images with various acquisition angles. Processing of tri-stereo images can be fully automated by filling a JSON configuration file with user defined settings (Region of Interest (ROI), terrain model resolution, homologous points' matching algorithm and tile processing size). Since panchromatic images Ground Sample Distance (GSD) of Pléiades tri-stereo panchromatic images is 0.5 m, 1-m resolution have been set for extracted DSM; Scale-invariant feature transform (SIFT) has been selected as homologous points matching method.

On the other hand, NASA AMES Stereo Pipeline grants to the user various options in selecting preferred matching parameters. Available stereo correlation methods are (a) standard, based on Local Search Window (b) Semi-Global Matching (SGM) [28] with 2D disparity search and (c) More Global Matching (MGM). Image alignment and sub-pixel correlation methods can also be fine-tuned by users, while tri-stereo DEMs generation can rely on a single-pass Multi-View reconstruction or on a two-pass process, combining all stereo terrain models obtained from 1-2, 1-3 and 2-3 stereo pairs. Level1A Pléiades images can be processed 'as is' or preprocessed by *mapproject* command using an external precision terrain model; in the latter case, 2017 LiDAR terrain model can be used as reference.

Both CNES s2p and NASA AMES Stereo Pipeline have been tested on a LUbuntu Virtual Machine with 4 GB of dedicated RAM memory, installed over an instance of Oracle© Virtual Box 6.1 virtual environment. The whole system has been hosted on a Windows 10 home PC with a 1.80 GHz/2 GHz dual core Intel © i7-8550U CPU and 8 GB of RAM.

The two stereo pipelines have been used to extract terrain models from tri-stereo images using both available single pairs combinations (left/right, left/center, right/center images) and the whole triplet (left/center/right images); various available stereo matching and sub-pixel refinement methods available in NASA AMES Stereo Pipeline have also been tested. Mid-2018 images have been processed as a single stereo pair in both s2p and AMES pipelines.

Coverage and quality of each terrain model have been assessed by comparison with reference 2017; *nodata* model cell percentage has been selected as Quality Assessment (QA) coverage indicator.

Models' elevations have been compared with the 2017 reference model over unchanged spatial locations, i.e. over the control points (CP) set described in Sect. 2.1.

4 Results

4.1 Terrain Models' Coverage

Terrain models' coverage has been found to be influenced by both site morphology, stereo pairs/triplets used (i.e., B/H ratio) and processing parameters: percentages of *nodata* values over all terrain cells for each test site, image pairs/triplets and processing parameters are shown in Table 5 and 6 for NASA AMES Stereo Pipeline (ASP) and CNES s2p. Merged terrain models percentages, referring to models obtained by combining single stereo pairs with the command *point2dem* are identified by columns 123.

Table 5. *nodata* cells' percentages in terrain models extracted with ASP for each 2020 Pléiades image pair/triplet (1: left image, 2: center image, 3: right image) compared to s2p for image pairs 1-3 (left/right) and whole 2020 triplet (left, center and right images).

Site	ASP *nodata* (%)					s2p *nodata* (%)		Reference model (2017 LiDAR survey)
	Basic ASP				MVS			
	12	23	13	123		13	123	
Site 1	1.83	1.70	6.64	0.59	2.20	17.84	23.0	0.26
Site 2	1.69	1.83	6.60	1.01	1.92	4.49	7.27	0.92
Site 3	4.40	2.84	11.28	1.32	6.33	20.14	30.16	0.78
Site 4	10.54	8.45	17.83	5.63	5.98	14.89	18.97	2.66

Terrain models extracted with NASA Ames Stereo Pipeline from pair 13, i.e. left and right images, are characterized by the worst coverage ratio, while terrain models extracted by pairs 12 and 23 (left/center and center/right images) show better coverage. Assembling the three image pairs allows to obtain the best coverage available, as expected from [1–3] (see column 123); coverage ratio of terrain models obtained by Multi-View stereo processing (MVS) is about two times lower than in combined model. s2p coverage percentage obtained in terrain model exyracted form stereo pair 13 (left and right image) is comparable with the one obtained by ASP only in test site 2 (best case scenario). In general, without proper parameter tuning s2p MVS terrain models are characterized by a lower coverage compared to the ones obtained with both image pairs and triplets in ASP.

As for ASP, simple assembly of terrain models from image pairs behaves slightly better comparing to terrain models extracted with Multi-View stereo reconstruction; only in test site 4 the two methods allow to extract models with identical *nodata* cells' percentage. Since tri-stereo extracted models from ASP have a better coverage with respect to s2p ones, further analysis are restricted to ASP tri-stereo models.

A quick look at spatial *nodata* cells distribution over each test site for ASP terrain models (Fig. 4, 5, 6, 7) highlights, as expected, that most of them are located over areas with sudden slope changes. This effect is notable in test sites 3 and 4 (Fig. 6 and 7): in worst-case scenarios, combining multiple terrain models generated from each stereo pair instead of using Multi-View stereo processing greatly enhances the coverage degree of the resulting model, thus minimizing *nodata* values due to incorrect matching.

Test case 4 combined terrain model map (Fig. 7) shows many *nodata* cells in north western zones thus showing an acceptable coverage of the central wall area; Multi-View terrain model shows a complementary behaviour, characterized by incorrect matching at the borders of the central vertical wall.

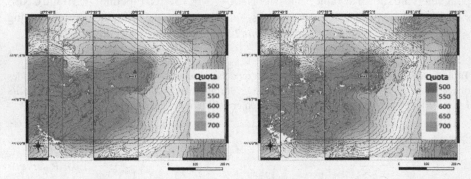

Fig. 4. Test site 1 terrain models extracted in ASP (1:2.000). Left: combined single-pairs terrain models, right: Multi-View stereo. Multi-View higher *nodata* cell values (in white) are mainly distributed along slope steep changes.

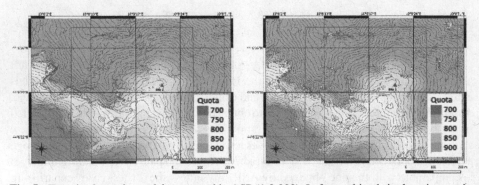

Fig. 5. Test site 2 terrain models extracted in ASP (1:2.000). Left: combined single-pairs terrain models, right: Multi-View stereo. Very few *nodata* cell values (in white) are visible (best-case scenario with regular slope).

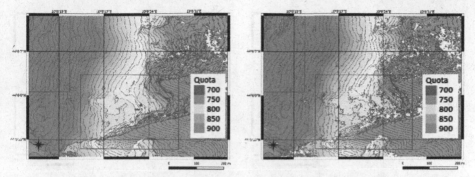

Fig. 6. Test site 3 terrain models extracted in ASP (1:2.000). Left: combined single-pairs terrain models, right: Multi-View stereo. Many *nodata* cells' values (in white) are visible around the main slope change area in the center of the image (worst-case scenario with vertical walls).

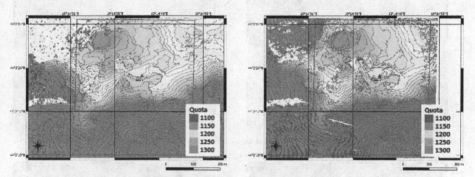

Fig. 7. Test site 4 terrain models extracted in ASP (1:2.000). Left: combined single-pairs terrain models, right: Multi-View stereo. Several *nodata* cell values (in white) are visible around the walls located in the center of the image (worst-case scenario: urban canyon-like morphology).

Both s2p and ASP have been tested over a limited area of test site 1 to extract terrain models from 2018 non-stereo acquisitions: though their global coverage is very poor (45% and 49% *nodata* cells), in this case (see Fig. 8) s2p pipeline behaves better showing a more regular pattern in reconstruction of marble cuts inside active area.

4.2 Elevation Accuracy

Precisions of tri-stereo APS terrain models derived by pairs combination and MVS have been assessed over the previously described set of Control Points (CP), each of them being located over unchanged elevations areas between 2017 and 2020. Elevation differences between the two models and the reference one, i.e., the 2017 LiDAR aerial survey terrain model, have been evaluated: mean values, RMSE and 3rd percentile for each site are showed in Table 6 (Fig. 9).

RMSE of both Multi-View stereo and combined stereo model is under 2.5 m in all test sites: these values are consistent with [1–3] (see Table 1). Both methods behave similarly in all test sites regards to RMSE.

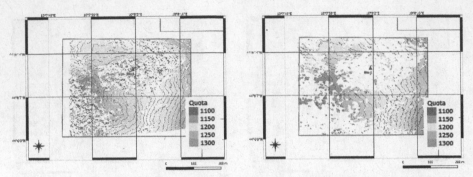

Fig. 8. Left: terrain models in Test Site 1 subarea extracted from 2018 non-stereo images. Left: s2p terrain model; right: ASP terrain model.

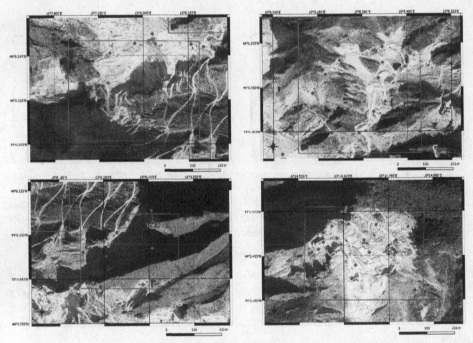

Fig. 9. Control Points (CP) digitized and used in terrain models QA (scale 1:2.000). Top left: Site 1, top right: Site 2, bottom left: Site 3, bottom right: Site 4.

Horizontal and vertical profiles over Test Sites' areas of 2020 ASP stereo models confirm that in unchanged areas elevation differences between 2017 and 2020 are largely under 5 m: in Fig. 10 the green profile, referring to 2017 terrain model, deviates from red (2020 combined model) and blue (2020 Multi-View terrain model) one deviates only in areas subjected to extraction activities or temporary MCW\MQW disposals.

Table 6. Elevation QA in control points over the four test sites.

Test site	GCPs	ASP tri-stereo models					
		123 combination			MVS		
		Mean	RMSE	3rd perc	Mean	RMSE	3rd perc
Site 1	13	0.52	2.03	0.84	−0.36	2.40	0.52
Site 2	14	0.21	1.90	1.02	−0.01	2.08	1.38
Site 3	7	−1.84	2.19	−0.90	−0.14	1.84	0.69
Site 4	15	−0.89	1.62	0.23	−1.31	1.12	0.92

Some deviations in unchanged areas between the two models in Site 4 can be found by evaluating horizontal and vertical profiles intersecting the main wall (see Fig. 10). Combined model, in red, shows a path quite similar to the reference model's one in green, while Multi-View stereo model, in blue, has some little artifacts clearly visible in horizontal profile: this surface roughness is in agreement with [33].

Found precisions, i.e. RMSE ranges assessed over control points an profiles' evaluation, confirm that the two models are suitable in evaluating surface and volume changes due to extraction activities in areas where marble cuts heights are over 10 m by using a 5 m threshold, i.e. two times the maximum RMSE found in all test sites.

4.3 Surface and Volume Changes Evaluation

Taking into account the vertical accuracy of extracted terrain models, maps of relevant elevation changes between 2017 reference model and 2020 combines ASP stereo models are shown in Fig. 11 for each test site: a threshold of 5 m – two times the assessed value of RMSE – has been used to highlight areas under intense extraction activities between 2017 and 2020. While red and orange areas are characterized by negative elevation changes (marble cuts), thus highlighting intense extraction activity over the years, green and cyan areas – being characterized by positive elevation differences – highlight areas used for temporary MCW/MQW disposals. In long-dated waste disposals, as in Test Site 2, negative and positive elevation changes allow identification of new waste disposals and/or the presence of relevant landslides; in these cases, as stated before, a slight lower threshold of 2–3 m can be used.

In Site 1 2017–2020 elevation differences correctly highlight areas subjected to marble cuts (in red) and temporary MCW/MQW disposals (in blue): marble cuts' areas are located near existing marble cuts, while temporary MCW/MQW disposals are located around service roads.

In Site 2 no notable extraction activity can be seen, except for a small MCW\MQW removal in the centre of the area, according to the absence of active quarries.

In Site 3 and Site 4, representing the worst-case scenarios, many artifacts can be visible near to the vertical walls: in both cases a precise visual interpretation of both marble cuts and waste disposals can be tricky, thus requiring deeper analysis.

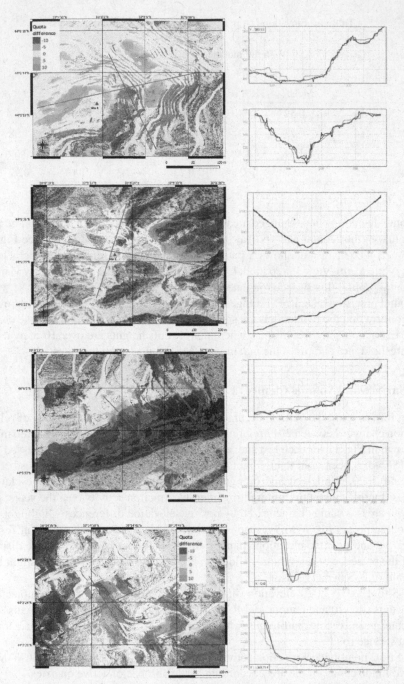

Fig. 10. 2017 reference-2020 ASP-combined terrain models' elevation changes maps and horizontal/vertical profiles for Test sites 1, 2, 3 and 4. Left images: 1:2.000 map with elevation differences and profile lines location, right images: horizontal profile (upper right image), vertical profile (lower right image). Profile lines are evaluated over 2017 LiDAR survey terrain model (reference model, in green), ASP combined model from stereo pairs (in red), ASP Multi-View stereo model (in blue). Site 4 profiles cover the central vertical wall. (Color figure online)

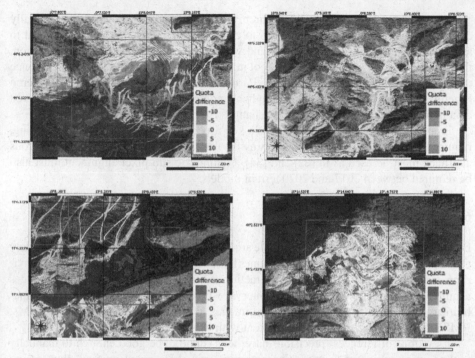

Fig. 11. 2017–2020 Test Sites' elevation differences (1:2.000). Top left: Site 1, top right: Site 2, bottom left: Site 3, bottom right: Site 4. Background: 2019 orthoimage. (Color figure online)

Elevation differences shown in Fig. 11 confirms that control points used in vertical QA are located over areas with minimal volume changes.

5 Discussion

Stereo extracted 2020 terrain model's coverage degree and vertical accuracies in all test sites is satisfactory with respect to extraction activity detection, making 2020 models currently suitable to obtain a rough evaluation of surface changes by simple models' differencing with 2017 reference model. Raster layer of differences between 2020 and 2017 models can be used in visual inspection of area changes between 2017 and 2020: while for Test Sites 1 and 2 area subjected to relevant changes could be automatically extracted with contouring operations followed by basic manual cleaning, identification of changed areas in Test Site 3 and 4 require additional visual inspection work over orthoimages and manual editing.

Artifacts in Site 4 and Site 5 2020 terrain models would require additional cleaning work over point clouds that is beyond the aim of this paper: since in presence of vertical walls TIN-based volume calculation are more indicated than GRID-based ones to achieve better precision, as stated in [31], future work on point could filtering and TIN creation would be recommended. In these cases, a combined stereo pairs terrain model would be slightly preferred to Multi-View unfiltered stereo one [33].

2018 stereo models extracted from archived images can only be useful in manually digitizing of quarry areas not subjected to extraction activities, but cannot be used to assess areas subjected to marble cuts and waste disposals. Even with this limitation, they can however represent a valuable tool in past years changes' monitoring in absence of stereo pairs/triplet's satellite images. Further tuning over both s2P and ASP Stereo Pipelines to improve stereo matching might be required to allow exploitation of archived data in monitoring surface and volume changes over the years.

Precise volume calculation, which is a key aspect in marble extraction monitoring, require more additional work to precisely assess uncertainty: in this case, a more rigorous approach must be used as in [32] and [34]. Planimetric sub-pixel alignment must also be required between 2017 and 2020 terrain models.

6 Conclusions

DSM extraction from tri-stereo and single archived Pléiades satellite images with widely used open-source stereo processing pipelines has been tested in a complex mountain environment with a notable presence of extraction activities. While single archive images acquired in different days (acquisition interval >60 days) showed poor matching capabilities, it has been shown that tri-stereo images allow to extract high quality DSMs. RMSE in all the four test sites is consistent with existing works [1–3, 29].

Elevations differences' precisions have been found to be good enough to manually outline areas subjected to extraction activities in a three years interval, thus easing monitoring activities at small scales, i.e. over the whole Carrara basin's area (1076 ha).

Tolerances of derived products – surface area of relevant volume changes and extracted volumes – must be further investigated, referring to both planimetric and vertical precision of both reference and stereo terrain models, in order to define confidence intervals of volume changes obtained by terrain models' raster differences.

Acknowledgements. The author wishes to thank the Soil Defense and Civil Protection Regional Directorate for granting the permission for LiDAR data usage in the project, and LAMMA Consortium (project manager of the LiDAR Survey for the Directorate) for data sharing.

Pléiades Data have been provided by the European Space Agency behind acceptance of Project Proposal ID-61779 "Quarry activity monitoring in the Apuan Alps".

This work has been completed under the Quarry Monitoring Special Project (Work Package 1) in charge to the Regional Environmental Agency of Tuscany, founded by Tuscany Regional Government.

References

1. Nasir, S., Iqbal, I.A., Ali, Z., Shahzad, A.: Accuracy assessment of digital elevation model generated from Pléiades tri stereo-pair. In: 2015 7th International Conference on Recent Advances in Space Technologies (RAST), Istanbul, Turkey, pp. 193–197 (2015). https://doi.org/10.1109/RAST.2015.7208340
2. Panagiotakis, E., Chrysoulakis, N., Charalampopoulou, V., Poursanidis, D.: Validation of pleiades tri-stereo DSM in urban areas. Int. J. Geo-Inf. **7**, 118 (2018). https://doi.org/10.3390/ijgi7030118

3. Poli, D., Remondino, F., Angiuli, E., Agugiaro, G.: Radiometric and geometric evaluation of GeoEye-1, WorldView-2 and Pléiades-1A stereo images for 3D information extraction. ISPRS J. Photogramm. Remote Sens. **100**, 35–47 (2015). https://doi.org/10.1016/j.isprsjprs. 2014.04.007

4. Poli, D., Caravaggi, I.: Digital surface modelling and 3D information extraction from space-borne very high-resolution stereo pairs. JRC Sci. Tech. Rep. (2012). ISSN 1831-9424. https:// doi.org/10.2788/15526

5. Jing, L., Yong-she, S., Jian-rong, W.: The research and design of the base-height ratio for the three linear array camera of satellite photogrammetry (2008)

6. Hasegawa, H., Matsuo, K., Koarai, M., Watanabe, N., Masaharu, H., Fukushima, Y.: DEM accuracy and the base to height (B/H) ratio of stereo images. Int. Arch. Photogramm. Remote Sens. **33**, 356–359 (2000)

7. Zhou, Y., Parsons, B., Elliott, J.R., Barisin, I., Walker, R.T.: Assessing the ability of Pleiades stereo imagery to determine height changes in earthquakes: a case study for the El Mayor-Cucapah epicentral area. J. Geophys. Res. Solid Earth **120**(12), 8793–8808 (2015). https:// doi.org/10.1002/2015JB012358

8. Aguilar, M.A., Saldana, M., Aguilar, F.: Generation and quality assessment of stereo-extracted DSM from GeoEye-1 and WorldView-2 imagery. IEEE Trans. Geosci. Remote Sens. **52**, 1259–1271 (2014). https://doi.org/10.1109/TGRS.2013.2249521

9. Perko, R., Raggam, H., Schardt, M., Roth, P.M.: Very high resolution mapping with the Pléiades satellite constellation. Am. J. Remote Sens. **6**(2), 89–99 (2018). https://doi.org/10. 11648/j.ajrs.20180602.14

10. de Franchis, C., Meinhardt-Llopis, E., Michel, J., Morel, J.-M., Facciolo, G.: An automatic and modular stereo pipeline for pushbroom images. ISPRS Ann. Photogramm. Remote Sens. Spat. Inf. Sci. **II–3**, 49–56 (2014). https://doi.org/10.5194/isprsannals-II-3-49-2014

11. Shean, D.E., et al.: An automated, open-source pipeline for mass production of digital eleva-tion models (DEMs) from very high-resolution commercial stereo satellite imagery. ISPRS J. Photogramm. Remote. Sens. **116**, 101–117 (2016). https://doi.org/10.1016/j.isprsjprs.2016. 03.012

12. Moratto, Z.M., Broxton, M.J., Beyer, R.A., Lundy, M., Husmann, K.: Ames stereo pipeline, NASA's open source automated stereogrammetry software. In: 41st Lunar and Planetary Science Conference (2010). Abstract #2364. https://ui.adsabs.harvard.edu/abs/2010LPI....41. 2364M/abstract

13. Broxton, M.J., Edwards, L.J.: The Ames stereo pipeline: automated 3D surface reconstruction from orbital imagery. In: 39th Lunar and Planetary Science Conference (2008). Abstract #2419. https://ui.adsabs.harvard.edu/abs/2008LPI....39.2419B

14. Beyer, R.A., Alexandrov, O., McMichael, S.: The AMES stereo pipeline: NASA's open source software for deriving and processing terrain data. Earth Space Sci. **5**, 537–548 (2018). https:// doi.org/10.1029/2018EA000409

15. Rupnik, E., Daakir, M., Pierrot Deseilligny, M.: MicMac – a free, open-source solution for photogrammetry. Open Geospatial Data Softw. Stan. **2**(1), 1–9 (2017). https://doi.org/10. 1186/s40965-017-0027-2

16. Gleyzes, M.A., Perret, L., Kubik, P.: Pleiades system architecture and main performances. Int. Arch. Photogramm. Remote Sens. Spat. Inf. Sci. **XXXIX-B1**, 537–542 (2012). https:// doi.org/10.5194/isprsarchives-XXXIX-B1-537-2012

17. Panem, C., Bignalet-Cazalet, F., Baillarin, S.: Pleiades-HR system products performance after in-orbit commissioning phase. Int. Arch. Photogramm. Remote Sens. Spat. Inf. Sci. **XXXIX-B1**, 567–572 (2012). https://doi.org/10.5194/isprsarchives-XXXIX-B1-567-2012

18. Poli, D., Remondino, F., Angiuli, E., Agugiaro, G.: Evaluation of Pleiades-1A triplet on Trento testfield. Int. Arch. Photogramm. Remote Sens. Spat. Inf. Sci. **XL-1/W1**, 287–292 (2013). https://doi.org/10.5194/isprsarchives-XL-1-W1-287-2013

19. Raggam, H.: Surface mapping using image triplets - case studies and benefit assessment in comparison to stereo image processing. Photogramm. Eng. Remote. Sens. **72**, 551–563 (2006)

20. Coeurdevey, L., Fernandez, K.: Pléiades Imagery. User Guide. Report No. USRPHR-DT-125-SPOT-2.0 (2012)

21. Abduelmola, A.E.: High resolution satellite image analysis and rapid 3D model extraction for urban change detection. Ph.D. thesis (2016)

22. de Franchis, C., Meinhardt-Llopis, E., Michel, J., Morel, J.-M., Facciolo, G.: An automatic and modular stereo pipeline for pushbroom images. Int. Arch. Photogramm. Remote Sens. Spat. Inf. Sci. **II–3**, 49–56 (2014). https://doi.org/10.5194/isprsannals-II-3-49-2014

23. Mandanici, E., Girelli, A.V., Poluzzi, L.: Metric accuracy of digital elevation models from WorldView-3 stereo-pairs in urban areas. Remote Sens. **11**(7), 878 (2019). https://doi.org/10.3390/rs11070878

24. Agiular, M.A., Nemmaoui, A., Aguilar, F.J., Qin, R.: Quality assessment of digital surface models extracted from WorldView-2 and WorldView-3 stereo pairs over different land covers. GISci. Remote Sens. **56**(1), 109–129 (2019). https://doi.org/10.1080/15481603.2018.1494408

25. Barbarella, M., Fiani, M., Zollo, C.: Assessment of DEM derived from very high-resolution stereo satellite imagery for geomorphometric analysis. Eur. J. Remote Sens. **50**, 534–549 (2017). https://doi.org/10.1080/22797254.2017.1372084

26. Facciolo, G., de Franchis, C., Meinhardt-Llopis, E.: MGM: a significantly more global matching for stereo-vision. In: 2015 Proceedings of the British Machine Vision Conference, pp. 1–90. British Machine Vision Association (2015)

27. Rothermel, M., Gong, K., Fritsch, D., Schindler, K., Haala, N.: Photometric multi-view mesh refinement for high-resolution satellite images. ISPRS J. Photogramm. Remote. Sens. **166**, 52–62 (2020). https://doi.org/10.1016/j.isprsjprs.2020.05.001

28. Hirschmüller, H.: Stereo processing by semiglobal matching and mutual information. IEEE Trans. Pattern Anal. Mach. Intell. **30**(2), 328–341 (2008). https://doi.org/10.1109/TPAMI.2007.1166

29. Palaseanu-Lovejoy, M., Bisson, M., Spinetti, C., Buongiorno, M.F., Alexandrov, O., Cecere, T.: High-resolution and accurate topography reconstruction of Mount Etna from Pleiades satellite data. Remote Sens. **11**(24), 2983 (2019). https://doi.org/10.3390/rs11242983

30. Sudalaimuthu, K., Kaliappan, S., Raja, K., Divya, C.: Surface area estimation, volume change detection in lime stone quarry, Tirunelveli District using Cartosat-1 generated digital elevation model (DEM). Circ. Syst. **07**, 849–858 (2016). https://doi.org/10.4236/cs.2016.76073

31. Pepe, M., Costantino, D., Alfio, V., Zannotti, N.: 4D Geomatics Monitoring of a quarry for the calculation of extracted volumes by TIN and GRID model: contribute to UAV photogrammetry. Geographia Technica. **16**, 1–14 (2020). https://doi.org/10.21163/GT_2021_163.01

32. Kramer Rhodes, R.: UAS as an inventory tool: a photogrammetric approach to volume estimation. University of Arkansas, Fayetteville. Thesis (2017)

33. Grohmann, C., Garcia, G., Affonso, A.A., Albuquerque, R.W.: Dune migration and volume change from airborne LiDAR, terrestrial LiDAR and structure from motion-multi view stereo. Comput. Geosci. **143**, 104569 (2020). https://doi.org/10.1016/j.cageo.2020.104569

34. Yilmaz, H.M.: Close range photogrammetry in volume computing. Exp. Tech. **34**(1), 48–54 (2010). https://doi.org/10.1111/j.1747-1567.2009.00476.x

Author Index

Printed in the United States
by Baker & Taylor Publisher Services